Peterson's
Hidden Job Market
1999

2,000 High-Growth Companies That Are Hiring at Four Times the National Average

Eighth Edition

**Selected from the
Corporate Technology Database
Compiled by CorpTech
(Woburn, Massachusetts)**

Peterson's
Princeton, New Jersey

About Peterson's

Peterson's is the country's largest educational information/communications company, providing the academic, consumer, and professional communities with books, software, and online services in support of lifelong education access and career choice. Well-known references include Peterson's annual guides to private schools, summer programs, colleges and universities, graduate and professional programs, financial aid, international study, adult learning, and career guidance. Peterson's Web site at petersons.com is the only comprehensive—and most heavily traveled—education resource on the Internet. The site carries all of Peterson's fully searchable major databases and includes financial aid sources, test-prep help, job postings, direct inquiry and application features, and specially created Virtual Campuses for every accredited academic institution and summer program in the U.S. and Canada that offers in-depth narratives, announcements, and multimedia features.

Visit Peterson's Education Center on the Internet (World Wide Web) at www.petersons.com

Copyright © 1998 by Peterson's

Previous editions © 1991, 1992, 1993, 1994, 1995, 1996, 1997

Data on technology companies © 1998 by Corporate Technology Information Services, Inc. (CorpTech). This material is compiled and copyrighted by CorpTech, 12 Alfred Street, Suite 200, Woburn, Massachusetts (Tel.: 781-932-3939). All rights reserved.

ISSN 1064-1769
ISBN 0-7689-0012-3

Printed in the United States of America

10 9 8 7 6 5 4 3 2 1

HIDDEN JOB MARKET 1999

Contents

Industry Icons and What They Mean

At the top of each profile in the main section of the book, a symbol appears that represents the major industry that each company is involved in. Find them listed below. A few companies don't have a corresponding icon. These companies are either holding companies or are companies that are so diverse that it is not possible to choose just one icon that represents what they do.

Advanced Materials

Biotechnology

Chemicals

Computer Hardware

Computer Software

Defense

Energy

Environmental

Factory Automation

Manufacturing Equipment

Medical Pharmaceuticals

Photonics

Subassemblies and
   Components

Telecoms & Internet

Test and Measurement

Transportation

The Thriving Technology Industry

Andrew Campbell
President, CorpTech

Manufacturers and developers of technology products are America's most successful business segment, the one major area that has expanded consistently over the past decade. With every facet of industry, commerce, and government looking to them to solve problems of productivity and competitiveness, technology companies are creating our tomorrow.

Small and midsize companies are better able to adapt to changing demands and consequently have been riding a steady wave of expansion. Technology manufacturers with under 1,000 employees now represent more than 27 percent of durable goods manufacturing employment.

Growth for these companies has been phenomenal and 1998 promises to be even more exciting. Between October and December 1997, CorpTech surveyed 4,285 emerging technology manufacturers with under 1,000 employees. These firms projected a combined job growth rate of 8.1 percent for 1998, with one in five expecting to grow at over 25 percent. The graph on page 2 gives the growth projections broken down by industry.

The *Hidden* Job Market

The 2,000 firms listed in *Peterson's Hidden Job Market 1999* have been selected from CorpTech's database of more than 45,000 technology manufacturers and developers. These are the firms with under 1,000 employees that added the most employees during the survey year. In fact, these 2,000 companies expanded their combined work force by 29 percent in the past year, creating more than 125,520 new jobs.

These are not just technical jobs that are being created. Expanding firms need people in all areas and at all levels of experience—from sales to clerical, from manufacturing to accounting, and from entry level to senior management. This is the hidden job market!

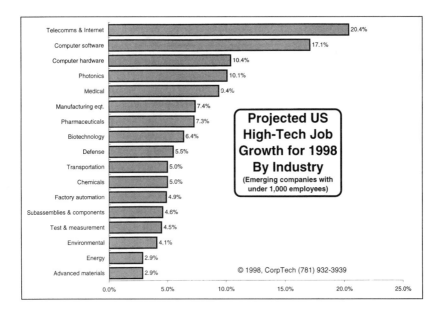

Telecomms & Internet — 20.4%
Computer software — 17.1%
Computer hardware — 10.4%
Photonics — 10.1%
Medical — 9.4%
Manufacturing eqt. — 7.4%
Pharmaceuticals — 7.3%
Biotechnology — 6.4%
Defense — 5.5%
Transportation — 5.0%
Chemicals — 5.0%
Factory automation — 4.9%
Subassemblies & components — 4.6%
Test & measurement — 4.5%
Environmental — 4.1%
Energy — 2.9%
Advanced materials — 2.9%

Projected US High-Tech Job Growth for 1998 By Industry
(Emerging companies with under 1,000 employees)

© 1998, CorpTech (781) 932-3939

What Does CorpTech Do?

Corporate Technology Information Services, Inc. (CorpTech), is the leading supplier of company information on America's manufacturers and developers of technology products. The company was formed in 1984 and is based in Woburn, Massachusetts.

CorpTech surveys more than 45,000 companies and updates the information on each company every year creating a uniquely comprehensive and detailed database. From this database we publish printed directories, CD-ROM databases, mailing lists, and custom reports. CorpTech's data are also available on the Internet (http://www.corptech.com).

CorpTech data are used to solve a wide range of business problems from technology transfer to sales to prospecting to job finding to economic development to venture capital research.

How Does CorpTech Collect Its Information?

CorpTech has assembled the country's most comprehensive source of information about technology companies. It tracks more than 45,000 technology manufacturers and developers with a unique five-stage research and checking process:

1. New and emerging firms are identified through local economic development groups, trade associations, the trade press, and other technology companies. Each is then entered into a central database.

2. Each new company is interviewed by phone for information on over 100 data elements, which are then entered into the database to form a comprehensive profile.

3. The profile is checked by sophisticated software and printed. Any errors detected are flagged on the printout.

4. The printed profile is edited by senior staff members, and corrections are made to the database.

5. A copy of the edited profile is faxed to the firm for verification, and any corrections are added to the database.

Steps 2 through 5 are repeated each year for each company to ensure the accuracy of the database, which has been continuously refined for twelve years at an investment of more than $5 million. Given this background on the methods CorpTech uses to collect and update the information for this book, the reader should make note that because these are fast-growing companies they may move to larger quarters or sometimes go out of business quickly. People may change titles, location, or jobs more frequently. A lot can happen between the time the company information is updated and the time the book is published.

What Information Can You Find in This Book?

The companies listed in this book are arranged alphabetically by state. Most profiles include:

- Company name and address

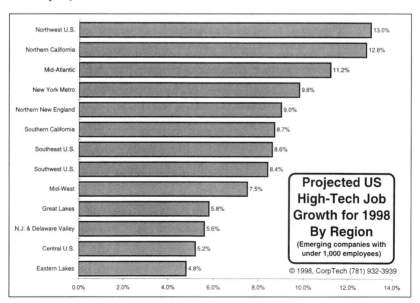

Projected US High-Tech Job Growth for 1998 By Region
(Emerging companies with under 1,000 employees)

© 1998, CorpTech (781) 932-3939

Region	Growth
Northwest U.S.	13.0%
Northern California	12.8%
Mid-Atlantic	11.2%
New York Metro	9.8%
Northern New England	9.0%
Southern California	8.7%
Southeast U.S.	8.6%
Southwest U.S.	8.4%
Mid-West	7.5%
Great Lakes	5.8%
N.J. & Delaware Valley	5.6%
Central U.S.	5.2%
Eastern Lakes	4.8%

- Year the company was founded
- Number of employees
- Annual sales revenue in the survey year
- The technology industries in which the company is active
- Number of employees added in the year prior to CorpTech's latest interview
- Contact name and title (usually the executive responsible for the personnel function or the chief executive officer)
- Telephone and fax numbers and e-mail and URL addresses

The company listings are followed by two indexes. The **Industry Index** lists the companies in this book according to the industry or industries in which they are active, along with their state and the page number of their profile. The seventeen categories of technology industries (plus holding companies) are as follows:

The Hidden Job Market
Technology Industries Ranked by Total Job Growth

#	Jobs	Industry	Comp.
1	27,317	Computer Software	499
2	8,480	Telecomms & Internet	218
3	7,604	Computer Hardware	173
4	7,550	Subassemblies & Components	249
5	3,594	Manufacturing Equipment	115
6	2,489	Medical	97
7	2,104	Factory Automation	118
8	2,027	Pharmaceuticals	43
9	1,629	Photonics	44
10	1,620	Environmental	63
11	1,599	Biotechnology	51
12	1,376	Transportation	56
13	1,373	Test & Measurement	77
14	1,358	Advanced Materials	62
15	1,008	Defense	36
16	965	Energy	40
17	501	Chemicals	25

Employment at technology manufacturers with under 1,000 employees where the home office is in this area. Jobs = new technology manufacturing jobs projected for the 12 months following the survey.
Source: CorpTech, Woburn, MA (800) 333-8036

- Advanced Materials
- Biotechnology
- Chemicals
- Computer Hardware
- Computer Software
- Defense
- Energy
- Environmental
- Factory Automation
- Holding Companies

- Manufacturing Equipment
- Medical
- Pharmaceuticals
- Photonics
- Subassemblies and Components
- Telecomms and Internet
- Test and Measurement
- Transportation

The **Company Index** lists companies alphabetically, giving their state and the page number on which their detailed information appears.

The **Metropolitan Area Index** sorts companies into major metropolitan areas, as defined by the U.S. Office of Management and Budget (OMB). Using population estimates and other criteria, the OMB updates the areas and cities that qualify as metropolitan areas in June each year. Of the 2,000 companies profiled in this book, 120 of them will not be found in this index because they are located in cities or towns outside the boundaries of these metropolitan areas. If your job search is focused on a particular region, you should start your research in this index.

The Hidden Job Markets Top 20 Cities
Ranked by High-Tech Employment

#	Emp	City	Comp.	Main high-tech activity ....Emp	
1	42,532	Houston, TX	431	Energy	9,903
2	41,842	San Diego, CA	371	Computer Software	6,726
3	40,841	San Jose, CA	347	Subassemblies & Components	8,295
4	30,097	New York, NY	319	Computer Software	9,455
5	28,254	Minneapolis, MN	197	Subassemblies & Components	7,178
6	27,135	Sunnyvale, CA	246	Computer Software	6,641
7	26,850	Dallas, TX	261	Computer Software	6,426
8	25,678	Irvine, CA	239	Computer Hardware	5,034
9	24,064	Chicago, IL	222	Subassemblies & Components	5,884
10	23,917	Santa Clara, CA	226	Computer Software	4,919
11	23,604	Saint Louis, MO	170	Pharmaceuticals	2,894
12	21,062	Pittsburgh, PA	248	Computer Software	3,574
13	19,434	Fremont, CA	195	Computer Hardware	4,498
14	18,726	Austin, TX	259	Computer Software	4,349
15	17,292	Atlanta, GA	170	Computer Software	7,547
16	17,173	Cambridge, MA	203	Computer Software	6,948
17	15,947	Phoenix, AZ	160	Computer Software	3,292
18	15,463	Cincinnati, OH	114	Subassemblies & Components	2,713
19	15,093	Cleveland, OH	137	Advanced Materials	3,524
20	14,287	Milwaukee, WI	87	Subassemblies & Components	2,729

Based on employment of emerging technology manufacturers with under 1,000 employees where the home office is in the city. **Main high-tech activity** = largest of 17 segments (tracked by CorpTech) by employment; **Emp** = total technology manufacturing employment within the main high-tech activity.

Source: CorpTech, Woburn, MA (800) 333-8036

The Hidden Job Market Technology Manufacturers
Sales and Employee Analysis by Primary Industry

Primary Industry	— Comp —		— Sales —		— Empl —		— Sales —	— Growth —	
	#	%	$m	%	#	%	PerEmpl	LstY	NxtY
Factory Automation	118	5.9%	$5,814	9.1%	26,491	6.2%	$153,111	19.7%	6.6%
Biotechnology	51	2.5%	$1,581	2.4%	11,634	2.7%	$107,710	24.9%	12.9%
Chemicals	25	1.2%	$1,093	1.7%	4,923	1.1%	$266,581	21.4%	7.0%
Computer Hardware	173	8.6%	$10,086	15.8%	37,861	8.8%	$206,389	30.9%	16.5%
Defense	36	1.8%	$1,519	2.3%	10,288	2.4%	$118,038	22.8%	7.7%
Energy	40	2.0%	$1,106	1.7%	8,511	1.9%	$231,343	26.2%	7.5%
Environmental	63	3.1%	$1,583	2.4%	16,575	3.8%	$123,185	19.0%	8.0%
Manufacturing Eqp	115	5.7%	$3,517	5.5%	25,505	5.9%	$125,361	28.1%	11.7%
Advanced Materials	62	3.1%	$2,668	4.2%	14,273	3.3%	$192,054	17.5%	6.7%
Medical	97	4.8%	$2,297	3.6%	21,112	4.9%	$122,242	24.2%	9.1%
Pharmaceuticals	43	2.1%	$1,138	1.7%	9,704	2.2%	$154,105	31.5%	18.7%
Photonics	44	2.2%	$1,079	1.6%	9,246	2.1%	$132,042	35.7%	14.3%
Computer Software	499	24.9%	$10,982	17.2%	97,321	22.8%	$129,449	40.3%	24.6%
Subassemblies & Components	249	12.4%	$7,624	12.0%	58,554	13.7%	$134,859	23.6%	9.3%
Test & Measurement	77	3.8%	$1,415	2.2%	11,396	2.6%	$135,778	27.2%	7.0%
Telecomm & Internet	218	10.9%	$8,384	13.2%	49,428	11.6%	$171,501	36.1%	14.7%
Transportation	56	2.8%	$520	0.8%	5,896	1.3%	$131,454	25.3%	7.9%
Not primarily high-tech	34	1.7%	$1,088	1.7%	7,332	1.7%	$178,094	26.4%	9.0%
	2,000	100.0%	$63,494	100.0%	426,050	100.0%	$152,647	28.5%	13.3%

Notes: **Sales PerEmpl** is a national average. **Growth** is based on employee growth reported by firms with under 1,000 employees. **LstY** is for the year prior to their interview. **NxtY** is their projected growth for the year following the interview.

Source: CorpTech, Woburn, MA (800) 333-8036

The Hidden Job Market's 20 Fastest-Growing Emerging Companies
Technology Producers Ranked by Projected Job Growth

#	Jobs	Company	City	Phone	Main high-tech activity	Sales($m)
1	750	Alydaar Software Corp.	Charlotte, NC	(704) 365-2324	Computer Software	$0
2	553	MicroStrategy, Inc.	Vienna, VA	(703) 848-8600	Computer Software	$25
3	350	Kendle International, Inc.	Cincinnati, OH	(513) 381-5550	Pharmaceuticals	$13
4	343	IXC Communications, Inc.	Austin, TX	(512) 328-1112	Telecomms & Internet	$203
5	330	KENDA Systems	Salem, NH	(603) 898-7884	Computer Software	$50
6	317	NCI Information Systems, Inc.	McLean, VA	(703) 903-0325	Computer Software	$52
7	309	Casella Waste Systems, Inc.	Rutland, VT	(802) 775-0325	Environmental	$73
8	280	Micros-to-Mainframes, Inc.	Valley Cottage, NY	(914) 268-5000	Computer Hardware	$58
9	250	The Indus Group	San Francisco, CA	(415) 904-5000	Computer Software	$76
10	235	Bowne Internet Solutions, Inc.	Birmingham, MI	(248) 642-0760	Telecomms & Internet	$5-10
11	220	Vertek International, Inc.	San Diego, CA	(619) 661-6868	Subassemblies & Components	$2.5-5
12	210	Nuclear Metals, Inc.	Concord, MA	(978) 369-5410	Advanced Materials	$29
13	200	Frontec AMT, Inc.	Stamford, CT	(203) 977-7100	Computer Software	$100
14	200	Indotronix International Corp.	Poughkeepsie, NY	(914) 473-1137	Computer Software	$45 e
15	200	AmeriPath, Inc.	Riviera Beach, FL	(561) 845-1850	Medical	$43
16	200	Siebel Systems, Inc.	San Mateo, CA	(650) 295-5000	Computer Software	$39
17	198	Sarif, Inc.	Vancouver, WA	(360) 750-0242	Telecomms & Internet	$17 e
18	190	Oce Printing Systems USA, Inc.	Boca Raton, FL	(561) 997-3100	Computer Hardware	$140 e
19	185	Paragon Computer Professionals, Inc.	Cranford, NJ	(908) 709-6767	Computer Hardware	$50-100
20	184	Computerpeople, Inc. / RPM Systems Div.	El Dorado Hills, CA	(916) 933-4033	Computer Software	$25-50

Based on employment at emerging technology manufacturers with under 1,000 employees. **Jobs** = number of new technology manufacturing jobs projected for the 12 months following the survey. **e** = estimated. **p** = parent.
Source: CorpTech, Woburn, MA (800) 333-8036

Who's Hiring Who at High-Growth Companies

Richard Thau and Jay Heflin

Purchasers of financial instruments, such as stocks and mutual funds, are often told, "Past performance is no guarantee of future return." This is a quick way to warn investors that it is impossible to know the future, even if the past seems, by all accounts, to be a clear guide.

But there's a big difference between knowing the future and attempting to anticipate its likely characteristics. To see what the next several years might hold for high-tech industries and the companies within, we should look at what has occurred in the past and view its impact on these industries. From this vantage point we can deduce the trends and the likely changes in a market's future.

The most thorough analysis of emerging technology markets comes from a study titled *Occupational Outlook Handbook, 1998–99* released by the U.S. Department of Labor's Bureau of Labor Statistics (BLS). In it, the BLS analyzes numerous fields, not just technologically related ones.

The chapter titled "Tomorrow's Jobs" offers an overview of future employment opportunities. It states, "The fastest growing occupations reflect growth in computer technology and health services." Positions for personal, home care, and health aides are expected to increase. This will be due to the number of baby boomers reaching elderhood early in the next century and swelling the size of the over 65 demographic. As for computer technology, engineers and analysts will be in demand for scientific research and other applications of the computer.

As for what might occur in other technical/professional fields, the following highlights provide some context for projecting likely job growth:

- Biotechnology: The study indicates that biological and medical scientist positions are expected to increase faster than the average for all occupations through the year 2005. Competition for these positions will also grow. Job seekers in this area can expect a lot of company when jockeying for an employment slot. The study also states that the field will continue to conduct genetic and biotechnological research and help develop and produce products developed by new biological methods. Careers related to AIDS, cancer, the environment, and the Human Genome Project will also grow.

  The report goes on to say that possession of a bachelor's degree in biological science will not qualify a person as a scientist. Rather, these people will have opportunities available to them within the field as science or engineering technicians or health technologists and technicians. Receiving a doctorate will not only ensure the title of scientist but will also guard against dwindling employment opportunities due to economic slumps. Most biological and medical scientists are employed on research projects or in agricultural research that is designed to be long term.

- Electronics: "Employment opportunities for electrical and electronics engineers are expected to be positive through 2005. Most job openings will result from job growth and the need to replace electrical engineers who transfer to other occupations or leave the labor force," the study says. The opportunities that will occur in the future will be in sync with the number of graduates and other entrants seeking employment within the field.

  Although many of the employees in this field are government workers and lay-offs do occur, particularly in the area of defense, the BLS report says there will be enough demand in the private sector for those looking there. The trick to staying competitive in this area is keeping abreast of the latest technical findings.

- Computers: The study states that computer scientists and system analysts will be among the fastest-growing occupations through the year 2005. In addition, tens of thousands of job openings will result annually from the need to replace workers who move into managerial positions or other occupations or who leave the labor force.

  As companies seek to maximize the efficiency of their computer systems to better control their bottom line and stay competitive with rival firms, technological advances in areas such as office and factory automation, telecommunications technology, and scientific research will be made. In doing this, the applications of systems will become more complex, allowing the demand for computer scientists and system analysts to increase. Their job will be "to design, develop and implement the new technology."

Interestingly, the common denominator to success in all these fields is education. Often, the more education and training a person gets, the more likely the highest-paying jobs will be available in their chosen field. The study states that "workers in jobs with low education and training requirements tend to have greater occupational mobility. Consequently, these jobs will provide a larger-than-proportional share of all job openings stemming from replacement needs. Jobs requiring the most education and training will grow faster than jobs with lower education and training requirements." Careers that will require the employee to have a bachelor's degree will increase 23 percent by the year 2005. This estimate is nearly double the 12 percent growth expected for the less-educated staff positions.

Some Firm Examples

Among various high-growth small and midsize technology firms, there have been specific areas of employment expansion over the last year or two.

Interviews with human resources people working for these fast-growing companies gives us a snapshot of the hiring patterns of both small and large companies with varying personnel needs:

- Symbiosis Corporation, a company in Miami, Florida, that manufactures and distributes disposable medical devices, has grown from 300 employees to 900 employees in the past five years. Tom McKenney, the Director of Human Resources, says he hires primarily development engineers such as mechanical, biotechnical, and manufacturing engineers and asssembly and production personnel. They have no sales or marketing staff at their location. Their parent company, Boston Scientific in Natick, Massachusetts, handles all of their sales, marketing, and product support needs.

- Mikohn Gaming Corporation, a computer hardware company located in Las Vegas, Nevada, employs nearly 930 workers and usually hires 60 people a year. "Right now we have 12 openings available; that's usually our norm for any given period," reports Helea Awoub. She is one of Mikohn's human resources professionals who screens potential employees. And though they do hire Ph.D.'s, a college degree will not always secure a position within their ranks. "We like to focus on people who have the right work history or skills—the ones who show an aptitude for the job. Sometimes a degree won't tell us enough about the person, which is why we don't limit ourselves to college graduates," states Ms. Awoub. Currently working within the company's computer science department are two IS employees who don't possess a college degree.

- PAR Technology Corporation also does not restrict itself to just hiring college graduates, but for different reasons. "By law we can't require the people we hire to have a college degree, but we do prefer it," said Bill Gaw, a recruiting professional for the company. PAR Tech is a computer hardware and holding company located in New Hartford, New York. Founded in 1968, it employs almost 1,000 workers and annually hires about 20 computer scientists who possess the right attributes. "We look to hire the candidates who have experience in specific languages for programming and design," says Gaw. We also seek those who have worked with the most updated programs like Windows 95 and Windows NT."

- Howmet Dover Casting, a company whose main activity is transportation, hires people with technical degrees, like mechanical or industrial engineering. They also seek those with industry experience, whose job skills are relevant to the position they are hiring for. The number of jobs that open within a given year varies, but, on average, the number hovers around fifty.

- Precision Interconnect, based in Portland, Oregon, specializes in subassemblies, components, and telecommunications. With sales estimated at $120 million and an employment growth rate of 20 percent, Interconnect hires about 100 new people each year.

Low-Tech Jobs at High-Tech Companies—
The *Hidden* Job Market

In today's changing technical industries, most nontechnical employment seekers are looking to satisfy one basic question: Will the nontechnical skills I have today still be applicable in tomorrow's technical job market?

The answer is simple. There is a general misconception about gaining employment in the high-tech industry. Many people believe a technical background is essential. This is not true. What most employers desire in a candidate is intelligence, curiosity, and a willingness to learn.

In areas ranging from contract administration to customer service to independent software vendor (ISV) relations, high-tech firms regularly hire people who bring a wealth of nontechnical knowledge, or sometimes just their open minds, to their positions. And interestingly, nontechnical employees, once hired, often find that they develop technical skills because their jobs require them. For example, a public relations person at a high-tech company cannot promote the company's line without understanding some of the intricacies of the products being manufactured.

There are many different positions at high-tech companies that in one way or another fit the description of low tech. These include account management, human resources, forecasting, publications management, sales support, and training management. Under marketing alone there are a variety of positions in areas such as advertising, public relations, and channels communication that fit the description of low-tech jobs.

Despite all of the segmentation in American life, workers who possess a multitude of skills and knowledge still have a place in today's workforce. Indeed, at small to midsize companies, where most of the growth in employment is occurring, employees must be able to handle a variety of disparate tasks.

Says the human resources administrator at one high-tech firm, "The nature of administrative jobs has widened. For example, accounting people are now doing finance and audits and maybe some program administration. You have a better understanding of your own job if you know how it affects everyone around you." This is also true for technical positions, she adds. "We used to have inspectors doing their work after the assembly on the production line. Now the positions of inspector and quality control supervisor have been eliminated and their responsibilities are embedded in other jobs."

But what happens within high-tech companies that grow quickly? Do CEOs still do the public relations? Are presidents handling all of the accounting requirements? Or do they find qualified professionals to pick up these responsibilities?

The answer is that these firms increasingly find themselves turning to nontechnical personnel to handle their ever-increasing business responsibilities. However, hiring is usually done sparingly, only when firms are pressed against the wall by client demands or changes in the business climate.

As the director of personnel for one medical products company put it, "When you're smaller, you have people who wear a lot of different hats."

Successful high-tech companies, many of which have grown phenomenally fast over the last several years, have increasingly found that they must turn to specialists in personnel, accounting, marketing, and advertising to handle the nontechnical aspects of their businesses. Aggressive start-up companies, such as the ones listed in this book, will most likely continue to thrive in the U.S. And as they do, they will continue to need support specialists.

One company that has been increasing its nontechnical workforce as fast as it has its technical workforce is Advanced Energy Industries, Inc., in Fort Collins, Colorado. This company manufactures power delivery and control systems for thin-film equipment manufacturers that produce such things as CD-ROMs, semiconductors, and flat display equipment. Dick Beck, Advanced Energy's president, says that his company is most likely to hire engineers and electronics technicians, but they hire sales and marketing people with technical backgrounds, software programmers, and manufacturing and product support personnel as well. With a 50 percent annual growth rate, his company is always looking for enthusiastic new people.

The story is the same for BASF Bioresearch Corporation, in Worcester, Massachusetts. This compay does research on diseases of the immune system and, according to Pamela Barney, the company's Manager of Human Resources, hires only research technologists. Their parent company provides them with nontechnical and product support from a different location.

Looking Forward

In researching the vast opportunities for possible employment at high-growth companies, one mustn't wear blinders. In looking ahead one must realize that global markets are here to stay, and the areas of highest activity reflect that reality.

As Labor Secretary Robert B. Reich says in his *Message from the Secretary*, "The rules for competing in a technologically advanced global economy are changing every day. The jobs of the future and the challenges posed by global competitiveness will require a skilled American workforce that can quickly adapt to a changing workplace."

How does a person catch a break in this climate? If you are seeking a high-tech job, stay educated about new findings in your industry, keep abreast of the status of the companies that you would like to work for, spend time at the firms themselves, look at the jobs posted on the employee-only bulletin boards, and use the library to study the company. If you are interested in a low-tech job at a high-tech company, be flexible, be prepared to be the wearer of many hats, learn as much as you can from the people who work in your company, and above all, learn to expect and cope with the unexpected.

Richard Thau and Jay Heflin are freelance business writers from New York City.

Getting the Job *You* Want

Using the Book to Your Advantage

This book has been developed to assist in all three phases of the job-hunting process:

1. Identifying potential employers
2. Persuading a potential employer that you are a good applicant
3. Convincing a potential employer that you would be a good employee

Identifying Potential Employers

For a company to be regarded as a potential employer, it must currently be hiring new staff, be in a location where you wish to work, and be an employer of people with your skills at your income level. No approach will guarantee success, but the following steps will help you identify potential employers.

1. *Concentrate on growing companies.* Simply by using this book, you have an advantage over other job seekers. The 2,000 firms profiled are those that have added the most new jobs in the past year and are active in the most dynamic sector of the country's economy.

2. *Find companies in your area.* Turn to your state in the book where the companies are listed alphabetically by name. Use the **Metropolitan Area Index** to find companies in specific areas within states.

3. *Find companies active in your industry.* If your job skills are specific to a particular industry, turn to the **Industry Index.** Firms active in specific areas of industry are listed alphabetically, with a page number directing you to their detailed description.

4. *Use the press.* Read the business section of your local paper and the regional and national business press. Look for stories about firms that are doing well. Notice which companies have just won a major contract, opened a new manufacturing plant, or are simply growing rapidly. When you find one that sounds interesting, look for it in the **Company Index**; if it is listed, the index will direct you to its profile.

Once you have found a firm that you would like to approach, call its sales department and request company sales literature. When this arrives, scan it to gain an overview of the company's products, noting questions that occur to you. If you are still interested, memorize the main facts—number of employees, growth, annual sales, and industries in which the company is active. (For the firms listed in *Peterson's Hidden Job Market 1999,* all of this information is featured.) Now you are ready to make contact.

Persuading a Potential Employer
That You Are a Good Applicant

Remember that companies receive job applications every day. Your task is to make your application stand out from the pack so that you get an interview. The good news it that 95 percent of job applications are poorly prepared, and yours won't be among them if you take this advice:

- Don't mail out a form letter to dozens of firms.

- Don't enclose a poorly copied resume—in fact, don't enclose a resume at all. The task at this phase is to get in the door, not to get hired. The more you say about yourself, the more reasons the employer will have to cross you off the list before even meeting you.

- Don't apply to a company unless you can think of several reasons you would be of value. Consider the job for which you are applying, and write down the skills and experience it requires. Then note your own skills and experience as they relate to the employer's needs. If your skills and experience are strong, make sure you communicate this to the company. If they are not, think about another job. If *you* can't think of some good reasons why you should be hired, it is certain the company won't either!

On the positive side, there are a number of things you can do to advance your application:

- Make a personal approach to a named executive, not just to a department. (The listings in this book usually give the name of the personnel director or CEO.)

- Make your initial contact a telephone call rather than a letter.

- Make sure you are sufficiently prepared *before* making your approach.

- Explain in as few words as possible what you have to offer the company, emphasizing your past accomplishments rather than future goals. The world is full of dreamers with goals, but companies hire people to do a job, and your list of actual accomplishments is your best selling tool. Even if you are looking for your first job, you should be able to cite accomplishments in community or leisure activities that demonstrate your ability to define a goal and work to achieve it.

- If you choose to approach the executive in writing, call first to double-check his or her name, title, and address and make sure that the person is still in the same position. Make your letter brief, and design it exclusively to get yourself in the door. There must be no typing or spelling errors. The letter should be perfect and attractively laid out.

Use a word processor with a good printer if you have them, or enlist the aid of a friend or professional who does. You will be judged by the impression the letter makes.

- If you phone as suggested, rehearse your technique with a friend until you know without thinking what you will say to a variety of responses, from "He's not in" to "We aren't hiring" to "Put your resume in the mail" to "Why should I see you?"
- Whether you call or write, use your knowledge of the firm's products to explain why you think that you would be of value to the company, and request an interview.

Convincing a Potential Employer That You Would Be a Good Employee

Take the sales literature you received to the interview together with the list of questions you compiled. Make a point of asking your questions as early in the interview as possible, showing the interviewer that you are serious and interested. Refer to the job analysis you made and ask if this accurately defines the skills and experience required. This demonstrates that you have made an effort to see the job from the employer's perspective, a valuable quality. The answers you receive to these questions will allow you to present yourself in a way that is relevant to the company's needs.

Most interviewees have little or no knowledge of the companies to which they apply. This comes across as a lack of interest. Those few who take the modest amount of time needed to do the kind of research described stand out head and shoulders above the rest. They are not simply *claiming* competence, they are *demonstrating* it! Finally, remember that the interviewer has the difficult job—choosing the best applicant. Make that job easier by showing exactly what you have to offer in terms of accomplishments and a proven willingness to work hard.

Quick Tips for Job Search Success

In the four checklists that follow, we've provided some proven tips, techniques, and reminders that we're sure will improve even an experienced job seeker's chances of success. To make these lists even more useful, we've left space on each page for you to personalize them by adding items based on your own hard-learned lessons from interviews that were less than perfect. Experience is a great teacher and, since you pay dearly for the lessons you learn, you might as well benefit by improving your checklist. It will be invaluable in your future job searches.

We recommend taking the "During the Interview" checklist with you to your job interview. A last-minute glance at it will remind you of the essential things to do to make a terrific first impression.

Good luck!

Applying for a Job

- Thoroughly research the companies you apply to—a good reference librarian can guide you to the best sources for your research, including annual reports, Web sites, trade press articles, and *Who's Who* for information on founders or top executives.

- Avoid form letters. Customize your letter to fit each company that you apply to.

- Send a query letter without a resume to companies listed in this book; your intent at this point is to gather information. You can follow up with a tailored resume once you learn more about the qualifications the company is seeking.

- Make your approach to the hiring manager. Research the person's name, title, and address and make sure you spell everything correctly in any correspondence.

- Don't apply to a company unless you can think of good reasons why you would be a valuable asset. If you can't, they probably won't be able to either.

- Give your letter a reasonable amount of time to be delivered to the recipient, then make a phone call. Be prepared to cite your accomplishments, potential value to the company, and the reasons you want to work there.

- Be sure your resume is current and that it has no typographical errors. Contact your references now so you will be ready to provide their names if asked during the interview.

NOTES

Preparing for the Interview

- Find out the exact names and titles of all the people who will interview you. Take extra copies of your resume with you in case some interviewers didn't receive a copy.

- Find out how long the interview is expected to last. This will help you to determine how much time you have to ask your questions and provide information about yourself.

- If you've never been to the company before, make a trial run the day before to see how long it will take to get there. The day of the interview, give yourself plenty of time and get there early.

- Make sure your hands, hair, and skin are clean and well-groomed and that your clothes are pressed.

- Dress professionally. Minimize accessories and excess baggage. Carry only a small portfolio with copies of your resume and any other materials that demonstrate your skills and accomplishments. You might want to take a magazine or book to read, in case you have to wait for your interviewer.

- Prepare a list of questions that you would like to have answered during the interview. If you don't have any questions, you may appear uninterested in the job.

- Be prepared for the many questions that might be asked of you, even inappropriate ones, and rehearse your responses. If possible, ask a friend to conduct a mock interview with you and focus on difficult questions.

NOTES

During the Interview

- Smile.

- Shake hands firmly and make eye contact.

- Exhibit poise, enthusiasm, and good manners.

- Think before you speak. It is perfectly OK to gather your thoughts before you respond to a question.

- Speak clearly, confidently, and in complete sentences. Avoid using slang expressions—they may make you appear unintelligent and immature.

- Listen attentively—sit forward in your chair. Don't interrupt, argue, tell jokes, fidget, chew your nails, or play with your hair or jewelry.

- Take notes and check *your* list of questions to make sure they have been answered.

- It is all right to ask about the salary *range* if your interviewer has not mentioned it. Don't ask about specifics and don't discuss it any further at this stage of the interview process.

- Never criticize or complain about your former employer, professors, or anyone for that matter. Nobody else can understand what it was really like in your last job, and you will come across as a disgruntled complainer.

- Never lie about your credentials or abilities.

NOTES

After the Interview

- Thank your interviewers for their time and the opportunity to learn something about their company and the job.

- Reiterate your interest in the job—if, indeed, you are still interested.

- Ask what the time frame is for filling the position and ask if it is OK for you to call your interviewer to check on the status of hiring.

- Send a thank you note the same day or the next day at the latest.

- If you haven't heard from the interviewer within a week, make a follow-up call to check on your status.

NOTES

2,000 High-Growth Companies That Are Hiring at Four Times the National Average

Alabama

ADS Environmental Services, Inc.
5025 Bradford Blvd.
Huntsville, AL 35805
http://www.adsenv.com
Founded: 1979
Total Employees: 325
Annual Sales: $40 million
Industry: Environmental
Growth: Openings in past year, 25
Contact Ms. Jennifer Goodman, Director of Human Resources; 205-430-3366; Fax: 205-430-3961

Boeing Cummings Research Park
689 Discovery Dr.
Huntsville, AL 35806
Founded: 1977
Total Employees: 850
Industries: Defense, Manufacturing Equipment, Transportation
Growth: Openings in past year, 98
Contact Ms. Nickee Reynolds-Mahoney, Senior Manager of Human Resources; 205-922-6600; Fax: 205-922-7070

CAS, Inc.
PO Box 11190
Huntsville, AL 35814
http://www.cas-inc.com
Founded: 1979
Total Employees: 550
Industry: Defense
Growth: Openings in past year, 100
Contact William H. Stender, Jr., Chief Executive Officer; 205-895-8600; Fax: 205-895-8668; E-mail: charlie.vaughn@cas-inc.com

Command Data, Incorporated
2204 Lake Shore Dr., Suite 206
Birmingham, AL 35209
http://www.commanddata.com
Founded: 1976
Total Employees: 185
Annual Sales: $23 million
Industries: Computer Hardware, Computer Software, Holding Companies
Growth: Openings in past year, 35
Contact Ken Robinson, President; 205-879-3282; Fax: 205-870-1405; E-mail: cdi@commanddata.com

CPSI
6600 Wall St.
Mobile, AL 36695
Founded: 1979
Total Employees: 272
Industry: Computer Software
Growth: Openings in past year, 46
Contact Dr. Dennis Wilkins, Ph.D., President; 334-639-8100; Fax: 334-639-8214

Dynetics, Inc.
PO Box 5500
Huntsville, AL 35814
http://www.dynetics.com
Founded: 1974
Total Employees: 412
Annual Sales: $42 million
Industries: Defense, Factory Automation, Photonics, Subassemblies and Components
Growth: Openings in past year, 96
Contact Ms. Donna Brewington, Human Resources Manager; 205-922-9230; Fax: 205-922-9255; E-mail: marketing.services@dynetics.com

Electro Design Manufacturing, Inc.
4603 Hwy. 31 South. PO Box 2208
Decatur, AL 35609
Founded: 1985
Total Employees: 140
Annual Sales: $17 million
Industries: Manufacturing Equipment, Subassemblies and Components
Growth: Openings in past year, 40
Contact Ms. Faith Ashwander, Personnel Administrator; 205-353-3855; Fax: 205-353-3979

MEVATEC Corporation
1525 Perimeter Pkwy., Suite 500
Huntsville, AL 35806
http://www.mevatec.com
Founded: 1985
Total Employees: 340
Industries: Computer Software, Defense
Growth: Openings in past year, 62
Contact Coy Gayle, VP of Human Resources; 205-890-8000; Fax: 205-890-0000

Quantum Research International, Inc.
991 Discovery Dr.
Huntsville, AL 35806
http://www.quantum-intl.com
Founded: 1987
Total Employees: 116
Industries: Defense, Manufacturing Equipment
Growth: Openings in past year, 31
Contact D. Frank Pitts, President; 205-971-1800; Fax: 205-971-1801; E-mail: quantum@quantum-intl.com

Revere, Inc.
3500 Blue Lake Dr., Suite 400
Birmingham, AL 35243
Founded: 1981
Total Employees: 105
Annual Sales: $10.5 million
Industry: Computer Software
Growth: Openings in past year, 45
Contact Chuck Jett, COB/CEO; 205-967-4905; Fax: 205-967-4751; E-mail: sales@immpower.com

Speedring, Inc.
6717 Alabama Hwy. 157
Cullman, AL 35056
Founded: 1947
Total Employees: 200
Annual Sales: $25 million
Industries: Defense, Energy, Manufacturing Equipment, Photonics, Transportation
Growth: Openings in past year, 28
Contact Ms. Judy Bradford, Director of Personnel; 205-737-5200; Fax: 205-739-8298

Techsonic Industries, Inc.
3 Humminbird Ln.
Eufaula, AL 36027
Founded: 1973
Total Employees: 350
Industries: Test and Measurement, Transportation
Growth: Openings in past year, 49
Contact Bobby Herring, Director of Human Resources; 334-687-6613; Fax: 334-687-4272

Vulcan Engineering Co.
Helena Industrial Park
PO Box 307
Helena, AL 35080
Founded: 1970
Total Employees: 400
Industries: Factory Automation, Holding Companies
Growth: Openings in past year, 100
Contact Phil Zettler, President; 205-663-0732; Fax: 205-663-9103

XANTE Corp.
4621 Springhill Ave.
Mobile, AL 36608
http://www.xante.com
Founded: 1988
Total Employees: 200
Annual Sales: $41 million
Industry: Computer Hardware
Growth: Openings in past year, 100
Contact Robert Ross, President; 334-342-4840; Fax: 334-342-3345

Arizona

ACCRAM, Inc.
2901 Clarendon Ave.
Phoenix, AZ 85017
Founded: 1981
Total Employees: 125
Industry: Computer Hardware
Growth: Openings in past year, 45
Contact Bob Daquilante, President; 602-264-0288; Fax: 602-264-1440

Anasazi, Inc.
7500 North Dreamy Draw Dr., Suite 120
Phoenix, AZ 85020
http://www.anasazi.com
Founded: 1980
Total Employees: 650

Annual Sales: $84 million
Industries: Computer Software, Telecommunications
Growth: Openings in past year, 223
Contact Tom Castleberry, Chief Executive Officer; 602-870-3330; Fax: 602-861-7687; E-mail: anasazi@anasazi.com

ASD-Simula
10220 South 51st St.
Phoenix, AZ 85044
Founded: 1995
Total Employees: 70
Annual Sales: $2.0 million
Industries: Test and Measurement, Transportation
Growth: Openings in past year, 55
Contact Ms. Lorrie Lane, Human Resource Specialist; 602-496-0105; Fax: 602-496-0250; E-mail: asd@enet.com

Bowmar Instrument Corp., White Microelectronics Division
4246 East Wood St.
Phoenix, AZ 85040
http://www.whitemicro.com
Founded: 1980
Total Employees: 107
Annual Sales: $19 million
Industries: Computer Hardware, Subassemblies and Components
Growth: Openings in past year, 32
Contact Ms. Karen Kock, Personnel Manager; 602-437-1520; Fax: 602-437-9120; E-mail: wminfo@whitemicro.com

Buzzeo, Inc.
4041 North Central Ave., Suite 1050
Phoenix, AZ 85012
http://www.buzzeo.com
Founded: 1993
Total Employees: 150

Annual Sales: $19 million
Industry: Computer Software
Growth: Openings in past year, 63
Contact Ms. Janine Buzzeo, VP of Human Resources; 602-234-2900; Fax: 602-234-0215; E-mail: zeologix@buzzeo.com

Cabaco, Inc.
PO Box 6445
Yuma, AZ 85366
http://www.cabaco.com
Founded: 1987
Total Employees: 513
Annual Sales: $27.2 million
Industries: Advanced Materials, Computer Hardware, Computer Software, Defense, Factory Automation, Manufacturing Equipment, Subassemblies and Components, Test and Measurement, Telecommunications
Growth: Openings in past year, 103
Contact Hector Armenta, President; 520-726-6560; Fax: 520-726-5254

Computer Information Technology Corp.
3101 West Peoria Ave., Suite A208
Phoenix, AZ 85029
Founded: 1982
Total Employees: 45
Industry: Computer Software
Growth: Openings in past year, 33
Contact Gurpreet Bains, President; 602-942-5778; Fax: 602-942-2678; E-mail: citc@primenet.com

D-Velco Manufacturing of Arizona, Inc.
401 South 36th St.
Phoenix, AZ 85034
Founded: 1954
Total Employees: 185
Annual Sales: $23 million
Industries: Manufacturing Equipment, Transportation
Growth: Openings in past year, 25
Contact John Maris, Vice President; 602-275-4406; Fax: 602-275-1071

EMTEK Health Care Systems, Inc.
1501 West Fountainhead Pkwy., Suite 190
Tempe, AZ 85282
Founded: 1985
Total Employees: 240
Annual Sales: $31 million
Industries: Computer Hardware, Computer Software
Growth: Openings in past year, 40
Contact Robert Nunamaker, President; 602-902-2600; Fax: 602-902-2616

GoodNet
3443 North Central Ave., 17th Floor
Phoenix, AZ 85012
http://www.good.net
Founded: 1994
Total Employees: 75
Industry: Telecommunications
Growth: Openings in past year, 35
Contact David Jemmett, Chief Executive Officer; 602-303-9500; Fax: 602-303-0550; E-mail: sales@good.net

Hypercom Corporation
2851 West Kathleen Rd.
Phoenix, AZ 85023
http://www.hypercom.com
Founded: 1978
Total Employees: 827
Annual Sales: $196.7 million
Industries: Computer Hardware, Telecommunications
Growth: Openings in past year, 276
Contact Tom Salamone, VP of Personnel; 602-504-5000; Fax: 602-866-5380; E-mail: info@hypercom.com

InfoImage, Inc.
100 West Clarendon, Suite 2310
Phoenix, AZ 85013
http://www.infoimage.com
Founded: 1992
Total Employees: 170
Annual Sales: $11.1 million
Industry: Computer Software
Growth: Openings in past year, 40
Contact Randy Eckeel, President; 602-234-6900; Fax: 602-234-6950; E-mail: info@infoimage.com

JDA Software Group, Inc.
11811 North Tatum Blvd., Suite 2000
Phoenix, AZ 85028
http://www.jdasoftware.com
Founded: 1985
Total Employees: 425
Annual Sales: $47.8 million
Industry: Computer Software
Growth: Openings in past year, 216
Contact James D. Armstrong, Chief Executive Officer; 602-404-5500;

Fax: 602-404-5520;
E-mail: sales@
jdasoftware.com

K-Tronics, Inc.
108 Naco Hwy.
PO Box 4398
Bisbee, AZ 85603
Founded: 1978
Total Employees: 200
Annual Sales: $5 million
Industry: Subassemblies
and Components
Growth: Openings in past
year, 50
Contact Ms. Issa Maley,
Human Resources
Manager; 520-432-5388;
Fax: 520-432-3354

Komando Corp.
2711 North 24th St.
Phoenix, AZ 85008
Founded: 1992
Total Employees: 50
Annual Sales: $6.4 million
Industry: Computer
Software
Growth: Openings in past
year, 35
Contact Ms. Kim
Komando, President/
CEO; 602-381-8200;
Fax: 602-381-8221

Modular Mining Systems, Inc.
3289 East Hemisphere
Loop
Tucson, AZ 85706
http://www.mmsi.com
Founded: 1979
Total Employees: 178
Industries: Computer
Hardware, Energy
Growth: Openings in past
year, 53
Contact Michael J. Arnold,
President; 520-746-9127;
Fax: 520-889-5790;
E-mail: pr@mmsi.com

National Health Enhancement Systems, Inc.
3200 North Central Ave.,
Suite 1750
Phoenix, AZ 85012
http://www.nhesinc.com
Founded: 1983
Total Employees: 225
Annual Sales: $25.2
million
Industries: Computer
Software, Holding
Companies
Growth: Openings in past
year, 36
Contact Gregory J.
Petras, President/CEO;
602-230-7575; Fax: 602-
274-6158

Ohlinger Industries, Inc.
1211 West Melinda Ln.
Phoenix, AZ 85027
Founded: 1963
Total Employees: 86
Industries: Manufacturing
Equipment,
Transportation
Growth: Openings in past
year, 29
Contact Ms. Janice L.
Sparks, Office Manager;
602-285-0911; Fax: 602-
581-1239; E-mail:
ohlinger@primenet.com

Opto Power Corporation
3321 East Global Loop
Tucson, AZ 85706
http://www.optopower.com
Founded: 1956
Total Employees: 200
Annual Sales: $24 million
Industry: Photonics
Growth: Openings in past
year, 100
Contact Ms. Linda Aguilar,
Human Resources
Manager; 520-746-1234;
Fax: 520-294-3300;
E-mail: opc-info@
optopwer.com

OrthoLogic Corp.
2850 South 36th St., Suite
16
Phoenix, AZ 85034
http://www.orthologic.com
Founded: 1987
Total Employees: 550
Annual Sales: $41.8
million
Industries: Medical,
Pharmaceuticals
Growth: Openings in past
year, 80
Contact Ms. maryAnn
Miller, VP of Human
Resources; 602-437-
5520; Fax: 602-437-5524

Pimalco, Inc.
6833 West Willis Rd.,
Suite 5050
Chandler, AZ 85226
Founded: 1888
Total Employees: 750
Annual Sales: $100 million
Industries: Manufacturing
Equipment,
Subassemblies and
Components,
Transportation
Growth: Openings in past
year, 50
Contact Jim Matthews,
Purchasing Agent; 520-
796-1098

MEGA Systems & Chemicals, Inc.
450 North McKemy Ave.
Chandler, AZ 85226
http://www.megasyschem.
com
Founded: 1986
Total Employees: 160
Annual Sales: $20 million
Industries: Holding
Companies,
Manufacturing Equipment
Growth: Openings in past
year, 30
Contact Doug Robertson,
Director of Human
Resources; 602-437-
9105; Fax: 602-437-2613

Progressive Electronics, Inc.
325 South El Dorado
Meεa, ΛZ 85202
Founded: 1971
Total Employees: 90
Annual Sales: $15 million
Industries: Factory
Automation, Test and
Measurement
Growth: Openings in past
year, 25
Contact Richard L.
Anderson, Chief Executive Officer; 602-966-2931; Fax: 602-967-8602

Prologic Management Systems, Inc.
2030 East Speedway
Tucson, AZ 85719
http://www.prologic.com
Founded: 1987
Total Employees: 65
Annual Sales: $2.623
million
Industries: Computer
Hardware, Computer
Software, Holding
Companies,
Telecommunications
Growth: Openings in past
year, 40
Contact James M. Heim,
COB/CEO; 520-320-1000; Fax: 520-320-1100;
E-mail: info-net@
prologic.com

Right Fax, Inc.
6303 East Tanque Verde
Rd. Suite 300
Tucson, AZ 85715
http://www.rightfax.com
Founded: 1987
Total Employees: 70
Annual Sales: $9.0 million
Industry: Computer
Software
Growth: Openings in past
year, 32
Contact Bradley Feder,
President; 520-320-7000;
Fax: 520-321-7456;
E-mail: sales@rightfax.
com

Spectrum Astro, Inc.
1440 North Fiesta Blvd.
Gilbert, AZ 85234
http://www.spectrumastro.
com
Founded: 1988
Total Employees: 200
Annual Sales: $26 million
Industries:
Subassemblies and
Components,
Telecommunications,
Transportation
Growth: Openings in past
year, 89
Contact Ms. Martha S.
Martin, COB/CEO; 602-892-8200; Fax: 602-892-2949; E-mail: info@
specastro.com

Speedfam International, Inc.
7406 West Detroit St.
Chandler, AZ 85226
Founded: 1959
Total Employees: 480
Annual Sales: $120 million
Industry: Holding
Companies
Growth: Openings in past
year, 28
Contact M. Kouzuma,
President/COO; 602-961-2175; Fax: 602-961-2171

Steris Laboratories
620 North 51st Ave.
PO Box 23160
Phoenix, AZ 85063
Founded: 1987
Total Employees: 650
Annual Sales: $250 million
Industry: Pharmaceuticals
Growth: Openings in past
year, 25
Contact Ron Crowe, VP
of Human Resources;
602-269-5120; Fax: 602-269-7468

Sunquest Information Systems, Inc.
4801 East Broadway
Tucson, AZ 85711
http://www.sunquest.com
Founded: 1979
Total Employees: 750
Annual Sales: $81 million
Industries: Computer
Software, Holding
Companies
Growth: Openings in past
year, 150
Contact Ms. Marsha
Morgan, VP of Human
Resources; 602-570-2000; Fax: 602-570-2492

Varian Tempe Electronics Center
615 South River Rd.
Tempe, AZ 85281
http://www.varian.com
Founded: 1984
Total Employees: 650
Annual Sales: $90 million
Industry: Subassemblies
and Components
Growth: Openings in past
year, 122
Contact Mel Erron,
Human Resources
Manager; 602-968-6790;
Fax: 602-829-4000;
E-mail: marketing@vtec.
varian.com

Veeco Process Meterology
2650 East Elvira Rd.
Tucson, AZ 85706
http://www.veeco.com
Founded: 1982
Total Employees: 135
Industries: Computer
Software, Factory
Automation, Photonics,
Test and Measurement
Growth: Openings in past
year, 45
Contact Ms. Helen
Cigrand, Human
Resources Manager;
520-741-1297; Fax: 520-294-1799; E-mail:
sales@wyko.com

WavePhore, Inc.
3311 North 44th St.
Phoenix, AZ 85018
http://www.wavephore.com
Founded: 1990
Total Employees: 200
Annual Sales: $19.020
million
Industries: Holding
Companies,
Telecommunications
Growth: Openings in past
year, 35
Contact David E. Deeds,
COB/President/CEO;
602-952-5500; Fax: 602-
952-5517

Arkansas

Hitech, Inc.
PO Box 3112
Camden, AR 71701
Founded: 1982
Total Employees: 220
Annual Sales: $39 million
Industry: Defense
Growth: Openings in past
year, 100
Contact Gene Hill,
President/CEO; 870-798-
4171; Fax: 870-798-4004

INDUTEC Corp.
PO Box 4328
Fayetteville, AR 72702
http://www.indutec.com
Founded: 1993
Total Employees: 57
Annual Sales: $2.9 million
Industries:
Subassemblies and
Components,
Telecommunications
Growth: Openings in past
year, 26
Contact James Penny,
COB/CEO; 501-444-
6548; Fax: 501-444-
6546; E-mail: penny@
ipa.net

Pel-Freez, Inc.
PO Box 68
Rogers, AR 72757
Founded: 1911
Total Employees: 171
Annual Sales: $18 million
Industry: Holding
Companies
Growth: Openings in past
year, 36
Contact David Dubbell,
Chief Executive Officer;
501-636-4361; Fax: 501-
636-4282

California

**3Com Corp., Palm
Computing, Inc.**
1565 Charleston Rd.
Mountain View, CA 94043
http://www.palmpilot.3com.
com/palm
Founded: 1992
Total Employees: 150
Industries: Computer
Hardware, Computer
Software
Growth: Openings in past
year, 122
Contact Jeff Hawkins,
Chief Technology Officer;
650-237-6000; Fax: 415-
968-9822

3D Systems, Inc.
26081 Ave. Hall
Valencia, CA 91355
http://www.3dsystems.com
Founded: 1987
Total Employees: 340
Annual Sales: $79.6
million
Industry: Manufacturing
Equipment
Growth: Openings in past
year, 140
Contact Arthur Sims,
Chief Executive Officer;
805-295-5600; Fax: 805-
257-1200

AAC Corp.
18300 Von Karman Ave.,
Suite 850
Irvine, CA 92715
http://www.aaccorp.com
Founded: 1972
Total Employees: 100
Annual Sales: $17 million
Industries: Computer
Software, Holding
Companies,
Telecommunications
Growth: Openings in past
year, 25
Contact Ricardo Brutocao,
President; 714-756-2700;
Fax: 714-851-6286;
E-mail: corpinfo@
aaccorp.com

AB Plastics
15730 South Figueroa St.
Gardena, CA 90248
Founded: 1952
Total Employees: 348
Annual Sales: $43 million
Industry: Manufacturing
Equipment
Growth: Openings in past
year, 63
Contact Michael A. Gibbs,
Chief Executive Officer;
213-770-8771; Fax: 310-
523-9859

**Accu-Fab California
Systems, Inc.**
4763 Bennett Dr.
Livermore, CA 94550
Founded: 1992
Total Employees: 90
Annual Sales: $13 million
Industry: Factory
Automation
Growth: Openings in past
year, 30
Contact Bill Robinson,
President; 510-606-1302;
Fax: 510-606-1305

**Acme Laundry Products,
Inc.**
21600 Lassen St.
Chatsworth, CA 91311
Founded: 1967
Total Employees: 170
Annual Sales: $22 million

Industries: Manufacturing Equipment, Test and Measurement
Growth: Openings in past year, 70
Contact Ms. Jan Rome, President; 818-341-0700; Fax: 818-341-1546

ACT Networks, Inc.
188 Camino Ruiz
Camarillo, CA 93012
http://www.acti.com
Founded: 1987
Total Employees: 200
Annual Sales: $28.4 million
Industries: Computer Hardware, Subassemblies and Components, Telecommunications
Growth: Openings in past year, 40
Contact Martin Shum, COB/President/CEO; 805-388-2474; Fax: 805-388-3504

ADAC Laboratories
540 Alder Dr.
Milpitas, CA 95035
Founded: 1970
Total Employees: 750
Annual Sales: $240.785 million
Industries: Holding Companies, Medical
Growth: Openings in past year, 98
Contact David L. Lowe, COB/CEO; 408-321-9100; Fax: 408-321-9536

AdiCom Wireless, Inc.
26142 Eden Landing Rd.
Hayward, CA 94545
http://www.adicomw.com
Founded: 1996
Total Employees: 60
Annual Sales: $10 million
Industry: Telecommunications
Growth: Openings in past year, 30

Contact Dr. Adel Ghamen, President/CEO; 510-781-5520; Fax: 510-781-5525

Advanced Aerodynamics & Structures, Inc.
3501 Lakewood Blvd.
Long Beach, CA 90808
http://www.aasiaircraft.com
Founded: 1990
Total Employees: 60
Industry: Transportation
Growth: Openings in past year, 34
Contact Dr. Carl Chen, COB/CEO; 562-938-8618; Fax: 562-938-8620

Advanced Bioresearch Associates
3377 North Torre Pines Ct.
La Jolla, CA 92037
http://www.advbio.com/~advbio
Founded: 1978
Total Employees: 50
Annual Sales: $5.3 million
Industry: Biotechnology
Growth: Openings in past year, 25
Contact Howard Asher, President; 619-535-1500; Fax: 619-535-1550; E-mail: advbio.com

Advanced Computer Communications
340 Storke Rd.
Santa Barbara, CA 93117
http://www.acc.com
Founded: 1987
Total Employees: 200
Annual Sales: $45 million
Industries: Computer Hardware, Telecommunications
Growth: Openings in past year, 30
Contact Ms. Kathy Gress, Human Resources Manager; 805-685-4455; Fax: 805-685-4465; E-mail: info@acc.com

Advanced Packaging Technology of America
6828 Nancy Ridge Dr.
San Diego, CA 92121
Founded: 1994
Total Employees: 150
Annual Sales: $20 million
Industries: Advanced Materials, Subassemblies and Components
Growth: Openings in past year, 50
Contact Per Tonnesen, President; 619-452-2700; Fax: 619-452-2325

Advent Software, Inc.
301 Brannan St., 6th Floor
San Francisco, CA 94107
http://www.advent.com
Founded: 1983
Total Employees: 315
Annual Sales: $36.744 million
Industries: Computer Hardware, Computer Software
Growth: Openings in past year, 65
Contact Ms. Stephanie DiMarco, CEO/COB; 415-543-7696; Fax: 415-543-5070; E-mail: info@advent.com

Aeronautical Systems, Inc.
16761 Via Del Camp Ct.
San Diego, CA 92127
Founded: 1993
Total Employees: 290
Annual Sales: $38 million
Industry: Transportation
Growth: Openings in past year, 40
Contact John Sullivan, Human Resources Manager; 619-455-2810; Fax: 619-455-4247

Affymetrix, Inc.
3380 Central Expwy.
Santa Clara, CA 95051

http://www.affymetrix.com
Founded: 1992
Total Employees: 161
Annual Sales: $11.9 million
Industry: Biotechnology
Growth: Openings in past year, 61
Contact Stephen P.A. Foder, Ph.D., President/CEO; 408-522-6000; Fax: 408-481-0422

Agile Software Corp.
1 Almaden Blvd., 12th Fl.
San Jose, CA 95113
http://www.agilesoft.com
Founded: 1994
Total Employees: 50
Industry: Computer Software
Growth: Openings in past year, 32
Contact Brian Stolle, President/CEO; 408-975-3900; Fax: 408-271-4862; E-mail: info@agilesoft.com

Ahntech, Inc.
5575 Ruffin Rd., Suite 100
San Diego, CA 92123
http://www.ahntech.com
Founded: 1984
Total Employees: 170
Annual Sales: $21 million
Industries: Computer Software, Manufacturing Equipment, Medical
Growth: Openings in past year, 34
Contact Dr. Sam Ahn, President; 619-565-1900; Fax: 619-277-0974

Airtronics Metal Products, Inc.
1980 Senter Rd.
San Jose, CA 95112
http://www.airtronics.com
Founded: 1962
Total Employees: 115
Annual Sales: $14 million
Industries: Computer Hardware, Manufacturing Equipment, Subassemblies and Components

Growth: Openings in past year, 37
Contact John S. Richardson, Jr., President; 408-977-7800; Fax: 408-977-7810; E-mail: info@airtronics.com

Alflex Corp.
2630 El Presidio St.
Long Beach, CA 90810
Founded: 1984
Total Employees: 360
Industry: Subassemblies and Components
Growth: Openings in past year, 60
Contact Steve Roush, VP of Human Resources; 310-886-8300; Fax: 310-631-3602

Alias, Wavefront
614 Chapala St.
Santa Barbara, CA 93101
http://www.wavefront.wti.com
Founded: 1984
Total Employees: 500
Annual Sales: $64 million
Industry: Computer Software
Growth: Openings in past year, 100
Contact Brian S. Allum, President/CEO; 805-884-7800; Fax: 805-963-0410; E-mail: info@aw.sgi.com

ALLDATA Corp.
9412 Big Horn Blvd.
Elk Grove, CA 95758
http://www.alldata.com
Founded: 1986
Total Employees: 300
Industry: Computer Hardware
Growth: Openings in past year, 50
Contact Mrs. Karlyn Oberg, Director of Finance and Administration; 916-684-5200; Fax: 916-684-5225

Alliance Pharmaceutical Corp.
3040 Science Park Rd.
San Diego, CA 92121
http://www.allp.com
Founded: 1983
Total Employees: 240
Annual Sales: $44.6 million
Industries: Advanced Materials, Chemicals, Medical, Pharmaceuticals
Growth: Openings in past year, 40
Contact Ms. Carole McWilson, Director of Human Resources; 619-558-4300; Fax: 619-678-4133; E-mail: corpcom@allp.com

AlliedSignal Inc., AlliedSignal Advanced Microelectronic Materials
3500 Garrett Dr.
Santa Clara, CA 95054
Founded: 1984
Total Employees: 160
Annual Sales: $30 million
Industries: Advanced Materials, Manufacturing Equipment
Growth: Openings in past year, 60
Contact Jim Gemmell, Human Resource Director; 408-562-0300; Fax: 408-980-1430

Alteon Networks, Inc.
6351 San Ignacio Ave.
San Jose, CA 95119
http://www.alteon.com
Founded: 1996
Total Employees: 50
Annual Sales: $6.7 million
Industries: Subassemblies and Components, Telecommunications
Growth: Openings in past year, 35
Contact Ms. Kathleen Nichols, Human Resources Manager; 408-360-5500

Amada Engineering Services, Inc.
14921 East Northam St.
La Mirada, CA 90638
http://www.amada.net
Founded: 1980
Total Employees: 250
Annual Sales: $78 million
Industry: Factory Automation
Growth: Openings in past year, 50
Contact Yasumasa Kageyama, President; 714-670-2111; Fax: 714-739-4634

American Business Service & Computer Technologies
9999 Rose Hills Rd.
Whittier, CA 90601
http://www.abscomputers.com
Founded: 1989
Total Employees: 140
Annual Sales: $60 million
Industry: Computer Hardware
Growth: Openings in past year, 75
Contact George Jiao, General Manager; 562-695-8823; Fax: 562-695-8923

American MSI Corp.
5245 Maureen Ln.
Moorpark, CA 93021
Founded: 1984
Total Employees: 100
Annual Sales: $13 million
Industry: Test and Measurement
Growth: Openings in past year, 40
Contact Ms. Beth Baker, Human Resources Director; 805-523-9593; Fax: 805-523-0575

Ameritec Corp.
760 Arrow Grand Cir.
Covina, CA 91722
Founded: 1980
Total Employees: 150
Industries: Factory Automation, Telecommunications
Growth: Openings in past year, 30
Contact John Van Der Goore, Personnel Manager; 626-915-5441; Fax: 626-915-7181; E-mail: ameritec@netcom.com

Anabolic, Inc.
17802 Gillette Ave.
Irvine, CA 92614
http://www.anaboliclabs.com
Founded: 1924
Total Employees: 180
Annual Sales: $26 million
Industry: Pharmaceuticals
Growth: Openings in past year, 30
Contact Steven R. Brown, President; 714-863-0340; Fax: 714-261-2928

Anchor Audio, Inc.
3415 Lomita Blvd.
Torrance, CA 90505
http://www.anchoraudio.com
Founded: 1984
Total Employees: 95
Industry: Telecommunications
Growth: Openings in past year, 30
Contact David Jacobs, President; 310-784-2300; Fax: 310-784-0066; E-mail: anchorjw@aol.com

ANDATACO
10140 Mesa Rim Rd.
San Diego, CA 92121
http://www.andataco.com

Founded: 1986
Total Employees: 310
Annual Sales: $100 million
Industry: Computer Hardware
Growth: Openings in past year, 74
Contact Ms. Lagaya Bowman, Human Resources Supervisor; 619-453-9191; Fax: 619-453-9294; E-mail: inquire@andataco.com

Application Group, Inc.
275 Battery St., 5th Floor
San Francisco, CA 94111
http://www.appgroup.com
Founded: 1978
Total Employees: 375
Annual Sales: $77 million
Industries: Computer Hardware, Computer Software
Growth: Openings in past year, 125
Contact Ms. Mary Helen Waldo, Director of Human Resources; 415-421-1627; Fax: 415-765-8190; E-mail: info@appgroup.com

Arbor Software Corp.
1344 Crossman Ave.
Sunnyvale, CA 94089
http://www.arborsoft.com
Founded: 1991
Total Employees: 300
Annual Sales: $47.4 million
Industry: Computer Software
Growth: Openings in past year, 165
Contact James Dorrian, COB/CEO; 408-744-9500; Fax: 408-744-0400; E-mail: info@arborsoft.com

Argonaut Technologies, Inc.
887 Industrial Rd., Suite G
San Carlos, CA 94070
http://www.argotech.com
Founded: 1994

Total Employees: 65
Annual Sales: $7.0 million
Industries: Biotechnology,
Chemicals
Growth: Openings in past
year, 35
Contact Dr. David D.
Binkley, Ph.D., President/
CEO; 650-598-1350;
Fax: 650-598-1359;
E-mail: info@argotech.
com

ArrayComm, Inc.
3141 Zanker Rd.
San Jose, CA 95134
http://www.arraycomm.com
Founded: 1992
Total Employees: 100
Industry: Computer
Software
Growth: Openings in past
year, 50
Contact Ms. Jill
Roumeliotis, Director of
Human Resources; 408-
428-9080; Fax: 408-428-
9083; E-mail: intellicell@
arraycomm.com

**Arris Pharmaceutical
Corp.**
180 Kimball Way
South San Francisco, CA
94080
http://www.arris.com
Founded: 1989
Total Employees: 182
Annual Sales: $21.560
million
Industries: Biotechnology,
Pharmaceuticals
Growth: Openings in past
year, 42
Contact J. Philip
Cunningham, VP of
Human Resources; 650-
829-1000; Fax: 650-829-
1001

ArthroCare Corp.
595 North Pastoria Ave.
Sunnyvale, CA 94086
http://www.arthrocare.com
Founded: 1993
Total Employees: 110
Annual Sales: $6.0 million

Industry: Medical
Growth: Openings in past
year, 31
Contact Michael Baker,
President/CEO; 408-736-
0224; Fax: 408-736-
0226; E-mail: info@
arthrocare.com

**Asante Technologies,
Inc.**
821 Fox Ln.
San Jose, CA 95131
http://www.asante.com
Founded: 1988
Total Employees: 190
Annual Sales: $67 million
Industries: Computer
Software,
Telecommunications
Growth: Openings in past
year, 25
Contact Jeff Lin, CEO/
President; 408-435-8388;
Fax: 408-432-1117;
E-mail: sales@asante.
com

Ashtech, Inc.
1170 Kifer Rd.
Sunnyvale, CA 94086
http://www.ashtech.com
Founded: 1987
Total Employees: 250
Annual Sales: $32 million
Industry: Transportation
Growth: Openings in past
year, 50
Contact Ms. Iris Barger,
Director of Personnel;
408-524-1400; Fax: 408-
524-1500; E-mail:
sales@ashtech.com

**Aspect Development,
Inc.**
1300 Charleston Rd.
Mountain View, CA 94043
http://www.aspectdv.com
Founded: 1991
Total Employees: 300
Annual Sales: $24.2
million
Industry: Computer
Software
Growth: Openings in past
year, 50

Contact Ms. Jill Beckman-
Donley, Human
Resources Manager;
650-428-2700; Fax: 650-
968-4335

Asymtek
2762 Loker Ave. West
Carlsbad, CA 92008
http://www.asymtek.com
Founded: 1983
Total Employees: 250
Annual Sales: $38 million
Industry: Factory
Automation
Growth: Openings in past
year, 100
Contact Ms. Laura Webb,
Employee Benefits
Coordinator; 760-431-
1919; Fax: 760-431-
2678; E-mail: info@
asymtek.com

Asyst Software, Inc.
2125 Zanker Rd.
San Jose, CA 95131
http://www.asyst.com
Founded: 1996
Total Employees: 68
Annual Sales: $8.8 million
Industries: Computer
Hardware, Computer
Software
Growth: Openings in past
year, 38
Contact William Leckonby,
President; 408-452-2500;
Fax: 408-452-2555

Asyst Technologies, Inc.
48761 Kato Rd.
Fremont, CA 94538
http://www.asyst.com
Founded: 1984
Total Employees: 800
Annual Sales: $137 million
Industries: Computer
Hardware, Holding
Companies,
Manufacturing Equipment
Growth: Openings in past
year, 99
Contact Ms. Debbie
Partridge, VP of Human
Resources; 510-661-
5000; Fax: 510-661-5166

Atcor Corporation
150 Great Oak Blvd.
San Jose, CA 95119
http://www.atcor.com
Founded: 1979
Total Employees: 350
Annual Sales: $15 million
Industries: Environmental,
Manufacturing
Equipment, Test and
Measurement
Growth: Openings in past
year, 240
Contact John Tidwell, VP
of Finance; 408-629-
6080; Fax: 408-629-9009

Autosplice, Inc.
10121 Barnes Canyon Rd.
San Diego, CA 92121
Founded: 1958
Total Employees: 270
Annual Sales: $40 million
Industries: Factory
Automation,
Subassemblies and
Components
Growth: Openings in past
year, 67
Contact Don Eisenberg,
President; 619-535-0077;
Fax: 619-535-0275

Avibank Mfg., Inc.
210 South Victory Blvd.
PO Box 391
Burbank, CA 91503
Founded: 1972
Total Employees: 625
Annual Sales: $60 million
Industries:
Subassemblies and
Components,
Transportation
Growth: Openings in past
year, 100
Contact Milton I. Berman,
President; 818-843-4330;
Fax: 818-846-1872

**Athena Neurosciences,
Inc.**
800 Gateway Blvd.
South San Francisco, CA
94080
http://www.athenaneuro.
com
Founded: 1986
Total Employees: 350
Annual Sales: $54 million
Industry: Pharmaceuticals
Growth: Openings in past
year, 81
Contact Jack Cummins,
Director of Human
Resources; 650-877-
0900; Fax: 650-877-
8370; E-mail: eliebler@
best.com

Avant! Corporation
46871 Bayside Pkwy.
Fremont, CA 94538
Founded: 1985
Total Employees: 444
Annual Sales: $70.608
million
Industries: Computer
Software, Holding
Companies
Growth: Openings in past
year, 224
Contact Gerald C. Hsu,
President/CEO; 510-413-
8000; Fax: 510-413-8080

Avigen, Inc.
1201 Harbor Bay Pkwy.,
Suite 1000
Alameda, CA 94502
http://www.avigen.com
Founded: 1992
Total Employees: 50
Industry: Biotechnology
Growth: Openings in past
year, 32
Contact John Monahan,
Ph.D., President/CEO;
510-748-7150; Fax: 510-
748-7155

Aurum Software, Inc.
2350 Mission College
Blvd., Suite 1300
Santa Clara, CA 95054
http://www.aurum.com
Founded: 1990
Total Employees: 350
Annual Sales: $28 million
Industry: Computer
Software
Growth: Openings in past
year, 210
Contact Ms. Mary
Coleman, President/
CEO; 408-986-8100;
Fax: 408-654-3400;
E-mail: prodinfo@aurum.
com

**AverMedia Technologies,
Inc.**
47923 A Warm Springs
Blvd.
Fremont, CA 94539
http://www.aver.com
Founded: 1992
Total Employees: 150
Annual Sales: $30 million
Industries: Computer
Hardware,
Telecommunications
Growth: Openings in past
year, 25
Contact Michael Kuo,
President; 510-770-9899;
Fax: 510-770-9901;
E-mail: alan@aver.com

**Bal Seal Engineering
Co., Inc.**
620 West Warner Ave.
Santa Ana, CA 92707
http://www.thomasregister.
com/balseal
Founded: 1960
Total Employees: 205
Industry: Subassemblies
and Components
Growth: Openings in past
year, 50
Contact Peter Bartheld,
Chief Executive Officer;
714-557-5192; Fax: 714-
241-0185; E-mail:
balseal@kaiwan.com

bd Systems, Inc.
385 Van Ness Ave., Suite 200
Torrance, CA 90501
http://www.bdsys.com
Founded: 1981
Total Employees: 300
Annual Sales: $37 million
Industries: Computer Hardware, Computer Software, Defense, Manufacturing Equipment, Transportation
Growth: Openings in past year, 50
Contact Ms. Clarisa F. Howard, President; 310-618-8798; Fax: 310-212-0753

BEA Systems, Inc.
385 Moffett Park Dr.
Sunnyvale, CA 94089
http://www.beasys.com
Founded: 1988
Total Employees: 635
Annual Sales: $61.5 million
Industry: Computer Software
Growth: Openings in past year, 143
Contact Ms. Jeanne Wu, Director of Human Resources; 408-743-4000; Fax: 408-734-9234; E-mail: info@beasys.com

BEI Sensors & Systems Co., Systron Donner Inertial Division
2700 Systron Dr.
Concord, CA 94518
http://www.beisensors.com
Founded: 1957
Total Employees: 242
Industries: Defense, Subassemblies and Components, Test and Measurement, Transportation
Growth: Openings in past year, 26

Contact Ms. Sandra Jenkins, Manager of Human Resources; 510-682-6161; Fax: 510-671-6590; E-mail: service@beisensors.com

Belkin Components
501 West Walnut St.
Compton, CA 90220
http://www.belkin.com
Founded: 1982
Total Employees: 250
Industries: Computer Hardware, Subassemblies and Components, Telecommunications
Growth: Openings in past year, 71
Contact Chet Pipkin, President; 310-898-1100; Fax: 310-898-1111; E-mail: info@belkin.com

Berghof/America
PO Box 6029
Concord, CA 94524
http://www.berghofusa.com
Founded: 1975
Total Employees: 57
Industries: Factory Automation, Subassemblies and Components, Test and Measurement
Growth: Openings in past year, 27
Contact Louis A. Rigali, President; 510-827-1868; Fax: 510-827-1189; E-mail: berghof@berghofusa.com

Biosite Diagnostics Incorporated
11030 Roselle St., Suite D
San Diego, CA 92121
Founded: 1988
Total Employees: 180
Annual Sales: $28.2 million
Industry: Medical
Growth: Openings in past year, 30
Contact Ms. Laura Weatherford, Director of

Human Resources; 619-455-4808; Fax: 619-455-4815

Bizcon Electronics, Inc.
2156 Zanker Rd.
San Jose, CA 95131
Founded: 1991
Total Employees: 05
Annual Sales: $11 million
Industry: Computer Hardware
Growth: Openings in past year, 35
Contact Duan Wang, General Manager; 408-526-0620; Fax: 408-526-1740; E-mail: bizcom@bignet.com

Black Sun Interactive, Inc.
50 Osgood Pl., Suite 100
San Francisco, CA 94133
http://www.blacksun.com
Founded: 1995
Total Employees: 55
Annual Sales: $7.1 million
Industry: Computer Software
Growth: Openings in past year, 30
Contact Franz Buchenberger, President; 415-273-7000; Fax: 415-273-7001; E-mail: info@blacksun.com

Brightware, Inc.
350 Ignacio Blvd.
Novato, CA 94949
http://www.brightware.com
Founded: 1995
Total Employees: 115
Annual Sales: $14 million
Industry: Computer Software
Growth: Openings in past year, 40
Contact Chuck Williams, President/CEO; 415-884-4744; Fax: 415-884-4740; E-mail: info@brightware.com

Brio Technology, Inc.
3950 Fabian Way, Suite
200
Palo Alto, CA 94303
http://www.brio.com
Founded: 1984
Total Employees: 150
Annual Sales: $19 million
Industry: Computer
Software
Growth: Openings in past
year, 95
Contact Yorgen Edholm,
CEO/President; 650-856-
8000; Fax: 650-856-
8020; E-mail: info@brio.
com

BroadVision, Inc.
333 Distel Cir.
Los Altos, CA 94022
http://www.broadvision.
com
Founded: 1993
Total Employees: 225
Annual Sales: $25 million
Industry: Computer
Software
Growth: Openings in past
year, 145
Contact Dr. Pehong Chen,
President/CEO; 650-943-
3600; Fax: 650-943-3699

**Broderbund Software,
Inc.**
500 Redwood Blvd.
PO Box 6121
Novato, CA 94948
http://www.broderbund.
com
Founded: 1980
Total Employees: 640
Annual Sales: $186.2
million
Industries: Computer
Software, Holding
Companies
Growth: Openings in past
year, 140
Contact Ms. Patricia
Murphy, VP of Human
Resources; 415-382-
4400; Fax: 415-382-4665

Burnham Institute
10901 North Torrey Pines
Rd.
La Jolla, CA 92037
http://www.ljcrf.edu
Founded: 1976
Total Employees: 350
Industry: Biotechnology
Growth: Openings in past
year, 29
Contact Dr. Erkki
Ruoslahti, President;
619-455-6480; Fax: 619-
646-3199

Business Objects, Inc.
2870 Zanker Rd.
San Jose, CA 95134
http://www.
businessobjects.com
Founded: 1989
Total Employees: 150
Annual Sales: $19 million
Industry: Computer
Software
Growth: Openings in past
year, 50
Contact Paul Doscher,
General Manager; 408-
953-6000; Fax: 408-953-
6001

**Cadence Design
Systems, Inc., Alta
Division**
555 North Mathilda Ave.
Sunnyvale, CA 94086
http://www.altagroup.com
Founded: 1969
Total Employees: 300
Industry: Computer
Software
Growth: Openings in past
year, 100
Contact Ms. Lori Prince,
Director of Human
Resources; 408-733-
1595; Fax: 408-523-4601

Caere Corp.
100 Cooper Ct.
Los Gatos, CA 95032
http://www.caere.com

Founded: 1973
Total Employees: 285
Annual Sales: $54.5
million
Industries: Computer
Hardware, Computer
Software
Growth: Openings in past
year, 54
Contact Robert G. Teresi,
COB/CEO/President;
408-395-7000; Fax: 408-
354-2743

**Cal Quality Electronics,
Inc.**
2700 South Fairview St.
Santa Ana, CA 92704
http://www.cal_quality.com
Founded: 1980
Total Employees: 230
Annual Sales: $31 million
Industry: Subassemblies
and Components
Growth: Openings in past
year, 55
Contact Thai Nguyen,
President; 714-545-8886;
Fax: 714-545-4975;
E-mail: eseidman@
pacbell.net

**Calex Manufacturing Co.,
Inc.**
2401 Stanwell Dr.
Concord, CA 94520
http://www.calex.com
Founded: 1962
Total Employees: 85
Industries:
Subassemblies and
Components, Test and
Measurement
Growth: Openings in past
year, 26
Contact S.P. Cuff,
President; 510-687-4411;
Fax: 510-687-3333;
E-mail: calex@best.com

**Capital Management
Sciences, Inc.**
11766 Wilshire Blvd., Suite
300
Los Angeles, CA 90025
http://www.bondvu.com
Founded: 1979

Total Employees: 115
Annual Sales: $14 million
Industry: Computer
Software
Growth: Openings in past
year, 30
Contact Ms. Amy
Hausthor, Personnel
Manager; 310-479-9715;
Fax: 310-479-6333

Cardiac Pathways Corp.
955 Benecia Ave.
Sunnyvale, CA 94086
Founded: 1991
Total Employees: 150
Annual Sales: $2.4 million
Industry: Medical
Growth: Openings in past
year, 78
Contact William N.
Starling, President/CEO;
408-737-0505; Fax: 408-
737-1700

**CardioThoracic Systems,
Inc.**
10600 North Tantau Ave.
Cupertino, CA 95014
http://www.cardioth.com
Founded: 1995
Total Employees: 120
Annual Sales: $1.5 million
Industry: Medical
Growth: Openings in past
year, 49
Contact Richard Ferrari,
President/CEO; 408-342-
1700; Fax: 408-342-
1717; E-mail: info@
cardioth.com

Carley Lamps, Inc.
1502 West 228th St.
Torrance, CA 90501
http://www.carleylamps.
com
Founded: 1975
Total Employees: 600
Industries: Medical,
Photonics,
Subassemblies and
Components
Growth: Openings in past
year, 149

Contact James A. Carley,
President; 310-325-8474;
Fax: 310-534-2912

CD Associates, Inc.
15375 Barranca Pkwy.,
Suite I-101
Irvine, CA 92718
http://www.cdassociates.
com
Founded: 1989
Total Employees: 60
Industry: Factory
Automation
Growth: Openings in past
year, 30
Contact Garret Ambrose,
Establishment Manager;
714-733-0850; Fax: 714-
453-0868; E-mail: cda@
cdassociates.com

Ceimic Corp.
8808 Balboa Ave.
San Diego, CA 92123
Founded: 1984
Total Employees: 150
Industries: Chemicals,
Environmental
Growth: Openings in past
year, 40
Contact John McGarry,
President; 619-637-7400;
Fax: 619-637-7401

CeLAN Technology, Inc.
2323 Calle Del Mundo
Santa Clara, CA 95054
http://www.celan.com
Founded: 1992
Total Employees: 150
Annual Sales: $10 million
Industry:
Telecommunications
Growth: Openings in past
year, 105
Contact Y.C. Lin, Chief
Executive Officer; 408-
988-8288; Fax: 408-988-
8289; E-mail: info@
celan.com

Celeritek, Inc.
3236 Scott Blvd.
Santa Clara, CA 95054
http://www.celeritek.com
Founded: 1985
Total Employees: 370
Annual Sales: $45.346
million
Industry: Subassemblies
and Components
Growth: Openings in past
year, 52
Contact Tamer Husseini,
COB/President; 408-986-
5060; Fax: 408-986-5095

**CellNet Data Systems,
Inc.**
125 Shoreway Rd.
San Carlos, CA 94070
http://www.cellnet.com
Founded: 1984
Total Employees: 600
Annual Sales: $1.7 million
Industry:
Telecommunications
Growth: Openings in past
year, 100
Contact John M. Seidl,
President/CEO; 650-508-
6000; Fax: 650-508-
6900; E-mail:
communications@cellnet.
com

Cemax-Icon, Inc.
47281 Mission Falls Ct.
Fremont, CA 94539
http://www.cemax-icon.com
Founded: 1982
Total Employees: 140
Annual Sales: $26 million
Industries: Computer
Software, Medical
Growth: Openings in past
year, 33
Contact Terry Ross,
President/CEO; 510-770-
8612; Fax: 510-770-
8555; E-mail: info@
cemax.com

Centigram Communications Corp.
91 East Tasman Dr.
San Jose, CA 95134
http://www.centigram.com
Founded: 1977
Total Employees: 449
Annual Sales: $104 million
Industries: Computer Software, Telecommunications
Growth: Openings in past year, 49
Contact Ms. Margaret A. Cuggino, VP of Sales; 408-944-0250; Fax: 408-428-3732

Century Analysis, Inc.
114 Center Ave.
Pacheco, CA 94553
http://www.cainc.com
Founded: 1975
Total Employees: 165
Annual Sales: $15 million
Industry: Computer Software
Growth: Openings in past year, 30
Contact Ross Hallberg, VP of Operations; 510-680-7800; Fax: 510-676-6857; E-mail: info@cainc.com

Ceradyne, Inc.
3169 Red Hill Ave.
Costa Mesa, CA 92626
Founded: 1967
Total Employees: 288
Annual Sales: $28.2 million
Industries: Advanced Materials, Defense, Factory Automation, Holding Companies, Medical, Subassemblies and Components, Transportation
Growth: Openings in past year, 38
Contact Joel P. Moskowitz, COB/CEO/President; 714-549-0421; Fax: 714-549-5787

Cesar Color, Inc.
880 Hinckley Rd.
Burlingame, CA 94010
Founded: 1988
Total Employees: 100
Annual Sales: $7.9 million
Industry: Advanced Materials
Growth: Openings in past year, 65
Contact Claudio Cesar, President; 650-259-9700; Fax: 650-259-7535

Channel Commercial Corp.
26040 Ynez Rd.
Temecula, CA 92591
http://www.channellcomm.com
Founded: 1990
Total Employees: 276
Annual Sales: $47.282 million
Industry: Factory Automation
Growth: Openings in past year, 30
Contact William H. Channel, Sr., COB/CEO; 909-694-9160; Fax: 909-694-9170

Chatsworth Data Corp.
20710 Lassen St.
Chatsworth, CA 91311
http://www.chatsworthdata.com
Founded: 1969
Total Employees: 89
Industries: Computer Hardware, Holding Companies
Growth: Openings in past year, 44
Contact Ms. Carol Lombard, Personnel Manager; 818-341-9200; Fax: 818-341-3002; E-mail: sales@chatsworth.com

Chip Express Corp.
2323 Owen St.
Santa Clara, CA 95054
http://www.chipexpress.com
Founded: 1990
Total Employees: 150
Annual Sales: $28 million
Industries: Manufacturing Equipment, Subassemblies and Components
Growth: Openings in past year, 50
Contact Ms. Anne Sledge, Director of Human Resources; 408-988-2445; Fax: 408-988-2449; E-mail: moreinfo@chipx.com

Chips and Technologies, Inc.
2950 Zanker Rd.
San Jose, CA 95134
http://www.chips.com
Founded: 1984
Total Employees: 260
Annual Sales: $168.334 million
Industries: Computer Hardware, Subassemblies and Components, Telecommunications
Growth: Openings in past year, 60
Contact Jim Strafford, President/CEO; 408-434-0600; Fax: 408-434-9315

CIDCO Incorporated
220 Cochrane Cir.
Morgan Hill, CA 95037
http://www.cidco.com
Founded: 1988
Total Employees: 600
Annual Sales: $214 million
Industry: Telecommunications
Growth: Openings in past year, 100
Contact Terry Dyckman, VP of Human Resources; 408-779-1162; Fax: 408-779-3106

Circle Seal Controls, Inc.
2301 Wardlow Cir.
Corona, CA 91720
http://www.circle-seal.com
Founded: 1947
Total Employees: 230
Annual Sales: $31 million
Industries:
Subassemblies and
Components,
Transportation
Growth: Openings in past
year, 30
Contact Ms. Elizabeth
Andrew, Manager of
Industrial Relations; 909-
270-6200; Fax: 909-270-
6201; E-mail: mktgsvcs@
circle-seal.com

Clayton Industries, Inc.
4213 Temple City Blvd.
El Monte, CA 91731
http://www.
claytonindustries.com
Founded: 1930
Total Employees: 800
Industries: Energy, Test
and Measurement
Growth: Openings in past
year, 99
Contact William Clayton,
Jr., President; 626-443-
9381; Fax: 626-442-1701

CliniComp International
9655 Towne Centre Dr.
San Diego, CA 92121
http://www.clinicomp.com
Founded: 1983
Total Employees: 70
Industry: Computer
Software
Growth: Openings in past
year, 30
Contact Ms. Marjorie
Roberts, Human
Resources Manager;
619-546-8202; Fax: 619-
546-1801; E-mail: info@
clinicomp.com

**CLONTECH
Laboratories, Inc.**
1020 East Meadow Cir.
Palo Alto, CA 94303
http://www.clontech.com
Founded: 1984
Total Employees: 215
Annual Sales: $23 million
Industries: Biotechnology,
Chemicals
Growth: Openings in past
year, 45
Contact Ms. Leslee
McLennan-Bonino,
Human Resources
Manager; 650-424-8222;
Fax: 650-424-0579;
E-mail: tech@clontech.
com

**CNET: The Computer
Network**
150 Chestnut St.
San Francisco, CA 94111
http://www.cnet.com
Founded: 1992
Total Employees: 450
Annual Sales: $10.134
million
Industry:
Telecommunications
Growth: Openings in past
year, 200
Contact Halsey Minor,
CEO/COB; 415-395-
7800; Fax: 415-395-
9205; E-mail: support@
cnet.com

**Coherent, Inc., Auburn
Group**
2303 Lindbergh St.
Auburn, CA 95602
http://www.cid.cohn.com
Founded: 1981
Total Employees: 428
Industries: Advanced
Materials, Factory
Automation,
Manufacturing
Equipment, Photonics
Growth: Openings in past
year, 28

Contact Robert Gelber,
Vice President/General
Manager; 916-823-9550;
Fax: 916-889-5353

Collagen Corp.
2500 Faber Pl.
Palo Alto, CA 94303
http://www.collagen.com
Founded: 1975
Total Employees: 379
Annual Sales: $71.8
million
Industries: Biotechnology,
Medical
Growth: Openings in past
year, 29
Contact Ms. Deborah
Berard, VP of Human
Resources & Admin.
Services; 650-856-0200;
Fax: 650-856-1430

**Communication
Intelligence Corp.**
275 Shoreline Dr., Suite
500
Redwood Shores, CA
94065
http://www.cic.com
Founded: 1981
Total Employees: 130
Annual Sales: $2.887
million
Industries: Computer
Hardware, Computer
Software
Growth: Openings in past
year, 45
Contact Ms. Karen
Kellenbach, VP of
Administration & Human
Resources; 650-802-
7888; Fax: 650-802-7777

**Compass Plastics &
Technologies, Inc.**
15730 South Figueroa St.
Gardena, CA 90248
Founded: 1952
Total Employees: 350
Annual Sales: $45 million
Industry: Holding
Companies
Growth: Openings in past
year, 64

Contact Michael A. Gibbs, Chief Executive Officer; 213-770-8771; Fax: 310-523-9859

Computer Intelligence
3344 North Torrey Pines Ct.
La Jolla, CA 92037
http://www.ci.zd.com
Founded: 1969
Total Employees: 650
Industry: Computer Hardware
Growth: Openings in past year, 150
Contact Ms. Joanne Clancy, Director of Human Resources; 619-450-1667; Fax: 619-450-1081

Computerized Structural Analysis & Research Corp.
28035 Dorothy Dr., Suite 100
Agoura Hills, CA 91300
http://www.csar.com
Founded: 1982
Total Employees: 52
Annual Sales: $6.7 million
Industry: Computer Software
Growth: Openings in past year, 27
Contact Dr. R. Narayanaswami, COB/President; 818-707-6060; Fax: 818-707-7722; E-mail: info@whq.csar.com

COMPUTERPEOPLE, Inc., RPM Systems Division
4987 Golden Foothill Pkwy.
El Dorado Hills, CA 95762
http://www.computerpeople.com
Founded: 1994
Total Employees: 460
Industry: Computer Software
Growth: Openings in past year, 260

Contact Paul Freudenberg, President/Owner; 916-933-4033; Fax: 916-933-4119

CONAM Inspection, Inc.
1875 Coronado Ave.
Signal Hill, CA 90804
Founded: 1959
Total Employees: 600
Annual Sales: $50 million
Industries: Advanced Materials, Manufacturing Equipment
Growth: Openings in past year, 100
Contact Mike Creech, President; 562-597-3932; Fax: 562-597-6570

Condor Reliability Services, Inc.
2921 Copper Rd.
Santa Clara, CA 95051
Founded: 1981
Total Employees: 120
Annual Sales: $4.5 million
Industries: Defense, Environmental, Subassemblies and Components
Growth: Openings in past year, 25
Contact Punam Patel, COB/President; 408-738-8375; Fax: 408-738-2757

Condor Systems, Inc.
2133 Samaritan Dr.
San Jose, CA 95124
http://www.condorsys.com
Founded: 1981
Total Employees: 375
Annual Sales: $60 million
Industries: Defense, Telecommunications, Transportation
Growth: Openings in past year, 75
Contact Ms. Leilli McPherson, Director of Human Resources; 408-371-9580; Fax: 408-371-9589; E-mail: busdev@condorsys.com

ConsenSys Software Corporation
111 North Market St., Suite 910
San Jose, CA 95113
http://www.consensoft.com
Founded: 1991
Total Employees: 60
Annual Sales: $7.7 million
Industry: Computer Software
Growth: Openings in past year, 30
Contact David Hurwitz, COB/CEO; 408-297-4500; Fax: 408-297-5382; E-mail: info@consensoft.com

Consolidated Devices, Inc.
19220 San Jose Ave.
City of Industry, CA 91748
Founded: 1970
Total Employees: 210
Annual Sales: $12 million
Industries: Factory Automation, Test and Measurement
Growth: Openings in past year, 60
Contact Gary Keefe, President; 818-965-0668; Fax: 818-810-2759

Constellar Corp.
1400 Bridge Pkwy., Suite 201
Redwood Shores, CA 94065
http://www.constellar.com
Founded: 1988
Total Employees: 110
Annual Sales: $14 million
Industry: Computer Software
Growth: Openings in past year, 35
Contact Paul Allman, Controller; 650-631-4800; Fax: 650-631-4802; E-mail: info@constellar.com

Continuum Electro Optics, Inc., Scientific Division
3150 Central Expwy.
Santa Clara, CA 95051
http://www.ceoi.com
Founded: 1975
Total Employees: 225
Annual Sales: $29 million
Industries: Photonics, Subassemblies and Components
Growth: Openings in past year, 45
Contact Steve Butcher, Ph.D., Director of Sales and Services; 408-727-3240; Fax: 408-727-3550; E-mail: continuum@ceoi.com

Copper Mountain Networks, Inc.
3931 Sorrento Valley Blvd.
San Diego, CA 92121
http://www.coppermountain.com
Founded: 1996
Total Employees: 50
Annual Sales: $8.5 million
Industry: Telecommunications
Growth: Openings in past year, 40
Contact Joe Markee, President/CEO; 619-453-8799; Fax: 619-453-9244; E-mail: info@coppermountain.com

Corsair Communications, Inc.
3408 Hillview Ave.
Palo Alto, CA 94304
http://www.corsair.com
Founded: 1994
Total Employees: 110
Annual Sales: $18.2 million
Industry: Telecommunications
Growth: Openings in past year, 55
Contact Ms. Jeanette Robinson, VP of Human Resources; 650-842-3300; Fax: 650-493-3588; E-mail: info@corsair.com

CoSystems Inc.
1263 Oakmead Pkwy., 2nd Fl.
Sunnyvale, CA 94086
http://www.cosystems.com
Founded: 1981
Total Employees: 55
Annual Sales: $7.1 million
Industries: Computer Hardware, Computer Software
Growth: Openings in past year, 35
Contact Shirish Patel, President; 408-522-0500; Fax: 408-720-9114

Crane Co., Hydro-Aire Division
3000 Winona Ave.
PO Box 7722
Burbank, CA 91510
Founded: 1943
Total Employees: 480
Annual Sales: $63 million
Industries: Subassemblies and Components, Transportation
Growth: Openings in past year, 28
Contact Ms. Elise Kopczick, Director of Human Resources; 818-842-6121; Fax: 818-842-6117; E-mail: boushier@hydroaire.com

Creative Computer Solutions, Inc.
5994 West Las Positas Blvd., Suite 123
Pleasanton, CA 94588
Founded: 1976
Total Employees: 91
Annual Sales: $10.2 million
Industries: Computer Hardware, Computer Software
Growth: Openings in past year, 31

Contact Ms. Susan King, Human Resource Manager; 510-847-3838; Fax: 510-847-8754; E-mail: bruce_jones@us-creative.com

Creative Labs, Inc.
1901 McCarthy Blvd.
Milpitas, CA 95035
http://www.creativelabs.com
Founded: 1985
Total Employees: 800
Annual Sales: $500 million
Industries: Computer Hardware, Telecommunications
Growth: Openings in past year, 99
Contact W.H. Sim, COB/CEO; 408-428-6600; Fax: 408-428-6611

Credence Systems Corp.
215 Fourier Ave.
Fremont, CA 94539
http://www.credence.com
Founded: 1977
Total Employees: 600
Annual Sales: $238.8 million
Industries: Factory Automation, Manufacturing Equipment
Growth: Openings in past year, 100
Contact Wilmer R. Bottoms, COB/CEO; 510-657-7400; Fax: 510-623-2560

Cristek Interconnects, Inc.
1301 South Lewis St.
Anaheim, CA 92805
Founded: 1985
Total Employees: 75
Annual Sales: $9.9 million
Industry: Subassemblies and Components
Growth: Openings in past year, 25
Contact Ms. Cristi Lyn Cristich, President/CEO; 714-535-1333; Fax: 714-535-4897

CSD Industries
540 South Pacific
San Marcos, CA 92069
Founded: 1984
Total Employees: 81
Industry: Subassemblies
and Components
Growth: Openings in past
year, 30
Contact Charles E. Black-
burn, President/CEO;
760-744-8182; Fax: 760-
744-1659

CSS Laboratories, Inc.
1641 McGaw Ave.
Irvine, CA 92714
http://www.csslabs.com
Founded: 1982
Total Employees: 100
Annual Sales: $35 million
Industries: Computer
Hardware,
Telecommunications
Growth: Openings in past
year, 25
Contact Ms. Amy Fu,
Payroll/Administration
Manager; 714-852-8161;
Fax: 714-852-0410;
E-mail: info@csslabs.
com

CyberMedia Inc.
3000 Ocean Park Blvd.,
Suite 2001
Santa Monica, CA 90405
http://www.cybermedia.
com
Founded: 1991
Total Employees: 190
Annual Sales: $38.5
million
Industries: Computer
Software, Holding
Companies
Growth: Openings in past
year, 144
Contact Ms. Andrea
Thompson, Human
Resources Manager;
310-581-4700; Fax: 310-
581-4761

Cyclades Corp.
41934 Christy St.
Fremont, CA 94538
http://www.cyclades.com
Founded: 1991
Total Employees: 100
Annual Sales: $10 million
Industries: Computer
Hardware, Computer
Software,
Telecommunications
Growth: Openings in past
year, 30
Contact John Lima,
President; 510-770-9727;
Fax: 510-770-0355;
E-mail: sales@cyclades.
com

Cygnus Solutions, Inc.
1325 Chesapeake Terr.
Sunnyvale, CA 94089
http://www.cygnus.com
Founded: 1989
Total Employees: 100
Annual Sales: $12 million
Industry: Computer
Software
Growth: Openings in past
year, 30
Contact Kaz Hashimoto,
President/CEO; 408-542-
9600; Fax: 408-542-
9699; E-mail: info@
cygnus.com

Cylink Corp.
910 Hermosa Court
Sunnyvale, CA 94086
http://www.cylink.com
Founded: 1984
Total Employees: 332
Annual Sales: $51.9
million
Industries: Computer
Software,
Telecommunications
Growth: Openings in past
year, 77
Contact Ms. Sara Engel,
VP of Human Resources;
408-735-5800; Fax: 408-
720-8294; E-mail: info@
cylink.com

Cymer, Inc.
16750 Via Del Campo Ct.
San Diego, CA 92127
http://www.cymer.com
Founded: 1986
Total Employees: 633
Annual Sales: $65 million
Industry: Photonics
Growth: Openings in past
year, 297
Contact Louis Kaplan, VP
of Human Resources;
619-451-7300; Fax: 619-
487-2441; E-mail:
marketing@cymer.com

D-Link Systems, Inc.
5 Musick
Irvine, CA 92618
http://www.dlink.com
Founded: 1986
Total Employees: 100
Annual Sales: $17 million
Industries: Computer
Software,
Telecommunications
Growth: Openings in past
year, 40
Contact Roger Kao,
President; 714-455-1688;
Fax: 714-455-2521;
E-mail: sales@dlink.com

Dako Corp.
6392 Via Real
Carpinteria, CA 93013
http://www.dakousa.com
Founded: 1979
Total Employees: 155
Annual Sales: $16 million
Industries: Biotechnology,
Medical
Growth: Openings in past
year, 25
Contact Viggo G. Harboe,
President; 805-566-6655;
Fax: 805-566-6688

DASCOM, Inc.
1509 Seabright Ave.
Santa Cruz, CA 95062
http://www.dascom.com
Founded: 1994

Total Employees: 70
Industry: Computer
Software
Growth: Openings in past
year, 50
Contact James Curtin,
President/CEO; 408-457-
4510; Fax: 408-457-
0710; E-mail: info@
dascom.com

Data Tree Corp.
550 West C St., Suite
2040
San Diego, CA 92101
http://www.datatree.com
Founded: 1987
Total Employees: 150
Annual Sales: $19 million
Industries: Computer
Hardware, Computer
Software
Growth: Openings in past
year, 30
Contact Harish Chopra,
President/CEO; 619-231-
3300; Fax: 619-231-3301

DataTools, Inc.
3340 Hillview Ave.
Palo Alto, CA 94304
http://www.datatools.com
Founded: 1991
Total Employees: 150
Annual Sales: $19 million
Industry: Computer
Software
Growth: Openings in past
year, 50
Contact Roger Ferguson,
President; 650-842-9100;
Fax: 650-842-9101;
E-mail: info@datatools.
com

DataWorks Corporation
5910 Pacific Center Blvd.
San Diego, CA 92121
http://www.dataworks.com
Founded: 1977
Total Employees: 530
Annual Sales: $61 million
Industries: Computer
Software, Holding
Companies
Growth: Openings in past
year, 100

Contact Ms. Pam Fettu,
Human Resources
Manager; 619-546-9600;
Fax: 619-546-9777;
E-mail: taytore@
dataworks.com

Datum, Inc.
9975 Toledo Way
Irvine, CA 92718
http://www.datum.com
Founded: 1968
Total Employees: 665
Annual Sales: $91.854
million
Industry: Holding
Companies
Growth: Openings in past
year, 125
Contact Ms. Laurie
Pedroza, Director of
Human Resources; 714-
380-8880; Fax: 714-380-
8555; E-mail: sales@
datum.com

**Davidson & Associates,
Inc.**
19840 Pioneer Ave.
Torrance, CA 90503
http://www.education.com
Founded: 1984
Total Employees: 800
Annual Sales: $100 million
Industries: Computer
Software, Holding
Companies
Growth: Openings in past
year, 99
Contact Larry Gross,
President; 310-793-0600;
Fax: 310-793-0601;
E-mail: sales@education.
com

DDL Electronics, Inc.
2151 Anchor Ct.
Newbury Park, CA 91320
Founded: 1959
Total Employees: 500
Annual Sales: $48.9
million
Industry: Holding
Companies
Growth: Openings in past
year, 50

Contact Gregory Horton,
President/CEO/COB;
805-376-9415; Fax: 805-
376-9015

**DePuy Orthopedic
Technology, Inc.**
1005 North MacArthur Dr.
Tracy, CA 95376
http://www.depuy.com
Founded: 1973
Total Employees: 350
Annual Sales: $42 million
Industry: Medical
Growth: Openings in past
year, 130
Contact Peter L. Wehrly,
Executive Vice President;
209-832-5200; Fax: 209-
832-8010

Details, Inc.
1231 North Simon Cir.
Anaheim, CA 92806
http://www.details.com
Founded: 1978
Total Employees: 450
Annual Sales: $80 million
Industry: Subassemblies
and Components
Growth: Openings in past
year, 129
Contact Bruce McMaster,
President; 714-630-4077;
Fax: 714-630-4270;
E-mail: sales@detailsinc.
com

**Diamond Lane
Communications Corp.**
1310 Redwood Way
Petaluma, CA 94954
http://www.dlcc.com
Founded: 1996
Total Employees: 88
Industry:
Telecommunications
Growth: Openings in past
year, 43
Contact George Hawley,
President/Founder; 707-
793-7000; Fax: 707-792-
0850

Diamond Multimedia Systems, Inc.
2880 Junction Ave.
San Jose, CA 95134
http://www.diamondmm.com
Founded: 1982
Total Employees: 841
Annual Sales: $598.050 million
Industries: Computer Hardware, Telecommunications
Growth: Openings in past year, 141
Contact Ms. Linda Shaw, Director of Human Resources; 408-325-7000; Fax: 408-325-7070; E-mail: diamondmm@diamondmm.com

Diba, Inc.
3355 Edison Way
Menlo Park, CA 94025
http://www.diba.com
Founded: 1995
Total Employees: 100
Annual Sales: $12 million
Industry: Computer Software
Growth: Openings in past year, 81
Contact Farzad Dibachi, President/CEO; 650-482-3300; Fax: 650-482-3400; E-mail: info@diba.com

Digirad Corp.
7408 Trade St.
San Diego, CA 92121
http://www.digirad.com
Founded: 1985
Total Employees: 65
Industries: Medical, Subassemblies and Components
Growth: Openings in past year, 30
Contact Ms. Karen Klause, President/CEO; 619-578-5300; Fax: 619-549-7714; E-mail: info@digirad.com

Digital Link Corp.
217 Humboldt Ct.
Sunnyvale, CA 94089
http://www.dl.com
Founded: 1985
Total Employees: 240
Annual Sales: $52 million
Industry: Telecommunications
Growth: Openings in past year, 40
Contact Alan Fraser, President/CEO; 408-745-6200; Fax: 408-745-6250; E-mail: info@dl.com

Digital Power Corp.
41920 Christy St.
Fremont, CA 94538
http://www.digipwr.com
Founded: 1969
Total Employees: 500
Annual Sales: $13.835 million
Industry: Subassemblies and Components
Growth: Openings in past year, 100
Contact Robert O. Smith, President/CEO; 510-657-2635; Fax: 510-657-6634; E-mail: sales@digipwr.com

Diodes, Inc.
3050 East Hillcrest Dr., Suite 200
Westlake Village, CA 91362
http://www.diodes.com
Founded: 1959
Total Employees: 200
Annual Sales: $56 million
Industries: Photonics, Subassemblies and Components
Growth: Openings in past year, 90
Contact Ms. Patricia Friou, Office Manager; 805-446-4800; Fax: 805-446-4850

DisCopyLabs, Inc.
48641 Milmont Dr.
Fremont, CA 94538
http://www.discopylabs.com
Founded: 1982
Total Employees: 300
Annual Sales: $26 million
Industries: Computer Software, Telecommunications
Growth: Openings in past year, 100
Contact Ms. Antonia Tu, VP of Customer Relations; 510-651-5100; Fax: 510-651-2261

DiviCom, Inc.
1708 McCarthy Blvd.
Milpitas, CA 95035
http://www.divi.com
Founded: 1993
Total Employees: 180
Annual Sales: $30 million
Industry: Telecommunications
Growth: Openings in past year, 30
Contact Nolan Daines, President/CEO; 408-944-6700; Fax: 408-944-6705; E-mail: info@divi.com

Documentum, Inc.
5671 Gibraltar Dr.
Pleasanton, CA 94588
http://www.documentum.com
Founded: 1990
Total Employees: 300
Annual Sales: $45.3 million
Industry: Computer Software
Growth: Openings in past year, 125
Contact Joe Gabbert, VP of Human Resources; 510-463-6800; Fax: 510-463-6850

Dolch Computer Systems, Inc.
3178 Laurelview Ct.
Fremont, CA 94538
Founded: 1987
Total Employees: 150
Industries: Computer Hardware, Photonics, Subassemblies and Components
Growth: Openings in past year, 25
Contact Volker Dolch, COB/CEO; 510-661-2220; Fax: 510-490-2360; E-mail: info@dolch.com

Dow-Key Microwave Corp.
1667 Walter St.
Ventura, CA 93003
Founded: 1945
Total Employees: 148
Annual Sales: $20 million
Industries:
Subassemblies and Components, Telecommunications
Growth: Openings in past year, 64
Contact Ms. Karen Tellou, Human Resources Manager; 805-650-0260; Fax: 805-650-1734

Duet Technologies, Inc.
2833 Junction Ave., Suite 100
San Jose, CA 95134
http://www.duettech.com
Founded: 1991
Total Employees: 350
Industries:
Subassemblies and Components, Telecommunications
Growth: Openings in past year, 49
Contact Naresh Nigam, President/CEO; 408-432-9200; Fax: 408-432-0907; E-mail: info@duettech.com

Dura Pharmaceuticals, Inc.
7474 Lusk Blvd.
San Diego, CA 92121
Founded: 1981
Total Employees: 400
Annual Sales: $79.5 million
Industries: Medical, Pharmaceuticals
Growth: Openings in past year, 90
Contact Rich Everett, Human Resources Director; 619-457-2553; Fax: 619-457-2555

E-TEK Dynamics, Inc.
1885 Lundy Ave.
San Jose, CA 95131
http://www.e-tek.com
Founded: 1983
Total Employees: 495
Annual Sales: $73 million
Industries: Factory Automation, Manufacturing Equipment, Photonics, Subassemblies and Components, Test and Measurement, Telecommunications
Growth: Openings in past year, 245
Contact Ms. Sherry Hsu Lee, Manager of General Administration; 408-432-6300; Fax: 408-432-8550; E-mail: info@e-tek.com

Econolite Control Products, Inc.
3360 East La Palma Ave.
Anaheim, CA 92806
http://www.econolite.com
Founded: 1978
Total Employees: 190
Annual Sales: $24 million
Industry: Transportation
Growth: Openings in past year, 60
Contact Ms. Jeannette Scalise, Director of

Human Resources; 714-630-3700; Fax: 714-630-6349

EG&G Astrophysics Research Corp.
4031 Via Oro Ave.
Long Beach, CA 90810
Founded: 1974
Total Employees: 200
Industries: Test and Measurement, Transportation
Growth: Openings in past year, 70
Contact Ms. Diane Paine, Human Resources Manager; 310-513-1411; Fax: 310-513-6593

Electroglas, Inc.
2901 Coronado Dr.
Santa Clara, CA 95054
http://www.electroglas.com
Founded: 1960
Total Employees: 650
Annual Sales: $152 million
Industries: Factory Automation, Subassemblies and Components
Growth: Openings in past year, 130
Contact Curtis S. Wozniak, Chief Executive Officer; 408-727-6500; Fax: 408-982-8025

Elo TouchSystems, Inc.
41752 Christy St.
Fremont, CA 94538
http://www.elotouch.com
Founded: 1971
Total Employees: 400
Annual Sales: $82 million
Industry: Computer Hardware
Growth: Openings in past year, 50
Contact Ms. Emily Liggett, President; 510-651-2340; Fax: 510-651-3511; E-mail: eloinfo@elotouch.com

Eltron International, Inc.
41 Moreland Rd.
Simi Valley, CA 93065
http://www.eltron.com
Founded: 1991
Total Employees: 500
Annual Sales: $88.5 million
Industry: Holding Companies
Growth: Openings in past year, 300
Contact Donald Skinner, COB/CEO; 805-579-1800; Fax: 805-579-1808; E-mail: sales@eltron.com

Embarcadero Systems Corp.
1255 Harbor Bay Pkwy.
Alameda, CA 94502
Founded: 1996
Total Employees: 60
Annual Sales: $7.7 million
Industries: Computer Software, Environmental
Growth: Openings in past year, 30
Contact Robert E. Verret, President; 510-749-7490; Fax: 510-749-3800; E-mail: info@esystem.com

Enclosures Engineering, Inc.
48350 Milmont Dr.
Fremont, CA 94538
Founded: 1994
Total Employees: 60
Industry: Manufacturing Equipment
Growth: Openings in past year, 30
Contact George Halldin, President; 510-657-8997; Fax: 510-657-8996

Endosonics Corp.
2870 Kilgore Rd.
Rancho Cordova, CA 95670

Founded: 1984
Total Employees: 190
Annual Sales: $20.3 million
Industry: Medical
Growth: Openings in past year, 40
Contact Reinhard Warnking, President/CEO; 916-638-8008; Fax: 916-638-8812

EndoVascular Technologies, Inc.
1360 O'Brien Dr.
Menlo Park, CA 94025
Founded: 1989
Total Employees: 143
Annual Sales: $1.159 million
Industry: Medical
Growth: Openings in past year, 53
Contact W. James Fitzsimmons, President/CEO; 650-325-1600; Fax: 650-325-4196

Epoch Internet, Inc.
18201 Von Karman Ave., Suite 500
Irvine, CA 92612
http://www.eni.net
Founded: 1994
Total Employees: 200
Industries: Computer Software, Telecommunications
Growth: Openings in past year, 120
Contact Scott Purcell, CEO/President/Founder; 714-474-4950; Fax: 714-474-8127; E-mail: info@eni.net

Equipe Technologies, Inc.
733 North Pastoria Ave.
Sunnyvale, CA 94086
http://www.equipetech.com
Founded: 1990
Total Employees: 120
Annual Sales: $18 million
Industry: Factory Automation

Growth: Openings in past year, 80
Contact James Cameron, President; 408-522-0350; Fax: 408-522-0358

ESS Technology, Inc.
48401 Fremont Blvd.
Fremont, CA 94538
http://www.esstech.com
Founded: 1984
Total Employees: 260
Annual Sales: $226.5 million
Industry: Subassemblies and Components
Growth: Openings in past year, 110
Contact Fred Chan, COB/CEO; 510-492-1088; Fax: 510-492-8868; E-mail: info@esstech.com

Etak, Inc.
1430 O'Brien Dr.
Menlo Park, CA 94025
http://www.etak.com
Founded: 1983
Total Employees: 660
Annual Sales: $85 million
Industries: Computer Hardware, Computer Software, Transportation
Growth: Openings in past year, 96
Contact Hirohito Kawada, President/COO; 650-328-3825; Fax: 650-328-3148

Etec Systems, Inc.
26460 Corporate Ave.
Hayward, CA 94545
http://www.etec.com
Founded: 1983
Total Employees: 800
Annual Sales: $240.9 million
Industries: Holding Companies, Manufacturing Equipment, Photonics
Growth: Openings in past year, 398

Contact Steve Cooper,
COB/President/CEO;
510-783-9210; Fax: 510-
883-2870

Excite, Inc.
555 Broadway
Redwood City, CA 94063
http://www.excite.com
Founded: 1993
Total Employees: 225
Annual Sales: $14.7
million
Industries: Computer
Software, Holding
Companies,
Telecommunications
Growth: Openings in past
year, 33
Contact George Bell,
Chief Executive Officer;
650-568-6000; Fax: 650-
568-6030; E-mail: info@
excite.com

**Exclusive Design Co.,
Inc.**
871 Fox Ln.
San Jose, CA 95131
http://www.goedc.com
Founded: 1978
Total Employees: 190
Annual Sales: $29 million
Industry: Factory
Automation
Growth: Openings in past
year, 100
Contact William Harry,
COB/President; 408-273-
2300; Fax: 408-273-
2329; E-mail: info@
goedc.com

**Extron Contract
Manufacturing**
47550 Kato Rd.
Fremont, CA 94538
Founded: 1980
Total Employees: 150
Industries: Computer
Hardware, Computer
Software
Growth: Openings in past
year, 30
Contact Andy Nguyen,
President; 510-353-0177;

Fax: 510-353-1319;
E-mail: extron@
packagingservices.com

EZaccess, Inc.
1000 Marina Blvd., 4th
Floor
Brisbane, CA 94005
http://www.ezaccess.com
Founded: 1993
Total Employees: 100
Annual Sales: $12 million
Industry: Computer
Software
Growth: Openings in past
year, 78
Contact Ankesh Kumar,
President; 415-829-6800;
Fax: 415-829-6801;
E-mail: info@ezaccess.
com

Failure Group, Inc.
149 Commonwealth Dr.
Menlo Park, CA 94025
http://www.fail.com
Founded: 1967
Total Employees: 600
Annual Sales: $60 million
Industries: Holding
Companies,
Manufacturing Equipment
Growth: Openings in past
year, 149
Contact Michael R.
Gaulke, President/CEO;
650-326-9400; Fax: 650-
326-8072; E-mail:
faainfo@fail.com

Finjan, Inc.
2620 Augustine Dr., Suite
250
Santa Clara, CA 95054
http://www.finjan.com
Founded: 1996
Total Employees: 40
Annual Sales: $5.1 million
Industry: Computer
Software
Growth: Openings in past
year, 37
Contact Emi Scliar,
Human Resource
Manager; 408-727-8120;
Fax: 408-727-8528;
E-mail: info@finjan.com

**First Virtual Holdings,
Inc.**
11975 El Camino Real,
Suite 200
San Diego, CA 92130
http://www.fv.com
Founded: 1994
Total Employees: 125
Industries: Computer
Software,
Telecommunications
Growth: Openings in past
year, 75
Contact Lee H. Stein,
COB/CEO/Director; 619-
793-2700; Fax: 619-793-
2950; E-mail: info@fv.
com

Flex Products, Inc.
1402 Mariner Way
Santa Rosa, CA 95407
Founded: 1988
Total Employees: 175
Annual Sales: $21 million
Industry: Manufacturing
Equipment
Growth: Openings in past
year, 50
Contact Michael Sullivan,
President; 707-525-9200;
Fax: 707-525-7533

**Focalink
Communications, Inc.**
2191 East Bayshore Rd.,
Suite 100
Palo Alto, CA 94303
http://www.focalink.com
Founded: 1995
Total Employees: 70
Industry:
Telecommunications
Growth: Openings in past
year, 47
Contact Ronald A. Kovas,
President/CEO; 650-842-
0660; Fax: 650-842-
0665; E-mail: info@
focalink.com

FORCE COMPUTERS, Inc.
2001 Logic Dr.
San Jose, CA 95124
http://www.forcecomputers.
com
Founded: 1981
Total Employees: 503
Industry: Computer
Hardware
Growth: Openings in past
year, 42
Contact Ms. Ursula Dinse,
Director of Human
Resources; 408-369-
6000; Fax: 408-371-
3382; E-mail: info@fci.
com

Forte Software, Inc.
1800 Harrison St., 24th
Floor
Oakland, CA 94612
http://www.forte.com
Founded: 1991
Total Employees: 450
Annual Sales: $63 million
Industry: Computer
Software
Growth: Openings in past
year, 200
Contact Marty Sprinzen,
President/CEO; 510-869-
3400; Fax: 510-869-
3480; E-mail: info@forte.
com

Four Media Co.
2813 West Alameda Ave.
Burbank, CA 91505
http://www.4mc.com
Founded: 1993
Total Employees: 650
Annual Sales: $84.5
million
Industry:
Telecommunications
Growth: Openings in past
year, 49
Contact Ms. Kristie
Klechner, Director of
Human Resources; 818-
840-7000; Fax: 818-846-
5197

Gadzoox Networks, Inc.
6840 via del Oro, Suite
290
San Jose, CA 95119
http://www.gadzoox.com
Founded: 1992
Total Employees: 63
Annual Sales: $10 million
Industry:
Telecommunications
Growth: Openings in past
year, 38
Contact Bill Sickler,
President; 408-360-4950;
Fax: 408-360-4951

**Genesys
Telecommunications
Laboratories, Inc.**
1155 Market St., 11th
Floor
San Francisco, CA 94103
http://www.genesyslab.com
Founded: 1990
Total Employees: 371
Annual Sales: $34.889
million
Industry: Computer
Software
Growth: Openings in past
year, 77
Contact Ms. Darlene J.
Fontaine, Director of
Human Resources; 415-
437-1100; Fax: 415-437-
1260; E-mail: info@
genesyslab.com

GENSET Corporation
875 Prospect St., Suite
206
La Jolla, CA 92037
http://www.genry.com
Founded: 1989
Total Employees: 290
Annual Sales: $31 million
Industry: Biotechnology
Growth: Openings in past
year, 64
Contact Pascal Brandys,
President/CEO; 619-551-
6551; Fax: 619-551-
6549; E-mail: oligos@
gensetlj.com

Gentry, Inc.
430 40th St.
Oakland, CA 94609
http://www.gentry.com
Founded: 1974
Total Employees: 120
Annual Sales: $10 million
Industry: Computer
Software
Growth: Openings in past
year, 30
Contact Ms. Grace H.
Gentry, President; 510-
547-6134; Fax: 510-547-
0978; E-mail: gentry@
dice.com

Geoworks
960 Atlantic Ave.
Alameda, CA 94501
http://www.geoworks.com
Founded: 1983
Total Employees: 230
Annual Sales: $11 million
Industry: Computer
Software
Growth: Openings in past
year, 49
Contact Gordon Mayer,
President/CEO; 510-814-
1660; Fax: 510-814-4250

Gigalabs, Inc.
290 Santa Ana Ct.
Sunnyvale, CA 94086
http://www.gigalabs.com
Founded: 1988
Total Employees: 120
Industries: Computer
Hardware,
Telecommunications
Growth: Openings in past
year, 100
Contact Dr. Simon K. Fok,
COB/CEO; 408-481-
3030; Fax: 408-481-
3045; E-mail: sfok@
gigalabs.com

Glentek, Inc.
208 Standard St.
El Segundo, CA 90245
http://www.glentek.com

Founded: 1964
Total Employees: 270
Annual Sales: $25 million
Industry: Subassemblies and Components
Growth: Openings in past year, 70
Contact Milt Vasak, Marketing Manager; 310-322-3026; Fax: 310-322-7709

Gold Shield, Inc.
1850 Atlanta Ave.
Riverside, CA 92507
http://www.goldshield.com
Founded: 1975
Total Employees: 205
Industries: Advanced Materials, Manufacturing Equipment
Growth: Openings in past year, 55
Contact Gary Davis, General Manager; 909-682-9715; Fax: 909-681-4874

GoldMine Software Corp.
17383 Sunset Blvd., Suite 301
Pacific Palisades, CA 90272
http://www.goldminesw.com
Founded: 1986
Total Employees: 80
Annual Sales: $10 million
Industry: Computer Software
Growth: Openings in past year, 25
Contact Elan Susser, President; 310-454-6800; Fax: 310-454-4848; E-mail: 74431.1624@compuserve.com

Group IPEX, Inc.
3675 MT. Diablo Blvd., Suite 200
Lafayette, CA 94549
http://www.ipex.com
Founded: 1984
Total Employees: 75
Annual Sales: $9.7 million

Industry: Computer Software
Growth: Openings in past year, 45
Contact Lalit M. Kapoor, President; 510-284-2741; Fax: 510-284-2744; E-mail: ipex@ipex.com

Hallmark Circuits, Inc.
5330 Eastgate Mall Rd.
San Diego, CA 92121
Founded: 1970
Total Employees: 200
Industry: Subassemblies and Components
Growth: Openings in past year, 25
Contact Ms. Debe White, Corporate Affairs Manager; 619-453-7800; Fax: 619-453-1409

Harmonic Lightwaves, Inc.
549 Baltic Way
Sunnyvale, CA 94089
http://www.harmonic-lightwaves.com
Founded: 1988
Total Employees: 230
Annual Sales: $60.8 million
Industries: Photonics, Telecommunications
Growth: Openings in past year, 30
Contact Ms. Anne Lynch, VP of Human Resources; 408-542-2500; Fax: 408-542-2511; E-mail: info@harmonic-lightwaves.com

Haskel International, Inc.
100 East Graham Pl.
Burbank, CA 91502
http://www.haskel.com/
Founded: 1946
Total Employees: 335
Annual Sales: $56 million
Industry: Subassemblies and Components
Growth: Openings in past year, 85

Contact Ms. Pam Karno, Personnel Manager; 818-843-4000; Fax: 818-556-2549

HC Power, Inc.
17032 Armstrong Ave
Irvine, CA 92714
Founded: 1984
Total Employees: 225
Industry: Subassemblies and Components
Growth: Openings in past year, 50
Contact Wallace Hersom, President; 714-261-2200; Fax: 714-261-6584

Headland Digital Media, Inc.
88 Rowland Way
Novato, CA 94945
http://www.headland-media.com
Founded: 1997
Total Employees: 80
Annual Sales: $16 million
Industry: Computer Hardware
Growth: Openings in past year, 50
Contact Mark Nieker, President; 415-898-1999; Fax: 415-897-8814; E-mail: info@headland-media.com

Heartport, Inc.
200 Chesapeake Dr.
Redwood City, CA 94063
Founded: 1991
Total Employees: 275
Industries: Medical, Pharmaceuticals
Growth: Openings in past year, 142
Contact Wesley D. Sterman, MD, President/CEO; 650-306-7900; Fax: 650-306-7905

Hewlett-Packard Company, Lightwave Division
1400 Fountain Grove Pkwy.
Santa Rosa, CA 95403
Founded: 1939
Total Employees: 180
Annual Sales: $24 million
Industry: Test and Measurement
Growth: Openings in past year, 50
Contact Kunio Hasebe, General Manager; 707-577-5280; Fax: 707-577-5221

Hewlett-Packard Company, Santa Clara Division
5301 Stevens Creek Blvd.
Santa Clara, CA 95052
Founded: 1969
Total Employees: 800
Annual Sales: $100 million
Industries: Photonics, Test and Measurement
Growth: Openings in past year, 300
Contact Marty Neil, General Manager; 408-246-4300; Fax: 408-246-7293

HID Corp.
9292 Jeronimo Rd.
Irvine, CA 92618
Founded: 1975
Total Employees: 250
Annual Sales: $51 million
Industries: Computer Hardware, Telecommunications
Growth: Openings in past year, 50
Contact Donald Nelson, President; 714-598-1600; Fax: 714-598-1690

HM Electronics, Inc.
6675 Mesa Ridge Rd.
San Diego, CA 92121

Founded: 1971
Total Employees: 340
Annual Sales: $58 million
Industries: Test and Measurement, Telecommunications
Growth: Openings in past year, 31
Contact Ms. Pauline Mraz, Personnel Manager; 619-535-6000; Fax: 619-452-7207

HNC Software Inc.
5930 Cornerstone Ct. West
San Diego, CA 92121
http://www.hnc.com
Founded: 1986
Total Employees: 400
Annual Sales: $53.833 million
Industries: Computer Software, Holding Companies
Growth: Openings in past year, 200
Contact Ms. Laurel Jones, Director of Human Resources; 619-546-8877; Fax: 619-452-6524; E-mail: info@hnc.com

Hotmail
1290 Oakmead Pkwy.
Sunnyvale, CA 94086
http://www.hotmail.com
Founded: 1995
Total Employees: 35
Annual Sales: $6.0 million
Industry: Telecommunications
Growth: Openings in past year, 30
Contact Sabeer Bhatia, Chief Executive Officer; 408-222-7000; Fax: 408-222-7020; E-mail: sales@hotmail.com

Hughes Electronics Corp., Electron Dynamics Division
3100 West Lomita Blvd.
PO Box 2999
Torrance, CA 90509

Founded: 1968
Total Employees: 950
Annual Sales: $120 million
Industry: Subassemblies and Components
Growth: Openings in past year, 124
Contact Ms. Barbara Shryack, Human Resources Manager; 310-517-6196; Fax: 310-517-6103; E-mail: lpthorose@ccgate.hac.com

I-Bus, Inc.
9174 Sky Park Ct.
San Diego, CA 92123
http://www.ibus.com
Founded: 1983
Total Employees: 170
Annual Sales: $35 million
Industry: Computer Hardware
Growth: Openings in past year, 50
Contact Ms. Debbie Borek, Human Resources Manager; 619-974-8400; Fax: 619-268-7863; E-mail: info@ibus.com

I-Flow Corp.
2532 White Rd.
Irvine, CA 92714
Founded: 1985
Total Employees: 235
Annual Sales: $9.1 million
Industries: Computer Software, Medical, Telecommunications
Growth: Openings in past year, 55
Contact Ms. Linda M. Bainbridge, Manager of Human Resources; 714-553-0888; Fax: 714-553-8056

i-Planet, Inc.
1390 Borregas Ave.
Sunnyvale, CA 94089
http://www.i-planet.com
Founded: 1996
Total Employees: 42
Annual Sales: $1.6 million

Industry: Computer
  Software
Growth: Openings in past
  year, 26
Contact Rich Preston,
  President/CEO; 408-745-
  1500; Fax: 408-745-
  6680; E-mail: info@i-
  planet.com

ICVERIFY, Inc.
473 Roland Way
Oakland, CA 94621
http://www.icverify.com
Founded: 1988
Total Employees: 90
Annual Sales: $11 million
Industry: Computer
  Software
Growth: Openings in past
  year, 30
Contact F. Thomas Aden,
  President/CEO; 510-553-
  7500; Fax: 510-553-
  7553; E-mail: info@
  icverify.com

Identix, Inc.
510 North Pastoria Ave.
Sunnyvale, CA 94086
http://www.identix.com
Founded: 1982
Total Employees: 361
Annual Sales: $52.3
  million
Industries: Computer
  Hardware, Computer
  Software, Holding
  Companies
Growth: Openings in past
  year, 36
Contact Randall C.
  Fowler, President/CEO;
  408-739-2000; Fax: 408-
  739-3308

IKOS Systems, Inc.
19050 Pruneridge Ave.
Cupertino, CA 95014
http://www.ikos.com
Founded: 1984
Total Employees: 184
Annual Sales: $45.341
  million
Industries: Computer
  Hardware, Computer
  Software

Growth: Openings in past
  year, 69
Contact Ramon Nunez,
  President/CEO; 408-255-
  4567; Fax: 408-366-8699

ILOG, Inc.
1901 Landings Dr.
Mountain View, CA 94043
http://www.ilog.com
Founded: 1992
Total Employees: 290
Annual Sales: $30.8
  million
Industry: Computer
  Software
Growth: Openings in past
  year, 60
Contact Pierre Haren,
  COB/CEO; 650-944-
  7100; Fax: 650-390-
  0946; E-mail: info@ilog.
  com

**Incyte Pharmaceuticals,
Inc.**
3174 Porter Dr.
Palo Alto, CA 94304
http://www.incyte.com
Founded: 1991
Total Employees: 510
Annual Sales: $41.8
  million
Industry: Computer
  Hardware
Growth: Openings in past
  year, 235
Contact Roy Whitfield,
  Chief Executive Officer;
  650-855-0555; Fax: 650-
  855-0572

Indigo Technologies, Inc.
3550 Stevens Creek Blvd.
San Jose, CA 95117
http://www.indigotech.com
Founded: 1992
Total Employees: 150
Annual Sales: $19 million
Industry: Computer
  Software
Growth: Openings in past
  year, 50
Contact Sashi Chimala,
  President/CEO; 408-261-
  6500; Fax: 408-261-6505

Indus Group
60 Spear St.
San Francisco, CA 94105
http://www.indusgroup.com
Founded: 1987
Total Employees: 463
Annual Sales: $75.939
  million
Industry: Computer
  Software
Growth: Openings in past
  year, 93
Contact Bob Felton,
  President; 415-904-5000;
  Fax: 415-904-5050;
  E-mail: info@indusgroup.
  com

**Industrial Computer
Source**
6260 Sequence Dr.
San Diego, CA 92121
http://www.indcompsrc.com
Founded: 1984
Total Employees: 250
Annual Sales: $60 million
Industries: Computer
  Hardware,
  Subassemblies and
  Components
Growth: Openings in past
  year, 80
Contact Steven Peltier,
  President/CEO; 619-677-
  0877; Fax: 619-677-
  0898; E-mail: sales@
  indcompsrc.com

**Infinity Financial
Technology, Inc.**
640 Clyde Ct.
Mountain View, CA 94043
http://www.infinity.com
Founded: 1989
Total Employees: 170
Annual Sales: $41.548
  million
Industry: Computer
  Software
Growth: Openings in past
  year, 45
Contact Roger A. Lang,
  Chief Executive Officer;
  650-940-6100; Fax: 650-
  964-9844; E-mail: info@
  infinity.com

Influence, Inc.
601 Montgomery St., Suite 845
San Francisco, CA 94111
http://www.influencemedical.com
Founded: 1994
Total Employees: 70
Industry: Medical
Growth: Openings in past year, 40
Contact John Harland, Chief Financial Officer; 415-421-5600; Fax: 415-421-5622; E-mail: influence@sfo.com

InnoMedia, Inc.
4800 Great America Pkwy., Suite 400
Santa Clara, CA 95054
http://www.innomedia.com
Founded: 1995
Total Employees: 62
Industries: Computer Software, Telecommunications
Growth: Openings in past year, 30
Contact Dr. Nan-Sheng Lin, Corporate Vice President/General Manager; 408-562-3535; Fax: 408-562-3545

Integrated Silicon Solution, Inc.
2231 Lawson Ln.
Santa Clara, CA 95054
http://www.issiusa.com
Founded: 1988
Total Employees: 385
Annual Sales: $108.3 million
Industries: Computer Hardware, Subassemblies and Components
Growth: Openings in past year, 85
Contact Jimmy Lee, COB/President; 408-588-0800; Fax: 408-588-0805

Infoseek Corporation
1399 Moffett Park Dr.
Sunnyvale, CA 94089
http://www.infoseek.com
Founded: 1994
Total Employees: 150
Annual Sales: $15 million
Industries: Holding Companies, Telecommunications
Growth: Openings in past year, 37
Contact Harry M. Motro, President/CEO; 408-543-6000; Fax: 408-734-9350; E-mail: comments@infoseek.com

InnovaCom, Inc.
2855 Kifer Rd., Suite 100
Santa Clara, CA 95051
http://www.innovacom-mpeg2.com
Founded: 1996
Total Employees: 36
Industries: Computer Hardware, Subassemblies and Components
Growth: Openings in past year, 28
Contact Mark Koz, President/CEO; 408-727-2447; Fax: 408-727-8778; E-mail: rmaier@innovacom.com

Integrated Systems, Inc.
201 Moffett Park Dr.
Sunnyvale, CA 94089
http://www.isi.com
Founded: 1980
Total Employees: 510
Annual Sales: $105.463 million
Industries: Computer Software, Holding Companies
Growth: Openings in past year, 109
Contact Ms. Janice Waterman, VP of Human Resources & Operations; 408-542-1500; Fax: 408-542-1950; E-mail: info@isi.com

Inhale Therapeutic Systems
1060 East Meadow Cir.
Palo Alto, CA 94303
http://www.inhale.com
Founded: 1990
Total Employees: 90
Annual Sales: $6.9 million
Industry: Pharmaceuticals
Growth: Openings in past year, 40
Contact Robert B. Chess, President; 650-354-0700; Fax: 650-354-0701

Integrated Microwave Corp.
11353 Sorento Valley Rd.
San Diego, CA 92121
Founded: 1982
Total Employees: 112
Industries: Subassemblies and Components, Telecommunications
Growth: Openings in past year, 37
Contact Stewart Grant, Human Resources Manager; 619-259-2600; Fax: 619-755-8679

Interactive Group, Inc.
5095 Murphy Canyon Rd.
San Diego, CA 92123
http://www.interactive-group.com
Founded: 1975
Total Employees: 350
Annual Sales: $56.2 million
Industries: Computer Hardware, Computer Software
Growth: Openings in past year, 95
Contact Robert C. Vernon, COB/CEO; 619-560-8525; Fax: 619-565-8570

Interlink Computer Sciences, Inc.
47370 Fremont Blvd.
Fremont, CA 94538
http://www.interlink.com
Founded: 1982
Total Employees: 163
Annual Sales: $39 million
Industry: Computer Software
Growth: Openings in past year, 43
Contact Mickey Satterwhite, VP of Human Resources; 510-657-9800; Fax: 510-659-6381

INTERSHOP Communications, Inc.
600 Townsend St.
San Francisco, CA 94103
http://www.intershop.com
Founded: 1992
Total Employees: 130
Annual Sales: $16 million
Industry: Computer Software
Growth: Openings in past year, 65
Contact Stephan Schambach, President/CEO; 415-373-1530; Fax: 415-373-1536; E-mail: info@intershop.com

Ipsilon Networks
232 Java Dr.
Sunnyvale, CA 94089
http://www.ipsilon.com
Founded: 1995
Total Employees: 125
Industry: Telecommunications
Growth: Openings in past year, 53
Contact Brian NeSmith, President/CEO; 408-990-2000; Fax: 408-743-5675; E-mail: info@ipsilon.com

International Circuits and Components, Inc.
3701 East Miraloma Ave.
Anaheim, CA 92806
Founded: 1981
Total Employees: 151
Annual Sales: $20 million
Industries: Manufacturing Equipment, Subassemblies and Components
Growth: Openings in past year, 36
Contact Richard Cheng, President; 714-572-1900; Fax: 714-527-2900

Interventional Technologies, Inc.
3574 Ruffin Rd.
San Diego, CA 92123
Founded: 1984
Total Employees: 165
Industry: Medical
Growth: Openings in past year, 50
Contact Ms. Kathe Houghtaling, Human Resources Director; 619-268-4488; Fax: 619-292-8381

Isis Pharmaceuticals, Inc.
2292 Faraday Ave.
Carlsbad, CA 92008
http://www.isip.com
Founded: 1989
Total Employees: 300
Industries: Biotechnology, Pharmaceuticals
Growth: Openings in past year, 40
Contact Ms. Patricia Lowenstam, VP of Human Resources; 760-931-9200; Fax: 760-931-9639; E-mail: info@isisph.com

International Microcomputer Software, Inc.
1895 East Francisco Blvd.
San Rafael, CA 94901
http://www.imsisoft.com
Founded: 1982
Total Employees: 215
Annual Sales: $41.8 million
Industries: Computer Hardware, Computer Software
Growth: Openings in past year, 71
Contact Ms. Chris Diesch, Director of Human Resources; 415-257-3000; Fax: 415-257-3565

Invitrogen Corp.
1600 Faraday Ave.
Carlsbad, CA 92008
http://www.invitrogen.com
Founded: 1987
Total Employees: 140
Annual Sales: $15 million
Industry: Biotechnology
Growth: Openings in past year, 25
Contact Ms. Denise Higgins, Human Resources Manager; 760-603-7200; Fax: 760-603-7201; E-mail: techservice@invitrogen.com

Janco Corp.
3111 Winona Ave.
Burbank, CA 91504
Founded: 1947
Total Employees: 140
Annual Sales: $7 million
Industry: Subassemblies and Components
Growth: Openings in past year, 38
Contact Robert J. Giove, COB/CEO; 818-846-1800; Fax: 818-842-3396; E-mail: jancocorp@aol.com

Jay-El Products, Inc.
23301 South Wilmington
Ave.
Carson, CA 90745
Founded: 1971
Total Employees: 231
Industries:
Subassemblies and
Components,
Telecommunications
Growth: Openings in past
year, 36
Contact Ken Pearson,
Director of Human
Resources; 310-513-
7200; Fax: 310-513-
7298; E-mail: sales@
jldmt.com

JetFax, Inc.
1376 Willow Rd.
Menlo Park, CA 94025
http://www.jetfax.com
Founded: 1988
Total Employees: 100
Annual Sales: $13.1
million
Industries: Computer
Software,
Telecommunications
Growth: Openings in past
year, 35
Contact Rudy Prince,
President; 650-324-0600;
Fax: 650-326-6003

Kaiser Electroprecision
17000 South Redhill Ave.
Irvine, CA 92714
Founded: 1963
Total Employees: 350
Annual Sales: $46 million
Industries:
Subassemblies and
Components, Test and
Measurement,
Transportation
Growth: Openings in past
year, 59
Contact Robert Oxeley,
Personnel Manager; 714-
250-1015; Fax: 714-250-
0497

KDS USA
12300 Edison Way
Garden Grove, CA 92841
http://www.kdsusa.com
Founded: 1993
Total Employees: 65
Industry: Computer
Hardware
Growth: Openings in past
year, 40
Contact John Hui, Chief
Executive Officer; 714-
379-5599; Fax: 714-891-
2661

Kingston Technology Co.
17600 Newhope St.
Fountain Valley, CA 92708
http://www.kingston.com
Founded: 1987
Total Employees: 550
Annual Sales: $1000
million
Industry: Computer
Hardware
Growth: Openings in past
year, 50
Contact John Tu,
President/Co-Founder;
714-435-2600; Fax: 714-
435-2699; E-mail:
sales@kingston.com

KIVA Software Corp.
2141 Landing Dr.
Mountain View, CA 94043
http://www.kivasoft.com
Founded: 1995
Total Employees: 100
Annual Sales: $12 million
Industry: Computer
Software
Growth: Openings in past
year, 60
Contact Keng Lim,
President; 650-526-3900;
Fax: 650-526-3919;
E-mail: info@kivasoft.
com

Kleinfelder, Inc.
2121 North California
Blvd., Suite 570
Walnut Creek, CA 94596
http://www.kleinfelder.com
Founded: 1961
Total Employees: 850
Industries: Advanced
Materials, Environmental
Growth: Openings in past
year, 124
Contact Larry Bienati, VP
of Human Resources;
510-938-5610; Fax: 510-
938-5419

Kobe Precision, Inc.
31031 Huntwood Ave.
Hayward, CA 94544
Founded: 1988
Total Employees: 450
Annual Sales: $60 million
Industry: Subassemblies
and Components
Growth: Openings in past
year, 38
Contact Ms. Toni
Hampton, VP of Human
Resources; 510-487-
3200; Fax: 510-487-9550

**Lambda Advanced
Analog, Inc.**
2270 Martin Ave.
Santa Clara, CA 95050
Founded: 1969
Total Employees: 170
Annual Sales: $25 million
Industries: Computer
Hardware,
Subassemblies and
Components,
Telecommunications
Growth: Openings in past
year, 34
Contact Ms. Sharon
Allansmith, Director of
Human Resources; 408-
727-0500; Fax: 408-748-
9489

Larscom Incorporated
1845 McCandless Dr.
Milpitas, CA 95035
http://www.larscom.com
Founded: 1970
Total Employees: 250
Annual Sales: $66.444
million
Industry:
Telecommunications
Growth: Openings in past
year, 25
Contact Ms. Marilyn
Zuercher, Director of
Human Resources; 408-
988-6600; Fax: 408-986-
8690; E-mail: info@
larscom.com

**Lightwave Electronics
Corp.**
1161 San Antonio Rd.
Mountain View, CA 94043
http://www.lwecorp.com
Founded: 1984
Total Employees: 120
Annual Sales: $15 million
Industry. Photonics
Growth: Openings in past
year, 25
Contact Ms. Sue Olsen,
Human Resources
Manager; 650-962-0755;
Fax: 650-962-1661;
E-mail: sales@lwecorp.
com

Litronic, Inc.
2950 Red Hill Ave.
Costa Mesa, CA 92626
http://www.litronic.com
Founded: 1969
Total Employees: 140
Annual Sales: $18 million
Industries: Computer
Hardware, Computer
Software
Growth: Openings in past
year, 60
Contact Christopher Shah,
President/CEO; 714-545-
6649; Fax: 714-545-
7616; E-mail: info@
litronic.com

LESCO
23555 Telo Ave.
Torrance, CA 90505
http://www.lescouv.com
Founded: 1982
Total Employees: 50
Annual Sales: $7.5 million
Industry: Factory
Automation
Growth: Openings in past
year, 25
Contact Ms. Janene
DeCoster, Human
Resources Manager;
310-784-2930; Fax: 310-
784-2929

**Lightwave Microsystems
Corp.**
2950 Scott Blvd.
Santa Clara, CA 95054
http://www.lightwavemicro.
com
Founded: 1989
Total Employees: 40
Industries: Photonics,
Subassemblies and
Components,
Telecommunications
Growth: Openings in past
year, 31
Contact Michael Hess,
President/CEO; 408-970-
8614; Fax: 408-970-
8615; E-mail: info@
lightwavemicro.com

Live Picture, Inc.
5617 Scotts Valley Dr.
Suite 180
Scotts Valley, CA 95066
http://www.livepicture.com
Founded: 1993
Total Employees: 75
Annual Sales: $9.7 million
Industry: Computer
Software
Growth: Openings in past
year, 40
Contact Ms. Kathleen M.
Mitchell, President/CEO;
408-438-9610; Fax: 408-
438-9604; E-mail: info@
livepicture.com

**Level One
Communications, Inc.**
9750 Goethe Rd.
Sacramento, CA 95827
http://www.level1.com
Founded: 1985
Total Employees: 408
Annual Sales: $111.987
million
Industry:
Telecommunications
Growth: Openings in past
year, 27
Contact Dr. Robert S.
Pepper, President/CEO;
916-855-5000; Fax: 916-
854-1110

**Linfinity Microelectronics
Inc.**
11861 Western Ave.
Garden Grove, CA 92841
http://www.linfinity.com
Founded: 1968
Total Employees: 280
Annual Sales: $55 million
Industry: Subassemblies
and Components
Growth: Openings in past
year, 30
Contact Dan Rasdal,
Chairman of the Board/
CEO; 714-898-8121;
Fax: 714-893-2570

Logos Corp.
5201 Great America
Pkwy., Suite 238
Santa Clara, CA 95054
http://www.logos-ca.com
Founded: 1969
Total Employees: 100
Annual Sales: $12 million
Industry: Computer
Software
Growth: Openings in past
year, 25
Contact Jens Thomas
Luck, CEO/President;
408-987-5900; Fax: 408-
987-6150; E-mail: info@
logos-usa.com

Lumisys, Inc.
225 Humboldt Ct.
Sunnyvale, CA 94089
http://www.lumisys.com
Founded: 1987
Total Employees: 80
Annual Sales: $23 million
Industries: Holding
Companies, Medical, Test
and Measurement
Growth: Openings in past
year, 30
Contact Stephen Weiss,
President; 408-733-6565;
Fax: 408-733-6567

Lyte Optronics, Inc.
3015 Main St., Suite 450
Santa Monica, CA 90405
Founded: 1987
Total Employees: 100
Annual Sales: $13 million
Industry: Photonics
Growth: Openings in past
year, 60
Contact Keith Halsey,
President; 310-450-8551;
Fax: 310-392-1754

M.C. Gill Corp.
4056 Easy St.
El Monte, CA 91731
http://www.mcgillcorp.com
Founded: 1945
Total Employees: 300
Annual Sales: $37 million
Industries: Advanced
Materials, Holding
Companies
Growth: Openings in past
year, 75
Contact Ron Long, Direc-
tor of Human Resources;
626-443-6094; Fax: 626-
350-5880; E-mail:
doorman@mcgillcorp.
com

**M/A-COM, Inc. / Power
Hybrid Operation**
1742 Crenshaw Blvd.
Torrance, CA 90501
Founded: 1972

Total Employees: 260
Annual Sales: $32 million
Industry: Subassemblies
and Components
Growth: Openings in past
year, 60
Contact Ms. Paula Cohn,
Human Resources
Manager; 310-320-6160;
Fax: 310-618-9191

MAG InnoVision Co., Inc.
2801 South Yale St.
Santa Ana, CA 92704
http://www.maginnovision.
com
Founded: 1990
Total Employees: 300
Annual Sales: $500 million
Industry: Computer
Hardware
Growth: Openings in past
year, 150
Contact Ms. Yvonne
Molnar, Human
Resources Manager;
714-751-2008; Fax: 714-
751-5522

Mag-Tek, Inc.
20725 South Annalee Ave.
Carson, CA 90746
http://www.magtek.com
Founded: 1972
Total Employees: 200
Annual Sales: $41 million
Industries: Computer
Hardware, Factory
Automation
Growth: Openings in past
year, 50
Contact Thomas
McGeary, President; 310-
631-8602; Fax: 310-631-
3956

**Manufacturers' Services
Ltd., Fremont Division**
6600 Stevenson Blvd.
Fremont, CA 94538
Founded: 1994
Total Employees: 180
Annual Sales: $24 million
Industries: Manufacturing
Equipment,
Subassemblies and
Components

Growth: Openings in past
year, 120
Contact Steve
Darendinger, Vice
President; 510-413-1800;
Fax: 510-413-1999

**Manufacturing
Technology, Inc.**
2226 Goodyear Ave.
Ventura, CA 93003
Founded: 1979
Total Employees: 200
Annual Sales: $25 million
Industries: Factory
Automation,
Manufacturing Equipment
Growth: Openings in past
year, 30
Contact Mike Cromer,
President; 805-644-9681;
Fax: 805-644-3541

Marimba, Inc.
445 Sherman Ave.
Palo Alto, CA 94306
http://www.marimba.com
Founded: 1996
Total Employees: 37
Annual Sales: $4.7 million
Industry: Computer
Software
Growth: Openings in past
year, 33
Contact Ms. Kim Polese,
President/CEO; 650-328-
5282; Fax: 650-328-
5295; E-mail: info@
marimba.com

**Matheson-Semi-Gas
Systems**
625 Wool Creek Dr., Suite
A
San Jose, CA 95112
Founded: 1980
Total Employees: 150
Annual Sales: $34 million
Industries: Energy,
Manufacturing
Equipment, Test and
Measurement
Growth: Openings in past
year, 50
Contact Rick Darlow,
President; 408-971-6500;
Fax: 408-275-8643

MatriDigm Corp.
4777 Hellyer Ave.
San Jose, CA 95138
http://www.matridigmusa.
 com
Founded: 1995
Total Employees: 120
Annual Sales: $24 million
Industry: Computer
 Hardware
Growth: Openings in past
 year, 100
Contact Ms. Toni Tonacci,
 Director of Human
 Resources; 408-360-
 3200; Fax: 408-225-
 0215; E-mail: info@
 matridigmusa.com

Maxtech Corp.
13915 Cerritos Corporate
 Dr.
Cerritos, CA 90703
http://www.maxcorp.com
Founded: 1978
Total Employees: 80
Annual Sales: $13 million
Industries: Computer
 Hardware,
 Telecommunications
Growth: Openings in past
 year, 29
Contact Gary Fan,
 President; 562-921-1698;
 Fax: 562-802-9605

Mercury Interactive Corp.
470 Potrero Ave.
Sunnyvale, CA 94086
http://www.merc-int.com
Founded: 1989
Total Employees: 400
Annual Sales: $54.6
 million
Industry: Computer
 Software
Growth: Openings in past
 year, 100
Contact Amnon Landan,
 President/CEO; 408-523-
 9900; Fax: 408-523-9911

**Matrix Pharmaceutical,
Inc.**
34700 Campus Dr.
Fremont, CA 94555
http://www.matx.com
Founded: 1985
Total Employees: 170
Industries: Biotechnology,
 Pharmaceuticals
Growth: Openings in past
 year, 40
Contact Craig R.
 McMullen, President/
 CEO; 510-742-9900;
 Fax: 510-742-8510

**MDL Information
Systems, Inc.**
14600 Catalina St.
San Leandro, CA 94577
http://www.mdli.com/
Founded: 1978
Total Employees: 400
Annual Sales: $51 million
Industry: Computer
 Software
Growth: Openings in past
 year, 47
Contact Dan E. Kingman,
 VP of Human Resources;
 510-895-1313; Fax: 510-
 352-2870

Metabyte, Inc.
39350 Civic Center Dr.,
 Suite 200
Fremont, CA 94538
http://www.metabyte.com
Founded: 1993
Total Employees: 100
Annual Sales: $12 million
Industry: Computer
 Software
Growth: Openings in past
 year, 50
Contact Manu Mehta,
 President; 510-494-9700;
 Fax: 510-494-9100

Maxis, Inc.
2121 North California
 Blvd., Suite 600
Walnut Creek, CA 94596
http://www.maxis.com
Founded: 1987
Total Employees: 236
Annual Sales: $48.262
 million
Industry: Computer
 Software
Growth: Openings in past
 year, 56
Contact Sam Poole,
 President/CEO; 510-933-
 5630; Fax: 510-927-3736

Mega Drive Systems, Inc.
9201 Oakdale Ave.
Chatsworth, CA 91311
http://www.megadrive.com
Founded: 1988
Total Employees: 180
Annual Sales: $37 million
Industry: Computer
 Hardware
Growth: Openings in past
 year, 30
Contact Paul Bloch, Chief
 Executive Officer; 818-
 700-7600; Fax: 818-700-
 7601; E-mail: sales@
 megadrive.com

Metricom, Inc.
980 University Ave.
Los Gatos, CA 95030
http://www.metricom.com
Founded: 1985
Total Employees: 250
Annual Sales: $7.2 million
Industry:
 Telecommunications
Growth: Openings in past
 year, 50
Contact Ms. Elaine
 Hamilton, Human
 Resources Director; 408-
 399-8200; Fax: 408-399-
 8274; E-mail: info@
 metricom.com

MICOM Communications Corp.
4100 Los Angeles Ave.
Simi Valley, CA 93063
http://www.micom.com
Founded: 1973
Total Employees: 450
Annual Sales: $77 million
Industry:
Telecommunications
Growth: Openings in past year, 49
Contact Ms. Nancy Shemwell, General Manager; 805-583-8600; Fax: 805-583-1997; E-mail: info@micom.com

Micro Lithography, Inc.
1247 Elko Dr.
Sunnyvale, CA 94089
Founded: 1982
Total Employees: 250
Annual Sales: $33 million
Industry: Photonics
Growth: Openings in past year, 50
Contact Ms. Stephanie Spiller, Manager of Human Resources; 408-747-1769; Fax: 408-747-1978

Micro Motors, Inc., Industrial Motors Division
151 East Columbine Ave.
Santa Ana, CA 92707
Founded: 1971
Total Employees: 100
Annual Sales: $13 million
Industry: Subassemblies and Components
Growth: Openings in past year, 30
Contact Bill Fitzpatrick, President; 714-546-4045; Fax: 714-546-1109

Microcide Pharmaceuticals, Inc.
850 Maude Ave.
Mountain View, CA 94043

http://www.microcide.com
Founded: 1992
Total Employees: 110
Annual Sales: $11.3 million
Industry: Pharmaceuticals
Growth: Openings in past year, 40
Contact Ms. Michelle Benjamin, Personnel Manager; 650-428-1550; Fax: 650-428-3550

MicroProse, Inc.
2490 Mariner Sq. Loop, Suite 100
Alameda, CA 94501
Founded: 1983
Total Employees: 455
Annual Sales: $100.3 million
Industries: Computer Software, Holding Companies
Growth: Openings in past year, 49
Contact Steven Race, Chief Executive Officer; 510-522-3584; Fax: 510-522-3587

MicroTel International, Inc.
2040 Fortune Dr.
San Jose, CA 95131
Founded: 1984
Total Employees: 390
Annual Sales: $38.3 million
Industry: Holding Companies
Growth: Openings in past year, 68
Contact Ms. Jen Height, Human Resource Manager; 408-435-8520; Fax: 408-435-1276

Mitsubishi Electronics America, Inc., Electronic Device Group
1050 East Arques Ave.
Sunnyvale, CA 94086
Founded: 1980
Total Employees: 350
Annual Sales: $47 million
Industries: Computer Hardware, Factory

Automation, Photonics, Subassemblies and Components, Test and Measurement
Growth: Openings in past year, 49
Contact T. Nishimura, Group President; 408-730-5900; Fax: 408-732-9382

ModaCAD, Inc.
1954 Cotner Ave.
Los Angeles, CA 90025
http://www.modacad.com
Founded: 1988
Total Employees: 59
Annual Sales: $3.370 million
Industry: Computer Software
Growth: Openings in past year, 29
Contact Ms. Joyce Freedman, COB/President; 310-312-9826; Fax: 310-444-9577; E-mail: modamaster@modacad.com

Modular Devices, Inc.
4115 Spencer St.
Torrance, CA 90503
Founded: 1963
Total Employees: 550
Industry: Subassemblies and Components
Growth: Openings in past year, 100
Contact Michael R. Dulion, President; 310-542-8561; Fax: 310-371-6331; E-mail: sales@modular.com

Molded Fiber Glass Companies West
9400 Holly Rd.
Adelanto, CA 92301
Founded: 1958
Total Employees: 100
Industry: Manufacturing Equipment
Growth: Openings in past year, 30

Contact Gerald Bender, President; 760-246-4042; Fax: 760-246-5500

Molecular Dynamics, Inc.
928 East Arques Ave.
Sunnyvale, CA 94086
http://www.mdyn.com
Founded: 1987
Total Employees: 280
Annual Sales: $50 million
Industries: Medical, Test and Measurement
Growth: Openings in past year, 51
Contact Jay Flatley, President/CEO; 408-773-1222; Fax: 408-773-8343

Monogram Aerospace Fasteners
3423 South Garfield Ave.
Los Angeles, CA 90040
Founded: 1945
Total Employees: 280
Industry: Subassemblies and Components
Growth: Openings in past year, 30
Contact Jim Lord, Industrial Relations Manager; 213-722-4760; Fax: 213-721-1851

Motorola Indala Corp.
3041 Orchard Pkwy.
San Jose, CA 95134
http://www.indala.mot.com
Founded: 1985
Total Employees: 250
Annual Sales: $49 million
Industry: Computer Hardware
Growth: Openings in past year, 90
Contact Ms. Kris Anderson, Personnel Manager; 408-383-4000; Fax: 408-434-7057

MRV Communications, Inc.
8943 Fullbright Ave.
Chatsworth, CA 91311

http://www.nbase.com
Founded: 1988
Total Employees: 350
Annual Sales: $88.8 million
Industries: Holding Companies, Photonics
Growth: Openings in past year, 114
Contact Noam Lotan, President; 818-773-0900; Fax: 818-773-8932

Multi-Pure Corp.
21339 Nordhoff St.
Chatsworth, CA 91311
Founded: 1970
Total Employees: 370
Annual Sales: $45 million
Industry: Environmental
Growth: Openings in past year, 199
Contact H. Allen Rice, Chief Executive Officer; 818-341-7577; Fax: 818-341-5275

Mustek, Inc.
121 Waterworks Way, Suite 100
Irvine, CA 92618
http://www.mustek.com
Founded: 1988
Total Employees: 100
Annual Sales: $89 million
Industry: Computer Hardware
Growth: Openings in past year, 25
Contact Mike Feng, President; 714-790-3800; Fax: 714-788-3636

National Technical Systems, Inc.
24007 Ventura Blvd., Suite 200
Calabasas, CA 91302
http://www.ntscorp.com
Founded: 1961
Total Employees: 450
Annual Sales: $47 million
Industries: Holding Companies, Manufacturing Equipment
Growth: Openings in past year, 150

Contact Jack Lin, President/CEO; 818-591-0776; Fax: 818-591-0899; E-mail: moreinfo@ntscorp.com

National Telephone & Communications, Inc.
2801 Main St.
Irvine, CA 92614
http://www.natltele.com.
Founded: 1988
Total Employees: 243
Annual Sales: $41 million
Industry: Telecommunications
Growth: Openings in past year, 83
Contact Ed Jacobs, Chief Executive Officer; 714-251-8000; Fax: 714-224-7474

NDC Systems
5314 North Irwindale Ave.
Irwindale, CA 91706
http://www.ndc.com
Founded: 1967
Total Employees: 140
Annual Sales: $24.3 million
Industries: Computer Software, Test and Measurement
Growth: Openings in past year, 25
Contact Yudie Fishman, President; 626-960-3300; Fax: 626-939-3870

NETCOM On-Line Communication Services, Inc.
2 North 2nd St., Plaza A
San Jose, CA 95113
http://www.netcom.com
Founded: 1988
Total Employees: 860
Annual Sales: $120.540 million
Industries: Computer Software, Telecommunications
Growth: Openings in past year, 156
Contact David W. Garrison, COB/CEO; 408-

881-2000; Fax: 408-881-3610; E-mail: info@netcom.com

NetDynamics, Inc.
185 Constitution Dr.
Menlo Park, CA 94025
http://www.netdynamics.com
Founded: 1995
Total Employees: 80
Annual Sales: $10 million
Industry: Computer Software
Growth: Openings in past year, 60
Contact Zack Rinat, President/CEO; 650-462-7600; Fax: 650-617-5920; E-mail: info@netdynamics.com

NetGravity, Inc.
1700 South Amphlett Blvd., Suite 350
San Mateo, CA 94402
http://www.netgravity.com
Founded: 1995
Total Employees: 80
Industry: Computer Software
Growth: Openings in past year, 27
Contact John Danner, President/CEO/Founder; 650-655-4777; Fax: 650-655-4776; E-mail: info@netgravity.com

NetPartners Internet Solutions, Inc.
9210 Sky Park Ct.
San Diego, CA 92123
http://www.netpart.com
Founded: 1994
Total Employees: 45
Industry: Computer Software
Growth: Openings in past year, 35
Contact Phil Trubey, President; 619-505-3020; Fax: 619-495-1950; E-mail: info@netpart.com

Netro Corp.
3200 Coronado Dr.
Santa Clara, CA 95054
http://www.netro-corp.com
Founded: 1994
Total Employees: 100
Annual Sales: $17 million
Industry: Telecommunications
Growth: Openings in past year, 70
Contact Gideon Ben-Efraim, COB/President/CEO; 408-654-7500; Fax: 408-654-7525; E-mail: webmaster@netro-corp.com

NetSoft
31 Technology Dr.
Irvine, CA 92618
http://www.netsoft.com
Founded: 1980
Total Employees: 200
Annual Sales: $25 million
Industries: Computer Hardware, Computer Software, Telecommunications
Growth: Openings in past year, 55
Contact Ms. Carol Carson, Human Resources Manager; 714-753-0800; Fax: 714-753-0810

Netwave Technologies, Inc.
6663 Owens Dr.
Pleasanton, CA 94588
http://www.netwave-wireless.com
Founded: 1996
Total Employees: 100
Industries: Computer Software, Telecommunications
Growth: Openings in past year, 93
Contact Jerry Ulrich, President/CEO; 510-737-1600; Fax: 510-847-8744; E-mail: lhaggerty@netwave-wireless.com

Network General Corp.
4200 Bohannon Dr.
Menlo Park, CA 94025
http://www.ngc.com/
Founded: 1986
Total Employees: 950
Annual Sales: $240.668 million
Industries: Computer Software, Holding Companies, Telecommunications
Growth: Openings in past year, 95
Contact Ms. Sally Takemoto, VP of Human Resources; 650-473-2000; Fax: 650-327-2145

Neurex Corp.
3760 Haven Ave.
Menlo Park, CA 94025
http://www.neurex.com
Founded: 1983
Total Employees: 95
Annual Sales: $4 million
Industry: Pharmaceuticals
Growth: Openings in past year, 30
Contact Paul Goddard, Ph.D., COB/CEO; 650-853-1500; Fax: 650-853-1538

NextLevel Communications
6085 State Farm Dr.
Rohnert Park, CA 94928
Founded: 1994
Total Employees: 300
Industries: Energy, Telecommunications
Growth: Openings in past year, 200
Contact Charles Seeback, Chief Financial Officer; 707-584-6811; Fax: 707-584-6653

Nichols Institute Diagnostics
33051 Calle Aviador
San Juan Capistrano, CA
  92675
http://www.nicholsdiag.com
Founded: 1974
Total Employees: 267
Annual Sales: $35 million
Industry: Medical
Growth: Openings in past
  year, 25
Contact David Macdonald,
  President/COO; 714-728-
  4610; Fax: 714-240-5273

NovaQuest InfoSystems
19950 Mariner Ave.
Torrance, CA 90503
http://www.novaquest.com
Founded: 1985
Total Employees: 350
Annual Sales: $270 million
Industries: Computer
  Software, Holding
  Companies
Growth: Openings in past
  year, 49
Contact Zeb Bhatti, COB/
  CEO; 310-793-4582;
  Fax: 310-793-4462;
  E-mail: webmaster@
  novaquest.com

Objectivity, Inc.
301B East Evelyn Ave.
Mountain View, CA 94041
http://www.objectivity.com
Founded: 1988
Total Employees: 100
Annual Sales: $12 million
Industry: Computer
  Software
Growth: Openings in past
  year, 30
Contact David Caplan,
  COB/President/CEO;
  650-254-7100; Fax: 650-
  254-7171; E-mail: info@
  objy.com

Nikon Precision, Inc.
1399 Shoreway Rd.
Belmont, CA 94002
Founded: 1982
Total Employees: 450
Industry: Subassemblies
  and Components
Growth: Openings in past
  year, 93
Contact Dr. David A.
  Huchital, President; 650-
  508-4674; Fax: 650-508-
  4600

Oacis Healthcare Holdings Corp.
100 Drakes Landing Rd.,
  Suite 100
Greenbrae, CA 94904
http://www.oacis.com
Founded: 1994
Total Employees: 175
Annual Sales: $20.4
  million
Industry: Holding
  Companies
Growth: Openings in past
  year, 35
Contact Jim McCord,
  COB/CEO; 415-925-
  0121; Fax: 415-925-4610

OEA Aerospace, Inc.
PO Box KK
Fairfield, CA 94533
Founded: 1961
Total Employees: 460
Annual Sales: $54 million
Industries: Defense,
  Subassemblies and
  Components,
  Transportation
Growth: Openings in past
  year, 109
Contact Ben E. Paul,
  President; 707-422-1880;
  Fax: 707-422-3242

NMB Technologies Inc.
9730 Independence Ave.
Chatsworth, CA 91311
http://www.nmbtech.com
Founded: 1971
Total Employees: 150
Annual Sales: $23.5
  million
Industries: Computer
  Hardware,
  Subassemblies and
  Components,
  Telecommunications
Growth: Openings in past
  year, 25
Contact David Morena,
  Director of Human
  Resources; 818-341-
  3355; Fax: 818-341-
  8207; E-mail: info@
  nmbtech.com

Objective Systems Integrators, Inc.
100 Blue Ravine Rd.
Folsom, CA 95630
http://www.osi.com
Founded: 1989
Total Employees: 481
Annual Sales: $57.712
  million
Industry: Computer
  Software
Growth: Openings in past
  year, 111
Contact Tom Johnson,
  Co-Founder/Co-
  Chairman/Co-CEO; 916-
  353-2400; Fax: 916-353-
  2424

Omega Power Systems, Inc.
8966 Mason Ave.
Chatsworth, CA 91311
http://www.omegapower.
  com/~omega
Founded: 1991
Total Employees: 151
Annual Sales: $20 million
Industries: Holding
  Companies,
  Subassemblies and
  Components
Growth: Openings in past
  year, 31
Contact Avi Bernstein,
  President; 818-727-2216;
  Fax: 818-727-2276;
  E-mail: sales1@
  omegapower.com

OmniCell Technologies, Inc.
1101 East Meadow Dr.
Palo Alto, CA 94313
http://www.omnicell.com
Founded: 1992
Total Employees: 180
Annual Sales: $23 million
Industry: Computer Software
Growth: Openings in past year, 50
Contact Shelly Asher, President; 650-843-6100; Fax: 650-843-6262

OnTrak Systems, Inc.
1010 Rincon Cir.
San Jose, CA 95131
Founded: 1988
Total Employees: 400
Annual Sales: $50 million
Industry: Manufacturing Equipment
Growth: Openings in past year, 100
Contact Jerry Cutini, President; 408-577-1010; Fax: 408-952-5441

Optivision, Inc.
3450 Hillview Ave.
Palo Alto, CA 94304
http://www.optivision.com
Founded: 1983
Total Employees: 104
Industries: Computer Hardware, Photonics
Growth: Openings in past year, 29
Contact Anita Reddy, Human Relations Manager; 650-855-0200; Fax: 650-855-0222; E-mail: info@optivision. com

OPTO 22
43044 Business Park Dr.
Temecula, CA 92590
http://www.opto22.com
Founded: 1974
Total Employees: 250

Annual Sales: $51 million
Industries: Computer Hardware, Computer Software, Subassemblies and Components
Growth: Openings in past year, 50
Contact R.G. Engman, President; 909-695-3000; Fax: 909-695-3095

Orbit Semiconductor, Inc.
169 Java Dr.
Sunnyvale, CA 94089
http://www.orbitsemi.com
Founded: 1982
Total Employees: 400
Annual Sales: $53 million
Industry: Subassemblies and Components
Growth: Openings in past year, 100
Contact Howard Pruitt, VP of Human Resources; 408-744-1800; Fax: 408-747-1263

Origin Medsystems, Inc.
135 Constitution Dr.
Menlo Park, CA 94025
Founded: 1988
Total Employees: 280
Annual Sales: $34 million
Industry: Medical
Growth: Openings in past year, 39
Contact Ms. Bev Mehlhoff, Director of Human Resources; 650-617-5000; Fax: 650-617-5200; E-mail: origin@guidant.com

Ortel Corp.
2015 West Chestnut St.
Alhambra, CA 91803
http://www.ortel.com
Founded: 1980
Total Employees: 600
Annual Sales: $82.55 million
Industries: Photonics, Telecommunications
Growth: Openings in past year, 100

Contact Wim H.J. Selders, President/CEO; 626-281-3636; Fax: 626-281-1007; E-mail: info@ortel. com

Overland Data, Inc.
8975 Balboa Ave.
San Diego, CA 92123
http://www.overlanddata. com
Founded: 1980
Total Employees: 208
Annual Sales: $59.146 million
Industry: Computer Hardware
Growth: Openings in past year, 32
Contact Scott McClendon, President/CEO; 619-571-5555; Fax: 619-571-3664; E-mail: odisales@overlanddata.com

OZ Interactive, Inc.
525 Brannan St.
San Francisco, CA 94107
http://www.oz.com
Founded: 1990
Total Employees: 70
Industry: Computer Software
Growth: Openings in past year, 30
Contact Skuli Mogenson, President; 415-536-0500; Fax: 415-536-0536

Pacific Device, Inc.
8572 Spectrum Ln.
San Diego, CA 92121
Founded: 1983
Total Employees: 330
Industry: Medical
Growth: Openings in past year, 30
Contact Randy Keene, President; 619-457-1988; Fax: 619-558-7264

Pacific Flued Systems, Inc.
2324 Del Monte St.
West Sacramento, CA 95691
Founded: 1978
Total Employees: 120
Annual Sales: $35 million
Industries: Holding Companies, Subassemblies and Components
Growth: Openings in past year, 70
Contact Gordon Pardy, President; 916-372-0660; Fax: 916-372-0492

Pacific Monolithics, Inc.
1308 Moffett Park Dr.
Sunnyvale, CA 94089
http://www.pacmono.com
Founded: 1984
Total Employees: 220
Annual Sales: $37 million
Industries: Subassemblies and Components, Telecommunications
Growth: Openings in past year, 40
Contact Ms. Katherine Watt, VP of Human Resources; 408-745-2700; Fax: 408-734-2656; E-mail: marketing@pacmono.com

PairGain Technologies, Inc.
14402 Franklin Ave.
Tustin, CA 92780
http://www.pairgain.com
Founded: 1988
Total Employees: 450
Annual Sales: $205.4 million
Industries: Holding Companies, Telecommunications
Growth: Openings in past year, 49
Contact Charles Strauch, COB/CEO; 714-832-9922; Fax: 714-832-9924; E-mail: info@pairgain.com

Pangea Systems, Inc.
1999 Harrison St., Suite 1100
Oakland, CA 94012
http://www.panbio.com
Founded: 1993
Total Employees: 60
Industries: Computer Hardware, Computer Software
Growth: Openings in past year, 48
Contact Jim Sampson, Human Resources Manager; 510-628-0100; Fax: 510-522-9394; E-mail: info@panbio.com

Parker Hannifin Corp., O-Seal Division
7664 Panasonic Way
San Diego, CA 92173
Founded: 1952
Total Employees: 300
Industry: Subassemblies and Components
Growth: Openings in past year, 40
Contact Ms. Lynne Ward, Human Resources Manager; 619-661-7000; Fax: 619-671-3202

Parpro, Inc.
11315 Rancho Bernardo Rd., Suite 148
San Diego, CA 92127
http://www.parpro.com
Founded: 1993
Total Employees: 200
Annual Sales: $3.7 million
Industry: Subassemblies and Components
Growth: Openings in past year, 120
Contact James Saint John, President; 619-673-7127; Fax: 619-673-8108

PASCO Scientific
10101 Foothills Blvd.
PO Box 619011
Roseville, CA 95678
http://www.pasco.com
Founded: 1964
Total Employees: 170
Annual Sales: $23 million
Industries: Computer Hardware, Computer Software, Energy, Factory Automation, Photonics, Subassemblies and Components, Test and Measurement
Growth: Openings in past year, 34
Contact Paul Stokstad, President/CEO; 916-786-3800; Fax: 916-786-8905; E-mail: sales@pasco.com

PC-TEL, Inc.
630 Alder Dr., Suite 202
Milpitas, CA 95035
http://www.pctel.com
Founded: 1994
Total Employees: 55
Annual Sales: $10 million
Industries: Computer Software, Subassemblies and Components, Telecommunications
Growth: Openings in past year, 30
Contact Peter Chen, President/CEO; 408-383-0452; Fax: 408-383-0455

PEDCOM, Inc.
5500 Stewart Ave.
Fremont, CA 94538
http://www.pedcom.com
Founded: 1981
Total Employees: 275
Industries: Photonics, Telecommunications
Growth: Openings in past year, 25
Contact Ms. Janet Migliore, Human Resources Manager;

510-490-3688; Fax: 510-490-0756; E-mail: fjp@pedcom.com

Penware, Inc.
500 Oakmead Pkwy.
Sunnyvale, CA 94086
http://www.penware.com
Founded: 1983
Total Employees: 50
Industries: Computer Hardware, Computer Software
Growth: Openings in past year, 25
Contact Aziz Valliani, President; 408-524-4200; Fax: 408-524-4299; E-mail: penware@penware.com

Peregrine Systems, Inc.
12670 High Bluff Dr.
San Diego, CA 92130
http://www.peregrine.com
Founded: 1980
Total Employees: 206
Annual Sales: $35 million
Industries: Computer Software, Holding Companies
Growth: Openings in past year, 96
Contact Ms. Diane Olivo, Personnel Manager; 619-481-5000; Fax: 619-481-1751; E-mail: info@peregrine.com

PharMingen
10975 Torreyana Rd.
San Diego, CA 92121
http://www.pharmingen.com
Founded: 1987
Total Employees: 270
Annual Sales: $35 million
Industry: Biotechnology
Growth: Openings in past year, 60
Contact Ms. Nancy Huang, VP of Human Resources & Administration; 619-812-8800; Fax: 619-812-8888; E-mail: info@pharmingen.com

Phaze Metrics, Inc.
10260 Sorrento Valley Blvd.
San Diego, CA 92101
http://www.phazemetrics.com
Founded: 1989
Total Employees: 535
Industries: Computer Software, Factory Automation, Holding Companies
Growth: Openings in past year, 70
Contact John F. Schaefer, COB/CEO/President/COO; 619-552-1115; Fax: 619-552-1132

Philips Key Modules, Inc.
2099 Gateway Pl., Suite 100
San Jose, CA 95110
http://www.philips.com
Founded: 1948
Total Employees: 200
Annual Sales: $25 million
Industries: Computer Hardware, Manufacturing Equipment, Photonics
Growth: Openings in past year, 50
Contact A. Verweij, Vice President/General Manager; 408-453-7373; Fax: 408-453-6444

Physical Optics Corp.
20600 Gramercy Pl., Suite 103
Torrance, CA 90501
Founded: 1985
Total Employees: 150
Annual Sales: $19 million
Industries: Factory Automation, Photonics, Test and Measurement, Telecommunications
Growth: Openings in past year, 46
Contact Ms. Joanna Jannson, President/CEO; 310-320-3088; Fax: 310-320-8067

Pilkington Aerospace, Inc.
12122 Western Ave.
Garden Grove, CA 92641
Founded: 1934
Total Employees: 750
Annual Sales: $71 million
Industries: Advanced Materials, Transportation
Growth: Openings in past year, 50
Contact Larry Valenti, Director of Human Resources; 714-893-7531; Fax: 714-892-7635

PinPoint Software Corp.
6155 Almaden Expwy., Suite 100
San Jose, CA 95120
http://www.pinpt.com
Founded: 1992
Total Employees: 40
Annual Sales: $5.1 million
Industry: Computer Software
Growth: Openings in past year, 30
Contact Lou Ryan, President/CEO; 408-997-6900; Fax: 408-323-2310; E-mail: sales@pinpt.com

Pioneer New Media Technologies, Inc.
2265 East 220th St.
Long Beach, CA 90810
Founded: 1973
Total Employees: 150
Industries: Computer Hardware, Photonics, Telecommunications
Growth: Openings in past year, 30
Contact Tom Haga, President; 310-952-2111; Fax: 310-952-2990

Plastic Engineered Components, Inc., PEC Los Angeles Division
1125 Beacon St.
Brea, CA 92821
http://www.pecplastics.com
Founded: 1946
Total Employees: 170
Annual Sales: $21 million
Industries: Factory Automation,
Manufacturing Equipment
Growth: Openings in past year, 70
Contact Steve Broadhead, General Manager; 714-672-0400; Fax: 714-672-0404

Play, Inc.
2890 Kilgore Rd.
Rancho Cordova, CA 95670
http://www.play.com
Founded: 1979
Total Employees: 99
Annual Sales: $20 million
Industries: Computer Hardware, Computer Software, Telecommunications
Growth: Openings in past year, 29
Contact Paul Montgomery, President; 916-851-0800; Fax: 916-851-0801

PointCast, Inc.
501 Macara Ave.
Sunnyvale, CA 94086
http://www.pointcast.com
Founded: 1992
Total Employees: 200
Industry: Telecommunications
Growth: Openings in past year, 130
Contact David Dorman, Chief Executive Officer; 408-990-7000; Fax: 408-990-0080

Poly-Flow Engineering, Inc.
15392 Cobalt St.
Sylmar, CA 91342
http://www.polyflow.com
Founded: 1974
Total Employees: 135
Annual Sales: $20 million
Industry: Factory Automation
Growth: Openings in past year, 30
Contact John Sweeney, President; 818-362-5891; Fax: 818-364-1259

Powerwave Technologies, Inc.
2026 McGaw Ave.
Irvine, CA 92614
http://www.powerwave.com
Founded: 1985
Total Employees: 330
Annual Sales: $60.331 million
Industry: Subassemblies and Components
Growth: Openings in past year, 80
Contact Bruce Edwards, Chief Executive Officer; 714-757-0530; Fax: 714-757-0941

PREMENOS
1000 Burnett Ave., Second Floor
Concord, CA 94520
http://www.premenos.com
Founded: 1987
Total Employees: 263
Annual Sales: $33.471 million
Industries: Computer Software, Holding Companies
Growth: Openings in past year, 66
Contact Ms. Ardene Fullerton, Director of Human Resources; 510-602-2000; Fax: 510-688-3096; E-mail: info@premenos.com

Premisys Communications, Inc.
48664 Milmont Dr.
Fremont, CA 94538
http://www.premisys.com
Founded: 1990
Total Employees: 245
Annual Sales: $78.358 million
Industry: Telecommunications
Growth: Openings in past year, 75
Contact Raymond C. Lin, Chief Executive Officer; 510-353-7600; Fax: 510-353-7601

Pretty Good Privacy, Inc.
21215 El Camino Real
San Mateo, CA 94403
http://www.pgp.com
Founded: 1996
Total Employees: 80
Industries: Computer Software, Holding Companies
Growth: Openings in past year, 30
Contact Phil Dunkelberger, President; 650-572-0430; Fax: 650-572-1932; E-mail: info@pgp.com

Printrak International Inc.
1250 North Tustin Ave.
Anaheim, CA 92807
http://www.printrakinternational.com
Founded: 1981
Total Employees: 300
Annual Sales: $65.6 million
Industries: Computer Hardware, Holding Companies
Growth: Openings in past year, 64
Contact Richard Giles, President/CEO; 714-666-2700; Fax: 714-666-1055

ProBusiness Services, Inc.
5934 Gibraltar Dr.
Pleasanton, CA 94566
Founded: 1993
Total Employees: 377
Annual Sales: $27.3 million
Industry: Computer Software
Growth: Openings in past year, 73
Contact Thomas H. Sinton, COB/CEO/President; 510-734-9990; Fax: 510-734-8811

Promex Industries, Inc.
3075 Oakmead Village Dr.
Santa Clara, CA 95051
Founded: 1975
Total Employees: 120
Industries: Medical, Subassemblies and Components
Growth: Openings in past year, 30
Contact Richard Otte, President; 408-496-0222; Fax: 408-496-0117

Proxim, Inc.
295 North Bernardo Ave.
Mountain View, CA 94043
http://www.proxim.com
Founded: 1984
Total Employees: 180
Annual Sales: $41.22 million
Industries: Computer Software, Telecommunications
Growth: Openings in past year, 50
Contact David C. King, COB/CEO/President; 650-960-1630; Fax: 650-960-1984

Psygnosis, Inc.
919 East Hillsdale Blvd.
Foster City, CA 94404
http://www.psygnosis.com

Founded: 1985
Total Employees: 120
Annual Sales: $7.8 million
Industry: Computer Software
Growth: Openings in past year, 60
Contact Mark Beumont, General Manager/CEO; 650-655-8000; Fax: 650-655-8031

PTI Technologies, Inc.
950 Rancho Conejo Blvd.
Newbury Park, CA 91320
http://www.ptitechnologies.com
Founded: 1924
Total Employees: 350
Annual Sales: $58 million
Industries: Biotechnology, Subassemblies and Components, Test and Measurement, Transportation
Growth: Openings in past year, 49
Contact Jim Littrell, VP of Human Resources; 805-499-2661; Fax: 805-375-2296; E-mail: filters@ptitechnologies.com

PUMA Technology, Inc.
2940 North First St.
San Jose, CA 95134
http://www.pumatech.com
Founded: 1993
Total Employees: 83
Annual Sales: $15.629 million
Industry: Computer Software
Growth: Openings in past year, 42
Contact Ms. Mitzi Zenger, Manager of Personnel; 408-321-7650; Fax: 408-433-2212; E-mail: webmaster@pumatech.com

Pyxis Corp.
9380 Carroll Park Dr.
San Diego, CA 92121
http://www.pyxis.com
Founded: 1987

Total Employees: 815
Annual Sales: $99 million
Industries: Computer Hardware, Medical
Growth: Openings in past year, 163
Contact Ms. Deborah Weaver, VP of Human Resources; 619-625-3300; Fax: 619-625-3310

Quadramed Corp.
80 East Sir Francis Drake Blvd., Suite 2A
Larkspur, CA 94939
http://www.quadramed.com
Founded: 1993
Total Employees: 350
Annual Sales: $19 million
Industry: Computer Software
Growth: Openings in past year, 175
Contact James D. Durham, COB/CEO/President; 415-461-7725; Fax: 415-461-7785

QUALCOMM, Incorporated, Eudora Division
6455 Lusk Blvd.
San Diego, CA 92121
http://www.eudora.com
Founded: 1993
Total Employees: 140
Annual Sales: $18 million
Industry: Computer Software
Growth: Openings in past year, 70
Contact Jeff Jacobs, Vice President/General Manager; 619-587-1121; Fax: 619-658-5879; E-mail: eudora-rep@eudora.com

Quality Assurance Engineering, Inc.
4464 Willow Rd., Suite C
Pleasanton, CA 94588
Founded: 1975
Total Employees: 220
Annual Sales: $16.2 million

Industries: Advanced Materials, Environmental
Growth: Openings in past year, 34
Contact Gary M. Cappa, President/CEO; 510-460-5100; Fax: 510-460-5118; E-mail: info@celhq.com

Quality Semiconductor, Inc.
851 Martin Ave.
Santa Clara, CA 95050
http://www.qualitysemi.com
Founded: 1989
Total Employees: 220
Annual Sales: $48 million
Industry: Subassemblies and Components
Growth: Openings in past year, 70
Contact R. Paul Gupta, Chief Executive Officer; 408-450-8000; Fax: 408-496-0591; E-mail: first_last@qualitysemi.com

Quality Systems, Inc.
17822 East 17th St.
Tustin, CA 92780
http://www.qsii.com
Founded: 1975
Total Employees: 250
Annual Sales: $20.127 million
Industry: Computer Software
Growth: Openings in past year, 50
Contact Ray Mead, Director of Human Resources; 714-731-7171; Fax: 714-731-9494; E-mail: qsi@qsii.com

Qualix Group, Inc.
1900 South Norfolk St., Suite 224
San Mateo, CA 94403
http://www.qualix.com
Founded: 1990
Total Employees: 110
Annual Sales: $32.1 million
Industries: Computer Hardware, Computer

Software, Holding Companies
Growth: Openings in past year, 25
Contact Richard Thau, President; 650-572-0200; Fax: 650-572-1300; E-mail: info@qualix.com

Quest International, Inc.
65 Parker
Irvine, CA 92618
http://www.questinc.com
Founded: 1984
Total Employees: 85
Annual Sales: $10 million
Industry: Subassemblies and Components
Growth: Openings in past year, 25
Contact Shawn Arshadi, President; 714-581-9900; Fax: 714-581-4011; E-mail: vince@questinc.com

Quester Technology, Inc.
47633 Westinghouse Dr.
Fremont, CA 94539
http://www.quester.com
Founded: 1989
Total Employees: 250
Industry: Manufacturing Equipment
Growth: Openings in past year, 35
Contact Aki Nagatoishi, President/CEO; 510-623-3400; Fax: 510-490-6993

Quote.com, Inc.
850 North Shoreline Blvd.
Mountain View, CA 94043
http://www.quote.com
Founded: 1993
Total Employees: 80
Annual Sales: $16 million
Industries: Computer Hardware, Telecommunications
Growth: Openings in past year, 50
Contact Tom Henry, President/CEO; 650-930-1000; Fax: 650-930-1111; E-mail: info@quote.com

Racal Instruments, Inc.
4 Goodyear St.
PO Box 19541
Irvine, CA 92618
http://www.racalate.com
Founded: 1961
Total Employees: 200
Annual Sales: $27 million
Industries: Factory Automation, Subassemblies and Components, Test and Measurement
Growth: Openings in past year, 73
Contact Ms. Karen O'Donnell, Director of Administration; 714-859-8999; Fax: 714-859-7139; E-mail: 72056.256@compuserve.com

Rainbow Technologies, Inc.
50 Technology Dr.
Irvine, CA 92618
http://www.rainbow.com
Founded: 1984
Total Employees: 360
Annual Sales: $81.71 million
Industries: Computer Hardware, Computer Software, Holding Companies
Growth: Openings in past year, 33
Contact Ms. Cheryl Baffa, Director of Human Resources; 714-450-7300; Fax: 714-450-7450; E-mail: info@rainbow.com

Rambus Inc.
2465 Latham St.
Mountain View, CA 94040
http://www.rambus.com
Founded: 1990
Total Employees: 135
Annual Sales: $11.3 million
Industry: Subassemblies and Components
Growth: Openings in past year, 55

Contact Ed Larson, VP of Human Resources; 650-903-3800; Fax: 650-965-1528

Rational Software Corp.
2800 San Tomas Expwy.
Santa Clara, CA 95051
http://www.rational.com
Founded: 1980
Total Employees: 680
Annual Sales: $145 million
Industries: Computer Software, Holding Companies
Growth: Openings in past year, 68
Contact Burr Gibbons, Director of Human Resources; 408-496-3600; Fax: 408-496-3636; E-mail: product_info@rational.com

Raytheon Co., Amber Division
5756 Thornwood Dr.
Goleta, CA 93117
http://www.amber-infrared.com
Founded: 1980
Total Employees: 230
Annual Sales: $30 million
Industries: Photonics, Test and Measurement
Growth: Openings in past year, 60
Contact Art Lockwood, President; 805-692-1348; Fax: 805-692-1403

Reasoning, Inc.
3260 Hillview Ave.
Palo Alto, CA 94304
http://www.reasoning.com/
Founded: 1984
Total Employees: 50
Industry: Computer Software
Growth: Openings in past year, 38
Contact Michael Crouch, Staffing Specualist; 650-494-6201; Fax: 650-494-8053; E-mail: info@reasoning.com

Red Brick Systems, Inc.
485 Alberto Way
Los Gatos, CA 95032
http://www.redbrick.com
Founded: 1986
Total Employees: 275
Annual Sales: $32 million
Industry: Computer Software
Growth: Openings in past year, 115
Contact Ms. Peggy Deleon, VP of Human Resources; 408-399-3200; Fax: 408-399-3277; E-mail: info@redbrick.com

RedCreek Communications, Inc.
3900 Newpark Mall Rd.
Newark, CA 94560
http://www.redcreek.com
Founded: 1996
Total Employees: 30
Annual Sales: $3.8 million
Industries: Computer Software, Telecommunications
Growth: Openings in past year, 27
Contact Ms. Diana Latour, Chief Executive Officer; 510-745-3900; Fax: 510-745-3999; E-mail: maggie@redcreek.com

Reinhold Industries, Inc.
12827 East Imperial Hwy.
Santa Fe Springs, CA 90670
Founded: 1928
Total Employees: 125
Annual Sales: $13.12 million
Industry: Advanced Materials
Growth: Openings in past year, 70
Contact Michael Furry, President; 562-944-3281; Fax: 562-944-7238

Remedy Corp.
1505 Salado Dr.
Mountain View, CA 94043
http://www.remedy.com
Founded: 1990
Total Employees: 485
Annual Sales: $80.635 million
Industry: Computer Software
Growth: Openings in past year, 97
Contact Ms. Carajane Finn, VP of Employee Services; 650-903-5200; Fax: 650-903-9001; E-mail: info@remedy.com

Repeater Technologies, Inc.
1150 Morse Ave.
Sunnyvale, CA 94089
http://www.repeaters.com
Founded: 1983
Total Employees: 100
Annual Sales: $17 million
Industry: Telecommunications
Growth: Openings in past year, 35
Contact Ms. Christine Thoel, Human Resources Manager; 408-747-1900; Fax: 408-747-0375; E-mail: davidb@repeaters.com

Research Engineers, Inc.
22700 Savi Ranch Pkwy.
Yorba Linda, CA 92687
http://www.reiusa.com
Founded: 1977
Total Employees: 126
Annual Sales: $11 million
Industry: Computer Software
Growth: Openings in past year, 51
Contact Amrit K. Das, President; 714-974-2500; Fax: 714-974-4771; E-mail: info@reiusa.com

RFI Enterprises, Inc.
360 Turtle Creek Ct.
San Jose, CA 95125
http://www.rfi-ent.com
Founded: 1979
Total Employees: 325
Annual Sales: $25 million
Industry: Holding
Companies
Growth: Openings in past
year, 25
Contact Ms. Christine
Burger, Human
Resources Manager;
408-298-5400; Fax: 408-
275-0156

**Roger Wagner
Publishing, Inc.**
1050 Pioneer Way, Suite P
El Cajon, CA 92020
http://www.hyperstudio.
com
Founded: 1983
Total Employees: 50
Annual Sales: $6.4 million
Industry: Computer
Software
Growth: Openings in past
year, 30
Contact Roger Wagner,
President; 619-442-0522;
Fax: 619-442-0525;
E-mail: rwagnerinc@
hyperstudio.com

**RSP Manufacturing
Corp.**
44980 South Grimmer
Blvd.
Fremont, CA 94538
Founded: 1977
Total Employees: 370
Annual Sales: $46 million
Industries: Manufacturing
Equipment,
Subassemblies and
Components
Growth: Openings in past
year, 130
Contact Ms. Judy Koch
Buchanan, President;
510-659-8665; Fax: 510-
659-8775

**Rhythm & Hues Studios,
Inc.**
5404 Jandy Pl.
Los Angeles, CA 90066
http://www.rhythm.com
Founded: 1987
Total Employees: 250
Annual Sales: $32 million
Industry: Computer
Hardware
Growth: Openings in past
year, 50
Contact Ms. Pauline Ts'o,
VP of Development; 310-
448-7500; Fax: 310-448-
7610

**Romic Environmental
Technology Corp.**
2081 Bay Rd.
East Palo Alto, CA 94303
http://www.romic.com
Founded: 1964
Total Employees: 280
Annual Sales: $34 million
Industries: Energy,
Environmental, Holding
Companies
Growth: Openings in past
year, 30
Contact Peter Schneider,
President; 650-324-1638;
Fax: 650-462-2411

**Safety Components
International, Inc.,
Automotive Division**
3190 Pullman St.
Costa Mesa, CA 92626
Founded: 1994
Total Employees: 850
Industries: Test and
Measurement,
Transportation
Growth: Openings in past
year, 148
Contact Tom Cresante,
COO/General Manager;
714-540-5432; Fax: 714-
662-7649; E-mail: asci@
earthlink.net

**RightAngle Systems and
Technology, Inc.**
12651 High Bluff Dr., Suite
100
San Diego, CA 92130
http://www.motivasoft.com
Founded: 1994
Total Employees: 40
Annual Sales: $5.1 million
Industry: Computer
Software
Growth: Openings in past
year, 30
Contact Bruce Carothers,
President/CEO; 619-481-
4822; Fax: 619-481-
8482; E-mail: info@
motivasoft.com

RSA Data Security, Inc.
100 Marine Pkwy., Suite
500
Redwood City, CA 94065
http://www.rsa.com
Founded: 1982
Total Employees: 90
Annual Sales: $11 million
Industry: Computer
Software
Growth: Openings in past
year, 40
Contact D. James Bidzos,
Chief Executive Officer;
650-595-8782; Fax: 650-
595-1873; E-mail: info@
rsa.com

**Samsung
Semiconductor, Inc.**
3655 North First St.
San Jose, CA 95134
http://www.samsung.com
Founded: 1983
Total Employees: 400
Annual Sales: $53 million
Industries: Computer
Hardware,
Subassemblies and
Components
Growth: Openings in past
year, 23
Contact J. Farnsworth,
Director of Human
Resources; 408-954-
7000; Fax: 408-954-7286

SanDisk Corp.
140 Caspian Ct.
Sunnyvale, CA 94089
http://www.sandisk.com
Founded: 1988
Total Employees: 500
Annual Sales: $97.599
million
Industry: Computer
Hardware
Growth: Openings in past
year, 215
Contact Ms. Marianne
Jackson, VP of Human
Resources; 408-562-
0500; Fax: 408-562-3403

**Sattel Communications
LLC.**
26025 Mureau Rd.
Calabasas, CA 91302
http://www.sattelcom.com
Founded: 1995
Total Employees: 90
Annual Sales: $15 million
Industry:
Telecommunications
Growth: Openings in past
year, 75
Contact James Fiedler,
COB/CEO; 818-878-
7711; Fax: 818-878-7632;
E-mail: info@sattelcom.
com

Scaled Composites, Inc.
1624 Flight Line
Mojave, CA 93501
http://www.scaled.com
Founded: 1982
Total Employees: 140
Annual Sales: $18 million
Industry: Transportation
Growth: Openings in past
year, 50
Contact Ms. Patricia
Storch, VP of Finance/
CFO; 805-824-4541; Fax:
805-824-4174; E-mail:
scaled@hughes.net

Scantron Corp.
1361 Valencia Ave.
Tustin, CA 92780
http://www.scantron.com
Founded: 1972
Total Employees: 581
Industries: Computer
Hardware, Computer
Software, Holding
Companies
Growth: Openings in past
year, 39
Contact Ms. Sherri
McKaig, Human
Resources Manager;
714-259-8887; Fax: 714-
259-8423; E-mail:
sales@scantron.com

Schumacher
1969 Palomar Oaks Way
Carlsbad, CA 92009
Founded: 1972
Total Employees: 380
Annual Sales: $100 million
Industries: Chemicals,
Test and Measurement
Growth: Openings in past
year, 180
Contact Joseph Quince,
Manager of Human
Resources; 760-931-
9555; Fax: 760-931-7819

**Science Applications
International Corp.,
Radeco Division**
4161 Campus Point Ct.
San Diego, CA 92121
Founded: 1969
Total Employees: 80
Industries: Environmental,
Test and Measurement
Growth: Openings in past
year, 40
Contact James Winso,
Division Manager; 619-
646-9830; Fax: 619-646-
9009

Scopus Technology, Inc.
1900 Powell St., 7th Floor
Emeryville, CA 94608

http://www.scopus.com
Founded: 1991
Total Employees: 340
Annual Sales: $63.1
million
Industry: Computer
Software
Growth: Openings in past
year, 254
Contact Ori Sasson,
President/CEO; 510-597-
5800; Fax: 510-428-
1027; E-mail: info@
scopus.com

**SELECT Software Tools,
Inc.**
19600 Fairchild, Suite 350
Santa Ana, CA 92705
http://www.selectst.com
Founded: 1988
Total Employees: 270
Annual Sales: $14.3
million
Industry: Computer
Software
Growth: Openings in past
year, 70
Contact Stuart Frost,
COB/CEO; 714-477-
4100; Fax: 714-477-3232

**Senior Flexonics,
Katema Division**
790 Greenfield Dr.
El Cajon, CA 92021
Founded: 1930
Total Employees: 500
Annual Sales: $65 million
Industries:
Subassemblies and
Components,
Telecommunications,
Transportation
Growth: Openings in past
year, 100
Contact Thomas Brooks,
General Manager; 619-
442-3451; Fax: 619-440-
1456

**Senior Systems
Technology, Inc.**
20150 Sunburst St.
Chatsworth, CA 91311
Founded: 1984
Total Employees: 335

Industries: Manufacturing Equipment, Subassemblies and Components
Growth: Openings in past year, 34
Contact Joseph Candella, President; 818-998-1818; Fax: 818-998-0664; E-mail: sales@ seniorsystems.com

Sequana Therapeutics, Inc.
11099 North Torrey Pines Rd., Suite 160
La Jolla, CA 92037
http://www.sequana.com
Founded: 1993
Total Employees: 200
Annual Sales: $11 million
Industry: Biotechnology
Growth: Openings in past year, 80
Contact Kevin Kinsella, President/CEO; 619-452-6550; Fax: 619-452-4378

SEQUUS Pharmaceuticals, Inc.
960 Hamilton Ct.
Menlo Park, CA 94025
http://www.sequus.com
Founded: 1981
Total Employees: 200
Annual Sales: $32.923 million
Industry: Pharmaceuticals
Growth: Openings in past year, 50
Contact Ms. Jeannine Niacaris, Director of Human Resources; 650-323-9011; Fax: 650-323-9106

SERENA Software International
500 Airport Blvd., 2nd Floor
Burlingame, CA 94010
http://www.serena.com
Founded: 1980
Total Employees: 130
Industry: Computer Software

Growth: Openings in past year, 40
Contact Richard Doerr, CEO/CFO; 650-696-1800; Fax: 650-696-1849; E-mail: info@ serena.com

SGI Technic, Inc.
28176 North Ave. Stanford
Santa Clarita, CA 91355
Founded: 1967
Total Employees: 270
Industry: Advanced Materials
Growth: Openings in past year, 29
Contact B.J. Schramm, Site Manager; 805-257-0500; Fax: 805-257-2755

ShareData, Inc.
2465 Augustine Dr.
Santa Clara, CA 95054
http://www.sharedata.com
Founded: 1983
Total Employees: 100
Annual Sales: $11.3 million
Industries: Computer Hardware, Computer Software
Growth: Openings in past year, 25
Contact Ms. Cheryl Breetwor, President; 408-746-3666; Fax: 408-746-0701; E-mail: interset@ sharedata.com

Shomiti Systems, Inc.
1800 Bering Dr.
San Jose, CA 95112
http://www.shomiti.com
Founded: 1995
Total Employees: 40
Industries: Computer Software, Factory Automation, Test and Measurement, Telecommunications
Growth: Openings in past year, 37
Contact Som Sikdar, CEO/President; 408-437-3940; Fax: 408-437-4041; E-mail: info@ shomiti.com

Siebel Systems, Inc.
1885 South Grand St.
San Mateo, CA 94402
http://www.siebel.com
Founded: 1993
Total Employees: 300
Annual Sales: $39.2 million
Industries: Computer Software, Holding Companies
Growth: Openings in past year, 209
Contact Tom Siebel, COB/CEO; 650-295-5000; Fax: 650-295-5111; E-mail: info@siebel.com

Sigma Circuits, Inc.
393 Mathew St.
Santa Clara, CA 95050
Founded: 1974
Total Employees: 740
Annual Sales: $79.98 million
Industries: Computer Hardware, Subassemblies and Components
Growth: Openings in past year, 240
Contact B. Kevin Kelly, President/CEO; 408-727-9169; Fax: 408-654-5806

SIIG, Inc.
6078 Stewart Ave.
Fremont, CA 94538
http://www.siig.com
Founded: 1985
Total Employees: 150
Annual Sales: $30 million
Industries: Computer Hardware, Telecommunications
Growth: Openings in past year, 41
Contact Ms. Nancy Liu, Controller; 510-657-8688; Fax: 510-657-5962

Silicon Gaming, Inc.
2800 West Bayshore Rd.
Palo Alto, CA 94303
http://www.silicongamıng.
com
Founded: 1994
Total Employees: 140
Annual Sales: $12 million
Industry: Computer
Hardware
Growth: Openings in past
year, 90
Contact Donald Massaro,
President/CEO; 650-842-
9000; Fax: 650-849-9001

Silvaco International, Inc.
4701 Patrick Henry Dr.,
Bldg. 1
Santa Clara, CA 95054
http://www.silvaco.com
Founded: 1984
Total Employees: 150
Annual Sales: $19 million
Industry: Computer
Software
Growth: Openings in past
year, 30
Contact Ms. Linda Leslie,
Personnel Manager; 408-
567-1000; Fax: 408-496-
6080; E-mail: sales@
silvaco.com

Simulation Sciences Inc.
601 Valencia Ave.
Brea, CA 92621
http://www.simsci.com
Founded: 1967
Total Employees: 380
Annual Sales: $46.9
million
Industries: Computer
Software, Holding
Companies
Growth: Openings in past
year, 50
Contact Dan Nichols, VP
of Human Resources;
714-579-0412; Fax: 714-
579-7468

Silicon Power Corp.
411 North Central Ave.
Glendale, CA 91203
http://www.crydom.com
Founded: 1980
Total Employees: 500
Industries: Holding
Companies,
Subassemblies and
Components, Test and
Measurement
Growth: Openings in past
year, 24
Contact John Royan,
President; 818-956-3900;
Fax: 818-956-3915;
E-mail: sales@crydom.
com

SIMCO Electronics
382 Martin Ave.
Santa Clara, CA 95050
Founded: 1962
Total Employees: 300
Industries: Factory
Automation,
Manufacturing Equipment
Growth: Openings in past
year, 64
Contact Ms. Janice Smith,
Human Resources
Manager/Corp.
Secretary; 408-727-3611;
Fax: 408-727-4084

**SMART Modular
Technologies, Inc.**
4305 Cushing Pkwy.
Fremont, CA 94538
http://www.smartm.com
Founded: 1988
Total Employees: 800
Annual Sales: $401.8
million
Industries: Computer
Hardware, Holding
Companies,
Telecommunications
Growth: Openings in past
year, 400
Contact Ajay Shah, COB/
CEO/President; 510-623-
1231; Fax: 510-623-
1434; E-mail: info@
smartm.com

**Silicon Storage
Technology, Inc.**
1171 Sonora Ct.
Sunnyvale, CA 94086
Founded: 1989
Total Employees: 150
Annual Sales: $93.3
million
Industry: Subassemblies
and Components
Growth: Openings in past
year, 30
Contact Bing Yeh,
President/CEO; 408-735-
9110; Fax: 408-735-9036

Simple Technology, Inc.
3001 Daimler St.
Santa Ana, CA 92705
http://www.simpletech.com
Founded: 1990
Total Employees: 450
Annual Sales: $165 million
Industries: Computer
Hardware,
Telecommunications
Growth: Openings in past
year, 99
Contact Manouch
Moshayedi, Chief Execu-
tive Officer; 714-476-
1180; Fax: 714-476-1209

Solatron Enterprises
3450 Fujita St.
Torrance, CA 90505
Founded: 1961
Total Employees: 68
Industry: Factory
Automation
Growth: Openings in past
year, 38
Contact Mahmood Izadi,
President; 310-325-0463;
Fax: 310-325-0416

Solec International, Inc.
12533 Chadron Ave.
Hawthorne, CA 90250
Founded: 1976
Total Employees: 150
Annual Sales: $34 million
Industries: Energy,
Photonics
Growth: Openings in past
year, 30
Contact Hiroyoshi
Sunatsu, President; 310-
970-0065; Fax: 310-970-
1065

**Somnus Medical
Technologies, Inc.**
285 North Wolfe Rd.
Sunnyvale, CA 94086
http://www.somnus.com
Founded: 1996
Total Employees: 38
Industries: Medical,
Subassemblies and
Components
Growth: Openings in past
year, 37
Contact Stewart Edwards,
CEO/President; 408-773-
9121; Fax: 408-773-
9137; E-mail: info@
somnus.com

SPARTA, Inc.
23041 Ave. de la Carlota,
Suite 325
Laguna Hills, CA 92653
http://www.mclean.sparta.
com
Founded: 1979
Total Employees: 565
Annual Sales: $66 million
Industries: Advanced
Materials, Defense
Growth: Openings in past
year, 102
Contact Wayne Winton,
President/CEO; 714-768-
8161; Fax: 714-583-9113

Specialty Laboratories
2211 Michigan Ave.
Santa Monica, CA 90404

http://www.specialtylabs.
com
Founded: 1977
Total Employees: 550
Annual Sales: $67 million
Industry: Medical
Growth: Openings in past
year, 50
Contact Ms. Gayel
Pitchford, VP of Human
Resources; 310-828-
6543; Fax: 310-828-6634

Spectrian Corp.
350 West Java Dr.
Sunnyvale, CA 94089
http://www.spectrian.com
Founded: 1984
Total Employees: 600
Annual Sales: $88 million
Industry: Subassemblies
and Components
Growth: Openings in past
year, 124
Contact Garrett
Garrettson, President/
COB/CEO; 408-745-
5400; Fax: 408-541-0262

Spiveco, Inc.
1700 East Via Burton
Anaheim, CA 92806
Founded: 1970
Total Employees: 150
Industry: Advanced
Materials
Growth: Openings in past
year, 33
Contact Ms. D.J. Carroll,
VP of Personnel; 714-
254-8300; Fax: 714-956-
4421

**SPL World Group
Consulting, Inc.**
75 Hawthorne Plaza, Suite
2000
San Francisco, CA 94105
http://www.splwg.com
Founded: 1969
Total Employees: 200
Industries: Computer
Hardware, Computer
Software, Holding
Companies
Growth: Openings in past
year, 30

Contact Ms. Yo
McDonald, President/
Acting GM of West; 415-
541-9462; Fax: 415-541-
0224

Sputtered Films, Inc.
320 Nopal St.
Santa Barbara, CA 93103
http://www.sputtered-films.
com
Founded: 1968
Total Employees: 135
Annual Sales: $16 million
Industry: Manufacturing
Equipment
Growth: Openings in past
year, 42
Contact Ms. Cresanna
Millegan, Human
Resources Manager;
805-963-9651; Fax: 805-
963-2959; E-mail:
sales@sputtered-films.
com

SSD, Inc.
1600 Riviera Ave., Suite
300
Walnut Creek, CA 94596
http://www.rebis.com
Founded: 1977
Total Employees: 70
Annual Sales: $9.0 million
Industry: Computer
Software
Growth: Openings in past
year, 40
Contact Bob Gardner,
President; 510-933-1930;
Fax: 510-933-1920

**Stanford
Telecommunications,
Inc.**
1221 Crossman Ave.
Sunnyvale, CA 94089
Founded: 1973
Total Employees: 951
Annual Sales: $167.002
million
Industries: Defense,
Holding Companies,
Subassemblies and
Components,
Telecommunications,
Transportation

Growth: Openings in past year, 54
Contact Ms. Joanne Lee, Personnel Director; 408-745-0818; Fax: 408-745-7756

Steri-Oss, Inc.
22895 Eastpark Dr.
Yorba Linda, CA 92887
http://www.steri-oss.com
Founded: 1984
Total Employees: 232
Annual Sales: $32.2 million
Industry: Medical
Growth: Openings in past year, 32
Contact Patrick Bolton, Human Resources Director; 714-282-4800; Fax: 714-998-9236

SteriGenics International
4020 Clipper Ct.
Fremont, CA 94538
http://www.sterigenics.com
Founded: 1978
Total Employees: 280
Annual Sales: $37.7 million
Industry: Medical
Growth: Openings in past year, 80
Contact Ms. Linda Gruehl, Human Resources Manager; 510-770-9000; Fax: 510-770-1499

Sterling Holding Co., Inc.
31186 LaBaya Dr.
Westlake Village, CA 91362
http://www.trompeter.com
Founded: 1960
Total Employees: 400
Industry: Holding Companies
Growth: Openings in past year, 100
Contact Don Meyers, Vice President/CFO; 818-707-2020; Fax: 818-706-1040; E-mail: trompeter@worldnet.att.net

StorMedia, Incorporated
385 Reed St.
Santa Clara, CA 95050
Founded: 1994
Total Employees: 670
Annual Sales: $211 million
Industry: Computer Hardware
Growth: Openings in past year, 67
Contact William Almon, COB/CEO; 408-327-8000; Fax: 408-727-4928

Structural North America, Codeline Division
2181 Meyers Ave.
Escondido, CA 92029
Founded: 1977
Total Employees: 210
Industries: Environmental, Subassemblies and Components
Growth: Openings in past year, 29
Contact Ms. Mary Manriquez, Director of Human Resources; 760-738-3000; Fax: 760-738-3031; E-mail: sales-as@4dcomm.com

Stryker Endoscopy
2590 Walsh Ave.
Santa Clara, CA 95051
Founded: 1946
Total Employees: 400
Annual Sales: $48 million
Industry: Medical
Growth: Openings in past year, 50
Contact Lee Lovely, Human Resources Manager; 408-567-9100; Fax: 408-567-2505

Subscriber Computing, Inc.
18881 Von Karman Ave., Suite 450
Irvine, CA 92715
http://www.subscriber.com

Founded: 1973
Total Employees: 170
Annual Sales: $22 million
Industry: Computer Software
Growth: Openings in past year, 50
Contact Ms. Patricia Howe, VP of Human Resources/General Counsel; 714-260-1500; Fax: 714-260-1500

Sugen, Inc.
351 Galveston Dr.
Redwood City, CA 94063
Founded: 1991
Total Employees: 180
Annual Sales: $13.7 million
Industries: Biotechnology, Pharmaceuticals
Growth: Openings in past year, 40
Contact Ms. Dorian Rinella, Director of Human Resources; 650-306-7700; Fax: 650-369-8984

Summa Industries, Inc.
1660 West Commonwealth Ave.
Fullerton, CA 92633
http://www.summa-ind.com
Founded: 1942
Total Employees: 366
Annual Sales: $45 million
Industry: Holding Companies
Growth: Openings in past year, 116
Contact James R. Swartwout, COB/President/CEO/CFO; 714-738-5000; Fax: 714-738-5960; E-mail: summa@konnections.com

Sundstrand Power Systems
4400 Ruffin Rd.
San Diego, CA 92123
http://www.sundstrand.com
Founded: 1985
Total Employees: 570

Annual Sales: $130 million
Industries: Energy, Transportation
Growth: Openings in past year, 28
Contact Ms. Kathy Fultz, Human Resources Manager; 619-627-6000; Fax: 619-627-6641

SUPERMICRO Computer, Inc.
2051 Junction Ave.
San Jose, CA 95131
http://www.supermicro.com
Founded: 1993
Total Employees: 100
Annual Sales: $20 million
Industries: Computer Hardware, Subassemblies and Components, Telecommunications
Growth: Openings in past year, 30
Contact Charles Liang, President; 408-895-2000; Fax: 408-895-2008; E-mail: marketing@supermicro.com

Supertex, Inc.
1235 Bordeaux Dr.
Sunnyvale, CA 94089
http://www.supertex.com
Founded: 1976
Total Employees: 421
Annual Sales: $48.935 million
Industries: Computer Hardware, Subassemblies and Components
Growth: Openings in past year, 131
Contact Ms. Melba Stathis, Personnel Manager; 408-744-0100; Fax: 408-745-4800; E-mail: investors@supertex.com

Synopsys, Inc., Physical Tools Group
310 North Mary Ave.
Sunnyvale, CA 94086
http://www.epic.com

Founded: 1986
Total Employees: 215
Annual Sales: $43.9 million
Industry: Computer Software
Growth: Openings in past year, 45
Contact Sang S. Wang, Ph.D., Senior Vice President; 408-731-2900; Fax: 408-733-8820; E-mail: mkt@epic.com

TA Manufacturing Co.
375 West Arden Ave.
PO Box 2500
Glendale, CA 91203
Founded: 1943
Total Employees: 200
Industries: Manufacturing Equipment, Subassemblies and Components
Growth: Openings in past year, 50
Contact Ms. Annette O'Neal, Personnel Manager; 818-240-4600; Fax: 818-241-3948

Tangent Computer, Inc.
197 Airport Blvd.
Burlingame, CA 94010
http://www.tangent.com
Founded: 1988
Total Employees: 100
Industries: Computer Hardware, Telecommunications
Growth: Openings in past year, 40
Contact Ms. Caroline Doyle, Account Manager; 650-342-9388; Fax: 650-342-9380; E-mail: sales@tangent.com

Tatung Co. of America
2850 El Presidio St.
Long Beach, CA 90810
http://www.tatung.com
Founded: 1980
Total Employees: 400
Annual Sales: $150 million

Industries: Computer Hardware, Telecommunications
Growth: Openings in past year, 220
Contact Hsin Chu Liu, President; 310-637-2105; Fax: 310-637-8484

Tecom Industries, Inc.
9324 Topanga Canyon Blvd.
Chatsworth, CA 91311
Founded: 1971
Total Employees: 125
Industry: Telecommunications
Growth: Openings in past year, 30
Contact Vito P. Minerva, President; 818-341-4010; Fax: 818-718-1402

Teknowledge Corp.
1810 Embarcadero Rd.
Palo Alto, CA 94303
http://www.teknowledge.com
Founded: 1981
Total Employees: 75
Annual Sales: $7.185763 million
Industry: Computer Software
Growth: Openings in past year, 35
Contact Benedict O'Mahoney, Corporate Counsel; 650-424-0500; Fax: 650-493-2645

TelCom Semiconductor, Inc.
1300 Terra Bella Ave.
PO Box 7267
Mountain View, CA 94039
Founded: 1993
Total Employees: 350
Annual Sales: $37 million
Industries: Computer Hardware, Subassemblies and Components, Test and Measurement
Growth: Openings in past year, 49

Contact Don Human, Manager of Human Resources; 650-968-9241; Fax: 650-967-1590

Telegen Corp.
101 Saginaw Dr.
Redwood City, CA 94063
http://www.telegen.com
Founded: 1990
Total Employees: 80
Annual Sales: $5.115 million
Industry: Holding Companies
Growth: Openings in past year, 40
Contact Warren Dillard, CFO/CEO; 650-261-9400; Fax: 650-261-9468

Telegra Corp.
2055 Gateway Place, Suite 400
San Jose, CA 95110
http://www.telegra.com
Founded: 1982
Total Employees: 35
Annual Sales: $4.5 million
Industries: Computer Software, Factory Automation
Growth: Openings in past year, 25
Contact Robert H. Welch, President; 408-970-9200; Fax: 408-970-9242; E-mail: sales@telegra.com

Teradyne, Inc., Assembly Test/Walnut Creek Division
2625 Shadelands Dr.
Walnut Creek, CA 94598
http://www.teradyne.com/cbt
Founded: 1966
Total Employees: 200
Industries: Computer Software, Factory Automation
Growth: Openings in past year, 50
Contact Joe Wrinn, General Manager; 510-

932-6900; Fax: 510-934-0540; E-mail: teranet@teradyne.com

Tessera, Inc.
3099 Orchard Dr.
San Jose, CA 95134
http://www.tessera.com
Founded: 1990
Total Employees: 107
Annual Sales: $14 million
Industry: Subassemblies and Components
Growth: Openings in past year, 62
Contact John Smith, President; 408-894-0700; Fax: 408-894-0768

Therma-Wave, Inc.
1250 Reliance Way
Fremont, CA 94539
http://www.thermawave.com
Founded: 1982
Total Employees: 387
Annual Sales: $109.5 million
Industry: Factory Automation
Growth: Openings in past year, 36
Contact Allen Rosencwaig, Chief Executive Officer; 510-490-3663; Fax: 510-656-3852

Thermogenesis Corp.
3146 Gold Camp Dr.
Rancho Cordova, CA 95742
http://www.thermogenesis.com
Founded: 1986
Total Employees: 85
Annual Sales: $6.6 million
Industry: Medical
Growth: Openings in past year, 31
Contact Philip H. Coelho, President/CEO; 916-858-5100; Fax: 916-858-5199

Thoratec Laboratories Corp.
6035 Stoneridge Dr.
Pleasanton, CA 94588
http://www.thoratec.com
Founded: 1976
Total Employees: 90
Annual Sales: $8.087 million
Industries: Biotechnology, Medical
Growth: Openings in past year, 30
Contact D. Keith Grossman, President/CEO; 510-841-1213; Fax: 510-845-3935; E-mail: sales@thoratec.com

TMCI Electronics, Inc.
1875 Dobbin Dr.
San Jose, CA 95133
Founded: 1995
Total Employees: 450
Annual Sales: $26 million
Industries: Manufacturing Equipment, Telecommunications
Growth: Openings in past year, 90
Contact Roland Loera, COB/President/CEO; 408-272-5700; Fax: 408-254-1537

TomaHawk II, Inc.
8315 Century Park Ct., Suite 200
San Diego, CA 92123
http://www.tomahawk.com
Founded: 1993
Total Employees: 100
Annual Sales: $1.1 million
Industries: Computer Hardware, Manufacturing Equipment
Growth: Openings in past year, 50
Contact Steve Caira, President/CEO; 619-874-7692; Fax: 619-874-2731

Trans-Ameritech
23424 Walsh Ave.
Santa Clara, CA 95051
http://www.transameritech.
 com
Founded: 1989
Total Employees: 96
Annual Sales: $15 million
Industry:
 Telecommunications
Growth: Openings in past
 year, 36
Contact Oleg Titov,
 Personnel Manager; 408-
 727-3883; Fax: 408-727-
 3882

Trek Industries, Inc.
701 South Azusa Ave.
Azusa, CA 91702
http://www.trek-ind.com
Founded: 1976
Total Employees: 130
Annual Sales: $17 million
Industries: Factory
 Automation, Holding
 Companies,
 Subassemblies and
 Components, Test and
 Measurement
Growth: Openings in past
 year, 30
Contact Ms. Sally Miller,
 Human Resources Direc-
 tor; 626-815-5555; Fax:
 626-815-8304

**Trident Microsystems,
Inc.**
189 North Bernardo Ave.
Mountain View, CA 94043
http://www.tridentmicro.
 com
Founded: 1987
Total Employees: 320
Annual Sales: $177 million
Industries: Computer
 Hardware, Computer
 Software, Subassemblies
 and Components
Growth: Openings in past
 year, 49
Contact W. Steven Rowe,
 VP of Human Resources;
 650-691-9211; Fax: 650-
 691-9265

Trigem America Corp.
48400 Fremont Blvd.
Fremont, CA 94538
Founded: 1991
Total Employees: 120
Annual Sales: $160 million
Industry: Computer
 Hardware
Growth: Openings in past
 year, 50
Contact Sam Muk,
 President; 510-770-8787

**Trillium Digital Systems,
Inc.**
12100 Wilshire Blvd., Suite
 1800
Los Angeles, CA 90025
http://www.trillium.com
Founded: 1988
Total Employees: 101
Annual Sales: $13 million
Industry: Computer
 Software
Growth: Openings in past
 year, 38
Contact Jeff Lawrence,
 COB/President/CEO;
 310-442-7222; Fax: 310-
 442-1162; E-mail:
 marketing@trillium.com

Trio-Tech International
355 Parkside Dr.
San Fernando, CA 91340
Founded: 1963
Total Employees: 684
Annual Sales: $21.5
 million
Industries: Factory
 Automation, Holding
 Companies
Growth: Openings in past
 year, 182
Contact Ms. Maria
 Chittim, Personnel Direc-
 tor; 818-365-9200; Fax:
 818-365-8210

**Trompeter Electronics,
Inc.**
31186 LaBaya Dr.
PO Box 5069
Westlake Village, CA
 91362
Founded: 1960
Total Employees: 250
Annual Sales: $33 million
Industries:
 Subassemblies and
 Components,
 Telecommunications
Growth: Openings in past
 year, 50
Contact Ms. Judith
 Shapiro, Human
 Resources Manager;
 818-707-2020; Fax: 818-
 706-1040; E-mail:
 trompeter.electronics@
 industry.net

**Tumbleweed Software
Corporation**
2010 Broadway
Redwood City, CA 94063
http://www.tumbleweed.
 com
Founded: 1993
Total Employees: 40
Industry: Computer
 Software
Growth: Openings in past
 year, 31
Contact Jeff Smith, Chief
 Executive Officer; 650-
 369-6790; Fax: 650-369-
 7197; E-mail: info@
 tumbleweed.com

Tut Systems, Inc.
2495 Estand Way
Pleasant Hill, CA 94523
http://www.tutsys.com
Founded: 1989
Total Employees: 64
Industry:
 Telecommunications
Growth: Openings in past
 year, 26
Contact Sal D'Auria,
 President/CEO; 510-682-
 6510; Fax: 510-682-4125

TV/COM International, Inc.
17066 Goldentop Rd.
San Diego, CA 92127
http://www.tvcom.com
Founded: 1973
Total Employees: 350
Industry:
Telecommunications
Growth: Openings in past year, 70
Contact Ms. Donna Kaptain, Director of Human Resources; 619-451-1500; Fax: 619-451-1505

TYAN Computer Corp.
1753 South Main St.
Milpitas, CA 95035
http://www.tyan.com
Founded: 1989
Total Employees: 70
Industry: Computer Hardware
Growth: Openings in past year, 40
Contact Larry Barber, President; 408-956-8000; Fax: 408-956-8044; E-mail: info@tyan.com

U.S. Wireless Corp.
2694 Bishop Dr., Suite 213
San Ramon, CA 94583
http://www.uswcorp.com
Founded: 1996
Total Employees: 30
Industry: Holding Companies
Growth: Openings in past year, 27
Contact Dr. Oliver Hilsenrath, CEO/President; 510-830-8801; Fax: 510-830-8821

UDT Sensors, Inc.
12525 Chadron Ave.
Hawthorne, CA 90250
Founded: 1956
Total Employees: 600

Industries: Factory Automation, Photonics, Subassemblies and Components, Test and Measurement
Growth: Openings in past year, 299
Contact Ms. Heather Zammitt, Human Resources Manager; 310-978-0516; Fax: 310-644-1727

Ulead Systems, Inc.
970 West 190th St., Suite 520
Torrance, CA 90502
http://www.ulead.com
Founded: 1989
Total Employees: 185
Industry: Computer Software
Growth: Openings in past year, 70
Contact Liming Chen, President; 310-523-9393; Fax: 310-523-9399; E-mail: info@ulead.com

Ultra Clean Technology
150 Independence Dr.
Menlo Park, CA 94025
http://www.uctnow.com
Founded: 1991
Total Employees: 85
Annual Sales: $10 million
Industry: Manufacturing Equipment
Growth: Openings in past year, 35
Contact Ms. Nancy Nelson, Human Resources Manager; 650-323-4100; Fax: 650-323-7159; E-mail: uctnow@ix.netcom.com

Ultradata Corporation
5020 Franklin Dr.
Pleasanton, CA 94588
http://www.ultradata.com
Founded: 1981
Total Employees: 300
Annual Sales: $40.4 million
Industry: Computer Software

Growth: Openings in past year, 75
Contact Ms. Brigit Garabedian, Director of Human Resources; 510-463-8356; Fax: 510-463-0394

Ultratech Stepper, Inc.
3050 Zanker Rd.
San Jose, CA 95134
Founded: 1979
Total Employees: 540
Annual Sales: $193.508 million
Industry: Manufacturing Equipment
Growth: Openings in past year, 63
Contact Robert Weston, VP of Human Resources; 408-321-8835; Fax: 408-325-6444

UltraViolet Devices, Inc.
28220 Industry Dr.
Valencia, CA 91355
Founded: 1992
Total Employees: 100
Annual Sales: $12 million
Industries: Environmental, Holding Companies
Growth: Openings in past year, 40
Contact Thomas Velloz, President; 805-295-8140; Fax: 805-257-4698

UMAX Technologies, Inc.
33561 Gateway Blvd.
Fremont, CA 94538
http://www.umax.com
Founded: 1989
Total Employees: 120
Industry: Computer Hardware
Growth: Openings in past year, 60
Contact Vincent Pai, President; 510-651-4000; Fax: 510-651-8834

Unison Software, Inc.
5101 Patrick Henry Dr.
Santa Clara, CA 95054
http://www.unison.com
Founded: 1978
Total Employees: 200
Annual Sales: $39.8
million
Industries: Computer
Hardware, Computer
Software
Growth: Openings in past
year, 25
Contact Don H. Lee,
COB/CEO; 408-988-
2800; Fax: 408-988-
2236; E-mail: info@
unison.com

Vadem, Inc.
1960 Zanker Rd.
San Jose, CA 95112
http://www.vadem.com
Founded: 1983
Total Employees: 90
Annual Sales: $18 million
Industries: Computer
Hardware,
Subassemblies and
Components,
Telecommunications
Growth: Openings in past
year, 50
Contact John Zhao,
President; 408-467-2100;
Fax: 408-467-2199;
E-mail: info@vadem.com

VeriSign, Inc.
2593 Coast Ave.
Mountain View, CA 94043
http://www.verisign.com
Founded: 1995
Total Employees: 110
Annual Sales: $14 million
Industries: Computer
Software,
Telecommunications
Growth: Openings in past
year, 75
Contact Stratton Sclavos,
President/CEO; 650-961-
7500; Fax: 650-961-
7300; E-mail: info@
verisign.com

USWeb Corp.
3000 Lakeside Dr.
Santa Clara, CA 95054
http://www.usweb.com
Founded: 1995
Total Employees: 250
Annual Sales: $1.8 million
Industries: Holding
Companies,
Telecommunications
Growth: Openings in past
year, 200
Contact Joseph Firmage,
COB/CEO; 408-987-
3200; Fax: 408-986-
6701; E-mail: info@
usweb.com

Valley-Todeco
12975 Bradley Ave.
Sylmar, CA 91342
Founded: 1866
Total Employees: 200
Annual Sales: $26 million
Industries:
Subassemblies and
Components,
Transportation
Growth: Openings in past
year, 25
Contact Samuel Contino,
Director of Human
Resources; 818-367-
2261; Fax: 818-364-6036

VERITAS Software Corp.
1600 Plymouth St.
Mountain View, CA 94043
http://www.veritas.com
Founded: 1982
Total Employees: 180
Annual Sales: $36 million
Industry: Computer
Software
Growth: Openings in past
year, 70
Contact Christopher Dier,
Controller; 650-335-8000;
Fax: 650-335-8050;
E-mail: vx-sales@veritas.
com

**Utopia Technology
Partners, Inc.**
125 East Sir Francis Drake
Blvd., 3rd Floor
Larkspur, CA 94939
http://www.utosoft.com
Founded: 1987
Total Employees: 90
Annual Sales: $11 million
Industry: Computer
Software
Growth: Openings in past
year, 30
Contact Steven A.
Hammersly, President/
CEO; 415-464-4500;
Fax: 415-464-4510;
E-mail: info@utosoft.com

Verilink Corp.
145 Baytech Dr.
San Jose, CA 95134
http://www.verilink.com
Founded: 1982
Total Employees: 219
Annual Sales: $57.2
million
Industry:
Telecommunications
Growth: Openings in past
year, 37
Contact Ms. Grace Griffin,
VP of Human Resources;
408-945-1199; Fax: 408-
945-3823

**Vernitron Corp., Motion
Controls Group**
1601 Precision Park Ln.
San Diego, CA 92173
Founded: 1959
Total Employees: 250
Annual Sales: $33 million
Industries: Computer
Hardware, Factory
Automation,
Subassemblies and
Components, Test and
Measurement
Growth: Openings in past
year, 100
Contact Brent Nelson,
President/Controller; 619-
428-5581; Fax: 619-428-
5090

Versant Object Technology
6539 Dumbarton Circle
Fremont, CA 94555
http://www.versant.com
Founded: 1988
Total Employees: 170
Annual Sales: $18 million
Industry: Computer Software
Growth: Openings in past year, 45
Contact Ms. Karin Churchill, HR and Administration Manager; 510-789-1500; Fax: 510-789-1515

Vertek International, Inc.
9465 Custom House Pl., Suite D
San Diego, CA 92173
Founded: 1983
Total Employees: 280
Industry: Subassemblies and Components
Growth: Openings in past year, 80
Contact Harry L. Veroba, COB/CEO/President; 619-661-6868; Fax: 619-661-1229

VertiCom, Inc.
2330 Circadian Way
Santa Rosa, CA 95407
http://www.verticom.com
Founded: 1994
Total Employees: 60
Annual Sales: $8.0 million
Industries: Subassemblies and Components, Telecommunications
Growth: Openings in past year, 30
Contact Doug DeVivo, Chief Executive Officer; 707-544-9757; Fax: 707-527-4087

ViaSat, Inc.
2290 Cosmos Ct.
Carlsbad, CA 92009
http://www.cerfnet.viasat.com
Founded: 1986
Total Employees: 280
Annual Sales: $47.7 million
Industries: Computer Software, Factory Automation, Telecommunications
Growth: Openings in past year, 80
Contact Ms. Valerie Agnew, Manager of Human Resources; 760-438-8099; Fax: 760-438-8489; E-mail: info@viasat.com

Viking Components, Inc.
30200 Avenida De Las Bandera
Rancho Santa Margarita, CA 92688
http://www.vikingcomponents.com
Founded: 1988
Total Employees: 400
Industries: Computer Hardware, Telecommunications
Growth: Openings in past year, 139
Contact Ms. Susie Lewis, Human Resource Manager; 714-643-7255; Fax: 714-643-7250

Visigenic Software, Inc.
951 Mariner's Island Blvd., Suite 120
San Mateo, CA 94404
http://www.visigenic.com
Founded: 1993
Total Employees: 175
Annual Sales: $17 million
Industries: Computer Software, Holding Companies
Growth: Openings in past year, 50
Contact Ms. Suzanne Guscott, Human

Resources Manager; 650-286-1900; Fax: 650-286-2464; E-mail: sales@visigenic.com

Vitesse Semiconductor Corporation
741 Calle Plano
Camarillo, CA 93012
http://www.vitesse.com
Founded: 1984
Total Employees: 350
Annual Sales: $104.8 million
Industry: Subassemblies and Components
Growth: Openings in past year, 79
Contact Ms. Jeanne Johnson, Director of Human Resources; 805-388-3700; Fax: 805-987-5896; E-mail: productinfo@vitesse.com

VIVUS, Inc.
545 Middlefield Rd., Suite 200
Menlo Park, CA 94025
http://www.vivus.com
Founded: 1991
Total Employees: 104
Industry: Pharmaceuticals
Growth: Openings in past year, 71
Contact Leland Wilson, President/CEO; 650-325-5511; Fax: 650-325-5546

VPNet Technologies, Inc.
1530 Meridian Ave.
San Jose, CA 95125
http://www.vpnet.com
Founded: 1995
Total Employees: 50
Annual Sales: $6.4 million
Industries: Computer Software, Telecommunications
Growth: Openings in past year, 30
Contact Michael Allen, President/CEO; 408-445-6600; Fax: 408-445-6611; E-mail: info@vpnet.com

VXtreme, Inc.
675 Almanor Ave.
Sunnyvale, CA 94086
http://www.vxtreme.com
Founded: 1995
Total Employees: 100
Annual Sales: $12 million
Industry: Computer
  Software
Growth: Openings in past
  year, 80
Contact Pete Mountanos,
  President/CEO; 408-617-
  2330; Fax: 408-245-
  9770; E-mail: info@
  vxtreme.com

**Watson Pharmaceuticals,
Inc.**
311 Bonnie Cir.
Corona, CA 91720
Founded: 1983
Total Employees: 828
Annual Sales: $250.8
  million
Industry: Holding
  Companies
Growth: Openings in past
  year, 224
Contact Dr. Allen Chao,
  COB/CEO; 909-270-
  1400; Fax: 909-270-1096

Wind River Systems, Inc.
1010 Atlantic Ave.
Alameda, CA 94501
http://www.wrs.com/
Founded: 1981
Total Employees: 385
Annual Sales: $64 million
Industry: Computer
  Software
Growth: Openings in past
  year, 165
Contact Ms. Nina Lau
  Branson, Treasurer; 510-
  748-4100; Fax: 510-749-
  2010; E-mail: inquiries@
  wrs.com

Winfield Medical
7737 Kenamar Ct.
San Diego, CA 92121

Founded: 1979
Total Employees: 300
Annual Sales: $36 million
Industry: Medical
Growth: Openings in past
  year, 50
Contact Jerry Englert,
  President; 619-271-4861;
  Fax: 619-578-4177

Wintec Industries, Inc.
4280 Technology Dr.
Fremont, CA 94538
http://www.wintecind.com
Founded: 1988
Total Employees: 135
Industry: Computer
  Hardware
Growth: Openings in past
  year, 40
Contact Ms. Sue Jeng,
  Controller/Operations
  Manager; 510-770-9239;
  Fax: 510-770-9338

Worldtalk Corp.
5155 Old Ironsides Dr.
Santa Clara, CA 95054
Founded: 1992
Total Employees: 100
Annual Sales: $14.2
  million
Industries: Computer
  Software, Holding
  Companies
Growth: Openings in past
  year, 40
Contact Mark A. Jung,
  COB/President/CEO;
  408-567-1500; Fax: 408-
  567-1501

XLNT Designs, Inc.
15050 Ave. of Sciences,
  Suite 106
San Diego, CA 92128
http://www.xlnt.com
Founded: 1989
Total Employees: 250
Annual Sales: $42 million
Industries: Computer
  Software,
  Telecommunications
Growth: Openings in past
  year, 209
Contact William Atkinson,
  President/CEO; 619-487-

9320; Fax: 619-487-
9768; E-mail: info@xlnt.
com

Xontech, Inc.
6862 Hayvenhurst Ave.
Van Nuys, CA 91406
http://www.xti.com
Founded: 1970
Total Employees: 276
Annual Sales: $36 million
Industries: Defense,
  Environmental
Growth: Openings in past
  year, 39
Contact Kenneth Schultz,
  President; 818-787-7380;
  Fax: 818-786-4275;
  E-mail: humres@xti.com

XYLAN Corporation
26679 West Agoura Rd.
Calabasas, CA 91302
http://www.xylan.com
Founded: 1993
Total Employees: 460
Annual Sales: $128.5
  million
Industry:
  Telecommunications
Growth: Openings in past
  year, 139
Contact Andy Jentis,
  Director of Human
  Resources; 818-880-
  3500; Fax: 818-880-
  3505; E-mail: info@xylan.
  com

Yardi Systems, Inc.
819 Reddick Ave.
Santa Barbara, CA 93103
http://www.yardi.com
Founded: 1982
Total Employees: 140
Annual Sales: $18 million
Industry: Computer
  Software
Growth: Openings in past
  year, 78
Contact Anant Yardi,
  President; 805-966-3666;
  Fax: 805-963-3155;
  E-mail: postmaster@
  yardi.com

YieldUP International Corp.
117 Easy St.
Mountain View, CA 94043
http://www.yieldup.com
Founded: 1994
Total Employees: 65
Annual Sales: $2.2 million
Industries: Environmental, Manufacturing Equipment
Growth: Openings in past year, 45
Contact Raj Mohindra, President/CEO; 415-964-0100; Fax: 415-940-4388; E-mail: sales@yieldup.com

Zoran Corp.
3112 Scott Blvd.
Santa Clara, CA 95054
http://www.zoran.com
Founded: 1981
Total Employees: 80
Annual Sales: $44.1 million
Industries: Computer Software, Subassemblies and Components
Growth: Openings in past year, 60
Contact Dr. Levy Gerzberg, President; 408-919-4111; Fax: 408-919-4122; E-mail: sales@zoran.com

Colorado

Access Graphics, Inc.
1426 Pearl St.
Boulder, CO 80302
http://www.access.com
Founded: 1988
Total Employees: 600
Annual Sales: $1000 million
Industry: Computer Hardware
Growth: Openings in past year, 230
Contact John Ramsey, Chief Executive Officer; 303-938-9333; Fax: 303-442-7415; E-mail: julanna@access.com

Advanced Energy Industries, Inc.
1625 Sharp Point Dr.
Fort Collins, CO 80525
http://www.advanced-energy.com
Founded: 1981
Total Employees: 900
Annual Sales: $98.9 million
Industry: Subassemblies and Components
Growth: Openings in past year, 131
Contact Ms. Sue Schell, VP of Human Resources; 970-221-4670; Fax: 970-221-5583

AMETEK, Inc., Dixson Division
287 27 Rd.
Grand Junction, CO 81503
http://www.ametekdixson.com
Founded: 1957
Total Employees: 550
Annual Sales: $74 million
Industries: Factory Automation, Manufacturing Equipment, Test and Measurement
Growth: Openings in past year, 250
Contact Ms. Sarah Hunt, Personnel Manager; 970-242-8863; Fax: 970-245-6267

Applied Films Corporation
6797 Winchester Cir.
Boulder, CO 80301
Founded: 1976
Total Employees: 220
Annual Sales: $34.1 million
Industries: Manufacturing Equipment, Photonics
Growth: Openings in past year, 70
Contact Ms. Heidi Bogner, Human Resource Manager; 303-530-1411; Fax: 303-530-3214

Atrix Laboratories, Inc.
2579 Midpoint Dr.
Fort Collins, CO 80525
Founded: 1987
Total Employees: 120
Annual Sales: $2.9 million
Industry: Medical
Growth: Openings in past year, 50
Contact John E. Urheim, Chief Executive Officer; 970-482-5868

Avedon Engineering, Inc.
811 South Sherman St.
PO Box 1018
Longmont, CO 80501
Founded: 1966
Total Employees: 200
Annual Sales: $23 million
Industry: Manufacturing Equipment
Growth: Openings in past year, 50
Contact Raymond Avedon, President; 303-772-2633; Fax: 303-772-8276

BI Incorporated
6400 Lookout Rd.
Boulder, CO 80301
http://www.bi.com
Founded: 1978
Total Employees: 711
Annual Sales: $48.4 million
Industries: Computer Software, Test and Measurement
Growth: Openings in past year, 261
Contact David J. Hunter, President/CEO; 303-530-2911; Fax: 303-530-5349

Carrier Access Corp.
5395 Pearl Pkwy.
Boulder, CO 80301
http://www.carrieraccess.com
Founded: 1992
Total Employees: 60

Annual Sales: $10 million
Industry:
Telecommunications
Growth: Openings in past
year, 30
Contact Roger Koenig,
President/CEO; 303-442-
5455; Fax: 303-546-
9724; E-mail: gerrys@
carrieraccess.com

**Colorado Memory
Systems, Inc.**
800 South Taft Ave.
Loveland, CO 80537
http://www.hpweb.corphp.
com
Founded: 1972
Total Employees: 800
Annual Sales: $160 million
Industries: Computer
Hardware, Computer
Software
Growth: Openings in past
year, 199
Contact John Boose,
General Manager; 970-
669-8000; Fax: 970-667-
0921

CommNet Cellular, Inc.
8350 East Crescent Pkwy.,
Suite 400
Englewood, CO 80111
Founded: 1983
Total Employees: 587
Annual Sales: $115.196
million
Industry:
Telecommunications
Growth: Openings in past
year, 81
Contact Arnold C. Pohs,
COB/CEO/President;
303-694-3234; Fax: 303-
694-3293

**CSG Systems
International, Inc.**
7887 East Belleview Ave.,
Suite 1000
Englewood, CO 80111
http://www.csgsys.com
Founded: 1994
Total Employees: 900
Annual Sales: $132.297
million

Industry: Holding
Companies
Growth: Openings in past
year, 43
Contact Neal C. Hansen,
COB/CEO; 303-796-
2850; Fax: 303-796-2881

**Engineered Data
Products, Inc.**
2550 West Midway Blvd.
Broomfield, CO 80020
http://www.edp-usa.com
Founded: 1969
Total Employees: 300
Industries: Computer
Hardware, Holding
Companies
Growth: Openings in past
year, 25
Contact Ms. Marilyn
Giroux, Human
Resources Manager;
303-465-2800; Fax: 303-
465-4936

**HBO & Company,
Clinical Systems Group**
4720 Walnut St.
Boulder, CO 80301
Founded: 1985
Total Employees: 150
Industries: Computer
Hardware, Computer
Software, Medical
Growth: Openings in past
year, 25
Contact Kris Wanamaker,
VP of Product Marketing;
303-443-9660; Fax: 303-
443-2455

Integral Peripherals, Inc.
5775 Flatiron Pkwy., Suite
100
Boulder, CO 80301
http://www.integralnet.com
Founded: 1990
Total Employees: 500
Annual Sales: $66 million
Industry: Computer
Hardware
Growth: Openings in past
year, 69

Contact Steven B. Volk,
Chief Executive Officer;
303-449-8009; Fax: 303-
449-8089

**Intergram International,
Inc.**
5655 South Yosemite St.,
Suite 105
Greenwood Village, CO
80111
http://www.intergram.com
Founded: 1996
Total Employees: 100
Annual Sales: $17 million
Industry:
Telecommunications
Growth: Openings in past
year, 75
Contact George Schad,
President/CEO; 303-741-
5777; Fax: 303-741-
4333; E-mail: info@
intergram.com

**Internet Communications
Corp.**
7100 East Belleview Ave.
Englewood, CO 80111
Founded: 1977
Total Employees: 300
Annual Sales: $28.001
million
Industries: Computer
Hardware,
Telecommunications
Growth: Openings in past
year, 33
Contact Thomas C. Gal-
ley, President/CEO/CFO;
303-770-7600; Fax: 303-
770-2706

Micromedex, Inc.
6200 South Syracuse
Way, Suite 300
Englewood, CO 80111
http://www.micromedex.
com
Founded: 1974
Total Employees: 300
Industry: Computer
Hardware
Growth: Openings in past
year, 100
Contact Ms. Dee Zall, VP
of Human Resources &

Admin.; 303-486-6400;
Fax: 303-486-6464;
E-mail: info@mdx.com

NaPro BioTherapeutics, Inc.
6304 Spine Rd., Unit A
Boulder, CO 80301
Founded: 1991
Total Employees: 125
Annual Sales: $3.473 million
Industries: Biotechnology, Pharmaceuticals
Growth: Openings in past year, 58
Contact Dr. Sterling K. Ainsworth, Ph.D., President/CEO; 303-530-3891; Fax: 303-530-1296

NETdelivery Corp.
4900 Pearl East Cir., Suite 109
Boulder, CO 80301
http://www.netdelivery.com
Founded: 1995
Total Employees: 40
Industries: Computer Software, Telecommunications
Growth: Openings in past year, 35
Contact Ms. Margaret Romeo, Human Resources Administrator; 303-448-1110; Fax: 303-442-5287; E-mail: deborah@netdelivery.com

NeXstar Pharmaceuticals, Inc.
2860 Wilderness Pl.
Boulder, CO 80301
http://www.nexstar.com
Founded: 1981
Total Employees: 550
Annual Sales: $90.522 million
Industry: Biotechnology
Growth: Openings in past year, 100
Contact Ms. Barbara Kazmier, VP of Human Resources; 303-444-5893; Fax: 303-444-0072

OHM Corp., Colorado Division
4897 Oakland St.
Denver, CO 80239
Founded: 1995
Total Employees: 200
Annual Sales: $24 million
Industry: Environmental
Growth: Openings in past year, 98
Contact Ms. Ann Dennis, Office Manager; 303-371-8175; Fax: 303-371-8702

Quality Education Data, Inc.
1700 Lincoln St., Suite 3600
Denver, CO 80203
http://www.qeddata.com
Founded: 1981
Total Employees: 75
Industry: Computer Hardware
Growth: Openings in past year, 25
Contact Ms. Jeanne Hayes, President; 303-860-1832; Fax: 303-860-0238; E-mail: qedinfo@qeddata.com

SSDS, Inc.
6595 South Dayton St., Suite 3000
Englewood, CO 80111
Founded: 1986
Total Employees: 370
Annual Sales: $36 million
Industries: Computer Hardware, Computer Software
Growth: Openings in past year, 70
Contact Jerry Parker, President/CEO; 303-790-0660; Fax: 303-790-1663

Sturman Industries
One Innovation Way
Woodland Park, CO 80863
Founded: 1989
Total Employees: 60

Annual Sales: $4 million
Industry: Subassemblies and Components
Growth: Openings in past year, 35
Contact Ms. Carol Sturman, President; 719-686-6000; Fax: 719-686-6050

T-NETIX Inc.
67 Inerness Dr. East
Englewood, CO 80112
http://www.t-netix.com
Founded: 1986
Total Employees: 325
Annual Sales: $36.2 million
Industries: Computer Software, Telecommunications
Growth: Openings in past year, 125
Contact Thomas Huzjak, Chief Executive Officer; 303-790-9111; Fax: 303-790-9540; E-mail: postmaster@t-netix.com

U S WEST Interactive
9000 East Nichols Ave., Suite 100
Englewood, CO 80112
http://www.usw-interactive.com
Founded: 1994
Total Employees: 60
Annual Sales: $10 million
Industry: Telecommunications
Growth: Openings in past year, 40
Contact Tom Cullen, President, US West Interactive; 303-705-7600; Fax: 303-705-5163; E-mail: webmstr@uswest.com

Connecticut

Accessory Controls and Equipment Corp.
805 Bloomfield Ave.
Windsor, CT 06095

Founded: 1966
Total Employees: 115
Annual Sales: $12 million
Industry: Transportation
Growth: Openings in past year, 40
Contact Richard F. Stern, President; 860-688-9520; Fax: 860-688-7773

Allied Group, Inc.
701 Hebron Ave.
Glastonbury, CT 06033
http://www.tag.com
Founded: 1984
Total Employees: 67
Industries: Computer Hardware, Computer Software, Telecommunications
Growth: Openings in past year, 42
Contact Ms. Nancy Florida, Human Resource Manager; 860-659-4235; Fax: 860-659-1402; E-mail: allied@tag.com

Aloka
10 Fairfield Blvd.
Wallingford, CT 06492
Founded: 1990
Total Employees: 65
Annual Sales: $7.9 million
Industry: Medical
Growth: Openings in past year, 30
Contact Shoichi Nakai, General Manager; 203-269-5088; Fax: 203-269-6075

Avidia Systems, Inc.
10 Fairfield Blvd.
Wallingford, CT 06492
http://www.avidia.com
Founded: 1995
Total Employees: 35
Industry: Telecommunications
Growth: Openings in past year, 30
Contact Charles Strauch, Chairman of the Board; 203-265-5612; Fax: 203-265-5614; E-mail: info@avidia.com

Bedford Associates, Inc.
101 Merritt 7
Norwalk, CT 06851
http://www.bedford.com
Founded: 1980
Total Employees: 175
Annual Sales: $15 million
Industries: Computer Hardware, Computer Software
Growth: Openings in past year, 75
Contact Henry Hoffman, President/COO; 203-846-0230; Fax: 203-846-1487

Berg Electronics Corp., Cable Assembly Division
650 Danbury Rd.
Ridgefield, CT 06877
Founded: 1976
Total Employees: 625
Annual Sales: $84 million
Industry: Subassemblies and Components
Growth: Openings in past year, 25
Contact Jeffrey L. Davis, Vice President/General Manager; 203-438-9625; Fax: 203-431-3001

Black & Decker Corp., Household Products Group
6 Armstrong Rd.
Shelton, CT 06484
Founded: 1984
Total Employees: 293
Annual Sales: $30 million
Industry: Photonics
Growth: Openings in past year, 43
Contact Bill Maxwell, VP of Personnel; 203-926-3000; Fax: 203-926-6304

Business Data Services, Inc.
78 Easter Blvd.
Glastonbury, CT 06033
http://www.bdsinc.com
Founded: 1985
Total Employees: 130
Annual Sales: $16 million
Industry: Computer Software

Growth: Openings in past year, 65
Contact Robert Huges, President; 860-633-3693; Fax: 860-633-5361; E-mail: jhuges@bdsine.com

BYK-Chemie, USA
524 South Cherry St.
PO Box 5670
Wallingford, CT 06492
http://www.gyk.com
Founded: 1963
Total Employees: 550
Annual Sales: $100 million
Industries: Advanced Materials, Chemicals
Growth: Openings in past year, 22
Contact Ms. Carol Foley, Employee Benefits Administrator; 203-265-2086; Fax: 203-284-9158; E-mail: gyklaa@connix.com

Chromalloy Gas Turbine Corp., Caval Tool Division
275 Richard St.
Newington, CT 06111
Founded: 1945
Total Employees: 226
Industries: Manufacturing Equipment, Transportation
Growth: Openings in past year, 67
Contact John Caval, President/General Manager; 860-667-2134; Fax: 860-667-0057

Command Systems, Inc.
76 Batterson Park Rd.
Farmington, CT 06032
http://www.commandsys.com
Founded: 1985
Total Employees: 350
Industry: Computer Hardware
Growth: Openings in past year, 150

Contact Ed Caputo, President/Owner; 860-409-2000; Fax: 860-409-2099

CuraGen Corp.
555 Long Wharf Dr., 11th Fl.
New Haven, CT 06511
http://www.curagen.com
Founded: 1990
Total Employees: 150
Annual Sales: $4.4 million
Industries: Biotechnology, Medical
Growth: Openings in past year, 50
Contact Dr. Jonathan Rothberg, President/CEO; 203-401-3330; Fax: 203-407-3331; E-mail: jrothberg@curagen.com

Devtec Corp.
812 Bloomfield Ave.
Windsor, CT 06095
Founded: 1966
Total Employees: 150
Industry: Holding Companies
Growth: Openings in past year, 40
Contact Richard F. Stern, President/CEO; 860-688-9520; Fax: 860-688-7895

Diagnostic Chemicals Limited (USA)
160 Christian St.
Oxford, CT 06478
Founded: 1983
Total Employees: 119
Industries: Biotechnology, Chemicals, Medical
Growth: Openings in past year, 29
Contact Dr. J. Regis Duffy, Chief Executive Officer; 203-881-2020; Fax: 203-888-1143; E-mail: sales@dclchem.com

Discas, Inc.
567-1 South Leonard St.
Waterbury, CT 06708
Founded: 1993

Total Employees: 65
Annual Sales: $9 million
Industries: Environmental, Holding Companies, Manufacturing Equipment
Growth: Openings in past year, 37
Contact Ms. Linda Conway, Controller; 203-753-5147; Fax: 203-755-5791; E-mail: discas@aol.com

ebm, PAPST, Inc.
110 Hyde Rd.
Farmington, CT 06034
http://www.ebm.com
Founded: 1981
Total Employees: 230
Industries: Computer Hardware, Subassemblies and Components
Growth: Openings in past year, 49
Contact Robert Sobolewski, General Manager; 860-674-1515; Fax: 860-674-8536; E-mail: sales@ebm.com

EDAC Technologies Corp.
1790 New Britain Ave.
Farmington, CT 06032
Founded: 1985
Total Employees: 180
Annual Sales: $25 million
Industries: Factory Automation, Holding Companies, Manufacturing Equipment, Transportation
Growth: Openings in past year, 30
Contact Ed McNerney, Chief Executive Officer; 860-677-2603; Fax: 860-677-6316

Electronic Retailing Systems International, Inc.
372 Danbury Rd.
Wilton, CT 06897
Founded: 1991

Total Employees: 90
Annual Sales: $5.002 million
Industry: Factory Automation
Growth: Openings in past year, 28
Contact Bruce F. Failing, Jr., Vice Chairman/President/CEO; 203-761-7900; Fax: 203-761-9928

Farmstead Telephone Group, Inc.
22 Prestige Park
East Hartford, CT 06108
http://www.farmstead.com
Founded: 1985
Total Employees: 110
Annual Sales: $20 million
Industry: Holding Companies
Growth: Openings in past year, 30
Contact George J. Taylor, Jr., COB/CEO/President; 860-282-0010; Fax: 860-282-9719; E-mail: acopo@farmstead.com

FlexiInternational Software, Inc.
2 Enterprise Dr.
Shelton, CT 06484
http://www.flexi.com
Founded: 1990
Total Employees: 138
Annual Sales: $8.3 million
Industry: Computer Software
Growth: Openings in past year, 38
Contact Ms. Rosemarrie Ferraro, Human Resources Manager; 203-925-3040; Fax: 203-925-3044; E-mail: info@flexi.com

Frontec AMT, Inc.
4 Landmark Sq., Suite 410
Stamford, CT 06901
http://www.frontec.com
Founded: 1992
Total Employees: 800
Annual Sales: $100 million
Industries: Computer Hardware, Computer Software
Growth: Openings in past year, 225

Contact Ms. Patricia
Kearney, Chief Executive
Officer; 203-977-7100;
Fax: 203-977-7134;
E-mail: webmaster@
frontec.com

Gerber Optical, Inc.
10 Gorbor Rd. East
South Windsor, CT 06074
http://www.gerberoptical.
com
Founded: 1987
Total Employees: 130
Annual Sales: $22 million
Industries: Factory
Automation,
Manufacturing Equipment
Growth: Openings in past
year, 29
Contact Michael Dolen,
Director of Human
Resources; 860-648-
6600; Fax: 860-648-
6601; E-mail: gerber@
gerberoptical.com

Hermell Products, Inc.
522 Cottage Grove Rd.,
Bldg. G
Bloomfield, CT 06002
http://www.hermell.com
Founded: 1968
Total Employees: 108
Industry: Medical
Growth: Openings in past
year, 58
Contact Ronald Pollack,
President; 860-242-6550;
Fax: 860-243-0361;
E-mail: hermell.prod@
snet.net

Hubbell Wiring Systems, Inc.
14 Prospect Dr.
Newtown, CT 06470
Founded: 1952
Total Employees: 200
Annual Sales: $23 million
Industry: Manufacturing
Equipment
Growth: Openings in past
year, 50
Contact Robert Hansen,
Plant Manager; 203-426-
2555; Fax: 203-270-7155

International Telecommunication Data Systems, Inc.
969 High Ridge Rd.
Stamford, CT 06905
http://www.itds.com
Founded: 1990
Total Employees: 188
Annual Sales: $16.689
million
Industry: Computer
Software
Growth: Openings in past
year, 28
Contact Peter P.
Basserman, President/
CEO; 203-329-3300;
Fax: 203-323-1314

Kaman Aerospace, Raymond Engineering Operations
217 Smith St.
Middletown, CT 06457
http://www.raymond-engrg.
com
Founded: 1939
Total Employees: 200
Industries: Computer
Hardware, Defense
Growth: Openings in past
year, 25
Contact Harry J. Hutchins,
Vice President/General
Manager; 860-632-1000;
Fax: 860-632-4329

Kamatics Corp.
PO Box 3
Bloomfield, CT 06002
Founded: 1945
Total Employees: 407
Annual Sales: $32 million
Industry: Subassemblies
and Components
Growth: Openings in past
year, 175
Contact Al Whitfield,
President; 860-243-9704;
Fax: 860-243-7993

KX Industries, LP
269 South Lambert Rd.
PO Box 545
Orange, CT 06477
http://www.kxindustries.
thomasregister.com
Founded: 1989
Total Employees: 140
Annual Sales: $17 million
Industry: Environmental
Growth: Openings in past
year, 65
Contact Richard Iannazzi,
Manager of Human
Resources; 203-799-
9000; Fax: 203-799-
7000; E-mail:
marketingmanager@
kxindustries.com

Lacey Manufacturing Co.
1146 Barnum Ave.
Bridgeport, CT 06610
Founded: 1921
Total Employees: 400
Annual Sales: $48 million
Industry: Medical
Growth: Openings in past
year, 50
Contact Robert A. Werner,
President; 203-336-0121;
Fax: 203-336-1774

Lifecodes Corp.
550 West Ave.
Stamford, CT 06902
http://www.lifecodes.com
Founded: 1982
Total Employees: 71
Industries: Biotechnology,
Holding Companies,
Medical
Growth: Openings in past
year, 41
Contact Ms. Kelly
Knoebel, Manager of
Human Resources; 203-
328-9500; Fax: 203-328-
9599; E-mail: lifecode@i-
2000.com

Linc Systems Corp.
310 West Newberry Rd.
Bloomfield, CT 06002
http://www.lincsys.com
Founded: 1985
Total Employees: 90
Annual Sales: $11 million
Industries: Computer
Hardware, Computer
Software
Growth: Openings in past
year, 35
Contact Rob Dillard,
Director of Personnel;
860-286-9060; Fax: 860-
286-9023

**Litton Industries, Inc.,
Winchester Electronics
Division**
400 Park Rd.
Watertown, CT 06795
http://www.litton-wed.com
Founded: 1953
Total Employees: 330
Industries: Photonics,
Subassemblies and
Components
Growth: Openings in past
year, 30
Contact Robert Beaucock,
Director of Human
Resources; 860-945-
5000; Fax: 860-945-5191

**Longview Holding, Inc.,
Sperry Rail Service**
46 Shelter Rock Rd.
Danbury, CT 06810
Founded: 1928
Total Employees: 250
Industry: Transportation
Growth: Openings in past
year, 80
Contact Ms. Debbie
Yachulke, Human
Resources Coordinator;
203-791-4500; Fax: 203-
797-8417

MECA Software, L.L.C.
115 Corporate Dr.
Trumbull, CT 06611

Founded: 1982
Total Employees: 350
Annual Sales: $45 million
Industry: Computer
Software
Growth: Openings in past
year, 160
Contact Ms. Lynn
Woodhall, Director of
Human Resources; 203-
452-2600; Fax: 203-268-
5257

**Methode New England
Co., Inc.**
50 McDermott Rd.
North Haven, CT 06473
Founded: 1950
Total Employees: 200
Industry: Subassemblies
and Components
Growth: Openings in past
year, 100
Contact Ms. Janet Fusco,
Human Resources; 203-
777-2541; Fax: 203-777-
3026; E-mail: methode@
attmail.com

**Microboard Processing,
Inc.**
4 Progress Ln..
Seymour, CT 06483
http://www.microboard.com
Founded: 1983
Total Employees: 215
Annual Sales: $18 million
Industry: Subassemblies
and Components
Growth: Openings in past
year, 70
Contact Craig T.
Hoekenga, President/
CEO; 203-881-1688;
Fax: 203-888-3017

North America O M C G
116 Front St.
Bridgeport, CT 06606
http://www.omcg.com/
omcg
Founded: 1982
Total Employees: 100
Annual Sales: $15 million
Industry: Factory
Automation

Growth: Openings in past
year, 50
Contact Robert Sears,
Vice President/General
Manager; 203-576-6948;
E-mail: bswire@flash.net

Numetrix, Inc.
101 Merrit 7
Norwalk, CT 06851
http://www.numetrix.com
Founded: 1977
Total Employees: 150
Industry: Computer
Software
Growth: Openings in past
year, 50
Contact Josef Schengili,
Founder/CEO; 203-847-
3452; Fax: 203-846-3537

OEM Controls, Inc.
10 Controls Dr.
Shelton, CT 06484
http://www.thomasregister.
com/joysticks
Founded: 1966
Total Employees: 180
Annual Sales: $24 million
Industries: Computer
Hardware, Test and
Measurement
Growth: Openings in past
year, 55
Contact Ms. Marge
Bennett, Personnel
Manager; 203-929-8431;
Fax: 203-929-3867

PanAmSat Corp.
One Pickwick Plaza
Greenwich, CT 06830
http://www.panamsat.com
Founded: 1992
Total Employees: 400
Annual Sales: $726.8
million
Industry:
Telecommunications
Growth: Openings in past
year, 50
Contact James W.
Cuminale, Senior Vice
President; 203-622-6664;
Fax: 203-622-9163

Phalo, CDT
90 Progress Dr.
Manchester, CT 06040
http://www.cdtc.com/phalo/
index.html
Founded: 1993
Total Employees: 90
Annual Sales: $12 million
Industry: Subassemblies
and Components
Growth: Openings in past
year, 30
Contact Jim Baker,
General Manager; 860-
649-6620; Fax: 860-649-
1698

**Rockbestos-Suprenant
Cable Corp.**
20 Bradley Park Rd.
PO Box 1102
East Granby, CT 06026
http://www.r-scc.com
Founded: 1918
Total Employees: 860
Industry: Subassemblies
and Components
Growth: Openings in past
year, 57
Contact Frederick
Schwelm, Jr., President/
General Manager; 860-
653-8300; Fax: 860-653-
8301

**Springborn Testing and
Research, Inc.**
10 Water St.
Enfield, CT 06082
Founded: 1944
Total Employees: 442
Industries: Advanced
Materials, Defense,
Holding Companies,
Subassemblies and
Components, Test and
Measurement
Growth: Openings in past
year, 133
Contact Ms. Carol A.
Dyjak, Human Resources
Manager; 860-749-8371;
Fax: 860-749-7533

Proto-Power Corporation
15 Thames St.
Groton, CT 06340
Founded: 1981
Total Employees: 220
Annual Sales: $17.7
million
Industries: Energy,
Environmental,
Manufacturing Equipment
Growth: Openings in past
year, 82
Contact Ms. Susan Lamb,
Manager of Human
Resources; 860-446-
9725; Fax: 860-446-8292

Seal Products, Inc.
550 Spring St.
Naugatuck, CT 06770
Founded: 1968
Total Employees: 190
Industries: Advanced
Materials, Factory
Automation, Photonics
Growth: Openings in past
year, 50
Contact Ms. Debra A.
Breski, Manager of
Human Resources; 203-
729-5201; Fax: 203-729-
5639

System Services, Inc.
835 Bloomfield Ave.
Windsor, CT 06095
Founded: 1991
Total Employees: 58
Annual Sales: $7.5 million
Industry: Computer
Software
Growth: Openings in past
year, 35
Contact Daniel A.
McMahon, President;
860-688-0033; Fax: 860-
683-2831; E-mail:
asesta@physicianbilling.
com

Quantel, Inc.
28 Thornval Cir.
Darien, CT 06820
Founded: 1975
Total Employees: 120
Industries:
Subassemblies and
Components,
Telecommunications
Growth: Openings in past
year, 25
Contact George A.
Grasso, Executive Chair-
man of the Board; 203-
656-3100; Fax: 203-656-
3459

**Semiconductor
Packaging Materials
Corp., Retconn Division**
199 West Pearl Rd.
Torrington, CT 06790
http://www.retconn.com
Founded: 1987
Total Employees: 190
Annual Sales: $12 million
Industry: Subassemblies
and Components
Growth: Openings in past
year, 90
Contact Dan Schreck,
President; 860-489-1220;
Fax: 860-496-7307

**Teleflex Fluid Systems,
Inc.**
1 Firestone Dr.
Suffield, CT 06078
http://www.teleflexhose.
com
Founded: 1980
Total Employees: 200
Annual Sales: $26 million
Industry: Subassemblies
and Components
Growth: Openings in past
year, 25
Contact David Guidetti,
Human Resources
Manager; 860-668-1285;
Fax: 860-668-2353;
E-mail: webmaster@
teleflexhose.com

Telepartner International North America, Inc.
900 Northrop Rd.
Wallingford, CT 06492
http://www.telepartner.com
Founded: 1985
Total Employees: 65
Annual Sales: $13 million
Industry: Computer Software
Growth: Openings in past year, 25
Contact Ms. Carol Barnett, Human Resources Manager; 203-265-2619; Fax: 203-284-2615; E-mail: sales@telepartner.com

TLF Associates, Inc.
415 Silas Dean Hwy., Suite 402
Wethersfield, CT 06109
Founded: 1993
Total Employees: 80
Annual Sales: $4.2 million
Industry: Computer Hardware
Growth: Openings in past year, 35
Contact Ms. Tammy L. Ferrauola, President; 860-563-6561; Fax: 860-563-7255; E-mail: tlfinc@compsol.net

Trans-Lux Corp.
110 Richards Ave.
Norwalk, CT 06854
http://www.trans-lux.com
Founded: 1920
Total Employees: 575
Annual Sales: $45.285 million
Industries: Holding Companies, Photonics
Growth: Openings in past year, 123
Contact Richard Kramer, VP of Human Resources; 203-853-4321; Fax: 203-855-8636; E-mail: mike. quirk@internetmci.net

Transact Technologies, Inc.
7 Laser Ln.
Wallingford, CT 06492
http://www.transact-tech. com
Founded: 1996
Total Employees: 280
Annual Sales: $42.1 million
Industry: Holding Companies
Growth: Openings in past year, 49
Contact Ms. Joanne Draper, VP of Human Resources; 203-269-1198; Fax: 203-949-9048

TRUMPF Inc.
Hyde Rd., Farmington Industrial Park
Farmington, CT 06032
http://www.trumpf.com
Founded: 1967
Total Employees: 372
Annual Sales: $49 million
Industries: Factory Automation, Photonics
Growth: Openings in past year, 57
Contact James Bento, VP of Finance and Administration; 860-677-9741; Fax: 860-678-1704

TSI International Software, Ltd.
45 Danbury Rd.
Wilton, CT 06897
http://www.tsisoft.com
Founded: 1979
Total Employees: 150
Annual Sales: $19.004 million
Industry: Computer Software
Growth: Openings in past year, 30
Contact Ms. Ann P. Curry, Manager of Administration and HR; 203-761-8600; Fax: 203-762-9677; E-mail: inquiry@tsisoft.com

United Oil Recovery, Inc.
136 Gracey Ave.
Meriden, CT 06451
Founded: 1976
Total Employees: 170
Industries: Environmental, Holding Companies
Growth: Openings in past year, 50
Contact David Carabetta, President; 203-238-6745; Fax: 203-238-6772

Utimaco Mergent
70 Inwood Rd.
Rocky Hill, CT 06067
http://www.utimaco.com
Founded: 1985
Total Employees: 130
Annual Sales: $16 million
Industry: Computer Software
Growth: Openings in past year, 50
Contact Ms. Sherri Turner, Director of Administration; 860-257-4223; Fax: 860-257-4245; E-mail: mergent.com

Warner Electric, Superior Electric Divsion
383 Middle St.
Bristol, CT 06010
http://www.warnernet.com
Founded: 1938
Total Employees: 550
Annual Sales: $74 million
Industries: Energy, Subassemblies and Components, Test and Measurement
Growth: Openings in past year, 50
Contact Lou Benien, Manager of Human Resources; 860-585-4500; Fax: 860-584-1483

Wentworth Laboratories, Inc.
500 Federal Rd.
Brookfield, CT 06804

Founded: 1967
Total Employees: 250
Annual Sales: $38 million
Industry: Factory
Automation
Growth: Openings in past
year, 25
Contact Arthur Evans,
President; 203-775-0448;
Fax: 203-775-8172

Whelen Engineering Co.
Rte. 145, Winthrop Rd.
Chester, CT 06412
http://www.whelen.com
Founded: 1952
Total Employees: 350
Annual Sales: $47 million
Industries: Photonics,
Test and Measurement,
Transportation
Growth: Openings in past
year, 49
Contact John Olson,
President; 860-526-9504;
Fax: 860-526-4078

**Yale Computing and
Information Systems**
175 Whitney Ave., Yale
Station
PO Box 208276
New Haven, CT 06520
Founded: 1979
Total Employees: 150
Industry: Computer
Software
Growth: Openings in past
year, 50
Contact Daniel
Updegrove, Acting Direc-
tor of Computing; 203-
432-6500; Fax: 203-432-
6165

Zygo Corp.
Laurel Brook Rd.
Middlefield, CT 06455
http://www.zygo.com
Founded: 1970
Total Employees: 420
Annual Sales: $87.2
million
Industries: Holding
Companies, Photonics,
Test and Measurement

Growth: Openings in past
year, 28
Contact Frank Pine,
Human Resource
Manager; 860-347-8506;
Fax: 860-347-8372;
E-mail: inquire@zygo.
com

Delaware

Rodel, Inc.
451 Bellevue Rd.
Newark, DE 19713
Founded: 1974
Total Employees: 675
Annual Sales: $120 million
Industry: Advanced
Materials
Growth: Openings in past
year, 20
Contact William Budinger,
COB/CEO; 302-366-
0500; Fax: 302-455-1216

District of Columbia

**American Petroleum
Institute**
1220 L St. Northwest
Washington, DC 20005
http://www.api.org
Founded: 1919
Total Employees: 500
Industry: Holding
Companies
Growth: Openings in past
year, 24
Contact Red Cavaney,
President; 202-682-8000;
Fax: 202-682-8232

**National Association of
Home Builders**
1201 15th St. Northwest
Washington, DC 20005
http://www.nahb.com
Founded: 1942
Total Employees: 330
Industry: Holding
Companies
Growth: Openings in past
year, 30
Contact Kent W. Colton,
CEO/Executive Vice
President; 202-822-0200;
Fax: 202-861-2131

Florida

**A&M Engineering
Plastics, Inc.**
10521 75th St. North
Largo, FL 34647
Founded: 1977
Total Employees: 150
Industry: Manufacturing
Equipment
Growth: Openings in past
year, 70
Contact Alan Caton,
President; 813-541-4482;
Fax: 813-546-4101

**ABB CEAG Power
Supplies**
1 Pine Lakes Pkwy. North
Palm Coast, FL 32137
http://www.abb.com/
americas/usa
Founded: 1976
Total Employees: 160
Industry: Subassemblies
and Components
Growth: Openings in past
year, 30
Contact George Golden,
Human Resources
Manager; 904-445-0311;
Fax: 904-445-0322;
E-mail: abbceag@aol.
com

**Advanced Manufacturing
Technologies, Inc.**
1216 East Prospect Ave.
Melbourne, FL 32901
Founded: 1982
Total Employees: 140
Annual Sales: $17 million
Industry: Manufacturing
Equipment
Growth: Openings in past
year, 70
Contact Karl Zurfluh,
President; 407-951-0828;
Fax: 407-951-0868

American Technical Molding Corp.
1351-B North Arcturas Ave.
Clearwater, FL 34625
http://www.a-t-m.com
Founded: 1984
Total Employees: 150
Annual Sales: $18 million
Industries: Factory Automation, Manufacturing Equipment
Growth: Openings in past year, 30
Contact Demetre Loulourgas, President; 813-447-7377; Fax: 813-447-0125; E-mail: engineering@a-t-m.com

AmeriPath, Inc.
7289 Garden Rd., Suite 200
Riviera Beach, FL 33404
Founded: 1996
Total Employees: 800
Annual Sales: $42.6 million
Industry: Medical
Growth: Openings in past year, 111
Contact Stephen V. Fuller, VP of Human Resources; 561-845-1850; Fax: 561-845-0129

AmPro Corp.
525 John Rodes Blvd.
Melbourne, FL 32934
http://www.amprocorp.com
Founded: 1972
Total Employees: 200
Annual Sales: $34 million
Industry: Telecommunications
Growth: Openings in past year, 30
Contact Charles Trippe, COB/CEO; 407-254-3000; Fax: 407-253-3001

Anchor
50 Industrial Loop North
Orange Park, FL 32073
Founded: 1948
Total Employees: 200
Industry: Chemicals
Growth: Openings in past year, 50
Contact Steven Zunde, President; 904-264-3500; Fax: 904-278-9697

Andrx Corp.
4001 Southwest 47th Ave., Suite 201
Fort Lauderdale, FL 33314
http://www.andrx.com
Founded: 1993
Total Employees: 325
Annual Sales: $89 million
Industry: Holding Companies
Growth: Openings in past year, 75
Contact Alan P. Cohen, COB/CEO; 954-584-0300; Fax: 954-792-1034

Andrx Pharmaceuticals, Inc.
4001 Southwest 47th Ave., Suite 201
Fort Lauderdale, FL 33314
Founded: 1991
Total Employees: 80
Annual Sales: $12 million
Industry: Pharmaceuticals
Growth: Openings in past year, 38
Contact Ronald Norris, Director of Human Resources; 954-581-7500; Fax: 954-587-1054

AquaCare Systems, Inc.
11820 Northwest 37th St.
Coral Springs, FL 33065
Founded: 1990
Total Employees: 160
Annual Sales: $31 million
Industry: Holding Companies

Growth: Openings in past year, 45
Contact William Mackey, COB/President; 954-796-3338; Fax: 954-796-3401

Aquagenix Land-Water Technology, Inc.
6500 Northwest 15th Ave.
Fort Lauderdale, FL 33309
Founded: 1990
Total Employees: 80
Annual Sales: $11.350 million
Industry: Environmental
Growth: Openings in past year, 30
Contact John P. Hart, President; 954-969-8000; Fax: 954-969-7700

Arnet Pharmaceutical Corp.
2280 West 77th St.
Hialeah, FL 33016
Founded: 1972
Total Employees: 120
Annual Sales: $14 million
Industry: Pharmaceuticals
Growth: Openings in past year, 50
Contact Adolfo Graubard, Controller; 305-558-2929; Fax: 305-558-4844

Arthur Andersen Technology Solutions
2805 Fruitville Rd.
Sarasota, FL 34237
Founded: 1984
Total Employees: 600
Industry: Computer Software
Growth: Openings in past year, 100
Contact James H. Shedivy, Chief Information Officer; 941-365-9469; Fax: 941-373-2900

Bell Technologies, Inc.
6120 Hanging Moss Rd.
Orlando, FL 32807
http://www.belltechinc.com

Founded: 1944
Total Employees: 550
Annual Sales: $74 million
Industries: Factory
  Automation,
  Subassemblies and
  Components, Test and
  Measurement,
  Telecommunications
Growth: Openings in past
  year, 50
Contact Ms. Rosanna D.
  Bolduc, Director of
  Human Resources; 407-
  678-6900; Fax: 407-678-
  0578; E-mail:
  belltechinc@belltechinc.
  com

Citrix Systems, Inc.
6400 Northwest 6th Way
Fort Lauderdale, FL 33309
http://www.citrix.com
Founded: 1989
Total Employees: 235
Annual Sales: $44.527
  million
Industry: Computer
  Software
Growth: Openings in past
  year, 123
Contact Roger W.
  Roberts, President/CEO;
  954-267-3000; Fax: 954-
  267-9319; E-mail:
  sales@citrix.com

COLLEGIS
2300 Maitland Center
  Pkwy., Suite 340
Maitland, FL 32751
http://www.collegis.com
Founded: 1986
Total Employees: 210
Annual Sales: $43 million
Industries: Computer
  Hardware,
  Telecommunications
Growth: Openings in past
  year, 60
Contact Bob Cominski,
  VP of Human Resources
  & Recruiting; 407-660-
  1199; Fax: 407-660-8008;
  E-mail: feellini@collegis.
  com

**Bentley Pharmaceuticals,
Inc.**
4830 West Kennedy Blvd.,
  Suite 548
Tampa, FL 33609
Founded: 1974
Total Employees: 110
Annual Sales: $23.133
  million
Industry: Pharmaceuticals
Growth: Openings in past
  year, 25
Contact Ms. Terri Kaiser,
  Director of Division of
  Medical Devices; 813-
  286-4401; Fax: 813-286-
  4402

Clairson Industries Corp.
2811 Northeast 14th St.
Ocala, FL 34470
Founded: 1979
Total Employees: 145
Annual Sales: $11 million
Industries: Holding
  Companies, Medical,
  Pharmaceuticals,
  Subassemblies and
  Components
Growth: Openings in past
  year, 25
Contact Philip K. Effinger,
  President; 352-732-3244;
  Fax: 352-368-1796;
  E-mail: clairson@praxis.
  net

**Command Software
Systems, Inc.**
1061 East Indiantown Rd.,
  Suite 500
Jupiter, FL 33477
http://www.commandcom.
  com
Founded: 1984
Total Employees: 110
Annual Sales: $14 million
Industry: Computer
  Software
Growth: Openings in past
  year, 35
Contact Ms. Sandra Egan,
  Director of Personnel;
  561-575-3200; Fax: 561-
  575-3026; E-mail:
  sales@commandcom.
  com

Catalina Marketing Corp.
11300 9th St. North
Saint Petersburg, FL
  33716
http://www.catalinamktg.
  com
Founded: 1983
Total Employees: 670
Annual Sales: $172.1
  million
Industry: Computer
  Software
Growth: Openings in past
  year, 67
Contact George Off,
  President/CEO; 813-579-
  5000; Fax: 813-570-8507

CMS, Inc.
4904 Eisenhower Blvd.,
  Suite 310
Tampa, FL 33634
Founded: 1988
Total Employees: 600
Annual Sales: $80 million
Industries: Defense,
  Environmental, Holding
  Companies
Growth: Openings in past
  year, 149
Contact F.P. Ragano,
  Chief Executive Officer;
  813-882-4477; Fax: 813-
  884-1876; E-mail:
  cms_inc@msn.com

Conax Florida Corp.
2801 75th St. North
Saint Petersburg, FL
  33710
Founded: 1983
Total Employees: 130
Annual Sales: $15 million
Industries: Defense,
  Subassemblies and
  Components
Growth: Openings in past
  year, 30
Contact Jeffrey Eckhart,
  President/CEO; 813-345-
  8000; Fax: 813-345-4217

Continental Circuits, Inc.
1150 Belle Ave.
Winter Springs, FL 32708
Founded: 1970
Total Employees: 250
Annual Sales: $33 million
Industry: Subassemblies
and Components
Growth: Openings in past
year, 29
Contact R. Leo Spotts, Jr.,
President; 407-699-5000;
Fax: 407-699-6871;
E-mail: http://www.
circuits.com

**Crestview Aerospace
Corp.**
5486 Fairchild Rd.
Crestview, FL 32539
Founded: 1991
Total Employees: 297
Industry: Transportation
Growth: Openings in past
year, 167
Contact Jack Owen,
President; 850-682-2746;
Fax: 850-682-0489

CyberGate, Inc.
1301 West Newport Dr.
Deerfield Beach, FL 33442
http://www.gate.net
Founded: 1993
Total Employees: 125
Annual Sales: $6 million
Industry:
Telecommunications
Growth: Openings in past
year, 95
Contact Ms. Cristy
Schimmoller, Director of
Personnel; 954-428-
4283; Fax: 954-429-
8001; E-mail: csales@
gate.net

Dalloz Safety
5300 Region Ct.
Lakeland, FL 33801
Founded: 1939
Total Employees: 300
Annual Sales: $50 million

Industries: Medical,
Photonics, Test and
Measurement
Growth: Openings in past
year, 100
Contact Herve Meillat,
President; 941-687-7266;
Fax: 941-687-0431

**Datamax International
Corp.**
4501 Parkway Commerce
Blvd.
Orlando, FL 32808
http://www.datamaxcorp.
com
Founded: 1977
Total Employees: 537
Annual Sales: $95.2
million
Industries: Computer
Hardware, Computer
Software
Growth: Openings in past
year, 36
Contact David Rogers,
Manager of Human
Resources; 407-578-
8007; Fax: 407-578-8377

Diamond Products, Inc.
PO Box 878
Seffner, FL 33584
Founded: 1972
Total Employees: 200
Annual Sales: $25 million
Industries: Chemicals,
Medical, Pharmaceuticals
Growth: Openings in past
year, 50
Contact Barton Bridges,
President; 813-622-8895;
Fax: 813-630-0318

**Dynacs Engineering Co.,
Inc.**
28870 US Hwy. 19 North,
Suite 405
Clearwater, FL 34621
http://www.dynacs.com
Founded: 1985
Total Employees: 275
Annual Sales: $15 million
Industries: Computer
Hardware, Computer
Software, Manufacturing

Equipment,
Transportation
Growth: Openings in past
year, 75
Contact Ramen Singh,
President; 813-725-3899;
Fax: 813-726-4755;
E-mail: dynacs@dynacs.
com

**Dynamic Healthcare
Technologies, Inc.**
101 Southhall Ln.
Maitland, FL 32751
http://www.dht.com
Founded: 1994
Total Employees: 300
Annual Sales: $26.2
million
Industries: Computer
Hardware, Computer
Software
Growth: Openings in past
year, 130
Contact Ms. Vicki Torres,
Director of Human
Resources; 407-875-
9991; Fax: 407-875-
9915; E-mail:
mmccabe@dht.com

Electro Corp.
1845 57th St.
Sarasota, FL 34243
http://www.electrocorp.com
Founded: 1936
Total Employees: 175
Annual Sales: $23 million
Industry: Test and
Measurement
Growth: Openings in past
year, 25
Contact Ms. Beverly Long,
Human Resources
Manager; 941-355-8411;
Fax: 941-355-3120

Equitrac Corp.
836 Ponce De Leon Blvd.
Coral Gables, FL 33134
http://www.equitrac.com
Founded: 1977
Total Employees: 350
Annual Sales: $40 million
Industry: Computer
Software

Growth: Openings in past year, 41
Contact Robert Diano, Director of Human Resources; 305-442-2060; Fax: 305-442-0687; E-mail: info@equitrac.com

FDP Corp.
2140 South Dixie Hwy.
Miami, FL 33133
http://www.fdpcorp.com
Founded: 1968
Total Employees: 293
Annual Sales: $26.5 million
Industry: Computer Software
Growth: Openings in past year, 30
Contact Ms. Carol Kincade, Personnel Manager; 305-858-8200; Fax: 305-854-6305

ForeFront Direct
25400 U.S. Hwy. 19 North, Suite 285
Clearwater, FL 33763
http://www.ffg.com
Founded: 1991
Total Employees: 180
Industry: Computer Software
Growth: Openings in past year, 80
Contact Tom Godfrey, Director of Personnel; 813-724-8994; Fax: 813-726-6922; E-mail: pctools@ffg.com

Geac VisionShift
3707 West Cherry St.
Tampa, FL 33607
http://www.geac.com/offices/vs/index.htm
Founded: 1975
Total Employees: 150
Annual Sales: $19 million
Industry: Computer Software
Growth: Openings in past year, 25
Contact Warren Fletcher, General Manager/CEO;

813-872-9990; Fax: 813-878-2751; E-mail: vsinfo@geac.com

Geltech, Inc.
3267 Progress Dr.
Orlando, FL 32826
http://www.geltech.com
Founded: 1985
Total Employees: 75
Annual Sales: $9.9 million
Industries: Advanced Materials, Photonics
Growth: Openings in past year, 45
Contact Todd Childress, VP of Administration; 407-382-4003; Fax: 407-382-4007; E-mail: geltech@sprynet.com

Guardian International, Inc.
3880 North 28th Terr.
Hollywood, FL 33020
http://www.guardianinternational.com
Founded: 1987
Total Employees: 80
Annual Sales: $3.6 million
Industry: Test and Measurement
Growth: Openings in past year, 40
Contact Richard Ginsberg, CEO/President; 954-926-5200; Fax: 954-926-1809; E-mail: rkn5200@aol.com

Hi-Rise Recycling Systems, Inc.
16255 Northwest 54th Ave.
Miami, FL 33015
http://www.hiri.com
Founded: 1991
Total Employees: 75
Annual Sales: $3.2 million
Industries: Environmental, Holding Companies
Growth: Openings in past year, 35
Contact Brad Hacker, Chief Financial Officer; 305-624-9222; Fax: 305-625-4666; E-mail: info@hiri.com

Holographic Dimensions, Inc.
2503 Northwest 36th St.
Miami, FL 33166
http://www.hgrm.com
Founded: 1985
Total Employees: 50
Industry: Photonics
Growth: Openings in past year, 42
Contact Kevin Brown, President/CEO; 305-994-7577; Fax: 305-994-7702; E-mail: info@hgrm.com

HotOffice Technologies, Inc.
5201 Congress Ave., Suite C-232
Boca Raton, FL 33487
http://www.hotoffice.com
Founded: 1995
Total Employees: 50
Annual Sales: $8.5 million
Industries: Computer Software, Telecommunications
Growth: Openings in past year, 40
Contact Stewart Padveen, COB/CEO; 561-995-0005; Fax: 561-995-5990; E-mail: info@hotoffice.com

Hughes Manufacturing, Inc.
11910 62nd St. North
Largo, FL 34643
http://www.hughesmfg.com
Founded: 1961
Total Employees: 175
Industries: Advanced Materials, Energy
Growth: Openings in past year, 55
Contact Ms. Kim Lestoric, Office Manager; 813-536-7891; Fax: 813-535-8199

Information Management Alternatives Plus, Inc.
9428 Baymeadows Rd., Suite 500
Jacksonville, FL 32256
http://www.imanet.com
Founded: 1984
Total Employees: 160
Annual Sales: $20 million
Industry: Computer Software
Growth: Openings in past year, 42
Contact Ms. Karen Kelley, Senior Business Partner, Human Resources; 904-636-6100; Fax: 904-737-0666

Intellitec, Inc.
2000 Brunswick Ln.
Deland, FL 32724
Founded: 1845
Total Employees: 270
Annual Sales: $38 million
Industries: Defense, Test and Measurement
Growth: Openings in past year, 40
Contact Hank Lattanzi, President; 904-736-1700; Fax: 904-736-2250

International Business Machines Corp., Manufacturing Technology Center
1798 Northwest 40th St.
Boca Raton, FL 33431
Founded: 1966
Total Employees: 250
Annual Sales: $31 million
Industries: Computer Software, Factory Automation, Manufacturing Equipment, Medical, Subassemblies and Components
Growth: Openings in past year, 50
Contact Mike Davis, Director; 561-443-6000; Fax: 561-443-6659

Internet Communications of America, Inc.
1020 Northwest 163rd. Dr.
Miami, FL 33169
http://www.icanect.com
Founded: 1995
Total Employees: 90
Annual Sales: $15 million
Industry: Telecommunications
Growth: Openings in past year, 50
Contact Robert Hurwitz, President; 305-621-9200; Fax: 305-621-2227; E-mail: sales@icanect.com

Johnson Matthey Electronic Assembly Services, Inc.
7100 Technology Dr.
West Melbourne, FL 32904
Founded: 1986
Total Employees: 550
Industry: Subassemblies and Components
Growth: Openings in past year, 174
Contact Jim Roberts, Manager of Human Resources; 407-725-6993; Fax: 407-724-6682

LaserSight Technologies, Inc.
12249 Science Dr., Suite 160
Orlando, FL 32826
http://www.lase.com
Founded: 1991
Total Employees: 70
Annual Sales: $8.5 million
Industries: Medical, Photonics
Growth: Openings in past year, 35
Contact Rick Crowley, President; 407-382-2700; Fax: 407-382-2701

Linvatec Corp.
11311 Concept Blvd.
Largo, FL 33773
Founded: 1991
Total Employees: 700
Annual Sales: $85 million
Industry: Medical
Growth: Openings in past year, 97
Contact George Kempsell, President; 813-392-6464

Mansur Industries Inc.
8425 Southwest 129th Terr.
Miami, FL 33156
Founded: 1990
Total Employees: 75
Industries: Environmental, Factory Automation
Growth: Openings in past year, 55
Contact Paul I. Mansur, Chief Executive Officer; 305-232-6768; Fax: 305-232-6818

Medical Technology Systems, Inc.
12920 Automobile Blvd.
Clearwater, FL 34622
Founded: 1984
Total Employees: 240
Annual Sales: $19.2 million
Industry: Holding Companies
Growth: Openings in past year, 80
Contact Peter Benjamin, Director of Human Resources; 813-576-6311; Fax: 813-579-8067

Memtec America Corp., Fluid Dynamics Division
1750 Memtec Dr.
Deland, FL 32724
Founded: 1972
Total Employees: 450
Annual Sales: $61 million
Industry: Test and Measurement

Growth: Openings in past year, 75
Contact Tom Hagan, President; 904-822-8000; Fax: 904-822-8010

Oce Printing Systems USA, Inc.
5500 Broken Sound Blvd.
Boca Raton, FL 33487
http://www.oceprinting.com
Founded: 1980
Total Employees: 710
Annual Sales: $140 million
Industry: Computer Hardware
Growth: Openings in past year, 65
Contact H. Werner Krause, President/CEO; 561-997-3100; Fax: 561-998-9160

Omega Research, Inc.
8700 West Flander St.
Miami, FL 33174
http://www.omegaresearch.com
Founded: 1982
Total Employees: 148
Annual Sales: $17.8 million
Industry: Computer Software
Growth: Openings in past year, 26
Contact William R. Cruz, COB/CEO; 305-551-9991; Fax: 305-551-2240; E-mail: sales@omegaresearch.com

PaySys International, Inc.
900 Winderly Pl., Suite 200
PO Box 5575
Maitland, FL 32751
http://www.paysys.com
Founded: 1981
Total Employees: 345
Annual Sales: $26.9 million
Industry: Computer Software
Growth: Openings in past year, 149

Contact Ms. Yvonne Mondragone, Director of Human Resources; 407-660-0343; Fax: 407-875-9936

Phasetronics, Inc.
13214 38th St. North
Clearwater, FL 34622
Founded: 1980
Total Employees: 150
Annual Sales: $20 million
Industry: Test and Measurement
Growth: Openings in past year, 50
Contact Jim Mitchell, President; 813-573-1900; Fax: 813-573-1803; E-mail: motorctrl@aol.com

Phoenix International Ltd., Inc.
500 International Dr.
Heathrow, FL 32746
http://www.phoenixint.com
Founded: 1993
Total Employees: 131
Annual Sales: $10.4 million
Industry: Computer Software
Growth: Openings in past year, 44
Contact Bahram Yusefzadeh, COB/CEO; 407-548-5100; Fax: 407-548-5295; E-mail: phoenix@int.com

PowerCerv Corp.
400 North Ashley Dr., Suite 2700
Tampa, FL 33602
http://www.powercerv.com
Founded: 1992
Total Employees: 410
Annual Sales: $38 million
Industry: Computer Software
Growth: Openings in past year, 100
Contact Mark Fartello, President; 813-226-2600;

Fax: 813-222-0886; E-mail: info@powercerv.com

Product Development Resources, Inc.
3 Old Meadow Way
Palm Beach Gardens, FL 33418
http://www.pdr-chiral.com
Founded: 1987
Total Employees: 38
Industries: Manufacturing Equipment, Test and Measurement
Growth: Openings in past year, 31
Contact Gary W. Yanik, President; 561-625-2645; Fax: 561-844-7663; E-mail: gwyanik@gde.net

ProxyMed, Inc.
2501 Davie Rd., Suite 230
Fort Lauderdale, FL 33317
http://www.proxymed.com
Founded: 1989
Total Employees: 75
Annual Sales: $3 million
Industries: Computer Software, Telecommunications
Growth: Openings in past year, 40
Contact John P. Guinan, President/CEO; 954-473-1001; Fax: 954-473-0620

Q-bit Corp.
2144 Franklin Dr. Northeast
Palm Bay, FL 32905
http://www.q-bit.com
Founded: 1972
Total Employees: 199
Industries: Subassemblies and Components, Telecommunications
Growth: Openings in past year, 39
Contact Phil Crews, Human Resources Manager; 407-727-1838; Fax: 407-727-3729; E-mail: sales@q-bit.com

Raltron Electronics Corp.
2315 Northwest 107th Ave.
Miami, FL 33172
http://www.raltron.com
Founded: 1983
Total Employees: 150
Industry: Subassemblies and Components
Growth: Openings in past year, 30
Contact Alexandre Wolloch, President; 305-594-3973; Fax: 305-594-3973; E-mail: sales@raltron.com

Soft Computer Consultants, Inc.
34350 US Hwy. 19 North
Palm Harbor, FL 34684
http://www.softcomputer.com
Founded: 1982
Total Employees: 305
Annual Sales: $18 million
Industry: Computer Software
Growth: Openings in past year, 84
Contact Armin Hakim, Director of Human Resources; 813-789-0100; Fax: 813-789-0110

Sun Hydraulics Corp.
1500 University Pkwy.
Sarasota, FL 34243
Founded: 1971
Total Employees: 500
Annual Sales: $55.4 million
Industries: Subassemblies and Components, Test and Measurement
Growth: Openings in past year, 100
Contact Ms. Kirsten Regal, Personnel Manager; 941-362-1200; Fax: 941-355-4497

Renex Corp.
2100 Ponce de Leon Blvd., Suite 950
Coral Gables, FL 33134
Founded: 1993
Total Employees: 258
Annual Sales: $18.6 million
Industry: Medical
Growth: Openings in past year, 32
Contact James P. Shea, CEO/President; 305-448-2044; Fax: 305-448-1154

Software Technology, Inc.
1225 Evans Rd.
Melbourne, FL 32904
http://www.sticomet.com
Founded: 1978
Total Employees: 300
Annual Sales: $38 million
Industry: Computer Software
Growth: Openings in past year, 33
Contact Jeff Clift, President; 407-723-3999; Fax: 407-676-4510

Sun MicroStamping, Inc.
14055 US Hwy. 19 North
Clearwater, FL 34624
Founded: 1987
Total Employees: 260
Annual Sales: $40 million
Industry: Manufacturing Equipment
Growth: Openings in past year, 73
Contact Ms. Jeanne Isacco, Human Resources Manager; 813-536-8822; Fax: 813-536-6667; E-mail: sunmic@mailhost.intnet.net

Sawtek, Inc.
PO Box 609501
Orlando, FL 32860
http://www.sawtek.com
Founded: 1979
Total Employees: 490
Annual Sales: $82 million
Industries: Subassemblies and Components, Test and Measurement, Telecommunications
Growth: Openings in past year, 37
Contact Ms. Sherri Walls, Manager of Human Resource; 407-886-8860; Fax: 407-886-7061; E-mail: mts@sawtek.com

Solitron, Vector Microwave Products, Inc.
3301 Electronics Way.
West Palm Beach, FL 33407
http://www.svmicro.com
Founded: 1993
Total Employees: 130
Annual Sales: $8.5 million
Industry: Subassemblies and Components
Growth: Openings in past year, 40
Contact Ms. Beth Willoughby, Human Resources Adminstrator; 561-840-1800; Fax: 561-844-8551; E-mail: sales@svmicro.com

Team Personnel, Inc.
3525 West Lake Mary Blvd., Suite 306
Lake Mary, FL 32746
Founded: 1990
Total Employees: 100
Annual Sales: $7.5 million
Industries: Holding Companies, Manufacturing Equipment, Telecommunications
Growth: Openings in past year, 39
Contact Matt Moore, President; 407-324-5111; Fax: 407-324-8566

Teltronics, Inc.
2150 Whitfield Industrial Way
Sarasota, FL 34243
http://www.teltronics.com
Founded: 1967
Total Employees: 240
Annual Sales: $28.8 million
Industries: Computer Software, Holding Companies, Telecommunications
Growth: Openings in past year, 40
Contact Ewen Cameron, President/CEO; 941-753-5000; Fax: 941-758-8469; E-mail: telt@teltronics.com

UCS, Inc.
2005 West Cypress Creek Rd., Suite 100
Fort Lauderdale, FL 33309
http://www.ucsworks.com
Founded: 1984
Total Employees: 150
Annual Sales: $19 million
Industries: Computer Hardware, Computer Software
Growth: Openings in past year, 30
Contact Ozzie Ramos, President; 954-771-8116; Fax: 954-771-8601; E-mail: bnelson@ucsworks.com

Vela Research, Inc.
2501 118th Ave. North
Saint Petersburg, FL 33716
http://www.vela.com
Founded: 1991
Total Employees: 70
Industry: Telecommunications
Growth: Openings in past year, 25
Contact Scott Cooper, President; 813-572-1230; Fax: 813-573-2508; E-mail: dedwards@vela.com

Vitech America, Inc.
8807 Northwest 23rd St.
Miami, FL 33172
http://www.vitech.net
Founded: 1993
Total Employees: 250
Annual Sales: $77 million
Industries: Computer Hardware, Telecommunications
Growth: Openings in past year, 100
Contact Georges C. St. Laurent, III, COB/CEO; 305-477-1161; Fax: 305-477-1379; E-mail: vitech@vitech.net

Georgia

Accu-Tech Corporation
200 Hembree Park Dr.
Roswell, GA 30076
Founded: 1984
Total Employees: 250
Annual Sales: $65 million
Industry: Subassemblies and Components
Growth: Openings in past year, 69
Contact Daniel G. Delavie, President; 770-751-9473; Fax: 770-475-4659

American Megatrends, Inc.
6145-F North Belt Pkwy.
Norcross, GA 30071
http://www.megatrends.com
Founded: 1985
Total Employees: 300
Annual Sales: $61 million
Industries: Computer Hardware, Computer Software, Holding Companies, Telecommunications
Growth: Openings in past year, 100
Contact S. Shankar, President; 770-263-8181; Fax: 770-246-8791

Amoco Polymer, Inc.
4500 McGinnis Ferry Rd.
Alpharetta, GA 30005
http://www.amoco.com
Founded: 1962
Total Employees: 450
Annual Sales: $86 million
Industry: Advanced Materials
Growth: Openings in past year, 49
Contact Bruce Carmichael, Director of Human Resources; 770-772-8200; Fax: 770-772-8547

Ayres Corp.
PO Box 3090
Albany, GA 31706
Founded: 1968
Total Employees: 525
Annual Sales: $31 million
Industry: Transportation
Growth: Openings in past year, 125
Contact Fred P. Ayres, President; 912-883-1440; Fax: 912-439-9790

Barco, Inc.
3240 Town Point Dr.
Kennesaw, GA 30144
http://www.barcousa.com
Founded: 1934
Total Employees: 250
Annual Sales: $42 million
Industries: Computer Hardware, Photonics, Telecommunications
Growth: Openings in past year, 50
Contact Guido VanLinden, Executive Vice President; 770-218-3200; Fax: 770-218-3250

Checkmate Electronics, Inc.
1003 Mansell Rd.
Roswell, GA 30076
Founded: 1987
Total Employees: 193

Annual Sales: $35 million
Industry: Computer Hardware
Growth: Openings in past year, 43
Contact Bruce Digby, Director of Human Resources; 770-594-6000; Fax: 770-594-6006

Compris Technologies, Inc.
1000 Cobb Place Blvd., Suite 300
Kennesaw, GA 30144
http://www.compristech.com
Founded: 1989
Total Employees: 180
Annual Sales: $23 million
Industry: Computer Software
Growth: Openings in past year, 100
Contact Paul Eurek, Chief Exexcutive Officer; 770-795-3300; Fax: 770-795-3333; E-mail: inform@compriscorp.com

Computone Corp.
1100 Northmeadow Pkwy.
Roswell, GA 30076
http://www.computone.com
Founded: 1984
Total Employees: 80
Annual Sales: $12.898 million
Industries: Computer Hardware, Computer Software
Growth: Openings in past year, 25
Contact Gregg Alba, VP of Finance; 770-475-2725; Fax: 770-664-1510; E-mail: sales@computone.com

Coopers & Lybrand, LLP, SysteCon Division
400 Northridge Rd., Suite 1000
Atlanta, GA 30350
http://www.systecon-clc.com
Founded: 1977

Total Employees: 110
Industry: Computer Hardware
Growth: Openings in past year, 60
Contact T. Ron Gable, Managing Partner; 770-643-5100; Fax: 770-643-5200

Display Solutions, Inc.
6301 Best Friend Rd.
Norcross, GA 30071
http://www.displaysolutionsinc.com
Founded: 1983
Total Employees: 125
Annual Sales: $16 million
Industries: Computer Software, Photonics, Transportation
Growth: Openings in past year, 40
Contact Ronald Turcotte, Chief Executive Officer; 770-662-5400; Fax: 770-263-8353; E-mail: display@america.net

Equifax, Inc., FBS Software Division
1150 Lake Hearn Dr. Northeast, Suite 500
Atlanta, GA 30342
Founded: 1899
Total Employees: 120
Annual Sales: $15 million
Industry: Computer Software
Growth: Openings in past year, 35
Contact Gary Shirley, President; 404-847-9988; Fax: 404-847-7606

Gate City Equipment Co., Inc.
2000 Northfield Ct.
Roswell, GA 30076
Founded: 1976
Total Employees: 40
Annual Sales: $5.4 million
Industry: Test and Measurement
Growth: Openings in past year, 30

Contact John Matthews, Electronics Manager; 770-475-1900; Fax: 770-475-1717

Harbinger Corp.
1055 Lenox Park Blvd.
Atlanta, GA 30319
http://www.harbinger.com
Founded: 1983
Total Employees: 800
Annual Sales: $40 million
Industry: Computer Software
Growth: Openings in past year, 99
Contact Mike Lieb, Director of Human Resources; 404-841-4334; Fax: 404-841-4399; E-mail: sales@harbinger.com

Healthdyne Technologies, Inc.
1255 Kenne Stone Cir.
Marietta, GA 30066
Founded: 1979
Total Employees: 600
Annual Sales: $118.318 million
Industry: Medical
Growth: Openings in past year, 24
Contact Craig Reynolds, President/CEO; 770-499-1212; Fax: 770-499-0117

Hepaco, Inc.
4745 Hugh Howell Rd.
Tucker, GA 30084
Founded: 1986
Total Employees: 200
Annual Sales: $10. million
Industry: Environmental
Growth: Openings in past year, 40
Contact Neville Anderson, Vice President; 770-934-1180; Fax: 770-621-0238

Heraeus Amersil, Inc.
3473 Satellite Blvd., Suite 300
Duluth, GA 30136

http://www.heraeus-amersil.com
Founded: 1916
Total Employees: 716
Annual Sales: $130 million
Industries: Advanced Materials, Photonics
Growth: Openings in past year, 105
Contact Dr. Peter Schultz, President; 770-623-6000; Fax: 770-623-5640

HomeCom Communications, Inc.
3535 Piedmont Rd., Suite 100
Atlanta, GA 30305
http://www.homecom.com
Founded: 1994
Total Employees: 80
Annual Sales: $2.299 million
Industries: Holding Companies, Telecommunications
Growth: Openings in past year, 55
Contact Harvey Sax, Founder/President/CEO; 404-237-4646; Fax: 404-237-3060; E-mail: sales@homecom.com

Immucor, Inc.
3130 Gateway Dr.
PO Box 5625
Norcross, GA 30091
http://www.immucor.com
Founded: 1982
Total Employees: 229
Annual Sales: $35.654 million
Industries: Chemicals, Medical
Growth: Openings in past year, 40
Contact Edward L. Gallup, President/CEO/COB; 770-441-2051; Fax: 770-441-3807; E-mail: immucor@immucor.com

IMNET Systems, Inc.
3015 Windward Plaza
Alpharetta, GA 30005
http://www.imnet.com

Founded: 1986
Total Employees: 350
Annual Sales: $50.92 million
Industries: Computer Software, Holding Companies
Growth: Openings in past year, 35
Contact Kenneth Rardin, COB/CEO; 770-521-5600; Fax: 770-521-5650

Information America, Inc.
245 Peachtree Center Ave., Suite 1400
Atlanta, GA 30308
http://www.infoam.com
Founded: 1982
Total Employees: 230
Annual Sales: $47 million
Industry: Computer Hardware
Growth: Openings in past year, 55
Contact Ed Porter, VP of Human Resources; 404-479-3500; Fax: 404-479-3300

Input Services International, Inc.
1090 North Chase Pkwy., Suite 300
Marietta, GA 30067
Founded: 1971
Total Employees: 600
Annual Sales: $10 million
Industry: Computer Hardware
Growth: Openings in past year, 299
Contact Albert H. Wiggins, Jr., President/COB; 770-952-8094; Fax: 770-784-1223

InterAG Technologies, Inc.
300 Grimes Bridge Rd.
Roswell, GA 30075
Founded: 1992
Total Employees: 600
Industries: Holding Companies, Test and Measurement
Growth: Openings in past year, 149

Contact Charles Stamp, Jr., President/CEO; 770-552-6522; Fax: 770-552-6577

Internet Security Systems, Inc.
41 Perimeter Ctr. East, Suite 660
Atlanta, GA 30346
http://www.iss.net
Founded: 1994
Total Employees: 60
Annual Sales: $5.5 million
Industry: Computer Software
Growth: Openings in past year, 54
Contact Christopher Klaus, CEO/Founder; 770-395-0150; Fax: 770-395-1972; E-mail: info@iss.net

LHS Group, Inc.
6 Concourse Pkwy., Suite 2700
Atlanta, GA 30328
http://www.lhsgroup.com
Founded: 1990
Total Employees: 523
Annual Sales: $56.864 million
Industries: Computer Hardware, Computer Software
Growth: Openings in past year, 65
Contact Vance Shaffer, VP of Human Resources; 770-280-3100; Fax: 770-280-3199; E-mail: info@lhsgroup.com

Logility, Inc.
470 East Paces Ferry Rd.
Atlanta, GA 30305
http://www.logility.com
Founded: 1997
Total Employees: 185
Annual Sales: $21.8 million
Industry: Computer Software
Growth: Openings in past year, 45

Contact Kevvon Burdette,
Human Resource
Manager; 404-261-9777;
Fax: 404-238-8450;
E-mail: ask@logility.com

**MindSpring Enterprises,
Inc.**
1430 West Peachtree St.
Northwest, Suite 400
Atlanta, GA 30309
http://www.mindspring.com
Founded: 1994
Total Employees: 317
Annual Sales: $18 million
Industry:
Telecommunications
Growth: Openings in past
year, 42
Contact Charles Brewer,
COB/CEO; 404-815-
0082; Fax: 404-815-
8805; E-mail: info@
mindspring.com

Optio Software, Inc.
4800 River Green Pkwy.
Duluth, GA 30096
http://www.optiosoftware.
com
Founded: 1981
Total Employees: 105
Annual Sales: $13 million
Industry: Computer
Software
Growth: Openings in past
year, 25
Contact Ms. Erin Davis,
Personnel Manager; 770-
283-8500; Fax: 770-283-
8699; E-mail: info@
optisoftware.com

Patterson Pump Co.
PO Box 790
Toccoa, GA 30577
Founded: 1874
Total Employees: 350
Annual Sales: $47 million
Industries: Factory
Automation,
Subassemblies and
Components, Test and
Measurement
Growth: Openings in past
year, 29

Contact Charles Craig,
Human Resources
Manager; 706-886-2101;
Fax: 706-886-0023

PCC Airfoils, Inc.
1400 Pope Dr.
Douglas, GA 31533
Founded: 1985
Total Employees: 550
Annual Sales: $72 million
Industry: Transportation
Growth: Openings in past
year, 100
Contact Ron Swymer,
Human Resources
Manager; 912-384-6633;
Fax: 912-384-0100

Peachtree Software, Inc.
1505 Pavilion Pl.
Norcross, GA 30093
http://www.peachtree.com
Founded: 1985
Total Employees: 300
Annual Sales: $38 million
Industry: Computer
Software
Growth: Openings in past
year, 100
Contact Ron Verni,
President; 770-724-4000;
Fax: 770-564-5888;
E-mail: sales@peachtree.
com

Piedmont Olsen Hensly
3200 Professional Pkwy.,
Suite 200
Atlanta, GA 30339
Founded: 1944
Total Employees: 475
Industries: Environmental,
Manufacturing Equipment
Growth: Openings in past
year, 40
Contact John Boyette,
President/COB; 770-952-
8861; Fax: 770-984-1160

**Premiere Technologies,
Inc.**
3399 Peachtree Rd.
Northeast, Lennox Bldg.,
#400
Atlanta, GA 30326
http://www.premtek.com
Founded: 1991
Total Employees: 170
Annual Sales: $52.1
million
Industries: Holding
Companies,
Telecommunications
Growth: Openings in past
year, 30
Contact Boland T. Jones,
COB/CEO/President;
404-262-8400; Fax: 404-
262-8540

Radiant Systems, Inc.
1000 Alderman Dr., Suite
A
Alpharetta, GA 30202
http://www.radiantsystems.
com
Founded: 1984
Total Employees: 250
Annual Sales: $35 million
Industry: Computer
Software
Growth: Openings in past
year, 110
Contact Eric Hinkle,
President; 770-772-3000;
Fax: 770-772-3052

Ross Systems, Inc.
Two Concourse Pkwy.,
Suite 800
Atlanta, GA 30328
http://www.rossinc.com
Founded: 1972
Total Employees: 500
Annual Sales: $78.773
million
Industries: Computer
Software, Holding
Companies
Growth: Openings in past
year, 50
Contact Stanley
Stoudenmire,
Secretary/VP of Finance

& Administration; 770-351-9600; Fax: 770-351-0036

Schlumberger Industries, Meter Communications Systems Division
5400 Metric Pl., Bldg. 300
Norcross, GA 30092
Founded: 1985
Total Employees: 150
Industries: Energy, Test and Measurement
Growth: Openings in past year, 50
Contact Alan Bojarski, Vice President/General Manager; 770-446-1991; Fax: 770-263-8104; E-mail: maps@slb.com

SecureIT, Inc.
3770-1 Data Dr.
Norcross, GA 30092
http://www.secure-it.net
Founded: 1996
Total Employees: 30
Annual Sales: $5.1 million
Industries: Computer Software, Telecommunications
Growth: Openings in past year, 26
Contact Jay Chaudhry, President/CEO; 770-248-1005; Fax: 770-248-1006; E-mail: info@secure-it.net

Security First Technologies
3390 Peachtree Rd. Northeast, Suite 1700
Atlanta, GA 30326
http://www.s-1.com
Founded: 1987
Total Employees: 180
Annual Sales: $23 million
Industries: Computer Software, Telecommunications
Growth: Openings in past year, 55
Contact Michael McChesney, Chief Executive Officer; 404-812-6200; Fax: 404-812-6616; E-mail: info@s-1.com

Software Technical Services, Inc.
4180 Phil Niekro Pkwy.
Norcross, GA 30093
Founded: 1900
Total Employees: 375
Annual Sales: $48 million
Industries: Computer Hardware, Computer Software
Growth: Openings in past year, 94
Contact Ms. LaQuenta Jacobs, Human Resources Manager; 770-449-8966; Fax: 770-923-3998

SpectRx, Inc.
6025-A Unity Dr.
Norcross, GA 30071
http://www.spectrx.com
Founded: 1992
Total Employees: 60
Industry: Medical
Growth: Openings in past year, 40
Contact Mark A. Samuels, President/CEO; 770-242-8723; Fax: 770-242-8723

Sun Data, Inc.
One Sun Ct.
PO Box 926020
Norcross, GA 30092
http://www.sundata.com
Founded: 1976
Total Employees: 240
Annual Sales: $200 million
Industry: Computer Hardware
Growth: Openings in past year, 40
Contact Eric Prockow, COB/CEO; 770-449-6116; Fax: 770-448-7726

Support Technologies, Inc.
Four Concourse Pkwy.
Atlanta, GA 30328
http://www.sti-help.com
Founded: 1995
Total Employees: 100

Annual Sales: $17 million
Industry: Holding Companies
Growth: Openings in past year, 80
Contact Ms. Harriet McCormick, VP of Human Resources; 770-280-2630; Fax: 770-280-2631; E-mail: info@sti-help.com

SynQuest, Inc.
3500 Parkway Ln., Suite 555
Norcross, GA 30092
http://www.synquest.com
Founded: 1986
Total Employees: 150
Annual Sales: $19 million
Industries: Computer Hardware, Computer Software
Growth: Openings in past year, 30
Contact Joe Trino, President; 770-447-8667; Fax: 770-447-4995; E-mail: info@synquest.com

TSW International, Inc.
3301 Windy Ridge Pkwy.
Atlanta, GA 30339
http://www.tswi.com
Founded: 1976
Total Employees: 450
Annual Sales: $70 million
Industry: Computer Software
Growth: Openings in past year, 49
Contact Christopher R. Lane, President/CEO; 770-952-8444; Fax: 770-955-2977

Unicomp, Inc.
1850 Parkway Pl., Suite 925
Marietta, GA 30067
http://www.unicomp.com/main.htm
Founded: 1985
Total Employees: 360
Annual Sales: $25.151 million

Industries: Computer Hardware, Computer Software, Holding Companies
Growth: Openings in past year, 162
Contact Stephen A. Hafer, COB/President/CEO; 770-424-3684; Fax: 770-424-5558

United States Filter Corp., Davis Fabrication Division
1828 Metcalf Ave.
Thomasville, GA 31792
http://www.usfilter.com
Founded: 1977
Total Employees: 175
Industries: Environmental, Manufacturing Equipment
Growth: Openings in past year, 25
Contact Wandell Hobbs, Contract Officer; 912-226-5733; Fax: 912-228-0526; E-mail: herndojh@usfilter.com

Universal Tax Systems, Inc.
6 Mathis Dr. Northwest
Rome, GA 30165
http://www.universalsystems.com
Founded: 1983
Total Employees: 150
Annual Sales: $19 million
Industry: Computer Software
Growth: Openings in past year, 30
Contact Steve Safigan, President; 706-232-7757; Fax: 706-236-9168; E-mail: info@universalsystems.com

World Access, Inc.
945 East Paces Ferry Rd., Suite 2240
Atlanta, GA 30326
Founded: 1988
Total Employees: 265
Annual Sales: $51 million

Industries: Holding Companies, Manufacturing Equipment, Subassemblies and Components, Telecommunications
Growth: Openings in past year, 29
Contact Steven A. Odom, COB/CEO; 404-231-2025; Fax: 404-232-2598

Hawaii

Cyanotech Corporation
73-4460 Queen Kaahumanu, Suite 102
Kailua Kona, HI 96745
http://www.cyanotech.com
Founded: 1983
Total Employees: 92
Annual Sales: $11.4 million
Industries: Biotechnology, Chemicals, Holding Companies, Pharmaceuticals
Growth: Openings in past year, 37
Contact Ronald P. Scott, Exec. VP of Finance and Administration; 808-326-1353; Fax: 808-329-3597; E-mail: info@cyanotech.com

Decision Research Corp.
1600 Kapiolani Blvd., Suite 730
Honolulu, HI 96814
Founded: 1972
Total Employees: 60
Annual Sales: $7.7 million
Industry: Computer Software
Growth: Openings in past year, 30
Contact Steve Johnson, Vice President; 808-949-8316; Fax: 808-942-4298

Illinois

AccuMed International, Inc.
900 North Franklin St., Suite 401
Chicago, IL 60610
http://www.accumed.com
Founded: 1988
Total Employees: 100
Annual Sales: $6 million
Industry: Holding Companies
Growth: Openings in past year, 25
Contact Peter Gombrich, Chief Executive Officer; 312-642-9200; Fax: 312-642-8684

Allied Products Corp., Verson Division
1355 East 93rd St.
Chicago, IL 60619
http://www.verson.com
Founded: 1920
Total Employees: 700
Annual Sales: $100 million
Industries: Factory Automation, Manufacturing Equipment
Growth: Openings in past year, 46
Contact John Perish, VP of Human Resources; 773-933-8200; Fax: 773-933-8225

Alloyd Co., Inc.
1401 Pleasant St.
De Kalb, IL 60115
http://www.alloyd.com
Founded: 1961
Total Employees: 500
Annual Sales: $62 million
Industries: Factory Automation, Manufacturing Equipment
Growth: Openings in past year, 50
Contact Martin Gabbert, Director of Human Resources; 815-756-8451; Fax: 815-756-5187; E-mail: alloyd@alloyd.com

American Information Systems, Inc.
161 North Clark St., Suite 1350
Chicago, IL 60601
http://www.ais.net
Founded: 1992
Total Employees: 50
Annual Sales: $5 million
Industries: Computer Software, Telecommunications
Growth: Openings in past year, 32
Contact P.J. Alfreid, Interim Human Resources Manager; 312-255-8500; Fax: 312-255-8501; E-mail: info@ais.net

Aquion Partners, Rainsoft Division
2080 Lunt Ave.
Elk Grove Village, IL 60007
http://www.aquion.com
Founded: 1953
Total Employees: 200
Annual Sales: $44 million
Industry: Environmental
Growth: Openings in past year, 75
Contact Dave Cole, Chief Executive Officer; 847-437-9400; Fax: 847-437-1594; E-mail: custserv@aquion.com

Atlas Electric Devices Co.
4114 North Ravenswood Ave.
Chicago, IL 60613
Founded: 1948
Total Employees: 275
Annual Sales: $37 million
Industries: Advanced Materials, Factory Automation, Holding Companies, Test and Measurement
Growth: Openings in past year, 50

Contact Ms. Charlene Engle, Personnel Manager; 773-327-4520; Fax: 773-327-5787

Berg Chilling Systems, Inc.
240 East Lake St.
Addison, IL 60101
http://www.berg-group.com
Founded: 1969
Total Employees: 104
Annual Sales: $20 million
Industries: Environmental, Factory Automation, Subassemblies and Components
Growth: Openings in past year, 29
Contact Lorne Berggren, President; 630-530-4644; Fax: 630-530-8988; E-mail: sales@berg-group.com

Bimba Manufacturing Co.
PO Box 68
Monee, IL 60449
http://www.bimba.com
Founded: 1967
Total Employees: 550
Annual Sales: $74 million
Industry: Subassemblies and Components
Growth: Openings in past year, 50
Contact Ms. Mary Fote, VP of Human Resources; 708-534-8544; Fax: 708-534-5767; E-mail: support@bimba.com

Bretford Manufacturing, Inc.
11000 Seymour Ave.
Franklin Park, IL 60131
http://www.bretford.com
Founded: 1948
Total Employees: 600
Industry: Telecommunications
Growth: Openings in past year, 100
Contact Ed Petrick, President; 847-678-2545; Fax: 800-343-1779

Clear Communications Corp.
100 Tri-State International
Lincolnshire, IL 60069
http://www.clear.com
Founded: 1988
Total Employees: 100
Annual Sales: $12 million
Industry: Computer Software
Growth: Openings in past year, 55
Contact Robert Copithorne, CEO/President; 847-317-2500; Fax: 847-317-2525

Climco Coils Co.
400 Oakwood Dr.
Morrison, IL 61270
Founded: 1950
Total Employees: 165
Industries: Energy, Subassemblies and Components
Growth: Openings in past year, 24
Contact Scott Selmon, General Manager; 815-772-2107; Fax: 815-772-2195

Compaction America, Inc.
2000 Kentville Rd.
Kewanee, IL 61443
Founded: 1880
Total Employees: 277
Industry: Environmental
Growth: Openings in past year, 26
Contact John Blake, Human Resources Manager; 309-853-3571; Fax: 309-852-0350

Computhink, Inc.
860 Parkview Blvd.
Lombard, IL 60148
http://www.computhink.com
Founded: 1994
Total Employees: 85

Annual Sales: $15 million
Industries: Computer Hardware, Computer Software
Growth: Openings in past year, 45
Contact K.J. Semikian, President; 630-705-9050; Fax: 630-705-9065; E-mail: cthinkinc@aol.com

Corcom, Inc.
844 East Rockland Rd.
Libertyville, IL 60048
http://www.cor.com
Founded: 1955
Total Employees: 710
Annual Sales: $33.166 million
Industry: Subassemblies and Components
Growth: Openings in past year, 21
Contact Ms. Sherril Bishop, VP of Human Resources; 847-680-7400; Fax: 847-680-8169; E-mail: info@cor.com

Cyborg Systems, Inc.
2 North Riverside Plaza
Chicago, IL 60606
http://www.cyborg.com
Founded: 1974
Total Employees: 460
Annual Sales: $49.9 million
Industry: Computer Software
Growth: Openings in past year, 98
Contact Ms. Patricia Christenson, Human Resources Director; 312-454-1865; Fax: 312-930-1033; E-mail: usa-info@cyborg.com

Daniel Woodhead Co.
3411 Woodhead Dr.
Northbrook, IL 60062
http://www.daniel/woodhead.com
Founded: 1922
Total Employees: 642

Annual Sales: $86 million
Industries: Energy, Factory Automation, Subassemblies and Components
Growth: Openings in past year, 141
Contact Will Barber, Manager of Human Resources; 847-272-7990; Fax: 847-272-8133; E-mail: dwinfo@intaraccess.com

Deublin Co.
2050 Norman Dr.
Waukegan, IL 60085
http://www.deublin.com
Founded: 1945
Total Employees: 420
Annual Sales: $56 million
Industries: Factory Automation, Subassemblies and Components
Growth: Openings in past year, 28
Contact Don Deubler, COB/CEO; 847-689-8600; Fax: 847-689-8690

DICKEY-john Corp.
5200 Dickey John Rd.
PO Box 10
Auburn, IL 62615
Founded: 1965
Total Employees: 450
Annual Sales: $68 million
Industries: Factory Automation, Test and Measurement, Transportation
Growth: Openings in past year, 49
Contact Ms. Jean Wheeler, Director of Human Resources; 217-438-3371; Fax: 217-438-6012

DSM Desotech Inc.
1122 Saint Charles St.
Elgin, IL 60120
http://www.dsmna.com
Founded: 1990
Total Employees: 130
Annual Sales: $24 million

Industry: Advanced Materials
Growth: Openings in past year, 50
Contact Dan Zacharski, Director of Human Resources; 847-697-0400; Fax: 847-468-7785

Electrodynamics, Inc.
1200 Hicks Rd.
Rolling Meadows, IL 60008
Founded: 1960
Total Employees: 250
Industries: Defense, Photonics, Test and Measurement, Transportation
Growth: Openings in past year, 50
Contact Ms. Diane Dichter, Director of Personnel; 847-259-0740; Fax: 847-255-3827

Enterprise Systems, Inc.
1400 South Wolf Rd., Suite 500
Wheeling, IL 60090
http://www.esicorp.com
Founded: 1981
Total Employees: 500
Annual Sales: $52.3 million
Industry: Computer Software
Growth: Openings in past year, 80
Contact Robert Rook, VP of Human Resources; 847-537-4800; Fax: 847-537-4866; E-mail: info@esicorp.com

Everpure, Inc.
660 Blackhawk Dr.
Westmont, IL 60559
http://www.everpure.com
Founded: 1933
Total Employees: 300
Annual Sales: $36 million
Industry: Environmental
Growth: Openings in past year, 100
Contact Ms. Norene Stimburis, Human

Resources Manager; 630-654-4000; Fax: 630-654-1115; E-mail: info@everepure.com

Fenner Fluid Power
5885 11th St.
Rockford, IL 61109
Founded: 1964
Total Employees: 350
Annual Sales: $47 million
Industry: Subassemblies and Components
Growth: Openings in past year, 75
Contact Ms. Candace Carlson, Personnel Manager; 815-874-5560; Fax: 815-874-7053

Greenbrier & Russel, Inc.
1450 East American Ln., Suite 1700
Schaumburg, IL 60173
http://www.gr.com
Founded: 1984
Total Employees: 500
Industry: Computer Software
Growth: Openings in past year, 50
Contact Ms. Maureen McLean, Human Resources Manager; 847-706-4000; Fax: 847-706-4020; E-mail: info@gr.com

Hanson Engineers, Inc.
1525 South 6th St.
Springfield, IL 62703
http://www.hansonengineers.com
Founded: 1954
Total Employees: 300
Annual Sales: $22 million
Industries: Advanced Materials, Environmental, Manufacturing Equipment
Growth: Openings in past year, 75
Contact Eugene R. Wilkinson, President/CEO/COB; 217-788-2450; Fax: 217-788-

2503; E-mail: marketing@hansonengineers.com

Harza Engineering Co.
Sears Tower, 233 South Wacker Dr.
Chicago, IL 60606
http://www.harza.com
Founded: 1920
Total Employees: 875
Industry: Environmental
Growth: Openings in past year, 58
Contact Ms. Jennifer Kohl, Human Resources Manager; 312-831-3000; Fax: 312-831-3999; E-mail: info@harza.com

Homaco, Inc.
1875 West Fullerton Ave.
Chicago, IL 60614
Founded: 1964
Total Employees: 165
Industries: Subassemblies and Components, Telecommunications
Growth: Openings in past year, 40
Contact Bruce D. Holcomb, President; 773-384-5575; Fax: 773-384-6080

Ingersoll Cutting Tool Co.
505 Fulton Ave.
Rockford, IL 61103
Founded: 1887
Total Employees: 500
Annual Sales: $76 million
Industry: Factory Automation
Growth: Openings in past year, 24
Contact Chuck Schultz, Manager of Human Resources; 815-987-6600; Fax: 815-987-6968

InterAccess Co.
168 North Clinton St., 2nd Floor
Chicago, IL 60661
http://www.interaccess.com
Founded: 1993
Total Employees: 60
Industry: Telecommunications
Growth: Openings in past year, 30
Contact Tom Simonds, President; 312-496-4400; Fax: 312-496-4499; E-mail: info@interaccess.com

InterPro, Inc.
10600 West Higgins Rd., Suite 710
Rosemont, IL 60018
http://www.interproinc.com
Founded: 1988
Total Employees: 80
Annual Sales: $15 million
Industries: Computer Software, Holding Companies
Growth: Openings in past year, 35
Contact Michael Hanna, President; 847-299-9090; Fax: 847-299-9095; E-mail: interpro@interproinc.com

James Electronics, Inc.
4050 North Rockwell St.
Chicago, IL 60618
Founded: 1948
Total Employees: 525
Industry: Subassemblies and Components
Growth: Openings in past year, 199
Contact Vincent Kennedy, President; 773-463-6500; Fax: 773-463-1504

Karmak, Inc.
One Karmak Plaza
Carlinville, IL 62626
http://www.karmak.com

Founded: 1981
Total Employees: 110
Industry: Computer Software
Growth: Openings in past year, 25
Contact J. Richard Schien, President; 217-854-4721; Fax: 217-854-9513; E-mail: service@karmak.com

Lakeview Technology, Inc.
2301 West 22nd St., Suite 206
Oak Brook, IL 60521
http://www.lakeviewtech.com
Founded: 1990
Total Employees: 100
Annual Sales: $12 million
Industry: Computer Software
Growth: Openings in past year, 30
Contact William Merchantz, President; 630-573-0440; Fax: 630-573-0015

Levi, Ray and Shoup, Inc.
2401 West Monroe St.
Springfield, IL 62704
http://www.lrs.com
Founded: 1979
Total Employees: 388
Annual Sales: $50 million
Industries: Computer Hardware, Computer Software
Growth: Openings in past year, 57
Contact Ms. Jenny Thieman, Human Resources Specialist; 217-793-3800; Fax: 217-787-3286

Lindgren RF Enclosures, Inc.
400 High Grove Blvd.
Glendale Heights, IL 60139
Founded: 1952
Total Employees: 200

Annual Sales: $30 million
Industries: Factory Automation, Holding Companies
Growth: Openings in past year, 40
Contact Ms. Joyce Curran, Treasurer; 630-307-7200; Fax: 630-307-7571; E-mail: lrfe@interserv.com

MAGNUM Technologies, Inc.
2017 West Hwy. 50
Fairview Heights, IL 62208
http://www.magnumtech.com
Founded: 1989
Total Employees: 140
Annual Sales: $8.6 million
Industries: Computer Hardware, Computer Software, Manufacturing Equipment
Growth: Openings in past year, 30
Contact Paul J. Galeski, PE, President; 618-628-3000; Fax: 618-628-3200; E-mail: info@magnumtech.com

Marsh Co.
707 East B St.
Belleville, IL 62221
http://www.marshco.com
Founded: 1920
Total Employees: 372
Annual Sales: $59 million
Industries: Chemicals, Computer Hardware, Factory Automation, Holding Companies
Growth: Openings in past year, 28
Contact John A. Marsh, COB/CEO; 618-234-1122; Fax: 618-234-1529

Material Sciences Corp.
2200 East Pratt Blvd.
Elk Grove Village, IL 60007
Founded: 1971
Total Employees: 988
Annual Sales: $278 million

Industry: Holding Companies
Growth: Openings in past year, 106
Contact Frank Lazowski, Jr., VP of Human Resources; 847 439 8270; Fax: 847-439-0737

Metamor Technologies, Ltd.
1 North Franklin St., Suite 1500
Chicago, IL 60606
http://www.metamor.com
Founded: 1985
Total Employees: 255
Industries: Computer Hardware, Computer Software
Growth: Openings in past year, 69
Contact Ms. Marcie Newman, Human Resources Manager; 312-251-2000; Fax: 312-251-2999

Mid-West Automation Systems, Inc.
1400 Busch Pkwy.
Buffalo Grove, IL 60089
Founded: 1965
Total Employees: 500
Annual Sales: $78 million
Industry: Factory Automation
Growth: Openings in past year, 73
Contact Dennis Schultz, Personnel Manager; 847-541-3570; Fax: 847-541-8562

Mitsubishi Electric Automation, Inc.
500 Corporate Woods Pkwy.
Vernon Hills, IL 60056
Founded: 1997
Total Employees: 380
Industry: Test and Measurement
Growth: Openings in past year, 74

Contact Charles Baum, Director of Administration; 847-478-2100; Fax: 847-478-0328

Nanophase Technologies Corporation
453 Commerce St.
Burr Ridge, IL 60521
http://www.nanophase.com
Founded: 1989
Total Employees: 75
Industries: Advanced Materials, Chemicals, Photonics
Growth: Openings in past year, 45
Contact Dennis W. Nowak, Chief Financial Officer; 630-323-1200; Fax: 630-323-1221; E-mail: info@nanophase.com

Nycomed Amersham, Inc.
2636 South Clearbrook Dr.
Arlington Heights, IL 60005
Founded: 1968
Total Employees: 340
Industries: Chemicals, Medical, Photonics
Growth: Openings in past year, 29
Contact James Reller, VP of Human Resources; 847-593-6300; Fax: 847-593-8075

Omron Electronics, Inc., Factory Automation Systems Division
One East Commerce Dr.
Schaumburg, IL 60173
http://www.oei.omron.com
Founded: 1984
Total Employees: 387
Industries: Factory Automation, Subassemblies and Components, Test and Measurement
Growth: Openings in past year, 87
Contact Shingo Akechi, President; 847-843-7900;

Fax: 847-843-7787; E-mail: omroninfo@oei.omron.com

Otto Engineering, Inc.
2 East Main St.
Carpentersville, IL 60110
http://www.ottoeng.com
Founded: 1962
Total Employees: 300
Annual Sales: $40 million
Industry: Holding Companies
Growth: Openings in past year, 35
Contact Jack Roeser, President; 847-428-7171; Fax: 847-428-1956; E-mail: sales@ottoeng.com

Parker Hannifin Corp., Cylinder Division
500 South Wolf Rd.
Des Plaines, IL 60016
Founded: 1938
Total Employees: 995
Industries: Factory Automation, Subassemblies and Components
Growth: Openings in past year, 66
Contact Louis Ford, Personnel Manager; 847-298-2400; Fax: 847-294-2640

Peoria Disposal Co. and Affiliates
4700 North Sterling Ave.
Peoria, IL 61615
Founded: 1965
Total Employees: 460
Industry: Environmental
Growth: Openings in past year, 160
Contact Royal J. Coulter, President/CEO; 309-688-0760; Fax: 309-688-0881

Plymouth Tube Co.
PO Box 768
Warrenville, IL 60555

http://www.plymouth.com
Founded: 1925
Total Employees: 975
Annual Sales: $130 million
Industries: Subassemblies and Components, Transportation
Growth: Openings in past year, 20
Contact Donald Van Pelt, Jr., President; 630-393-3550; Fax: 630-393-3551; E-mail: sales@plymouth.com

Portec, Inc.
100 Field Dr., Suite 120
Lake Forest, IL 60045
Founded: 1928
Total Employees: 669
Annual Sales: $97.338 million
Industry: Holding Companies
Growth: Openings in past year, 32
Contact Ms. Pat Riccio, Manager of Human Resources; 847-735-2800; Fax: 847-735-2828

Quest International Flavors & Food Ingredients
5115 Sedge Blvd.
Hoffman Estates, IL 60192
Founded: 1905
Total Employees: 150
Annual Sales: $39 million
Industries: Advanced Materials, Biotechnology, Chemicals
Growth: Openings in past year, 25
Contact Joe Dunne, President; 847-645-7000; Fax: 847-645-7070

Reis Machines, Inc.
1320 Holmes Rd.
Elgin, IL 60123
Founded: 1958
Total Employees: 600
Industry: Factory Automation

Growth: Openings in past year, 200
Contact Walter Reis, President/CEO; 847-741-9500; Fax: 847-888-2762

Rexnord Corp., Rex Bearing Operation
2400 Curtiss St.
Downers Grove, IL 60515
http://www.rexnord.com
Founded: 1924
Total Employees: 450
Annual Sales: $60 million
Industry: Subassemblies and Components
Growth: Openings in past year, 49
Contact Arthur Denklau, Personnel Manager; 630-969-1770; Fax: 630-969-8827

Rexroth Corp., Indramat Division
5150 Prairie Stone Pkwy.
Hoffman Estates, IL 60192
Founded: 1979
Total Employees: 225
Annual Sales: $75 million
Industries: Factory Automation, Subassemblies and Components, Test and Measurement
Growth: Openings in past year, 45
Contact Ms. Ronna Greene, Human Resources Manager; 847-645-3600; Fax: 847-645-6201

Roesch, Inc.
100 North 24th St.
PO Box 328
Belleville, IL 62222
http://www.thomasregister.com/roeschinc
Founded: 1916
Total Employees: 150
Industries: Energy, Manufacturing Equipment
Growth: Openings in past year, 40
Contact W. Robert Voges, President; 618-233-2760;

Fax: 618-233-1186;
E-mail: sales@roeschinc.com

Sage Products, Inc.
815 Tek Dr.
Crystal Lake, IL 60014
Founded: 1971
Total Employees: 750
Annual Sales: $91 million
Industries: Environmental, Medical
Growth: Openings in past year, 50
Contact Vincent Foglia, President; 815-455-4700; Fax: 815-455-5599

SEI Information Technologies
212 East Ohio, Suite 200
Chicago, IL 60611
http://www.sei-it.com
Founded: 1970
Total Employees: 435
Industries: Computer Hardware, Computer Software
Growth: Openings in past year, 33
Contact Russell Shields, Owner; 312-440-8300; Fax: 312-440-8373

SERFILCO, Ltd.
1777 Shermer Rd.
Northbrook, IL 60062
http://www.serfilco.com
Founded: 1961
Total Employees: 250
Annual Sales: $23 million
Industry: Holding Companies
Growth: Openings in past year, 60
Contact James Ringel, Human Resources; 847-559-1777; Fax: 847-559-1995; E-mail: sales@serfilco.com

SPSS, Inc.
444 North Michigan Ave., Suite 3000
Chicago, IL 60611
http://www.spss.com
Founded: 1975
Total Employees: 535
Annual Sales: $83.989 million
Industry: Computer Software
Growth: Openings in past year, 82
Contact Jack Noonan, President/CEO; 312-329-2400; Fax: 800-841-0064; E-mail: sales@spss.com

Spyglass, Inc.
1240 East Diehl Rd., 4th Floor
Naperville, IL 60563
http://www.spyglass.com
Founded: 1990
Total Employees: 200
Annual Sales: $21.2 million
Industries: Computer Software, Holding Companies
Growth: Openings in past year, 95
Contact Lee Nelson, VP of Human Resources; 630-505-1010; Fax: 630-505-4944

Terasys, Inc.
1771 West Diehl Rd., Suite 320
Naperville, IL 60563
http://www.terasys.com
Founded: 1990
Total Employees: 100
Annual Sales: $20 million
Industries: Computer Hardware, Computer Software, Telecommunications
Growth: Openings in past year, 50
Contact Greg Sutton, President; 630-961-9100; Fax: 630-961-9122; E-mail: info@terasys.com

Total Control Products, Inc.
2001 North Janice Ave.
Melrose Park, IL 60160
http://www.total-control.com
Founded: 1982
Total Employees: 210
Annual Sales: $40.821 million
Industries: Computer Hardware, Manufacturing Equipment, Photonics, Subassemblies and Components, Test and Measurement
Growth: Openings in past year, 60
Contact Ms. Nancy Doherty, Human Resources Administrator; 708-345-5500; Fax: 708-345-5670

Tricon Industries, Inc.
1600 Eisenhower Ln.
Lisle, IL 60532
Founded: 1944
Total Employees: 500
Annual Sales: $67 million
Industry: Holding Companies
Growth: Openings in past year, 38
Contact Mal Wadland, Human Resources Manager; 630-964-2330; Fax: 630-964-5179

UIP Engineered Products
5501 West Grand Ave.
Chicago, IL 60639
http://www.uipe.com
Founded: 1910
Total Employees: 48
Industries: Energy, Factory Automation, Subassemblies and Components
Growth: Openings in past year, 28
Contact Sam Amin, President; 773-237-6004; Fax: 773-237-5730; E-mail: rplescia@uipe.com

Unitech Systems, Inc.
1240 East Diehl Rd.
Naperville, IL 60563
http://www.unitechsys.com
Founded: 1982
Total Employees: 155
Annual Sales: $30 million
Industry: Computer Software
Growth: Openings in past year, 40
Contact Madhavan K. Nayar, President; 630-505-1800; Fax: 630-505-1812

United States Diamond Wheel Co.
101 Kendall Point Dr.
Oswego, IL 60543
Founded: 1947
Total Employees: 174
Annual Sales: $22 million
Industry: Factory Automation
Growth: Openings in past year, 99
Contact Peter Mertens, General Manager; 630-898-9000; Fax: 630-898-1796

Vasco Corp.
1919 South Highland Ave., Suite 118C
Lombard, IL 60148
http://www.vasco.com
Founded: 1985
Total Employees: 48
Annual Sales: $14 million
Industries: Computer Hardware, Computer Software, Test and Measurement
Growth: Openings in past year, 28
Contact Ms. Cindy Harris, Office Manager; 630-932-8844; Fax: 630-495-0279; E-mail: info@vasco.com

Velsicol Chemical Corp.
10400 West Higgins Rd., Suite 600
Rosemont, IL 60018
Founded: 1986
Total Employees: 750
Annual Sales: $185 million
Industries: Advanced Materials, Chemicals
Growth: Openings in past year, 50
Contact Ms. Donna Jennings, VP of HR and Communications; 847-298-9000; Fax: 847-298-9014

Viktron West Chicago
475 Industrial Dr.
West Chicago, IL 60185
Founded: 1986
Total Employees: 800
Annual Sales: $100 million
Industries: Holding Companies, Subassemblies and Components
Growth: Openings in past year, 99
Contact Ms. Carol Lewis, Human Resources and Credit Manager; 630-293-7300; Fax: 630-293-7176

Wilton Corp.
300 South Hicks Rd.
Palatine, IL 60067
http://www.wiltoncorp.com
Founded: 1928
Total Employees: 450
Annual Sales: $68 million
Industry: Holding Companies
Growth: Openings in past year, 99
Contact Alexander Vogl, COB/CEO; 847-934-6000; Fax: 847-934-6730

Indiana

Allomatic Products Co., Inc.
609 East Cheney St.
PO Box 267
Sullivan, IN 47882
http://www.allomatic.com
Founded: 1954
Total Employees: 170
Industry: Subassemblies and Components
Growth: Openings in past year, 30
Contact Bob Fink, Personnel Manager; 812-268-0322; Fax: 812-268-0417

Baker Hill Corp.
655 West Carmel Dr., Suite 100
Carmel, IN 46032
Founded: 1983
Total Employees: 53
Annual Sales: $6.8 million
Industry: Computer Software
Growth: Openings in past year, 27
Contact Ms. Karen A. Hill, Chief Executive Officer; 317-571-2000; Fax: 317-571-5125

Bioanalytical Systems, Inc.
2701 Kent Ave.
West Lafayette, IN 47906
http://www.bioanalytical.com
Founded: 1974
Total Employees: 170
Annual Sales: $23 million
Industries: Biotechnology, Holding Companies, Test and Measurement
Growth: Openings in past year, 25
Contact Ms. Lina Reeves-Kerner, VP of Human Resources; 765-463-4527; Fax: 765-497-1102; E-mail: bas@bioanalytical.com

Burge Electronics, Inc., RF Coaxial Division
2100 Early Wood Dr.
PO Box 547
Franklin, IN 46131
http://www.burgeelect.com/rfcoaxial
Founded: 1967
Total Employees: 200
Annual Sales: $26 million
Industry: Subassemblies and Components
Growth: Openings in past year, 45
Contact Jim Anderson, General Manager; 317-738-2800; Fax: 317-738-2858

Casting Technology Co.
1450 Musicland Dr.
Franklin, IN 46131
Founded: 1991
Total Employees: 260
Annual Sales: $49 million
Industries: Advanced Materials, Manufacturing Equipment
Growth: Openings in past year, 130
Contact John Garratt, President; 317-738-0282; Fax: 317-738-0262

CTS Corp., Microelectronics
1201 Cumberland Ave.
West Lafayette, IN 47906
http://www.ctscorp.com
Founded: 1964
Total Employees: 500
Annual Sales: $67 million
Industries: Subassemblies and Components, Telecommunications
Growth: Openings in past year, 148
Contact Ed Higgins, Human Resources Manager; 765-463-2565; Fax: 765-497-5399

EAS Technologies, Inc.
4345 Security Park Way
New Albany, IN 47150
http://www.eastech.com
Founded: 1985
Total Employees: 132
Annual Sales: $17 million
Industry: Computer Software
Growth: Openings in past year, 82
Contact Ms. Karen Kuchen, Manager of Human Resources; 812-941-9360; Fax: 812-941-9368

EMF Corp.
505 Pokagon Trail
PO Box 389
Angola, IN 46703
Founded: 1970
Total Employees: 250
Industry: Subassemblies and Components
Growth: Openings in past year, 50
Contact Richard N. Poe, President; 219-665-9541; Fax: 219-665-3040

Endress & Hauser, Inc.
PO Box 246
Greenwood, IN 46143
http://www.endress.com
Founded: 1970
Total Employees: 250
Industry: Test and Measurement
Growth: Openings in past year, 50
Contact Ms. Patty Harmon, Personnel Manager; 317-535-7138; Fax: 317-535-8498; E-mail: info@endress.com

Fiserv, Inc., Mortgage Product Division
1818 Commerce Dr.
South Bend, IN 46628
http://www.fiserv.com

Founded: 1972
Total Employees: 250
Annual Sales: $32 million
Industries: Computer Hardware, Computer Software
Growth: Openings in past year, 100
Contact Ms. Lora Bentley, Human Resources Manager; 219-282-3300; Fax 219-202-0000

General Devices Co., Inc.
1410 South Post Rd.
PO Box 39100
Indianapolis, IN 46239
http://www.gendevco.com
Founded: 1953
Total Employees: 450
Industries: Computer Hardware, Manufacturing Equipment
Growth: Openings in past year, 49
Contact Ms. Rita Stonestreet, Director of Personnel; 317-897-7000; Fax 317-898-2917

Industrial Dielectrics, Inc.
PO Box 357
Noblesville, IN 46060
http://www.idiplastic.com
Founded: 1966
Total Employees: 450
Annual Sales: $75 million
Industries: Advanced Materials, Manufacturing Equipment
Growth: Openings in past year, 99
Contact Jon Coleman, Personnel Manager; 317-773-1766; Fax: 317-773-3877; E-mail: plastics@iquest.com

Made2Manage Systems, Inc.
9002 Purdue Rd., Suite 200
Indianapolis, IN 46268
http://www.made2manage.com
Founded: 1986

Total Employees: 105
Annual Sales: $9.4 million
Industry: Computer Software
Growth: Openings in past year, 42
Contact David Wortman, President; 317-875-9750; Fax: 317-872-6454; E-mail: info@made2manage.com

Pierce Co., Inc.
201 North 8th St.
PO Box 2000
Upland, IN 46989
Founded: 1913
Total Employees: 200
Industries: Subassemblies and Components, Test and Measurement, Transportation
Growth: Openings in past year, 40
Contact S. Bowser, General Manager; 765-998-2712; Fax: 765-998-3348

Point Medical Corp.
871 East Summit St.
Crown Point, IN 46307
Founded: 1990
Total Employees: 130
Industry: Medical
Growth: Openings in past year, 60
Contact Rick Ferraro, President; 219-663-1775; Fax: 219-663-2877

POWERWAY, Inc.
6919 Hillsdale Ct.
Indianapolis, IN 46250
http://www.powerway.com
Founded: 1987
Total Employees: 90
Annual Sales: $11 million
Industry: Computer Software
Growth: Openings in past year, 45
Contact Kevin O'Callaghan, VP of Operations; 317-598-1760; Fax: 317-598-1740

SMC Pneumatics, Inc.
3011 North Franklin Rd.
Indianapolis, IN 46226
http://www.smcusa.com
Founded: 1972
Total Employees: 400
Annual Sales: $53 million
Industry: Subassemblies and Components
Growth: Openings in past year, 100
Contact Dave Robinson, General Manager; 317-899-4440; Fax: 317-899-3102

South Bend Lathe Corp.
400 West Sample St.
South Bend, IN 46601
Founded: 1906
Total Employees: 100
Annual Sales: $1.250 million
Industry: Factory Automation
Growth: Openings in past year, 25
Contact Norbert Toubes, President; 219-289-7771; Fax: 219-236-1210

Steel Parts Corp.
801 Berryman Rd.
Tipton, IN 46702
Founded: 1946
Total Employees: 382
Annual Sales: $50 million
Industries: Manufacturing Equipment, Subassemblies and Components, Transportation
Growth: Openings in past year, 32
Contact Dennis French, President/CEO; 765-675-2191; Fax: 765-675-4232

T.M. Morris Manufacturing Co., Inc.
830 State Rd. 25 South
PO Box 658
Logansport, IN 46947

Founded: 1965
Total Employees: 800
Industry: Subassemblies and Components
Growth: Openings in past year, 99
Contact David Wihebrink, Vice President/CFO; 219-722-4040; Fax: 219-722-5723

Thermwood Corp.
904 Old Buffaloville Rd.
Dale, IN 47523
http://www.thermwood.com
Founded: 1975
Total Employees: 130
Annual Sales: $14 million
Industry: Factory Automation
Growth: Openings in past year, 30
Contact Ken Susnajara, President; 812-937-4476; Fax: 812-937-2956; E-mail: thrmwood@thermwood.com

Tri-Industries, Inc.
333 South 3rd St.
Terre Haute, IN 47807
Founded: 1953
Total Employees: 300
Annual Sales: $43 million
Industry: Transportation
Growth: Openings in past year, 80
Contact Dave Heavin, Director of Personnel; 812-234-1591; Fax: 812-231-7272

VITCO, Inc.
PO Box 407
Nappanee, IN 46550
Founded: 1986
Total Employees: 105
Industry: Manufacturing Equipment
Growth: Openings in past year, 35
Contact Ms. Patricia Lintner, Human Resources Director; 219-773-3181; Fax: 219-773-3186

Wells Electronics, Inc.
52940 Olive Rd.
South Bend, IN 46628
Founded: 1959
Total Employees: 200
Industries: Factory Automation, Subassemblies and Components
Growth: Openings in past year, 40
Contact Ms. Julie Sparayznski, Human Resources Manager; 219-287-5941; Fax: 219-287-0356

Iowa

Barnstead, Thermolyne Corp.
2555 Kerper Blvd.
PO Box 797
Dubuque, IA 52004
http://www.barnsteadthermolyne.com
Founded: 1942
Total Employees: 440
Annual Sales: $59 million
Industries: Environmental, Factory Automation, Subassemblies and Components, Test and Measurement
Growth: Openings in past year, 40
Contact Stephen R. Schmieder, Human Resources Manager; 319-556-2241; Fax: 319-556-0695

Chantland Co.
Hwy. 3 East
PO Box 69
Humboldt, IA 50548
Founded: 1961
Total Employees: 425
Annual Sales: $65 million
Industries: Factory Automation, Subassemblies and Components

Growth: Openings in past year, 25
Contact George Flurey, General Manager; 515-332-4040; Fax: 515-332-4923

Compressor Controls Corp.
11359 Aurora Ave.
Des Moines, IA 50322
Founded: 1975
Total Employees: 350
Industries: Energy, Subassemblies and Components, Test and Measurement
Growth: Openings in past year, 49
Contact Ms. Ellen Iverson, Human Resources Manager; 515-270-0857; Fax: 515-270-1331

Engineering Animation, Inc.
2321 North Loop Dr., ISU Research Park
Ames, IA 50010
http://www.eai.com
Founded: 1988
Total Employees: 300
Annual Sales: $20.4 million
Industries: Computer Hardware, Computer Software, Holding Companies
Growth: Openings in past year, 83
Contact Ms. Patricia Johnson, Executive Director of Human Resources; 515-296-9908; Fax: 515-296-7025; E-mail: eaii@eai.com

Fansteel, Inc., Wellman Dynamics Division
Hwy. 34 East
Creston, IA 50801
http://www.fansteelweldyn.com
Founded: 1943
Total Employees: 260
Annual Sales: $16 million

Industry: Advanced
Materials
Growth: Openings in past
year, 30
Contact Mike Mead,
General Manager; 515-
782-8521; Fax: 515-782-
4844

Genesis Systems Group
8900 Harrison St.
Davenport, IA 52806
http://www.genesis-
systems.com
Founded: 1983
Total Employees: 190
Annual Sales: $36 million
Industries: Factory
Automation, Holding
Companies
Growth: Openings in past
year, 80
Contact Richard Litt,
President/CEO; 319-445-
5600; Fax: 319-445-
5699; E-mail: robots@
genesis-systems.com

GMT Corp.
PO Box 358
Waverly, IA 50677
http://www.gmtcorporation.
com
Founded: 1973
Total Employees: 300
Annual Sales: $37.5
million
Industries: Factory
Automation,
Manufacturing Equipment
Growth: Openings in past
year, 50
Contact Larry Graening,
President; 319-352-1509;
Fax: 319-352-3354;
E-mail: info@
gmtcorporation.com

**Iowa Laser Technology,
Inc.**
6122 Nordic Dr.
Cedar Falls, IA 50613
Founded: 1979
Total Employees: 120
Industry: Photonics
Growth: Openings in past
year, 25

Contact Ms. Joan Rickard,
Human Resources
Manager; 319-266-3561;
Fax: 319-266-8203

**Kind & Knox Gelatine,
Inc.**
PO Box 927
Sioux City, IA 51102
Founded: 1964
Total Employees: 250
Annual Sales: $66 million
Industry: Chemicals
Growth: Openings in past
year, 25
Contact Larry Weaver,
Human Resources
Manager; 712-943-5516;
Fax: 712-943-3372

**Litton Industries, Inc.,
Life Support Division**
2734 Hickory Grove Rd.
PO Box 4508
Davenport, IA 52808
Founded: 1982
Total Employees: 300
Annual Sales: $40 million
Industries: Medical,
Subassemblies and
Components, Test and
Measurement,
Transportation
Growth: Openings in past
year, 25
Contact Ms. Victoria
Kaularich, Director of
Human Resources; 319-
383-6000; Fax: 319-383-
6323

Norand Corp.
550 Second St. Southeast
Cedar Rapids, IA 52401
http://www.norand.com
Founded: 1968
Total Employees: 950
Annual Sales: $235 million
Industries: Computer
Hardware, Computer
Software, Factory
Automation
Growth: Openings in past
year, 46

Contact Jim Harrington,
Human Resources Direc-
tor; 319-369-3100; Fax:
319-369-3453

Telegroup, Inc.
2098 Nutmeg Ave.
Fairfield, IA 52556
http://www.telegroup.com
Founded: 1990
Total Employees: 600
Annual Sales: $213.2
million
Industry:
Telecommunications
Growth: Openings in past
year, 113
Contact Clifford Rees,
President/CEO; 515-472-
5000; Fax: 515-472-
4747; E-mail: savings@
telegroup.com

**Wayne Engineering
Corp.**
701 Performance Dr.
Cedar Falls, IA 50613
http://www.wayneeng.com
Founded: 1963
Total Employees: 115
Annual Sales: $14 million
Industries: Environmental,
Factory Automation
Growth: Openings in past
year, 40
Contact Ms. Cynthia
Goro, President; 319-
266-1721; Fax: 319-266-
8207; E-mail: info@
wayneeng.com

Kansas

**Airport Systems
International, Inc.**
11300 West 89th St.
Overland Park, KS 66214
Founded: 1991
Total Employees: 140
Annual Sales: $20.098
million
Industry: Transportation
Growth: Openings in past
year, 40

Contact Tom Cargin, VP of Finance and Administration; 913-492-0861; Fax: 913-492-0870

B.F. Goodrich Aerospace Test Systems, JCAir
PO Box 9
New Century, KS 66031
http://www.jcair.com
Founded: 1980
Total Employees: 187
Annual Sales: $16 million
Industries: Factory Automation, Test and Measurement
Growth: Openings in past year, 30
Contact Ms. Janet Smith, Director of Human Resources; 913-764-2452; Fax: 913-782-5104; E-mail: x400*misc@bfg-aerospace.sprint.com

Buderus Sell Aviation, Inc.
9800 West York St.
Wichita, KS 67215
Founded: 1991
Total Employees: 45
Industry: Transportation
Growth: Openings in past year, 33
Contact Helmut Hallenberger, Plant Manager; 316-524-3300; Fax: 316-524-3370

Burnham Products, Inc.
PO Box 2950
Wichita, KS 67277
Founded: 1953
Total Employees: 240
Industries: Factory Automation, Subassemblies and Components, Transportation
Growth: Openings in past year, 130
Contact Ms. Marsha Brown, Manager of Human Resources; 316-942-3208; Fax: 316-942-5044

Foster Design Co., Inc.
1999 North Amidon, Suite 222
Wichita, KS 67201
Founded: 1965
Total Employees: 249
Industries: Computer Software, Manufacturing Equipment
Growth: Openings in past year, 49
Contact Ms. Barbara Taggart, VP of Contract Staffing; 316-832-9700; Fax: 316-832-9357; E-mail: fdci@southwind.net

Global Engineering & Technology, Inc.
1720 South 151st St.
Goddard, KS 67052
Founded: 1991
Total Employees: 85
Annual Sales: $11 million
Industry: Transportation
Growth: Openings in past year, 50
Contact Ms. Delores Nevin, CEO/Secretary; 316-729-9232; Fax: 316-729-7927

Latshaw Enterprises
2533 South West St.
Wichita, KS 67217
Founded: 1940
Total Employees: 449
Annual Sales: $44 million
Industry: Holding Companies
Growth: Openings in past year, 49
Contact Michael E. Bukaty, President; 316-942-7266; Fax: 316-942-5114

Midwest Grain Products, Inc.
1300 Main St.
Atchison, KS 66002
Founded: 1941
Total Employees: 411
Annual Sales: $224 million
Industries: Biotechnology, Chemicals

Growth: Openings in past year, 24
Contact Dave Rindom, Director of Human Resources; 913-367-1480; Fax: 913-367-0192

Midwestern Electronics, Inc.
11714 Blackbob Rd.
Olathe, KS 66062
http://www.midwestelec.com
Founded: 1972
Total Employees: 210
Industry: Subassemblies and Components
Growth: Openings in past year, 102
Contact David Anderson, President; 913-768-6300; Fax: 913-768-6139; E-mail: comml@midwestelec.com

Mobile Data Solutions, Inc.
8717 West 110th St., Suite 600
Overland Park, KS 66210
http://www.mdsi-advantex.com
Founded: 1979
Total Employees: 327
Annual Sales: $42 million
Industries: Computer Hardware, Computer Software, Telecommunications
Growth: Openings in past year, 80
Contact Ms. Debbie Allen, Office Manager; 913-661-0190; Fax: 913-661-0220; E-mail: 75162.255@compuserve.com

Oread Laboratories
1501 Wakarusa Dr.
Lawrence, KS 66047
Founded: 1983
Total Employees: 156
Annual Sales: $24 million
Industries: Biotechnology, Chemicals, Pharmaceuticals

Growth: Openings in past year, 76
Contact Dave Johnson, President; 785-749-0034; Fax: 785-841-1991

Oread, Inc.
1501 Wakarusa Dr.
Lawrence, KS 66047
http://www.oread.com
Founded: 1994
Total Employees: 467
Industry: Holding Companies
Growth: Openings in past year, 85
Contact David Pumphrey, Manager of Human Resources; 785-749-0034; Fax: 785-749-1882; E-mail: inform@oread.com

Plastic Fabricating Co., Inc.
1650 South McComas St.
Wichita, KS 67277
Founded: 1948
Total Employees: 200
Industries: Advanced Materials, Transportation
Growth: Openings in past year, 40
Contact Ms. Lisa McAlexander, Human Relations Manager; 316-942-1241; Fax: 316-942-0687

Power Flame, Inc.
2001 South 21st St.
Parsons, KS 67357
http://www.power-flame.com
Founded: 1977
Total Employees: 250
Industry: Test and Measurement
Growth: Openings in past year, 25
Contact William Wiener, President; 316-421-0480; Fax: 316-421-0948; E-mail: csd@power-flame.com

Professional Engineering Consultants PA
303 South Topeka
Wichita, KS 67202
http://www.pecl.com
Founded: 1965
Total Employees: 200
Annual Sales: $23 million
Industry: Manufacturing Equipment
Growth: Openings in past year, 40
Contact Dale E. Maltbie, PE, President; 316-262-2691; Fax: 316-262-3003; E-mail: designers@pecl.com

Remel, Inc.
12076 Santa Fe Dr.
Lenexa, KS 66215
Founded: 1973
Total Employees: 500
Annual Sales: $60 million
Industries: Advanced Materials, Biotechnology, Chemicals, Medical
Growth: Openings in past year, 100
Contact Mike Dunn, Manager of Human Resources; 913-888-0939; Fax: 913-888-5884

Terracon Companies, Inc.
16000 College Blvd.
Lenexa, KS 66219
http://www.terracon.com
Founded: 1965
Total Employees: 750
Annual Sales: $63 million
Industry: Holding Companies
Growth: Openings in past year, 29
Contact Robert Costigan, Chief Operating Officer; 913-599-6886; Fax: 913-599-0574

Topeka Metal Specialties, Inc.
5600 South Topeka Blvd.
Topeka, KS 66619
Founded: 1965
Total Employees: 230
Industry: Manufacturing Equipment
Growth: Openings in past year, 60
Contact Gary Gerdes, President; 785-862-1071; Fax: 785-862-1138

Triple-I, Inc.
6330 Lamar, Suite 230
Overland Park, KS 66202
http://www.triplei.com
Founded: 1971
Total Employees: 450
Industry: Computer Hardware
Growth: Openings in past year, 150
Contact Robert Spachman, President; 913-262-6500; Fax: 913-262-4224

Kentucky

AdminStar, Inc.
10180 Linn Station Rd., Suite C200
Louisville, KY 40223
Founded: 1976
Total Employees: 70
Annual Sales: $9.0 million
Industry: Computer Software
Growth: Openings in past year, 30
Contact Ms. Mariam Paramore, Vice President; 502-423-6767; Fax: 502-423-6746

Advanced Filtration Concepts, Inc.
7070 International Dr.
Louisville, KY 40258

Founded: 1978
Total Employees: 140
Annual Sales: $18 million
Industry: Subassemblies and Components
Growth: Openings in past year, 68
Contact Frank Croket, President; 502-935-9333; Fax: 502-935-5885

American Synthetic Rubber Corp.
PO Box 32960
Louisville, KY 40232
Founded: 1955
Total Employees: 400
Industry: Advanced Materials
Growth: Openings in past year, 50
Contact Jim McGraw, Director of Human Relations; 502-449-8300; Fax: 502-449-8305

Blue Grass Manufacturing Co. of Lexington, Inc.
1454 Jingle Bell Ln.
Lexington, KY 40509
Founded: 1966
Total Employees: 230
Annual Sales: $22 million
Industries: Factory Automation, Manufacturing Equipment
Growth: Openings in past year, 40
Contact Don Bundy, President; 606-233-7445; Fax: 606-233-0081; E-mail: blue.grass.mfg. co@worldnet.att.net

Blue Star Plastics, Inc.
801 Nandino Blvd.
Lexington, KY 40511
Founded: 1984
Total Employees: 150
Industry: Manufacturing Equipment
Growth: Openings in past year, 50
Contact Roger Storch, President; 606-255-0714; Fax: 606-255-0716

CDR Pigments and Dispersions
305 Ring Rd.
Elizabethtown, KY 42701
Founded: 1948
Total Employees: 500
Annual Sales: $130 million
Industry: Chemicals
Growth: Openings in past year, 38
Contact W. Rucker Wickline, President; 502-737-1700; Fax: 502-737-0318

Commonwealth Technology, Inc.
2520 Regency Rd.
Lexington, KY 40503
Founded: 1977
Total Employees: 140
Annual Sales: $7.4 million
Industry: Environmental
Growth: Openings in past year, 40
Contact Ms. Cindy Peters, Controller; 606-276-3506; Fax: 606-278-5665

Contract Machining & Manufacturing Co., Inc.
2425 Over Dr.
Lexington, KY 40511
Founded: 1981
Total Employees: 65
Annual Sales: $8.1 million
Industry: Manufacturing Equipment
Growth: Openings in past year, 35
Contact Fred Lawson, President; 606-253-9700; Fax: 606-231-7688

Ellison Surface Technologies
1780 Anderson Blvd.
Hebron, KY 41048
Founded: 1986
Total Employees: 100
Annual Sales: $19 million

Industries: Advanced Materials, Manufacturing Equipment, Photonics
Growth: Openings in past year, 55
Contact C. Michael Ellison, President; 606-586-9300; Fax: 606-586-8585

Fisher-Klosterman, Inc.
2900 West Broadway, Second Floor
Louisville, KY 40211
Founded: 1948
Total Employees: 100
Annual Sales: $12 million
Industries: Environmental, Test and Measurement
Growth: Openings in past year, 25
Contact Rob Haydon, Purchasing and Personnel Manager; 502-776-1505; Fax: 502-774-4157

Kuhlman Electric Corp.
101 Kuhlman Blvd.
Versailles, KY 40383
http://www.keco.com
Founded: 1894
Total Employees: 600
Annual Sales: $100 million
Industries: Energy, Subassemblies and Components
Growth: Openings in past year, 29
Contact John Zvolensky, President/CEO; 606-879-2999; Fax: 606-873-8032; E-mail: kuhlman@keco.com

Mazak Corp.
8025 Production Dr.
Florence, KY 41042
http://www.mazakusa.com
Founded: 1968
Total Employees: 900
Industry: Factory Automation
Growth: Openings in past year, 43
Contact Mike Vogt, VP of Personnel; 606-342-1700; Fax: 606-342-1865

Star Manufacturing, Inc.
1306 Russell Cave Rd.
Lexington, KY 40505
Founded: 1957
Total Employees: 75
Industries: Factory Automation, Manufacturing Equipment
Growth: Openings in past year, 25
Contact Mark Stanley, President; 606-252-6741; Fax: 606-252-6744

Teklogix, Inc.
1810 Airport Exchange Blvd., Suite 500
Erlanger, KY 41018
http://www.teklogix.com
Founded: 1967
Total Employees: 580
Annual Sales: $120 million
Industry: Telecommunications
Growth: Openings in past year, 80
Contact John Janetos, VP of Human Resources; 606-371-6006; Fax: 606-372-4334

Tekno, Inc.
One Wall St.
Cave City, KY 42127
http://www.tekno.com
Founded: 1988
Total Employees: 100
Annual Sales: $15 million
Industry: Factory Automation
Growth: Openings in past year, 30
Contact Ms. Vickie Monroe, Personnel Manager; 502-773-4181; Fax: 502-773-4180; E-mail: sales@tekno.com

Louisiana

Global Divers and Contractors, Inc.
5319 Port Rd.
New Iberia, LA 70560
Founded: 1992
Total Employees: 300
Annual Sales: $29 million
Industry: Energy
Growth: Openings in past year, 37
Contact Mike Stark, General Manager; 318-367-3483; Fax: 318-374-3210

Specialty Plastics, Inc.
15915 Perkins Rd.
Baton Rouge, LA 70810
Founded: 1973
Total Employees: 87
Annual Sales: $11 million
Industry: Subassemblies and Components
Growth: Openings in past year, 27
Contact Richard H. Lea, President; 504-752-2705; Fax: 504-752-2757; E-mail: fiberbond@aol.com

UNIFAB International, Inc.
PO Box 11308
New Iberia, LA 70562
Founded: 1980
Total Employees: 425
Annual Sales: $66 million
Industry: Energy
Growth: Openings in past year, 93
Contact Dailey J. Berard, COB/CEO/President; 318-367-8291; Fax: 318-365-3711

Maine

Mestek, Inc., Cooper-Weymouth, Peterson Division
Hinckley Rd.
Clinton, ME 04927
Founded: 1972
Total Employees: 150
Annual Sales: $22 million
Industry: Factory Automation
Growth: Openings in past year, 50
Contact Stephen Staples, Office Manager; 207-426-2351; Fax: 207-426-8868

Soleras, Ltd.
589 Elm St.
Biddeford, ME 04005
http://www.soleras.com
Founded: 1978
Total Employees: 70
Annual Sales: $8.7 million
Industry: Manufacturing Equipment
Growth: Openings in past year, 25
Contact Dean Plaisted, President; 207-282-5699; Fax: 207-284-6118; E-mail: soleras@soleras.com

Maryland

ACE*COMM Corp.
704 Quince Orchard Rd.
Gaithersburg, MD 20878
http://www.acecomm.com
Founded: 1983
Total Employees: 160
Annual Sales: $32.8 million
Industries: Computer Software, Test and Measurement, Telecommunications
Growth: Openings in past year, 45
Contact George T. Jimenez, COB/President/CEO; 301-721-3000;

Fax: 301-721-3001;
E-mail: info@acecomm.
com

**ADP-Integrated Medical
Solutions, Inc.**
10401 Fernwood Rd.
Bethesda, MD 20817
Founded: 1988
Total Employees: 300
Annual Sales: $38 million
Industry: Computer
Software
Growth: Openings in past
year, 100
Contact Ms. Stella Tittle,
Human Resources
Manager; 301-564-6696;
Fax: 301-571-4761

**American Environmental
Network, Inc.**
9151 Rumsey Rd., Suite
150
Columbia, MD 21045
Founded: 1992
Total Employees: 400
Annual Sales: $49 million
Industries: Environmental,
Holding Companies
Growth: Openings in past
year, 40
Contact Larry Frantz,
General Manager; 410-
730-8525; Fax: 410-997-
2586

**American Personal
Communications, L.P.**
6905 Rockledge Dr., Suite
100
Bethesda, MD 20817
Founded: 1988
Total Employees: 800
Annual Sales: $130 million
Industry:
Telecommunications
Growth: Openings in past
year, 400
Contact W. Scott Schelle,
Chief Executive Officer;
301-214-9200; Fax: 301-
214-9490

**Annapolis Micro
Systems, Inc.**
190 Admiral Cochrane Dr.,
Suite 130
Annapolis, MD 21401
http://www.annapmicro.
com
Founded: 1982
Total Employees: 55
Industries: Computer
Hardware, Computer
Software, Manufacturing
Equipment,
Subassemblies and
Components
Growth: Openings in past
year, 25
Contact Ms. Betsy
Jenkins, Human
Resources and Marketing
Manager; 410-841-2514;
Fax: 410-841-2518

**Aspen Systems Corp.,
Applied Management
Sciences Group**
2277 Research Blvd., Mail
Stop 4-B
Rockville, MD 20850
Founded: 1970
Total Employees: 140
Annual Sales: $28 million
Industries: Computer
Hardware, Computer
Software, Defense,
Energy, Environmental,
Medical
Growth: Openings in past
year, 50
Contact Ms. Georgette
Semick, Vice President/
General Manager; 301-
519-5000; Fax: 301-947-
8666

**Boehringer Mannheim
Corp., Therapeutics
Division**
101 Orchard Ridge Dr.
Gaithersburg, MD 20878
http://www.thera.
boehringer-mannheim.
com
Founded: 1985
Total Employees: 430
Annual Sales: $66 million

Industry: Pharmaceuticals
Growth: Openings in past
year, 29
Contact Al Lichenstein,
Director of Human
Resources; 301-216-
3900; Fax: 301-990-3815

**California Microwave,
Inc., Airborne Systems
Integration**
1362 Brass Mill Rd.
Belcamp, MD 21017
Founded: 1993
Total Employees: 241
Annual Sales: $59 million
Industries: Computer
Hardware, Defense
Growth: Openings in past
year, 91
Contact William G.
Shaver, President/
General Manager; 410-
272-2228; Fax: 410-272-
9272; E-mail: info@cmi-
asi.com

**CDA Investment
Technologies**
1355 Piccard Dr.
Rockville, MD 20850
http://www.cda.com
Founded: 1962
Total Employees: 500
Industries: Computer
Hardware, Computer
Software
Growth: Openings in past
year, 100
Contact Jeff Kramer, VP
of Human Resources;
301-975-9600; Fax: 301-
590-1350; E-mail: cda-
info@cda.com

Cellular One
7855 Walker Dr.
Greenbelt, MD 20770
http://www.getcellone.com
Founded: 1983
Total Employees: 700
Annual Sales: $120 million
Industry:
Telecommunications
Growth: Openings in past
year, 97

Contact Denny Boresow, Director of Human Resources; 301-489-3600; Fax: 301-489-3800

Century Technologies, Inc.
8405 Colesville Rd., Suite 400
Silver Spring, MD 20910
http://www.centech.com
Founded: 1977
Total Employees: 250
Annual Sales: $25 million
Industries: Computer Hardware, Computer Software, Telecommunications
Growth: Openings in past year, 25
Contact Donald Campbell, President/CEO; 301-585-4800; Fax: 301-588-1619

Communication Systems Technology, Inc.
8975 Guilford Rd., Suite 100
Columbia, MD 21046
Founded: 1986
Total Employees: 140
Annual Sales: $23 million
Industries: Computer Software, Holding Companies, Telecommunications, Transportation
Growth: Openings in past year, 25
Contact Steven Brucker, President/CEO; 410-381-5080; Fax: 410-381-3589

COMNET Corporation
4200 Parliament Pl., Suite 600
Lanham, MD 20706
Founded: 1967
Total Employees: 400
Annual Sales: $54.547 million
Industry: Holding Companies
Growth: Openings in past year, 164

Contact Trent Lutz, Director of Human Resources; 301-918-0400; Fax: 301-918-0430

Computech, Inc.
4800 Hampton Ln., Suite 600
Bethesda, MD 20014
http://www.computechinc.com
Founded: 1979
Total Employees: 65
Annual Sales: $5 million
Industry: Computer Software
Growth: Openings in past year, 25
Contact James D. Murphy, Jr., President; 301-656-4030; Fax: 301-656-7060; E-mail: hr@computech.com

Credit Management Solutions, Inc.
5950 Symphony Woods Rd., Suite 301
Columbia, MD 21044
http://www.cmsinc.com
Founded: 1987
Total Employees: 210
Annual Sales: $14.3 million
Industry: Computer Software
Growth: Openings in past year, 80
Contact Wyatt Cook, Director of Human Resources; 410-740-6789; Fax: 410-884-5297; E-mail: nancyw@cmsinc.com

Data Systems Marketing Corp.
375 Prince George's Blvd.
Upper Marlboro, MD 20774
http://www.dsmc.com
Founded: 1976
Total Employees: 80
Industries: Computer Hardware, Telecommunications

Growth: Openings in past year, 30
Contact Allen Dolgoff, President; 301-390-7000; Fax: 301-390-7035; E-mail: info@dsmc.com

Denro, Inc.
9318 Gaither Rd.
Gaithersburg, MD 20877
http://www.denro.com
Founded: 1966
Total Employees: 326
Annual Sales: $34 million
Industries: Defense, Subassemblies and Components, Transportation
Growth: Openings in past year, 35
Contact Jack Hix, Human Resources Manager; 301-840-1597; Fax: 301-869-3192; E-mail: denro@denro.com

Digene Corporation
2301-B Broadbirch Dr.
Silver Spring, MD 20904
http://www.digene.com
Founded: 1985
Total Employees: 120
Annual Sales: $10.1 million
Industries: Biotechnology, Chemicals, Medical
Growth: Openings in past year, 37
Contact Evan Jones, President/CEO; 301-470-6505; Fax: 301-680-0696; E-mail: inforceq@digene.com

Eagan, McAllister Associates, Inc.
PO Box 986
Lexington Park, MD 20653
http://www.emainc.com
Founded: 1984
Total Employees: 500
Industries: Computer Software, Defense
Growth: Openings in past year, 148
Contact Ms. Julie McAllister, Human

Resources Director; 301-863-2192; Fax: 301-863-2308

EOG, Inc.
10947 Golden West Dr.
Hunt Valley, MD 21031
Founded: 1961
Total Employees: 300
Annual Sales: $40 million
Industries: Manufacturing
 Equipment,
 Subassemblies and
 Components
Growth: Openings in past
 year, 140
Contact Ms. Carol Tracy,
 Human Resources
 Manager; 410-785-3000;
 Fax: 410-771-5814

Estimation, Inc.
805-L Barkwood Ct.
PO Box 488
Linthicum Heights, MD
 21090
http://www.estimation.com
Founded: 1973
Total Employees: 90
Annual Sales: $11 million
Industry: Computer
 Software
Growth: Openings in past
 year, 25
Contact James T. Jubb,
 Chief Financial Officer;
 410-636-4566; Fax: 410-789-3207; E-mail:
 estimkrt@ix.netcom.com

FiberTech Medical, Inc.
5020 Campbell Blvd.,
 Suite K
Baltimore, MD 21236
Founded: 1989
Total Employees: 100
Industry: Medical
Growth: Openings in past
 year, 46
Contact Frank
 Majerowicz, President;
 410-931-4411; Fax: 410-931-4414

**Forensic Technologies
International Corp.**
2021 Research Dr.
Annapolis, MD 21401

http://www.fticorp.com
Founded: 1982
Total Employees: 200
Annual Sales: $30.647
 million
Industry: Holding
 Companies
Growth: Openings in past
 year, 32
Contact Gary Sindler,
 Executive Vice President/
 CFO/Treasurer; 410-224-8770; Fax: 410-266-0765

**Fusion Semiconductor
Systems**
7600 Standish Pl.
Rockville, MD 20855
Founded: 1971
Total Employees: 364
Industries: Factory
 Automation,
 Manufacturing Equipment
Growth: Openings in past
 year, 64
Contact John C.
 Matthews, President;
 301-251-0300; Fax: 301-340-9351

Genetic Therapy, Inc.
938 Clopper Rd.
Gaithersburg, MD 20878
Founded: 1986
Total Employees: 190
Annual Sales: $22 million
Industry: Biotechnology
Growth: Openings in past
 year, 35
Contact Ms. Rachael
 King, Chief Executive
 Officer; 301-590-2626;
 Fax: 301-948-0503

GSE Systems, Inc.
8930 Stanford Blvd.
Columbia, MD 21045
http://www.gses.com
Founded: 1995
Total Employees: 610
Annual Sales: $96.033
 million
Industries: Computer
 Hardware, Computer
 Software, Factory
 Automation, Holding

Companies,
 Telecommunications
Growth: Openings in past
 year, 80
Contact Rolf M.G.
 Falkenberg, President/
 COO; 410-312-3500;
 Fax: 410-312-3611;
 E-mail: info@gses.com

**Guilford Pharmaceuticals
Inc.**
6611 Tributary St.
Baltimore, MD 21224
http://www.guilfordpharm.
 com
Founded: 1994
Total Employees: 190
Annual Sales: $28 million
Industries: Biotechnology,
 Medical
Growth: Openings in past
 year, 100
Contact Craig R. Smith,
 MD, COB/CEO/
 President; 410-631-6300;
 Fax: 410-631-6338

**Hittman Materials &
Medical Components,
Inc.**
9190 Red Branch Rd.
Columbia, MD 21045
Founded: 1962
Total Employees: 95
Annual Sales: $12 million
Industry: Subassemblies
 and Components
Growth: Openings in past
 year, 30
Contact Ms. Jane Riley,
 Human Resources
 Administrator; 410-730-7800; Fax: 410-730-7837

**Human Genome
Sciences, Inc.**
9410 Key West Ave.
Rockville, MD 20850
http://www.hgsi.com
Founded: 1992
Total Employees: 316
Industries: Biotechnology,
 Medical, Pharmaceuticals
Growth: Openings in past
 year, 66

Contact Ms. Susan Bateson-McKay, VP of Human Resources; 301-309-8504; Fax: 301-309-8512

Hunter Group
100 East Pratt St., Suite 1600
Baltimore, MD 21202
http://www.hunter-group.com
Founded: 1989
Total Employees: 500
Industry: Computer Software
Growth: Openings in past year, 73
Contact Terry Hunter, President/CEO; 410-576-1515; Fax: 410-752-2879

J.F. Taylor, Inc.
PO Box 760
Lexington Park, MD 20653
Founded: 1984
Total Employees: 106
Industries: Defense, Manufacturing Equipment
Growth: Openings in past year, 26
Contact John F. Taylor, Sr., COB/President; 301-862-3939; Fax: 301-862-4069

LB & B Associates
9891 Broken Land Pkwy., Suite 400
Columbia, MD 21046
Founded: 1992
Total Employees: 400
Industries: Subassemblies and Components, Telecommunications
Growth: Openings in past year, 100
Contact Ms. Susan Payme, Human Resources Administrator; 301-596-2440; Fax: 301-596-7879

Macfadden and Associates, Inc.
1320 Fenwick Ln., Suite 600
Silver Spring, MD 20910
Founded: 1986
Total Employees: 500
Industries: Computer Hardware, Computer Software
Growth: Openings in past year, 300
Contact James R. Macfadden, President; 301-588-5900; Fax: 301-588-0390

Macro International Inc.
11785 Beltsville Dr.
Calverton, MD 20705
http://www.macroint.com
Founded: 1966
Total Employees: 450
Annual Sales: $56.1 million
Industries: Computer Software, Holding Companies
Growth: Openings in past year, 49
Contact Ms. Millie M. Ambrosia, VP of Human Resources; 301-572-0200; Fax: 301-572-0999; E-mail: lastname@macroint.com

Manugistics, Inc.
2115 East Jefferson St.
Rockville, MD 20852
http://www.manugistics.com
Founded: 1969
Total Employees: 600
Annual Sales: $94.7 million
Industry: Computer Software
Growth: Openings in past year, 65
Contact William M. Gibson, President/COB/CEO; 301-984-5000; Fax: 301-984-5370

MCI Systemhouse Lerning Technology
10025 Governor Warfield Pkwy.
Columbia, MD 21044
Founded: 1968
Total Employees: 353
Industry: Computer Software
Growth: Openings in past year, 88
Contact Roger St. Germain, Vice President; 410-910-8600; Fax: 410-715-5574; E-mail: kee@shl.com

MedImmune, Inc.
35 West Watkins Mill Rd.
Gaithersburg, MD 20878
http://www.medimmune.com
Founded: 1988
Total Employees: 250
Annual Sales: $41.1 million
Industries: Biotechnology, Pharmaceuticals
Growth: Openings in past year, 105
Contact Wayne T. Hockmeyer, Ph.D., COB/CEO; 301-417-0770; Fax: 301-527-4200

Meridian Medical Technologies, Inc.
10240 Old Columbia Rd.
Columbia, MD 21046
http://www.meridianmeds.com
Founded: 1969
Total Employees: 286
Annual Sales: $31.385 million
Industries: Holding Companies, Medical, Pharmaceuticals
Growth: Openings in past year, 38
Contact Peter Garbis, Executive Dir. of Organizational Dev.; 410-309-6830; Fax: 410-309-1475; E-mail: info@meridianmt.com

Microlog Corporation
20270 Goldenrod Ln.
Germantown, MD 20876
http://www.mlog.com
Founded: 1969
Total Employees: 315
Annual Sales: $25.7 million
Industries: Defense, Telecommunications
Growth: Openings in past year, 84
Contact Ms. Linda Cononie, Director of Personnel; 301-428-9100; Fax: 301-540-5557

Nichols Research, CSSI
10260 Old Columbia Rd.
Columbia, MD 21046
http://www.cssi.net
Founded: 1982
Total Employees: 170
Annual Sales: $12 million
Industry: Computer Software
Growth: Openings in past year, 75
Contact Ms. Janet Campenella, Human Resources Manager; 410-290-9500; Fax: 410-290-7012

Osiris Therapeutics, Inc.
2001 Aliceanna St.
Baltimore, MD 21231
http://www.osiristx.com
Founded: 1992
Total Employees: 70
Annual Sales: $1.6 million
Industry: Biotechnology
Growth: Openings in past year, 30
Contact Michael Demchuk, Vice President/CFO; 410-522-5005; Fax: 410-522-6999

PATS, Inc.
9570 Berger Rd.
Columbia, MD 21046
Founded: 1976

Total Employees: 160
Industry: Holding Companies
Growth: Openings in past year, 60
Contact Harvey Patrick, Chief Executive Officer; 410-381-5533; Fax: 410-290-6966; E-mail: frostj@pats.com

Peri Formwork Systems, Inc.
2031 Inverness Ave.
Baltimore, MD 21230
Founded: 1969
Total Employees: 70
Annual Sales: $12 million
Industry: Factory Automation
Growth: Openings in past year, 35
Contact Harvey Evans, President; 410-646-5010; Fax: 410-646-5018

PRB Associates, Inc.
43865 Airport View Dr.
Hollywood, MD 20636
http://www.prb.net
Founded: 1977
Total Employees: 262
Annual Sales: $28 million
Industries: Computer Hardware, Computer Software, Defense
Growth: Openings in past year, 26
Contact Richard Bos, Executive Vice President; 301-373-2360; Fax: 301-373-3421

Pulse Electronics, Inc.
5706 Frederick Ave.
Rockville, MD 20852
Founded: 1976
Total Employees: 300
Annual Sales: $61 million
Industries: Computer Hardware, Photonics
Growth: Openings in past year, 100
Contact Emilio A. Fernandez, President; 301-230-0600; Fax: 301-984-6615

RDA Consultants, Ltd.
1966 Green Spring Dr.
Timonium, MD 21093
http://www.rdaconsultants.com
Founded: 1988
Total Employees: 105
Annual Sales: $16 million
Industries: Computer Hardware, Computer Software
Growth: Openings in past year, 30
Contact Donald Awalt, President; 410-561-9028; Fax: 410-561-9031; E-mail: landsman@rdaconsultants.com

RPM Consulting, Inc.
7130 Minstrel Way, Suite 230
Columbia, MD 21045
http://www.rpm.com
Founded: 1992
Total Employees: 120
Annual Sales: $8.6 million
Industry: Telecommunications
Growth: Openings in past year, 60
Contact Robert Miller, President; 410-309-6000; Fax: 410-309-6070; E-mail: www-rpm@rpm.com

RWD Technologies, Inc.
10480 Little Patuxent Pkwy., Suite 1200
Columbia, MD 21044
http://www.rwd.com
Founded: 1988
Total Employees: 719
Annual Sales: $65 million
Industries: Computer Software, Manufacturing Equipment
Growth: Openings in past year, 115
Contact Dr. Robert W. Deutsch, COB/CEO/Founder; 410-730-4377

Sherwin-Williams Co., Cleaning Solutions Group
1354 Old Post Rd.
Havre De Grace, MD 21078
Founded: 1977
Total Employees: 300
Annual Sales: $79 million
Industry: Chemicals
Growth: Openings in past year, 50
Contact Mark Spifito, President; 410-939-1234; Fax: 410-939-3028

Statistica, Inc.
800 South Frederick Ave., Suite 204
Gaithersburg, MD 20877
http://www.statistica.com
Founded: 1977
Total Employees: 320
Annual Sales: $36 million
Industries: Computer Hardware, Computer Software
Growth: Openings in past year, 70
Contact Ray Oleson, President; 301-926-9000; Fax: 301-926-8864; E-mail: rbruce@statistica. com

Swales and Associates, Inc.
5050 Powder Mill Rd.
Beltsville, MD 20705
Founded: 1978
Total Employees: 590
Annual Sales: $63 million
Industries: Defense, Manufacturing Equipment, Transportation
Growth: Openings in past year, 99
Contact Thomas G. Swales, Chief Executive Officer; 301-595-5500; Fax: 301-902-4114; E-mail: http://www. swales.com

Sylvest Management Systems Corp.
10001 Derekwood Ln.
Lanham, MD 20706
http://www.sylvest.com
Founded: 1987
Total Employees: 140
Annual Sales: $106 million
Industry: Computer Hardware
Growth: Openings in past year, 30
Contact Gary Murray, President/CEO; 301-459-2700; Fax: 301-459-5558

Tenax Corporation
4800 East Monument Dr.
Baltimore, MD 21205
http://www.tenax.com
Founded: 1985
Total Employees: 125
Annual Sales: $80 million
Industry: Manufacturing Equipment
Growth: Openings in past year, 45
Contact Cesare Berreta, President; 410-522-7000; Fax: 410-522-3977; E-mail: tenaxusa@ix. netcom.com

Trusted Information Systems, Inc.
3060 Washington Rd.
Glenwood, MD 21738
http://www.tis.com
Founded: 1983
Total Employees: 290
Annual Sales: $26.3 million
Industries: Computer Hardware, Computer Software, Telecommunications
Growth: Openings in past year, 130
Contact Alan Burke, Director of Human Resources; 301-854-6889; Fax: 301-854-5363; E-mail: tis@tis.com

Universal Security Instruments, Inc.
10324 South Dolfield Rd.
Owings Mills, MD 21117
Founded: 1969
Total Employees: 600
Annual Sales: $16 million
Industries: Energy, Subassemblies and Components, Test and Measurement, Telecommunications
Growth: Openings in past year, 100
Contact Stephen Knepper, President; 410-363-3000; Fax: 410-363-2218; E-mail: 72731.1433@ compuserve.com

VEDA Systems, Inc.
44417 Pecan Ct., Suite A
California, MD 20619
http://www.vedasystems. com
Founded: 1989
Total Employees: 80
Industries: Test and Measurement, Telecommunications
Growth: Openings in past year, 30
Contact David E. Butler, President; 301-737-1555; Fax: 301-737-1564; E-mail: sales.vsys@veda. com

Visual Networks, Inc.
2092 Gaither Rd.
Rockville, MD 20850
http://www.visualnetworks. com
Founded: 1993
Total Employees: 110
Annual Sales: $18 million
Industry: Telecommunications
Growth: Openings in past year, 65
Contact Scott Stouffer, President/CEO; 301-296-2300; Fax: 301-296-2301; E-mail: info@ visualnetworks.com

Massachusetts

Ward Machinery Co.
10615 Beaver Dam Rd.
Cockeysville, MD 21030
http://www.wardmach.com
Founded: 1957
Total Employees: 500
Annual Sales: $76 million
Industry: Factory
 Automation
Growth: Openings in past
 year, 24
Contact Dick Bailey, VP of
 Human Resources; 410-
 584-7700; Fax: 410-771-
 8406

XDB Systems, Inc.
9861 Broken Land Pkwy,
 Suite 156
Columbia, MD 21046
http://www.xdb.com
Founded: 1982
Total Employees: 150
Annual Sales: $19 million
Industries: Computer
 Software,
 Telecommunications
Growth: Openings in past
 year, 30
Contact Duncan McClain,
 President; 410-312-9300;
 Fax: 410-312-9500;
 E-mail: moreinfo@xdb.
 com

Yurie Systems, Inc.
10000 Derekwood Ln.
Lanham, MD 20706
http://www.yurie.com
Founded: 1992
Total Employees: 168
Annual Sales: $21.6
 million
Industry:
 Telecommunications
Growth: Openings in past
 year, 49
Contact Jeong H. Kim,
 COB/CEO; 301-352-
 4600; Fax: 301-352-
 4679; E-mail: info@yurie.
 com

**Ace Metal Fabricators,
Inc.**
137 Armory St.
Springfield, MA 01105
Founded: 1973
Total Employees: 70
Industries: Factory
 Automation,
 Manufacturing Equipment
Growth: Openings in past
 year, 38
Contact Maurice A. Boyer,
 President; 413-732-8724;
 Fax: 413-732-8848

**Adaptive Optics
Associates, Inc.**
54 Cambridge Park Dr.
Cambridge, MA 02140
http://www.aoainc.com
Founded: 1976
Total Employees: 160
Industries: Computer
 Hardware, Factory
 Automation, Photonics,
 Test and Measurement,
 Telecommunications
Growth: Openings in past
 year, 60
Contact Lawrence
 Schmutz, President; 617-
 864-0201; Fax: 617-484-
 5549; E-mail: info@
 aoainc.com

**Advanced Modular
Solutions, Inc.**
60 Codman Hill Rd.
Boxboro, MA 01719
http://www.mod.com
Founded: 1992
Total Employees: 100
Annual Sales: $19 million
Industries: Computer
 Hardware, Computer
 Software,
 Telecommunications
Growth: Openings in past
 year, 25
Contact Ms. Bonnie
 Bedell, Director of
 Personnel; 978-266-
 9700; Fax: 978-266-
 1601; E-mail: info@mod.
 com

**Advanced Visual
Systems, Inc.**
300 Fifth Ave.
Waltham, MA 02154
http://www.avs.com
Founded: 1992
Total Employees: 140
Annual Sales: $18 million
Industry: Computer
 Software
Growth: Openings in past
 year, 30
Contact Harry Cochran,
 President/CEO; 781-890-
 4300; Fax: 781-890-
 8287; E-mail: info@avs.
 com

Allaire Corp.
One Alewife Ctr.
Cambridge, MA 02140
http://www.allaire.com
Founded: 1995
Total Employees: 80
Industry: Computer
 Software
Growth: Openings in past
 year, 65
Contact Ms. Victoria Reiff,
 Director of Human
 Resources; 617-761-
 2000; Fax: 617-761-
 2001; E-mail: info@
 allaire.com

Alpha Industries, Inc.
20 Sylvan Rd.
Woburn, MA 01801
http://www.alphaind.com
Founded: 1962
Total Employees: 800
Annual Sales: $85 million
Industries: Holding
 Companies,
 Subassemblies and
 Components, Test and
 Measurement,
 Telecommunications
Growth: Openings in past
 year, 46
Contact Thomas Leonard,
 President/CEO; 781-935-
 5150; Fax: 617-824-4564

Alphatech, Inc.
50 Mall Rd.
Burlington, MA 01803
Founded: 1979
Total Employees: 100
Industries: Computer
Software, Manufacturing
Equipment
Growth: Openings in past
year, 30
Contact Dr. Nils Sandell,
President; 781-273-3388;
Fax: 781-273-9345

**Alpine Computer
Systems, Inc.**
125 Jeffrey Ave.
Holliston, MA 01746
http://www.alpinecsi.com
Founded: 1989
Total Employees: 200
Industry:
Telecommunications
Growth: Openings in past
year, 50
Contact Ken Smith, VP of
Human Resources; 508-
429-0700; Fax: 508-429-
0500; E-mail:
webmaster@alpinecsi.
com

**American Science and
Engineering, Inc.**
829 Middlesex Tpke.
Billerica, MA 01821
http://www.as-e.com
Founded: 1958
Total Employees: 166
Annual Sales: $17.815
million
Industries: Factory
Automation, Test and
Measurement,
Transportation
Growth: Openings in past
year, 43
Contact Ms. Paige Ryan,
Human Resources
Manager; 978-262-8700;
Fax: 978-262-8804

Andover Controls Corp.
300 Brickstone Sq.
Andover, MA 01810
http://www.
andovercontrols.com
Founded: 1976
Total Employees: 400
Annual Sales: $92 million
Industry: Energy
Growth: Openings in past
year, 100
Contact Ms. Patricia
Abate, Personnel
Manager; 978-470-0555;
Fax: 978-470-0946

**Applied Science and
Technology, Inc.**
35 Cabot Rd.
Woburn, MA 01801
Founded: 1987
Total Employees: 427
Annual Sales: $47.9
million
Industries: Holding
Companies,
Manufacturing
Equipment,
Subassemblies and
Components
Growth: Openings in past
year, 137
Contact Ms. Lorrie
Ferraro, Director of
Human Resources; 781-
933-5560; Fax: 781-933-
0750; E-mail: sales@
astex.com

**Artisoft, Inc., Telephony
Product Group**
5 Cambridge Ctr., 3rd
Floor
Cambridge, MA 02142
http://www.stylus.com
Founded: 1990
Total Employees: 60
Annual Sales: $7.7 million
Industry: Computer
Software
Growth: Openings in past
year, 30
Contact Chris Brookins,
VP of Development; 617-

354-0600; Fax: 617-354-
7744; E-mail: sales@
stylus.com

Avici Systems, Inc.
12 Elizabeth Dr.
Chelmsford, MA 01824
http://www.avici.com
Founded: 1996
Total Employees: 30
Industry:
Telecommunications
Growth: Openings in past
year, 27
Contact Surya Panditi,
President/CEO; 978-250-
3344; Fax: 978-250-
3377; E-mail: info@avici.
com

BASF Bioresearch Corp.
100 Research Dr.
Worcester, MA 01605
Founded: 1989
Total Employees: 258
Annual Sales: $27 million
Industry: Biotechnology
Growth: Openings in past
year, 34
Contact Ms. Pamela
Barney, Manager of
Human Resources; 508-
849-2500; Fax: 508-752-
6506

**Bay State Computer
Group, Inc.**
52 Roland St.
Boston, MA 02129
http://www.bscg.com
Founded: 1984
Total Employees: 150
Annual Sales: $100 million
Industry: Computer
Hardware
Growth: Openings in past
year, 25
Contact James Claypoole,
President; 617-623-3100;
Fax: 617-628-6211;
E-mail: info@bscg.com

Baystate/Sterling, Inc.
12 Union St.
Westborough, MA 01581
http://www.thomasregister.
com/baystate
Founded: 1922
Total Employees: 435
Annual Sales: $66 million
Industry: Factory
Automation
Growth: Openings in past
year, 33
Contact Ms. Lucia
Hackett, Human
Resources Manager;
508-366-4431; Fax: 800-
366-4311; E-mail: mkt@
baystatesterling.com

BGS Systems, Inc.
1 First Ave.
Waltham, MA 02254
http://www.bgs.com
Founded: 1975
Total Employees: 265
Annual Sales: $41.056
million
Industry: Computer
Software
Growth: Openings in past
year, 55
Contact Dr. Harold S.
Schwenk, Jr., President/
CEO; 781-891-0000;
Fax: 781-890-0000

Biogen, Inc.
14 Cambridge Ctr.
Cambridge, MA 02142
http://www.biogen.com
Founded: 1978
Total Employees: 796
Annual Sales: $277 million
Industries: Biotechnology,
Pharmaceuticals
Growth: Openings in past
year, 92
Contact Frank A. Burke,
VP of Human Resources;
617-679-2000; Fax: 617-
679-2617

Brainstorm Technologies
219 Vassar St.
Cambridge, MA 02139
http://www.braintech.com
Founded: 1993
Total Employees: 100
Industries: Computer
Hardware, Computer
Software,
Telecommunications
Growth: Openings in past
year, 50
Contact Ms. Amy Kessler,
VP of Worldwide Sales;
617-588-0800; Fax: 617-
588-0806; E-mail:
sales@braintech.com

Brooks Automation, Inc.
15 Elizabeth Dr.
Chelmsford, MA 01824
Founded: 1978
Total Employees: 459
Annual Sales: $90.432
million
Industry: Manufacturing
Equipment
Growth: Openings in past
year, 139
Contact Bob Therrien,
President; 978-262-2400;
Fax: 978-262-2500

**Brooktrout Technology,
Inc.**
410 First Ave.
Needham, MA 02194
http://www.brooktrout.com
Founded: 1984
Total Employees: 183
Annual Sales: $58.8
million
Industries: Computer
Hardware, Computer
Software, Holding
Companies,
Telecommunications
Growth: Openings in past
year, 90
Contact Eric Giler,
President/Founder; 781-
449-4100; Fax: 781-449-
3171; E-mail: info@
brooktrout.com

**C.W. Costello &
Associates, Inc.**
40 William St.
Wellesley, MA 02181
http://www.cwcboston.com
Founded: 1986
Total Employees: 100
Annual Sales: $20 million
Industry: Computer
Hardware
Growth: Openings in past
year, 55
Contact C.W. Costello,
Owner; 781-239-1414;
Fax: 781-237-4336

Candela Corp.
530 Boston Post Rd.
Wayland, MA 01778
Founded: 1970
Total Employees: 231
Annual Sales: $35.5
million
Industry: Medical
Growth: Openings in past
year, 51
Contact Gerard E. Puorro,
President/CEO; 508-358-
7400; Fax: 508-358-2791

Cascade Systems, Inc.
300 Brickstone Sq.
Andover, MA 01810
http://www.cascadenet.
com
Founded: 1993
Total Employees: 109
Industries: Computer
Hardware, Computer
Software
Growth: Openings in past
year, 34
Contact Malcolm McGrory,
President/CEO; 508-749-
7000; Fax: 508-749-7199

**Cerulean Technology,
Inc.**
300 Nickerson Rd.
Marlborough, MA 01752
http://www.cerulean.com
Founded: 1992
Total Employees: 80

Annual Sales: $10 million
Industry: Computer Software
Growth: Openings in past year, 25
Contact Robert P. Badavas, President; 508-460-4000; Fax: 508-460-4099; E-mail: info@cerulean.com

Chemineer Kenics
125 Flagship Dr.
North Andover, MA 01845
Founded: 1963
Total Employees: 100
Annual Sales: $23 million
Industries: Energy, Environmental, Test and Measurement
Growth: Openings in past year, 30
Contact Leonard Graziano, President; 978-687-0101; Fax: 978-687-8500

Cognex Corp.
One Vision Dr.
Natick, MA 01760
http://www.cognex.com
Founded: 1981
Total Employees: 350
Annual Sales: $130 million
Industries: Computer Software, Factory Automation, Holding Companies
Growth: Openings in past year, 61
Contact Robert Shillman, President/CEO; 508-650-3000; Fax: 508-650-3333

Collagenesis, Inc.
500 Cummings Ctr., Suite 464C
Beverly, MA 01915
Founded: 1996
Total Employees: 40
Industry: Medical
Growth: Openings in past year, 36
Contact Louis R. Frisina, President; 978-232-9333; Fax: 978-232-9601

Columbia Technical Services
17 Briden St.
Worcester, MA 01615
Founded: 1992
Total Employees: 175
Annual Sales: $23 million
Industry: Subassemblies and Components
Growth: Openings in past year, 25
Contact James Coghlin, Sr., President/Chief Quality Officer; 508-753-2354; Fax: 508-753-4310

Computer Merchant Ltd.
80 Washington St., Bldg. S
Norwell, MA 02061
http://www.tcml.com
Founded: 1978
Total Employees: 750
Annual Sales: $53 million
Industry: Computer Hardware
Growth: Openings in past year, 250
Contact Ms. Karin Bresnahan, Director of Human Resources; 781-878-1070; Fax: 781-878-4712

Computer Products Power Conversion America
7 Elkins St.
South Boston, MA 02127
http://www.computerproducts.com
Founded: 1947
Total Employees: 325
Industry: Subassemblies and Components
Growth: Openings in past year, 100
Contact Ms. Anne Jones, Director of Human Resources; 617-464-6600; Fax: 617-464-6612; E-mail: webmaster@computerproducts.com

Concord Communications, Inc.
33 Boston Post Rd., West Marlborough, MA 01752
http://www.concord.com
Founded: 1981
Total Employees: 97
Annual Sales: $9 million
Industry: Computer Software
Growth: Openings in past year, 37
Contact John Blaeser, President; 508-460-4646; Fax: 508-481-9772; E-mail: info@concord.com

Continental Resources, Inc.
175 Middlesex Tpke.
Bedford, MA 01730
http://www.conres.com
Founded: 1962
Total Employees: 350
Industry: Holding Companies
Growth: Openings in past year, 100
Contact Ms. Janet MacPherson, Recruitment Manager; 781-275-0850; Fax: 781-275-6563; E-mail: adempsey@conres.com

Cuming Corp.
230 Bodwell St.
Avon, MA 02322
Founded: 1980
Total Employees: 80
Annual Sales: $10 million
Industries: Advanced Materials, Photonics
Growth: Openings in past year, 40
Contact William Cuming, President; 508-580-2660; Fax: 508-580-0960; E-mail: mtkocsik@aol.com

Cynosure, Inc.
10 Elizabeth Dr.
Chelmsford, MA 01824
Founded: 1991
Total Employees: 95
Annual Sales: $12 million
Industries: Medical,
Photonics
Growth: Openings in past
year, 39
Contact Dr. Horace W.
Furumoto, President/
CEO; 978-256-4200;
Fax: 978-256-6556

Cytyc Corp.
85 Swanson Rd.
Boxboro, MA 01719
http://www.cytyc.com
Founded: 1987
Total Employees: 180
Annual Sales: $8.198
million
Industries: Biotechnology,
Medical
Growth: Openings in past
year, 118
Contact Ms. Christine
Pattison, Manager of
Personnel; 978-263-
8000; Fax: 978-635-
1033; E-mail: info@cytyc.
com

**Database Technologies,
Inc.**
27 Mica Ln., 2nd Fl.
Wellesley Hills, MA 02181
http://www.dbtinc.com
Founded: 1986
Total Employees: 75
Industry:
Telecommunications
Growth: Openings in past
year, 35
Contact David Teplo,
Chief Executive Officer;
781-431-2300; Fax: 781-
431-8444; E-mail: info@
dbtinc.com

**Dr Solomon's Software,
Inc.**
1 New England Executive
Pk.
Burlington, MA 01803
http://www.drsolomon.com
Founded: 1984
Total Employees: 330
Annual Sales: $44 million
Industry: Computer
Software
Growth: Openings in past
year, 110
Contact Ms. Suzanne
Bishop, Human
Resources Manager;
781-273-7400; Fax: 781-
273-7474; E-mail: info@
us.drsolomon.com

Dragon Systems, Inc.
320 Nevada St.
Newton, MA 02160
http://www.dragonsys.com
Founded: 1982
Total Employees: 230
Annual Sales: $29 million
Industries: Computer
Hardware, Computer
Software
Growth: Openings in past
year, 49
Contact Ms. Tamah
Rosker, Director of
Human Resources; 617-
965-5200; Fax: 617-527-
0372

Draka (USA), Inc.
9 Forge Park
Franklin, MA 02038
Founded: 1984
Total Employees: 530
Industry: Holding
Companies
Growth: Openings in past
year, 78
Contact Garo Artinian,
President/CEO; 508-520-
1200; Fax: 508-541-6790

**Eaton Thermal
Processing Systems**
2 Centennial Dr.
Peabody, MA 01960
Founded: 1987
Total Employees: 45
Annual Sales: $5.6 million
Industries: Manufacturing
Equipment,
Subassemblies and
Components
Growth: Openings in past
year, 25
Contact Ms. MiAnne Liu,
Office Manager; 978-524-
6400; Fax: 978-524-6444

EBSCO Publishing
10 Estes St.
PO Box 682
Ipswich, MA 01938
http://www.epnet.com
Founded: 1987
Total Employees: 350
Industries: Computer
Software,
Telecommunications
Growth: Openings in past
year, 100
Contact Tom Miller,
Human Resources
Manager; 978-356-6500;
Fax: 978-356-6565;
E-mail: ep@epnet.com

**EDS Personal
Communications**
1601 Trapelo Rd.
Waltham, MA 02154
Founded: 1986
Total Employees: 500
Annual Sales: $85 million
Industry:
Telecommunications
Growth: Openings in past
year, 100
Contact Bruce T. Leonard,
President/CEO; 781-890-
1000; Fax: 781-890-0367

Electronic Designs, Inc.
1 Research Dr.
Westborough, MA 01581

http://www.electronic-designs.com
Founded: 1981
Total Employees: 125
Annual Sales: $59.223 million
Industries: Advanced Materials, Computer Hardware, Factory Automation, Photonics, Subassemblies and Components
Growth: Openings in past year, 25
Contact Ms. Sally Baronian, Personnel Administrator; 508-366-5151; Fax: 508-836-4850

Electronic Products, Inc.
85 Parker St.
Newburyport, MA 01950
Founded: 1961
Total Employees: 125
Annual Sales: $16 million
Industry: Subassemblies and Components
Growth: Openings in past year, 25
Contact Joseph Urbanetti, President; 978-462-8101; Fax: 978-462-4071

Emerson and Cuming Composite Materials, Inc.
59 Walpole St.
Canton, MA 02021
Founded: 1981
Total Employees: 175
Industry: Advanced Materials
Growth: Openings in past year, 70
Contact Ms. Ali Gillespie, Human Resources Manager; 781-821-4250; Fax: 781-828-0124; E-mail: snakleoil@emerson.com

Endogen, Inc.
30 Commerce Way
Woburn, MA 01801
http://www.endogen.com
Founded: 1983
Total Employees: 75

Annual Sales: $9.589 million
Industry: Biotechnology
Growth: Openings in past year, 25
Contact Owen A. Dempsey, President/CEO; 781-937-0890; Fax: 781-937-3096; E-mail: ir@endogen.com

Energy Sciences, Inc.
42 Industrial Way
Wilmington, MA 01887
http://www.ebeam.com
Founded: 1970
Total Employees: 100
Annual Sales: $12 million
Industries: Factory Automation, Manufacturing Equipment
Growth: Openings in past year, 40
Contact Harvey Clough, President/COO; 978-694-9000; Fax: 978-694-9046

Exchange Applications, Inc.
695 Atlantic Ave.
Boston, MA 02111
http://www.exapps.com
Founded: 1995
Total Employees: 70
Annual Sales: $9.0 million
Industries: Computer Hardware, Computer Software
Growth: Openings in past year, 45
Contact Andrew Frawley, President/CEO; 617-737-2244; Fax: 617-443-9143; E-mail: info@exapps.com

Fiber Optic Network Solutions Corp.
71 Lyman St.
Northborough, MA 01532
http://www.fons.com
Founded: 1992
Total Employees: 130
Industries: Photonics, Telecommunications
Growth: Openings in past year, 70

Contact Ms. Cathy Twiss, Human Resources Manager; 508-393-4268; Fax: 508-393-3657; E-mail: sales@fons.com

Firefly Network, Inc.
1 Broadway, 6th Floor
Cambridge, MA 02142
http://www.firefly.net
Founded: 1995
Total Employees: 85
Annual Sales: $11 million
Industry: Computer Software
Growth: Openings in past year, 55
Contact Ms. Kathleen McCarthy, Director of Human Resources; 617-528-1000; Fax: 617-577-7220; E-mail: feedback@firefly.net

Focal, Inc.
4 Maguire Rd.
Lexington, MA 02173
Founded: 1991
Total Employees: 100
Annual Sales: $3.1 million
Industry: Medical
Growth: Openings in past year, 40
Contact David Clapper, President/CEO; 781-280-7800; Fax: 781-280-7801; E-mail: info@focalinc.com

General Scanning, Inc.
500 Arsenal St.
Watertown, MA 02172
Founded: 1968
Total Employees: 800
Annual Sales: $131.867 million
Industries: Computer Hardware, Holding Companies
Growth: Openings in past year, 117
Contact Ms. Linda Palmer, Vice President; 617-924-1010; Fax: 617-926-0708

Genome Therapeutics Corp.
100 Beaver St.
Waltham, MA 02154
Founded: 1961
Total Employees: 190
Annual Sales: $21 million
Industry: Pharmaceuticals
Growth: Openings in past year, 84
Contact Joseph Pane, VP of Human Resources; 781-893-5007; Fax: 781-893-8277

Gensym Corp.
125 Cambridge Park Dr.
Cambridge, MA 02140
http://www.gensym.com
Founded: 1986
Total Employees: 305
Annual Sales: $37.2 million
Industry: Computer Software
Growth: Openings in past year, 23
Contact Ms. Louise Callahan, Director of Human Resources; 617-547-2500; Fax: 617-547-1962; E-mail: info@gensym.com

Gentex Optics, Inc.
PO Box 307, 183 West Main St.
Dudley, MA 01571
Founded: 1932
Total Employees: 300
Annual Sales: $36 million
Industry: Medical
Growth: Openings in past year, 50
Contact Philip Sator, Human Resources Manager; 508-943-3860; Fax: 508-949-3701

Geo-Centers, Inc.
7 Wells Ave.
Newton, MA 02159
Founded: 1975

Total Employees: 600
Annual Sales: $55 million
Industries: Biotechnology, Chemicals, Environmental, Holding Companies, Manufacturing Equipment, Medical, Test and Measurement
Growth: Openings in past year, 50
Contact James T. Kimble, Dir. of Human Resources & Administration; 617-964-7070; Fax: 617-527-7592

Haley & Aldrich, Inc.
58 Charles St.
Cambridge, MA 02141
Founded: 1957
Total Employees: 297
Annual Sales: $33.3 million
Industries: Environmental, Manufacturing Equipment
Growth: Openings in past year, 27
Contact Edward E. Kinner, President; 617-494-1606; Fax: 617-577-8142; E-mail: bos@haleyaldrich.com

Harlequin, Inc.
One Cambridge Ctr.
Cambridge, MA 02142
http://www.harlequin.com
Founded: 1986
Total Employees: 280
Annual Sales: $36 million
Industry: Computer Software
Growth: Openings in past year, 30
Contact Jo Bragger, Personnel Manager; 617-374-2400; Fax: 617-252-6505; E-mail: web@harlequin.com

Harte-Hanks Data Technologies, Inc.
25 Linnell Cir.
Billerica, MA 01821
Founded: 1968
Total Employees: 500

Annual Sales: $64 million
Industries: Computer Hardware, Computer Software
Growth: Openings in past year, 100
Contact Ms. Trish Clark, VP of Human Resources; 978-663-9955; Fax: 978-667-7297

Helix Technology Corp.
Mansfield Corporate Ctr., 9 Hampshire St.
Mansfield, MA 02048
Founded: 1967
Total Employees: 450
Annual Sales: $128.383 million
Industry: Subassemblies and Components
Growth: Openings in past year, 49
Contact Christopher J. Madden, VP of Human Resources; 508-337-5500; Fax: 508-337-5669

Hottinger Baldwin Measurements, Inc.
19 Bartlett St.
Marlborough, MA 01752
http://www.hbmwt.com
Founded: 1973
Total Employees: 196
Annual Sales: $20 million
Industries: Subassemblies and Components, Test and Measurement
Growth: Openings in past year, 40
Contact Joseph Antkowiak, CEO/President; 508-624-4500; Fax: 508-485-7480

ICI
PO Box 332
Mansfield, MA 02048
http://www.ici.net
Founded: 1994
Total Employees: 50
Annual Sales: $8.5 million
Industry: Telecommunications

Growth: Openings in past year, 30
Contact Burke Anderson, President; 508-261-0383; Fax: 508-261-0430; E-mail: info@ici.net

Infinium Software, Inc.
25 Communications Way
Hyannis, MA 02601
http://www.infinium.com
Founded: 1981
Total Employees: 540
Annual Sales: $72 million
Industry: Computer Software
Growth: Openings in past year, 79
Contact Dan Kossmann, Chief Financial Officer; 508-778-2000; Fax: 508-775-3764; E-mail: webteam@infinium.com

Inspex, Inc.
47 Manning Rd.
Billerica, MA 01821
Founded: 1974
Total Employees: 150
Industries: Computer Software, Factory Automation
Growth: Openings in past year, 30
Contact Ms. Roberta Benson, Director of Human Resources; 978-667-5500; Fax: 978-663-0011

Intellution, Inc.
1 Edgewater Dr.
Norwood, MA 02062
http://www.intellution.com
Founded: 1980
Total Employees: 300
Annual Sales: $65 million
Industry: Computer Software
Growth: Openings in past year, 100
Contact Michael Jacobi, VP of Human Resources; 781-769-8878; Fax: 781-769-1990; E-mail: info@intellution.com

Interactive Video Systems, Inc.
45 Winthrop St.
Concord, MA 01742
http://www.ivsinc.com
Founded: 1982
Total Employees: 100
Annual Sales: $15 million
Industries: Factory Automation, Photonics
Growth: Openings in past year, 25
Contact Hans F. Hoyer, Chief Executive Officer; 978-371-2600; Fax: 978-369-0850

Internet Access Co., Inc.
175 Great Rd.
Bedford, MA 01730
http://www.tiac.net/
Founded: 1993
Total Employees: 200
Annual Sales: $11.5 million
Industry: Telecommunications
Growth: Openings in past year, 75
Contact Ms. Linda Vaughan, Human Resources Manager; 781-276-7200; Fax: 781-275-2224; E-mail: sales@tiac.net

Invention Machine Corp.
200 Portland St.
Boston, MA 02114
http://www.invention-machine.com
Founded: 1992
Total Employees: 100
Industry: Computer Software
Growth: Openings in past year, 49
Contact Dr. Val Tsourikov, CEO/Chief Scientist; 617-305-9250; Fax: 617-305-9255; E-mail: info@invention-machine.com

Iris Associates, Inc.
1 Technology Park
Westford, MA 01886
http://www.iris.com
Founded: 1984
Total Employees: 160
Annual Sales: $20 million
Industry: Computer Software
Growth: Openings in past year, 64
Contact Raymond Ozzie, President; 978-692-2800; Fax: 978-692-7365

ISI Systems, Inc.
Two Tech Dr.
Andover, MA 01810
http://www.isisys.com
Founded: 1969
Total Employees: 900
Annual Sales: $110 million
Industry: Computer Software
Growth: Openings in past year, 97
Contact Ms. Lucia Valente, VP of Human Resources; 978-682-5500; Fax: 978-686-0130; E-mail: info@isisys.com

Katahdin Industries, Inc.
61 North Ave.
Natick, MA 01760
Founded: 1965
Total Employees: 95
Industry: Holding Companies
Growth: Openings in past year, 39
Contact Roger Huebsch, President; 508-653-7380; Fax: 508-653-7832

Kenan Systems Corp.
1 Main St.
Cambridge, MA 02142
http://www.kenan.com
Founded: 1982
Total Employees: 250
Annual Sales: $32 million

Industry: Computer Software
Growth: Openings in past year, 69
Contact Ms. Eileen Winnick, Director of Human Resources; 617-225-2200; Fax: 617-225-2220

Krohne America, Inc.
7 Dearborn Rd.
Peabody, MA 01960
http://www.krohne.com
Founded: 1980
Total Employees: 100
Annual Sales: $13 million
Industry: Test and Measurement
Growth: Openings in past year, 25
Contact Horst Focks, CEO/President; 978-535-6060; Fax: 978-535-1720; E-mail: info@krohne.com

Lasertron, Inc.
11 Oak Park Dr.
Bedford, MA 01730
Founded: 1980
Total Employees: 285
Annual Sales: $28 million
Industry: Photonics
Growth: Openings in past year, 59
Contact Dr. Robert Hannemann, President; 781-280-9000; Fax: 781-280-3300

Levine-Fricke-Recon Group
25 Mathewson Dr.
Weymouth, MA 02189
Founded: 1969
Total Employees: 461
Annual Sales: $56 million
Industry: Environmental
Growth: Openings in past year, 50
Contact Robert J. Kelly, Executive Vice President/General Manager; 781-337-7887; Fax: 781-337-8237

Lifeline Systems, Inc.
640 Memorial Dr.
Cambridge, MA 02139
Founded: 1974
Total Employees: 425
Annual Sales: $50 million
Industries: Medical, Telecommunications
Growth: Openings in past year, 99
Contact Ms. Heather F. Edelman, VP of Human Resources; 617-679-1000; Fax: 617-679-1384

Lycos, Inc.
293 Boston Post Rd. West
Marlborough, MA 01752
http://www.lycos.com
Founded: 1995
Total Employees: 100
Annual Sales: $5.3 million
Industries: Computer Software, Telecommunications
Growth: Openings in past year, 70
Contact Robert Davis, President/CEO; 508-424-0400; Fax: 508-229-2866; E-mail: webmaster@lycos.com

Madison Cable Corp.
125 Goddard Memorial Dr.
Worcester, MA 01603
Founded: 1976
Total Employees: 370
Industries: Photonics, Subassemblies and Components
Growth: Openings in past year, 54
Contact Ed Hamilton, Director of Human Resources; 508-752-2884; Fax: 508-798-4194

Matec Corp.
75 South St.
Hopkinton, MA 01748
Founded: 1948
Total Employees: 324

Annual Sales: $30.857 million
Industry: Holding Companies
Growth: Openings in past year, 84
Contact Ted Valpey, Jr., COB/President/CEO; 508-435-9039; Fax: 508-435-4496

MathWorks, Inc.
24 Prime Park Way
Natick, MA 01760
http://www.mathworks.com
Founded: 1984
Total Employees: 420
Industry: Computer Software
Growth: Openings in past year, 100
Contact John N. Little, President; 508-647-7000; Fax: 508-647-7001; E-mail: info@mathworks.com

Medical Systems Management, Inc.
100 Main St.
Reading, MA 01867
http://www.med-sys.com
Founded: 1973
Total Employees: 95
Annual Sales: $8.9 million
Industry: Computer Software
Growth: Openings in past year, 31
Contact Raymond Forgit, President; 781-942-1700; Fax: 781-942-0917; E-mail: info@med-sys.com

Metfab Engineering, Inc.
332 John Dietsch Blvd.
Attleboro Falls, MA 02763
Founded: 1979
Total Employees: 90
Industries: Holding Companies, Manufacturing Equipment
Growth: Openings in past year, 30

Contact Edward Urquhart, President; 508-695-1007; Fax: 508-695-6335

Microsemi Corp., Semiconductor Products Division
580 Pleasant St.
Watertown, MA 02172
Founded: 1960
Total Employees: 350
Annual Sales: $47 million
Industry: Subassemblies and Components
Growth: Openings in past year, 23
Contact Ms. Lois Needham, Human Resources Manager; 617-926-0404; Fax: 617-924-1235

MicroTouch Systems, Inc.
300 Griffin Park
Methuen, MA 01844
http://www.microtouch.com
Founded: 1982
Total Employees: 700
Annual Sales: $95.045 million
Industries: Computer Hardware, Computer Software, Holding Companies
Growth: Openings in past year, 149
Contact Ms. Anne Marie Bell, Manager of Human Resources; 978-659-9000; Fax: 978-659-9100; E-mail: touch@microtouch.com

Millennium Pharmaceuticals, Inc.
640 Memorial Dr.
Cambridge, MA 02139
Founded: 1993
Total Employees: 375
Industries: Biotechnology, Pharmaceuticals
Growth: Openings in past year, 120

Contact Ms. Linda K. Pine, VP of Human Resources; 617-679-7000; Fax: 617-374-9379

Mod-Tap Corp.
285 Ayer Rd.
PO Box 706
Harvard, MA 01451
http://www.mod-tap.com
Founded: 1977
Total Employees: 350
Industry: Subassemblies and Components
Growth: Openings in past year, 38
Contact David Bundy, President; 978-772-5630; Fax: 978-772-2011

Molten Metal Technology, Inc.
400-2 Totten Pond Rd.
Waltham, MA 02154
http://www.mmt.com
Founded: 1989
Total Employees: 500
Annual Sales: $44.181 million
Industry: Environmental
Growth: Openings in past year, 69
Contact Ms. Katharyn Santoro, VP of Human Resources; 781-487-9700; Fax: 781-487-7870

MRSI
25 Industrial Ave.
Chelmsford, MA 01824
Founded: 1983
Total Employees: 120
Annual Sales: $15 million
Industries: Factory Automation, Holding Companies, Manufacturing Equipment
Growth: Openings in past year, 35
Contact Neil Srivastava, President/CEO; 978-256-4950; Fax: 978-256-5120; E-mail: mrsi1@ma.ultranet.com

Nabnasset Corp.
15 Craig Rd.
Acton, MA 01720
Founded: 1990
Total Employees: 63
Annual Sales: $8.1 million
Industry: Computer Software
Growth: Openings in past year, 28
Contact Richard J. Davis, President/CEO; 508-787-2800; Fax: 508-787-2834

Natural MicroSystems Corp.
100 Crossing Blvd.
Framingham, MA 01702
http://www.nmss.com
Founded: 1983
Total Employees: 250
Annual Sales: $51.46 million
Industries: Computer Hardware, Computer Software, Holding Companies, Telecommunications
Growth: Openings in past year, 50
Contact Ms. Kay Meekes, VP of Human Resources; 508-620-9300; Fax: 508-620-9313; E-mail: info@nmss.com

NetScout Systems, Inc.
4 Technology Park Dr.
Westford, MA 01886
http://www.netscout.com
Founded: 1984
Total Employees: 140
Industry: Computer Software
Growth: Openings in past year, 90
Contact Anil Singhal, COB/CEO; 978-244-4000; Fax: 978-244-4004; E-mail: webmaster@netscout.com

NewsEDGE Corp.
80 Blanchard Rd.
Burlington, MA 01803
http://newsedge.
 desktopdata.com
Founded: 1988
Total Employees: 436
Annual Sales: $75 million
Industries: Computer
 Software,
 Telecommunications
Growth: Openings in past
 year, 116
Contact Don McLagan,
 COB/CEO/President;
 781-229-3000; Fax: 781-
 229-3030

Nexar Technologies, Inc.
182 Turnpike Rd.
Westborough, MA 01581
http://www.nexarpc.com
Founded: 1995
Total Employees: 70
Annual Sales: $18.6
 million
Industry: Computer
 Hardware
Growth: Openings in past
 year, 40
Contact Albert J. Agbay,
 COB/CEO; 508-836-
 8700; Fax: 508-836-8729

NovaSoft Systems, Inc.
10 Burlington Mall Rd.
Burlington, MA 01803
http://www.novasoft.com
Founded: 1988
Total Employees: 100
Industry: Computer
 Software
Growth: Openings in past
 year, 25
Contact Bruce Cohen,
 President; 781-221-0300;
 Fax: 781-221-0465;
 E-mail: info@novasoft.
 com

Nuclear Metals, Inc.
2229 Main St.
Concord, MA 01742

http://www.nucmet.com
Founded: 1972
Total Employees: 210
Annual Sales: $28.69
 million
Industries: Advanced
 Materials, Holding
 Companies,
 Subassemblies and
 Components
Growth: Openings in past
 year, 40
Contact Ms. Judith
 Stephenson, Personnel
 Manager; 978-369-5410;
 Fax: 978-369-4045;
 E-mail: sales@nucmet.
 com

**Oberon Software
Incorporated**
215 First St.
Cambridge, MA 02142
http://www.oberon.com
Founded: 1989
Total Employees: 51
Industry: Computer
 Software
Growth: Openings in past
 year, 31
Contact Joseph Chappel,
 President; 617-494-0990;
 Fax: 617-494-0414;
 E-mail: info@oberon.com

Object Design, Inc.
25 Burlington Mall Rd.
Burlington, MA 01803
http://www.odi.com
Founded: 1988
Total Employees: 270
Annual Sales: $38 million
Industry: Computer
 Software
Growth: Openings in past
 year, 54
Contact Robert N.
 Goldman, COB/CEO/
 President; 781-674-5000;
 Fax: 781-674-5262;
 E-mail: info@odi.com

**Onward Technologies,
Inc.**
313 Speen St., Suite 202
Natick, MA 01760

http://www.onwardtech.
 com
Founded: 1994
Total Employees: 50
Annual Sales: $6 million
Industries: Computer
 Hardware, Computer
 Software
Growth: Openings in past
 year, 35
Contact David Reske,
 President/CEO; 508-651-
 0070; Fax: 508-651-
 0080; E-mail: sales@
 onwardtech.com

Open Group
11 Cambridge Ctr.
Cambridge, MA 02142
http://www.opengroup.org
Founded: 1988
Total Employees: 250
Annual Sales: $32 million
Industry: Computer
 Software
Growth: Openings in past
 year, 50
Contact Christian Mar, VP
 of Human Resources and
 Administration; 617-621-
 8700; Fax: 617-621-
 0631; E-mail: direct@
 opengroup.org

Open Market, Inc.
245 1st St.
Cambridge, MA 02142
http://www.openmarket.
 com
Founded: 1993
Total Employees: 550
Annual Sales: $23 million
Industries: Holding
 Companies,
 Telecommunications
Growth: Openings in past
 year, 229
Contact Ms. Joanne
 Conrad, VP of Human
 Resources; 617-949-
 7000; Fax: 617-621-
 1703; E-mail: sales@
 openmarket.com

Optical Corporation of America
170 Locke Dr.
Marlborough, MA 01752
http://www.oca.com
Founded: 1985
Total Employees: 160
Annual Sales: $30 million
Industries: Manufacturing
Equipment, Photonics
Growth: Openings in past
year, 55
Contact Ms. Pauline
Stephens, Human
Resources Manager;
508-481-9860; Fax: 508-485-0526

Pacer Infotec, Inc.
900 Technology Park Dr.
Billerica, MA 01821
http://www.pacerinfotec.com
Founded: 1968
Total Employees: 552
Annual Sales: $41.3
million
Industries: Computer
Hardware, Computer
Software, Defense,
Manufacturing
Equipment,
Transportation
Growth: Openings in past
year, 27
Contact Ms. Roberta
Steinberg, VP of Human
Resources; 978-667-8800; Fax: 978-667-8873; E-mail: shareinfo@pacerinfotec.com

Parlex Corp.
145 Milk St.
Methuen, MA 01844
http://www.parlex.com
Founded: 1970
Total Employees: 475
Annual Sales: $55 million
Industry: Subassemblies
and Components
Growth: Openings in past
year, 23
Contact Ms. Frances
Spechts, Director of
Human Resources; 978-685-4341; Fax: 978-685-8809; E-mail:
infomaster@parlex.com

PC DOCS, Inc.
25 Burlington Mall Rd.
Burlington, MA 01803
http://www.pcdocs.com
Founded: 1990
Total Employees: 270
Industry: Computer
Software
Growth: Openings in past
year, 49
Contact Rubin Oston,
COB/CEO; 781-273-3800; Fax: 781-272-3693

Precise Software Solutions, Inc.
50 Braintree Hill Office
Pk., Suite 110
Braintree, MA 02184
http://www.precisesoft.com
Founded: 1991
Total Employees: 60
Annual Sales: $7.7 million
Industry: Computer
Software
Growth: Openings in past
year, 30
Contact Dan Haley,
President; 781-380-3300;
Fax: 781-380-3349;
E-mail: corporate@precisesoft.com

Priority Call Management
110 Fordham Rd.
Wilmington, MA 01887
http://www.prioritycall.com
Founded: 1992
Total Employees: 100
Annual Sales: $11 million
Industry:
Telecommunications
Growth: Openings in past
year, 50
Contact Andrew Ory,
President; 978-658-4400;
Fax: 978-658-3809;
E-mail: info@prioritycall.com

Process Software Corp.
959 Concord St.
Framingham, MA 01701
http://www.process.com
Founded: 1984
Total Employees: 150
Annual Sales: $19 million
Industry: Computer
Software
Growth: Openings in past
year, 25
Contact Dean
Goodermote, President;
508-879-6994; Fax: 508-879-0042

Programart Corporation
124 Mount Auburn St.
Cambridge, MA 02138
http://www.programart.com
Founded: 1969
Total Employees: 210
Annual Sales: $27 million
Industry: Computer
Software
Growth: Openings in past
year, 45
Contact Bill Mrachek,
Director of Human
Resources; 617-661-3020; Fax: 617-498-4010

Project Software & Development, Inc.
20 University Rd.
Cambridge, MA 02138
http://www.psdi.com
Founded: 1968
Total Employees: 520
Annual Sales: $73.329
million
Industry: Computer
Software
Growth: Openings in past
year, 135
Contact Bob Clancy,
Director of Human
Resources; 617-661-1444; Fax: 617-661-1642; E-mail:
grace_ferry@psdi.com

Prominet Corp.
100 Nickerson Rd.
Marlborough, MA 01752
http://www.prominet.com
Founded: 1996
Total Employees: 50
Industries:
  Subassemblies and
  Components,
  Telecommunications
Growth: Openings in past
  year, 45
Contact Menachem E.
  Abraham, President/
  CEO; 508-303-8885;
  Fax: 508-303-8161;
  E-mail: info@prominet.
  com

Psychemedics Corp.
1280 Massachusetts Ave.,
  Suite 200
Cambridge, MA 02138
Founded: 1986
Total Employees: 120
Annual Sales: $12.2
  million
Industry: Pharmaceuticals
Growth: Openings in past
  year, 50
Contact Raymond C.
  Kubacki, Jr., President/
  CEO; 617-868-7455;
  Fax: 617-864-1639

**R.G. Vanderweil
Engineers, Inc.**
274 Summer St.
Boston, MA 02210
Founded: 1947
Total Employees: 450
Annual Sales: $38.8
  million
Industry: Manufacturing
  Equipment
Growth: Openings in past
  year, 75
Contact Gary Vanderweil,
  Chief Executive Officer;
  617-423-7423; Fax: 617-
  423-7401; E-mail: info@
  vanderweil.com

Raptor Systems, Inc.
69 Hickory Dr.
Waltham, MA 02154
http://www.raptor.com
Founded: 1992
Total Employees: 110
Annual Sales: $14 million
Industry: Computer
  Software
Growth: Openings in past
  year, 30
Contact Robert
  Steinkrauss, COB/CEO;
  781-487-7700; Fax: 781-
  487-6755; E-mail: info@
  raptor.com

Reed National Co.
260 North Elm St.
Westfield, MA 01085
Founded: 1946
Total Employees: 275
Annual Sales: $63 million
Industry: Energy
Growth: Openings in past
  year, 25
Contact John E. Reed,
  President; 413-568-9571;
  Fax: 413-568-2969

Roll Systems, Inc.
63 2nd Ave.
Burlington, MA 01803
Founded: 1987
Total Employees: 160
Annual Sales: $38 million
Industries: Computer
  Hardware, Factory
  Automation
Growth: Openings in past
  year, 40
Contact Ms. Christine
  Balba, Operations
  Manager; 781-229-2266;
  Fax: 781-229-0486

**Safesite Records
Management Corp.**
96 High St.
PO Box 330
North Billerica, MA 01862
http://www.safe-site.com
Founded: 1986
Total Employees: 325
Annual Sales: $42 million
Industry: Computer
  Software

Growth: Openings in past
  year, 50
Contact Charles Estes,
  Marketing Manager; 978-
  663-7100; Fax: 978-670-
  5406; E-mail: safesite@
  tiac.com

Sapient Corp.
1 Memorial Dr.
Cambridge, MA 02142
http://www.sapient.com
Founded: 1991
Total Employees: 721
Annual Sales: $44.6
  million
Industry: Computer
  Software
Growth: Openings in past
  year, 228
Contact J. Stuart Moore,
  Co-Chairman/Co-CEO;
  617-621-0200; Fax: 617-
  374-1300

Schaefer, Inc.
251 West Central St.
Natick, MA 01760
Founded: 1987
Total Employees: 145
Annual Sales: $19 million
Industries: Energy,
  Subassemblies and
  Components
Growth: Openings in past
  year, 30
Contact Dr. J. Schafer,
  President; 508-652-0884;
  Fax: 508-879-0885

**SeaChange International,
Inc.**
124 Acton St.
Maynard, MA 01754
http://www.schange.com
Founded: 1993
Total Employees: 160
Annual Sales: $49.3
  million
Industry:
  Telecommunications
Growth: Openings in past
  year, 60
Contact Bill Styslinger,
  President/CEO; 978-897-
  0100; Fax: 978-897-0132

Security Dynamics Technologies, Inc.
20 Crosby Dr.
Bedford, MA 01730
http://www.securitydynamics.com
Founded: 1984
Total Employees: 530
Annual Sales: $70 million
Industries: Computer Hardware, Computer Software, Holding Companies
Growth: Openings in past year, 199
Contact Ms. Vivian Vitale, VP of Human Resources; 781-687-7000; Fax: 781-687-7010

Segue Software, Inc.
1320 Centre St.
Newton Center, MA 02159
http://www.segue.com
Founded: 1988
Total Employees: 150
Annual Sales: $16.972 million
Industries: Computer Hardware, Computer Software
Growth: Openings in past year, 50
Contact Ms. Betsy R. Rudnick, VP of Human Resources and Administration; 617-796-1000; Fax: 617-796-1621; E-mail: info@segue.com

Selfcare, Inc.
200 Prospect St.
Waltham, MA 02154
Founded: 1992
Total Employees: 300
Annual Sales: $14 million
Industry: Medical
Growth: Openings in past year, 210
Contact Ron Zwanziger, President; 781-647-3900; Fax: 781-647-3939

SENCORP SYSTEMS, Inc.
400 Kidds Hill Rd.
Hyannis, MA 02601
Founded: 1942
Total Employees: 180
Annual Sales: $22 million
Industry: Manufacturing Equipment
Growth: Openings in past year, 40
Contact Anthony Giovannone, President; 508-771-9400; Fax: 508-790-0002

Sensitech, Inc.
123 Brimbal Ave.
Beverly, MA 01915
http://www.sensitech.com
Founded: 1990
Total Employees: 70
Annual Sales: $9.5 million
Industries: Computer Software, Test and Measurement
Growth: Openings in past year, 36
Contact Ernest M. Santin, Chief Executive Officer; 978-927-7033; Fax: 978-921-2112; E-mail: marketing@sensitech.com

Software Pundits, Inc.
20 Mall Rd., Suite 200
Burlington, MA 01803
http://www.softwarepundits.com
Founded: 1989
Total Employees: 80
Industry: Computer Software
Growth: Openings in past year, 43
Contact Durga Rao, President; 781-229-6655; Fax: 781-229-6660

Solutions 2000 International, Inc.
120 Stafford St.
Worcester, MA 01603
http://www.solutions2000.com
Founded: 1996
Total Employees: 45
Annual Sales: $5.8 million
Industry: Computer Software
Growth: Openings in past year, 40
Contact Prabhakar Agrawal, President; 508-754-8566; Fax: 508-754-8973; E-mail: info@solutions2000.com

Specialized Software International, Inc.
120 Stafford St.
Worcester, MA 01603
http://www.s2ii.com
Founded: 1982
Total Employees: 55
Annual Sales: $7.1 million
Industries: Computer Software, Holding Companies
Growth: Openings in past year, 45
Contact Prabhakar Agrawal, President; 508-754-8566; Fax: 508-754-8973; E-mail: info@solutions2000.com

SpecTran Corp.
SpecTran Industrial Park, 50 Hall Rd.
Sturbridge, MA 01566
http://www.spectran.com
Founded: 1982
Total Employees: 454
Annual Sales: $61.571 million
Industries: Holding Companies, Photonics, Subassemblies and Components
Growth: Openings in past year, 82
Contact Glenn Moore, President/CEO; 508-347-2261; Fax: 508-347-2747

SSG, Inc.
150 Bear Hill Rd.
Waltham, MA 02154
Founded: 1977
Total Employees: 95
Industries: Holding
Companies, Photonics
Growth: Openings in past
year, 40
Contact Dexter Wang,
President; 781-890-0204;
Fax: 781-890-1267;
E-mail: ssg1@ssginc.
com

Sumaria Systems, Inc.
18 Lakeside Office Park
Wakefield, MA 01880
http://www.sumaria.com
Founded: 1982
Total Employees: 220
Industries: Computer
Hardware, Computer
Software
Growth: Openings in past
year, 90
Contact Venilal Sumaria,
President; 781-245-9810

SystemSoft Corp.
313 Speen St.
Natick, MA 01760
http://www.systemsoft.com
Founded: 1990
Total Employees: 280
Annual Sales: $39.7
million
Industry: Computer
Software
Growth: Openings in past
year, 30
Contact Robert F. Angelo,
COB/President/CEO;
508-651-0088; Fax: 508-
651-8188

**TAXWARE International,
Inc.**
27 Congress St.
Salem, MA 01970
http://www.taxware.com
Founded: 1964
Total Employees: 110

Industry: Computer
Software
Growth: Openings in past
year, 25
Contact Dan Sullivan,
Chief Executive Officer;
978-741-0101; Fax: 978-
741-0222; E-mail: info@
taxware.com

Tech Etch, Inc.
45 Aldrin Rd.
Plymouth, MA 02360
Founded: 1961
Total Employees: 480
Industries: Manufacturing
Equipment,
Subassemblies and
Components
Growth: Openings in past
year, 200
Contact George Keeler,
President; 508-747-0300;
Fax: 508-746-9639

Telco Systems, Inc.
63 Nahatan St.
Norwood, MA 02062
http://www.telco.com
Founded: 1972
Total Employees: 425
Annual Sales: $117 million
Industries: Computer
Software, Holding
Companies,
Telecommunications
Growth: Openings in past
year, 36
Contact Richard Nardone,
VP of Corporate
Resources; 781-551-
0300; Fax: 781-551-
0534; E-mail:
marketing@nad.telco.
com

**Thermedics Detection,
Inc.**
220 Mill Rd.
Chelmsford, MA 01824
http://www.thermedics.com
Founded: 1991
Total Employees: 230
Annual Sales: $43.750
million
Industries: Factory
Automation, Holding

Companies, Test and
Measurement
Growth: Openings in past
year, 30
Contact Jeffrey J. Langan,
President/CEO; 978-251-
2000; Fax: 978-251-
2091; E-mail: sales@
thermedics.com

Tom Snyder Productions
80 Coolidge Hill Rd.
Watertown, MA 02172
Founded: 1980
Total Employees: 75
Industries: Computer
Hardware, Computer
Software,
Telecommunications
Growth: Openings in past
year, 25
Contact Thomas F.
Snyder, COB/CEO; 617-
926-6000; Fax: 617-926-
6222

**Transcon Technologies,
Inc.**
PO Box 1536
Westfield, MA 01086
http://www.eciworld.com
Founded: 1943
Total Employees: 320
Industry: Subassemblies
and Components
Growth: Openings in past
year, 240
Contact Pablo Nyarady,
President; 413-562-7684;
Fax: 413-562-7749;
E-mail: sales@eciworld.
com

True Software, Inc.
300 Fifth Ave.
Waltham, MA 02154
http://www.truesoft.com
Founded: 1981
Total Employees: 65
Industry: Computer
Software
Growth: Openings in past
year, 35
Contact Bob Torino,
President/CEO; 781-890-

4450; Fax: 781-890-4452; E-mail: info@truesoft.com

TUV Product Service, Inc.
Five Cherry Hill Dr.
Danvers, MA 01923
http://www.tuvps.com
Founded: 1989
Total Employees: 210
Industries: Medical, Subassemblies and Components, Test and Measurement, Telecommunications
Growth: Openings in past year, 40
Contact Matthias Popp, Chief Executive Officer; 978-777-7999; Fax: 978-777-8441; E-mail: info@tuvps.com

U.S. Assemblies New England
PO Box 690
Middleboro, MA 02346
Founded: 1988
Total Employees: 120
Annual Sales: $30 million
Industries: Manufacturing Equipment, Subassemblies and Components
Growth: Openings in past year, 50
Contact John Piseski, General Manager; 508-946-3300; Fax: 508-946-3305; E-mail: usane@world.std.com

Ultranet Communications, Inc.
313 Boston Post Rd. West, Suite 190
Marlborough, MA 01752
http://www.ultranet.com
Founded: 1994
Total Employees: 92
Annual Sales: $15 million
Industry: Telecommunications
Growth: Openings in past year, 47

Contact Geoffrey Schultz, President; 508-229-8400; Fax: 508-229-2375; E-mail: info@ultranet.com

UNIFI Communications, Inc.
900 Chelmsford, Suite 312
Lowell, MA 01851
http://www.unifi.com
Founded: 1990
Total Employees: 600
Industry: Telecommunications
Growth: Openings in past year, 100
Contact Douglas J. Ranalli, President/CEO; 978-551-7500; Fax: 978-551-7505

Unisyn Technologies, Inc.
25 South St.
Hopkinton, MA 01748
http://www.unisyntech.com
Founded: 1990
Total Employees: 85
Annual Sales: $9.1 million
Industries: Biotechnology, Test and Measurement
Growth: Openings in past year, 35
Contact Peter Savas, CEO/President; 508-435-2000; Fax: 508-435-8111; E-mail: unisyn@unisyntech.com

UroMed Corporation
64 A St.
Needham, MA 02194
http://www.uromed.com
Founded: 1990
Total Employees: 170
Annual Sales: $2.6 million
Industry: Medical
Growth: Openings in past year, 70
Contact John G. Simon, COB/CEO/President; 781-433-0033; Fax: 781-433-0032

V-Tron Electronics Corp.
10 Venus Way
PO Box 3297
South Attleboro, MA 02703
Founded: 1971
Total Employees: 200
Annual Sales: $10.5 million
Industry: Subassemblies and Components
Growth: Openings in past year, 25
Contact Joseph Rheaume, President; 508-761-9100; Fax: 508-761-4727

Vality(R) Technology, Inc.
One Financial Ctr., 6th Floor
Boston, MA 02111
http://www.vality.com
Founded: 1991
Total Employees: 65
Annual Sales: $8.4 million
Industry: Computer Software
Growth: Openings in past year, 30
Contact Mark Atkins, President; 617-338-0300; Fax: 617-338-0338; E-mail: info@vality.com

VideoServer, Inc.
Northwest Park, 63 Third Ave.
Burlington, MA 01803
Founded: 1990
Total Employees: 133
Annual Sales: $48 million
Industry: Telecommunications
Growth: Openings in past year, 35
Contact Robert L. Castle, President; 781-229-2000; Fax: 781-229-2101

Viewlogic Systems, Inc.
293 Boston Post Rd. West
Marlborough, MA 01752
http://www.viewlogic.com

Founded: 1984
Total Employees: 680
Annual Sales: $133 million
Industry: Computer Software
Growth: Openings in past year, 79
Contact David Adey, Director of Human Resources; 508-480-0881; Fax: 508-480-0882; E-mail: viewdirect@viewlogic.com

Viisage Technology, Inc.
30 Porter Rd.
Littleton, MA 01460
http://www.viisage.com
Founded: 1995
Total Employees: 86
Annual Sales: $24.9 million
Industries: Computer Hardware, Factory Automation
Growth: Openings in past year, 44
Contact Bob Hughes, President; 978-952-2200; Fax: 978-952-2225; E-mail: info@viisage.com

Visibility Inc.
100 Fordham Rd.
Wilmington, MA 01887
http://www.visibility.com
Founded: 1979
Total Employees: 200
Annual Sales: $25 million
Industry: Computer Software
Growth: Openings in past year, 35
Contact Dunley Moore, President; 978-694-8000; Fax: 978-694-8020

Voicetek Corporation
19 Alpha Rd.
Chelmsford, MA 01824
http://www.voicetek.com
Founded: 1981
Total Employees: 175
Annual Sales: $25 million

Industries: Computer Software, Telecommunications
Growth: Openings in past year, 55
Contact Sheldon L. Dinkes, President; 978-250-9393; Fax: 978-250-9378; E-mail: info@voicetek.com

Walbar Metals, Inc.
5th St.
Peabody, MA 01960
Founded: 1970
Total Employees: 200
Annual Sales: $25 million
Industry: Manufacturing Equipment
Growth: Openings in past year, 60
Contact Peter Challinor, President; 978-532-2350; Fax: 978-532-6867

Weather Services International
4 Federal St.
Billerica, MA 01821
http://www.wsicorp.com
Founded: 1978
Total Employees: 150
Annual Sales: $30 million
Industry: Computer Hardware
Growth: Openings in past year, 25
Contact Peter McKallagat, Human Resource Manager; 978-670-5000; Fax: 978-670-5100

Workgroup Technology Corp.
91 Hartwell Ave.
Lexington, MA 02173
http://www.workgroup.com
Founded: 1986
Total Employees: 108
Annual Sales: $12 million
Industry: Computer Software
Growth: Openings in past year, 43
Contact James Carney, COB/CEO/President; 781-674-2000; Fax: 781-674-0034; E-mail: glebanc@workgroup.com

Michigan

ACMI Michigan Casting Center
14638 Apple Dr.
Fruitport, MI 49415
Founded: 1995
Total Employees: 176
Industries: Advanced Materials, Manufacturing Equipment
Growth: Openings in past year, 31
Contact Bob Fors, General Manager; 616-842-3500; Fax: 616-842-5872

Altair Computing, Inc.
1757 Maple Lawn
Troy, MI 48084
http://www.altair.com
Founded: 1985
Total Employees: 350
Annual Sales: $45 million
Industries: Computer Software, Holding Companies
Growth: Openings in past year, 100
Contact James Scapa, Chief Executive Officer; 248-614-2400; Fax: 248-614-2411; E-mail: sales@altair.com

ArborText, Inc.
1000 Victors Way, Suite 100
Ann Arbor, MI 48108
http://www.arbortext.com
Founded: 1982
Total Employees: 100
Industry: Computer Software
Growth: Openings in past year, 27
Contact Jim Sterken, President; 313-997-0200; Fax: 313-997-0201; E-mail: info@arbortext.com

Auto-Air Composites, Inc.
5640 Enterprise Dr.
Lansing, MI 48911
http://www.autoair.com
Founded: 1984
Total Employees: 170
Annual Sales: $20 million
Industries: Advanced
  Materials, Transportation
Growth: Openings in past
  year, 25
Contact Arnold Kartub,
  Personnel Director; 517-
  393-4040; Fax: 517-393-
  2164

Bowne Internet Solutions, Inc.
330 Hamilton Row
Birmingham, MI 48009
http://www.bowneinternet.
  com
Founded: 1994
Total Employees: 65
Industry:
  Telecommunications
Growth: Openings in past
  year, 50
Contact P.J. Stafford,
  President; 248-642-0760;
  Fax: 248-642-0594

Clover Communications
41290 Vincenti Ct.
Novi, MI 48375
Founded: 1952
Total Employees: 260
Industries: Computer
  Hardware,
  Telecommunications
Growth: Openings in past
  year, 80
Contact Ms. Sue Croteau,
  Human Resources
  Manager; 810-471-0200;
  Fax: 810-471-0530;
  E-mail: clover@clover.
  com

CMI-Competitive Solutions, Inc.
3940 Peninsula Dr. SE,
  Suite 100
Grand Rapids, MI 49546
http://www.cmi.com
Founded: 1980
Total Employees: 110
Annual Sales: $14 million
Industry: Computer
  Software
Growth: Openings in past
  year, 55
Contact Rich Naworicki,
  Chief Executive Officer;
  616-957-4444; Fax: 616-
  957-3924; E-mail: info@
  cs.cmi.com

Computech, Inc.
30600 North Telegraph
  Rd., Suite 2121
Bingham Farms, MI 48025
http://www.computechcorp.
  com
Founded: 1994
Total Employees: 190
Annual Sales: $24 million
Industries: Computer
  Hardware, Computer
  Software,
  Telecommunications
Growth: Openings in past
  year, 90
Contact Rao R.
  Kancharia, Chief Execu-
  tive Officer; 248-594-
  6500; Fax: 248-594-
  4855; E-mail: david@
  computechcorp.com

Counter Point Furniture Products, Inc.
17237 Van Wagoner Rd.
Spring Lake, MI 49456
Founded: 1990
Total Employees: 139
Annual Sales: $22 million
Industries: Advanced
  Materials, Manufacturing
  Equipment
Growth: Openings in past
  year, 29
Contact Ms. Kristy
  Carmean, Manager of
  Human Resources; 616-
  847-7000; Fax: 616-847-
  3109

Data Systems Network Corp.
34705 West 12 Mile Rd.,
  Suite 300
Farmington Hills, MI 48331
http://www.datasystems.
  com
Founded: 1986
Total Employees: 260
Annual Sales: $34.7
  million
Industries: Computer
  Hardware, Holding
  Companies,
  Telecommunications
Growth: Openings in past
  year, 49
Contact Ms. Jannie
  Jacobs, Director of
  Human Resources; 248-
  489-8700; Fax: 248-489-
  1007; E-mail: info@
  datasystems.com

Detroit Tool and Engineering, Peer Division
2100 East Empire Ave.
Benton Harbor, MI 49022
Founded: 1925
Total Employees: 95
Annual Sales: $14 million
Industry: Factory
  Automation
Growth: Openings in past
  year, 41
Contact Ms. Sally
  Kavanaugh, Supervisor
  of Personnel; 616-925-
  8828; Fax: 616-925-7756

DSP Technology Inc., Transportation Group
795 Highland Dr.
Ann Arbor, MI 48108
http://www.dspt.com
Founded: 1982
Total Employees: 100
Industries: Energy,
  Subassemblies and
  Components, Test and
  Measurement
Growth: Openings in past
  year, 55

Contact F. Gil Troutman, Jr., President; 313-973-1111; Fax: 313-973-1103

Durr Automation, Inc.
50055 Pontiac Trail
PO Box 1014
Wixom, MI 48393
http://www.durr.com
Founded: 1970
Total Employees: 135
Annual Sales: $30 million
Industry: Factory Automation
Growth: Openings in past year, 35
Contact Dan Zinger, Vice President/General Manager; 248-960-4630; Fax: 248-960-4633; E-mail: durr.automation@durr.com

edcor Data Services
31000 Northwestern Hwy.
Farmington Hills, MI 48334
Founded: 1970
Total Employees: 125
Industry: Computer Software
Growth: Openings in past year, 35
Contact Daniel Rose, Chief Executive Officer; 248-626-1110; Fax: 248-626-2011

Federal APD, Inc.
42775 West Nine Mile Rd.
Novi, MI 48375
Founded: 1953
Total Employees: 150
Annual Sales: $19 million
Industries: Computer Hardware, Computer Software, Test and Measurement, Transportation
Growth: Openings in past year, 30
Contact Jesse N. Polan, President; 248-374-9600; Fax: 248-374-9610

GHSP
1250 Beechtree St.
Grand Haven, MI 49417
http://www.ghsp.com
Founded: 1994
Total Employees: 500
Annual Sales: $80 million
Industries:
Subassemblies and Components, Test and Measurement, Transportation
Growth: Openings in past year, 138
Contact Joe Martella, Director of Personnel; 616-842-5500; Fax: 616-842-7230

Giffels Associates, Inc.
25200 Telegraph Rd.
Southfield, MI 48034
http://www.giffels-usa.com
Founded: 1925
Total Employees: 460
Annual Sales: $57 million
Industries: Environmental, Holding Companies, Manufacturing Equipment
Growth: Openings in past year, 109
Contact Francis A. Murad, Ph.D., VP of Human Resources; 248-936-8300; Fax: 248-936-8333; E-mail: info@giffels-usa.com

H.O. Trerice, Inc.
12950 West Eight Mile Rd.
Oak Park, MI 48237
Founded: 1923
Total Employees: 200
Annual Sales: $17 million
Industries:
Subassemblies and Components, Test and Measurement
Growth: Openings in past year, 25
Contact Ms. Debbie Mackie, Human Resource Manager; 248-399-8000; Fax: 248-399-7246; E-mail: pkrich@msn.com

Harman Automotive, Inc.
30665 Northwestern Hwy.
Farmington Hills, MI 48334
Founded: 1912
Total Employees: 600
Annual Sales: $79 million
Industry: Photonics
Growth: Openings in past year, 50
Contact Gary Dopirak, Personnel Manager; 248-626-4300; Fax: 248-932-8105

Hemlock Semiconductor Corp.
12334 Geddes Rd.
PO Box 80
Hemlock, MI 48626
Founded: 1961
Total Employees: 450
Industry: Advanced Materials
Growth: Openings in past year, 99
Contact Don Pfuehler, COB/CEO; 517-642-5201; Fax: 517-642-2091

Howmet Corp., Ti-Cast Division
1600 South Warner St.
Whitehall, MI 49461
Founded: 1974
Total Employees: 200
Industries: Advanced Materials, Medical, Transportation
Growth: Openings in past year, 65
Contact Dennis Albrechtsen, General Manager; 616-894-7112; Fax: 616-894-7106

Humphrey Products Co.
Kilgore at Sprinkle Rd.
PO Box 2008
Kalamazoo, MI 49003
http://www.humphrey.com/air
Founded: 1901
Total Employees: 415

Annual Sales: $46 million
Industries: Holding Companies, Subassemblies and Components, Test and Measurement
Growth: Openings in past year, 38
Contact Patrick Aldworth, Human Resources Manager; 616-381-5500; Fax: 616-381-4110; E-mail: humphrey@ humphreypc.com

Immuno U.S., Inc.
1200 Parkdale Rd.
Rochester, MI 48307
Founded: 1982
Total Employees: 178
Industry: Pharmaceuticals
Growth: Openings in past year, 28
Contact Dr. Mark Philip, Chief Executive Officer; 248-652-7872; Fax: 248-652-0670

MARELCO Power Systems, Inc.
317 Catrell Dr.
PO Box 440
Howell, MI 48844
Founded: 1942
Total Employees: 130
Annual Sales: $17 million
Industries: Energy, Subassemblies and Components
Growth: Openings in past year, 33
Contact Harold E. Fryer, Human Resources and Materials Manager; 517-546-6330; Fax: 517-546-9565; E-mail: marelco@ htonline.com

Maxitrol Company
PO Box 2230
Southfield, MI 48037
Founded: 1956
Total Employees: 300
Annual Sales: $40 million
Industries: Holding Companies, Subassemblies and

Components, Test and Measurement
Growth: Openings in past year, 50
Contact Frank Kern, President; 248-356-1400; Fax: 248-356-0829

McClain Industries, Inc.
PO Box 180913
Utica, MI 48318
Founded: 1968
Total Employees: 735
Annual Sales: $82 million
Industries: Environmental, Factory Automation
Growth: Openings in past year, 73
Contact Kenneth McClain, President; 810-264-3611; Fax: 810-264-7191

Medar, Inc.
38700 Grand River Ave.
Farmington Hills, MI 48335
http://www.medar.com
Founded: 1978
Total Employees: 325
Annual Sales: $41.5 million
Industries: Factory Automation, Holding Companies
Growth: Openings in past year, 90
Contact Charles J. Drake, President/COB; 248-471-2660; Fax: 248-615-2971; E-mail: vision@ medar.com

Montronix, Inc.
3600 Green Court, Suite 200
Ann Arbor, MI 48105
http://www.montronix.com
Founded: 1990
Total Employees: 80
Annual Sales: $9 million
Industry: Factory Automation
Growth: Openings in past year, 35
Contact Ashok Varma, President; 313-665-4500; Fax: 313-665-4515

NTK Cutting Tools
39205 Country Club Dr., Suite C30
Farmington Hills, MI 48331
Founded: 1972
Total Employees: 300
Industry: Factory Automation
Growth: Openings in past year, 50
Contact Max Tatematsu, General Manager; 248-489-0123; Fax: 248-489-0095

Owosso Corp., Motor Products
201 South Delaney Rd.
Owosso, MI 48867
Founded: 1973
Total Employees: 225
Annual Sales: $28 million
Industry: Subassemblies and Components
Growth: Openings in past year, 50
Contact Ms. Johnelle Fouts, Human Resources Administrator; 517-725-5151; Fax: 517-723-6035; E-mail: mpoc@ shianet.org

Perceptron, Inc.
47827 Halyard Dr.
Plymouth, MI 48170
Founded: 1981
Total Employees: 200
Annual Sales: $49.7 million
Industries: Computer Software, Factory Automation, Telecommunications
Growth: Openings in past year, 25
Contact Tom Williams, Director of Human Resources; 313-414-6100; Fax: 313-414-4700

Prein & Newhof, Inc.
3355 Evergreen Dr., NE
Grand Rapids, MI 49525
Founded: 1969
Total Employees: 110
Industry: Environmental
Growth: Openings in past year, 30
Contact Tom Newhof, President; 616-364-8491; Fax: 616-364-6955

PVS Chemicals, Inc.
10900 Harper Ave.
Detroit, MI 48213
Founded: 1945
Total Employees: 400
Annual Sales: $100 million
Industries: Chemicals, Environmental, Holding Companies
Growth: Openings in past year, 50
Contact James B. Nicholson, President; 313-921-1200; Fax: 313-921-1378

Rockwell International Suspension Systems Company, Inc.
2135 West Maple Rd.
Troy, MI 48084
Founded: 1986
Total Employees: 600
Industry: Subassemblies and Components
Growth: Openings in past year, 198
Contact Bob Patrician, President; 248-435-1000; Fax: 248-435-1224

Somanetics Corp.
1653 East Maple Rd.
Troy, MI 48083
Founded: 1982
Total Employees: 47
Industries: Medical, Test and Measurement
Growth: Openings in past year, 30

Contact Ms. Julie Thompson, Director of Human Resources; 248-689-3050; Fax: 248-689-4272

Star Cutter Co.
PO Box 376
Farmington, MI 48332
Founded: 1927
Total Employees: 750
Industries: Factory Automation, Manufacturing Equipment
Growth: Openings in past year, 150
Contact Tim Zoia, Human Resources Manager; 248-474-8200; Fax: 248-474-9518

Terex Handlers
455 North Superior Ave.
PO Box 248
Baraga, MI 49908
http://www.sqshooter.com
Founded: 1984
Total Employees: 76
Annual Sales: $11 million
Industry: Factory Automation
Growth: Openings in past year, 26
Contact James W. Mayo, President; 906-353-6675; Fax: 906-353-7543; E-mail: bpi@up.net

Tru-Turn Corp.
2991 M60 East
Homer, MI 49245
Founded: 1946
Total Employees: 235
Annual Sales: $90 million
Industries: Subassemblies and Components, Transportation
Growth: Openings in past year, 110
Contact Jim Lownsbery, General Manager; 517-568-4398; Fax: 517-568-4207

TRW Inc., Automotive Electronics Group
24175 Research Dr.
Farmington Hills, MI 48335
Founded: 1978
Total Employees: 650
Annual Sales: $88 million
Industries: Photonics, Subassemblies and Components, Test and Measurement, Transportation
Growth: Openings in past year, 100
Contact Tom Doyle, Vice President/General Manager; 248-478-7210; Fax: 248-478-7241

UNC Johnson Technology
2034 Latimer Dr.
Muskegon, MI 49442
Founded: 1962
Total Employees: 483
Annual Sales: $57 million
Industries: Manufacturing Equipment, Photonics, Transportation
Growth: Openings in past year, 81
Contact Dick Klein, Director of Human Resources; 616-777-2685; Fax: 616-773-1397; E-mail: dick_jeannot@uncmfg.com

Unitrac Software Corporation
141 East Michigan Ave.
Kalamazoo, MI 49007
http://www.unitrac.com
Founded: 1980
Total Employees: 80
Industry: Computer Software
Growth: Openings in past year, 35
Contact Gregory Ozuzu, President; 616-344-0220; Fax: 616-344-2027; E-mail: sales@unitrac.com

Minnesota

AETRIUM, Incorporated
2350 Helen St.
North Saint Paul, MN
55109
Founded: 1982
Total Employees: 375
Annual Sales: $58 million
Industry: Holding
Companies
Growth: Openings in past
year, 49
Contact Michael J. Jaeb,
VP of Corporate
Administration; 612-770-
2000; Fax: 612-770-7975

Angeion Corp.
3650 Annapolis Ln., Suite
170
Plymouth, MN 55447
Founded: 1986
Total Employees: 233
Annual Sales: $4.505
million
Industry: Medical
Growth: Openings in past
year, 133
Contact Bob Garin, VP of
Human Resources; 612-
550-9388; Fax: 612-550-
9487

BTD Manufacturing, Inc.
PO Box 1107
Detroit Lakes, MN 56502
Founded: 1907
Total Employees: 160
Annual Sales: $20 million
Industry: Manufacturing
Equipment
Growth: Openings in past
year, 70
Contact Paul White,
Co-CEO/President; 218-
847-4446; Fax: 218-847-
4448

Caire, Inc.
3505 County Rd. 42 West
Burnsville, MN 55306
Founded: 1979

Total Employees: 150
Industry: Medical
Growth: Openings in past
year, 35
Contact Warren Wilk,
Director of Human
Resources; 612-882-
5000; Fax: 612-882-5172

Carl Zeiss IMT Corp.
7008 Northland Dr.
Minneapolis, MN 55428
http://www.zeis.com/imt
Founded: 1925
Total Employees: 180
Annual Sales: $27 million
Industry: Factory
Automation
Growth: Openings in past
year, 30
Contact Greg Lee, Acting
Gen'l Manager/National
Sales Mgr.; 612-533-
9990; Fax: 612-533-4903

**Computer Network
Technology Corp.**
605 North Hwy. 169
Minneapolis, MN 55441
http://www.cnt.com
Founded: 1983
Total Employees: 500
Annual Sales: $97.1
million
Industry: Computer
Software
Growth: Openings in past
year, 42
Contact Thomas G. Hud-
son, President/CEO; 612-
797-6000; Fax: 612-797-
6813

Connect Computer Co.
7101 Metro Blvd.
Edina, MN 55439
Founded: 1986
Total Employees: 356
Industry: Computer
Hardware
Growth: Openings in past
year, 181
Contact Tom Kieffer, Chief
Executive Officer; 612-
944-0181; Fax: 612-946-
0390

Decision Systems, Inc.
60 South Sixth St.
Minneapolis, MN 55402
http://www.decisionsys.
com
Founded: 1974
Total Employees: 212
Industry: Computer
Software
Growth: Openings in past
year, 42
Contact Ms. Shelley Chell,
Human Relations
Manager; 612-338-2585;
Fax: 612-349-6722;
E-mail: info@decisionsys.
com

Digital River, Inc.
5198 West 76th St.
Minneapolis, MN 55439
http://www.digitalriver.com
Founded: 1994
Total Employees: 41
Industry:
Telecommunications
Growth: Openings in past
year, 34
Contact Joel Ronning,
President/CEO; 612-830-
9042; Fax: 612-830-1154;
E-mail: sales@
digitalriver.com

DISC Acquisition Corp.
9555 James Ave. South,
Suite 270
Bloomington, MN 55431
Founded: 1980
Total Employees: 140
Industry: Computer
Hardware
Growth: Openings in past
year, 55
Contact Ms. Rita Miller-
Daugherty, Chief Execu-
tive Officer; 612-881-
7000; Fax: 612-881-5303

**DRS Ahead Technology,
Inc.**
3550 Annapolis Ln.
Plymouth, MN 55447

http://www.drs.com
Founded: 1954
Total Employees: 150
Industries: Computer
Hardware,
Telecommunications
Growth: Openings in past
year, 50
Contact William
Musgrave, Vice
President/General
Manager; 612-519-9129;
Fax: 612-519-9138

EMA Services, Inc.
1970 Oakcrest Ave.
Saint Paul, MN 55113
http://www.ema-inc.com
Founded: 1975
Total Employees: 180
Industries: Computer
Hardware, Manufacturing
Equipment
Growth: Openings in past
year, 30
Contact Alan W. Manning,
Chief Executive Officer;
612-639-5600; Fax: 612-
639-5730; E-mail: info@
ema-inc.com

ENStar Inc.
6479 City West Pkwy.
Eden Prairie, MN 55344
http://www.transition.com
Founded: 1928
Total Employees: 275
Annual Sales: $64 million
Industry: Holding
Companies
Growth: Openings in past
year, 25
Contact Jeffrey J.
Michael, President/CEO;
612-941-3200; Fax: 612-
947-8660

Fourth Shift Corp.
7900 International Dr.,
Suite 450
Minneapolis, MN 55425
http://www.fs.com
Founded: 1984
Total Employees: 500
Annual Sales: $49.3
million

Industry: Computer
Software
Growth: Openings in past
year, 100
Contact M.M. Stuckey,
COB/CEO; 612-851-
1500; Fax: 612-851-
1560; E-mail: fs.info@fs.
com

**Honeywell Inc., Solid
State Electronic Center**
12001 State Hwy. 55
Plymouth, MN 55441
Founded: 1883
Total Employees: 600
Annual Sales: $80 million
Industries:
Subassemblies and
Components, Test and
Measurement
Growth: Openings in past
year, 100
Contact Bryan Johnson,
Director of Human
Resources & Facilities;
612-954-2300; Fax: 612-
954-2040

Hunt Technologies, Inc.
HC 2, Box 17H
Pequot Lakes, MN 56472
http://www.turtletech.com
Founded: 1985
Total Employees: 60
Industry: Energy
Growth: Openings in past
year, 33
Contact Ms. Pat Tweed,
Human Resources
Manager; 218-562-4877;
Fax: 218-562-4878;
E-mail: hunttech@
turtletech.com

Hypro Corporation
375 Fifth Ave. Northwest
New Brighton, MN 55112
Founded: 1947
Total Employees: 225
Annual Sales: $30 million
Industries: Holding
Companies,
Subassemblies and
Components
Growth: Openings in past
year, 25

Contact Robert Lamp,
Vice President/CFO; 612-
633-9300; Fax: 612-633-
6864

**Innovex, Inc., Precision
Products Division**
1313 Fifth St. South
Hopkins, MN 55343
http://www.innovexinc.com
Founded: 1972
Total Employees: 700
Annual Sales: $94 million
Industry: Subassemblies
and Components
Growth: Openings in past
year, 149
Contact Allan Chan, Vice
President/General
Manager; 612-938-4155;
Fax: 612-938-7718

Integ Incorporated
2800 Patton Rd.
Saint Paul, MN 55113
http://www.integonline.com
Founded: 1990
Total Employees: 76
Industry: Medical
Growth: Openings in past
year, 26
Contact Frank A.
Solomon, CEO/President/
Director; 612-639-8816;
Fax: 612-639-9042

INTERCIM Corp.
501 East Hwy. 13
Burnsville, MN 55337
http://www.intercim.com
Founded: 1983
Total Employees: 90
Annual Sales: $8 million
Industry: Computer
Software
Growth: Openings in past
year, 30
Contact Ms. Barbara
Balcom, Human Rela-
tions Manager; 612-894-
9010; Fax: 612-894-
0399; E-mail: hsherry@
intercim.com

IntraNet Solutions, Inc.
9625 West 76th St., Suite 150
Minneapolis, MN 55344
http://www.intranetsol.com
Founded: 1990
Total Employees: 120
Annual Sales: $20 million
Industries: Computer Hardware, Computer Software, Telecommunications
Growth: Openings in past year, 30
Contact Robert F. Olson, COB/CEO; 612-903-2000; Fax: 612-829-5424

ITI Technologies, Inc.
2266 North Second St.
North Saint Paul, MN 55109
Founded: 1992
Total Employees: 477
Annual Sales: $93.3 million
Industry: Holding Companies
Growth: Openings in past year, 27
Contact Thomas Auth, Chief Executive Officer; 612-777-2690; Fax: 612-779-4890

Lifecore Biomedical, Inc., Oral Restorative Division
3515 Lyman Blvd.
Chaska, MN 55318
Founded: 1987
Total Employees: 75
Annual Sales: $9.1 million
Industries: Advanced Materials, Medical
Growth: Openings in past year, 25
Contact Mark J. McKoskey, Vice President/General Manager; 612-368-4300; Fax: 612-368-3411

Lucht, Inc.
11201 Hampshire Ave. South
Bloomington, MN 55438
http://www.lucht.com
Founded: 1972
Total Employees: 180
Industries: Computer Hardware, Photonics
Growth: Openings in past year, 25
Contact Brian Johnson, Personnel Manager; 612-829-5444; Fax: 612-829-7544

Ludlow Corp., Uni-Patch Division
1313 Grant Blvd. West
Wabasha, MN 55981
Founded: 1978
Total Employees: 160
Annual Sales: $19 million
Industry: Medical
Growth: Openings in past year, 40
Contact Ms. Dianne Scholberg, Executive Vice President; 612-565-2601; Fax: 612-565-3971

Manufacturers' Services Ltd., Central US Operations
4300 Round Lake Rd.
Arden Hills, MN 55112
Founded: 1994
Total Employees: 350
Annual Sales: $47 million
Industry: Subassemblies and Components
Growth: Openings in past year, 125
Contact Tony Cammarano, Site Vice President; 612-604-2400; Fax: 612-604-2410

McKechnie Plastic Components
7309 West 27th St.
Minneapolis, MN 55426
Founded: 1959

Total Employees: 250
Annual Sales: $31 million
Industry: Manufacturing Equipment
Growth: Openings in past year, 50
Contact Brian Evenson, President; 612-929-3312; Fax: 612-929-8404; E-mail: mpc.sales@aol.com

MEANS Telcom
10300 Sixth Ave. North
Plymouth, MN 55441
http://www.means.net
Founded: 1988
Total Employees: 140
Annual Sales: $26 million
Industry: Telecommunications
Growth: Openings in past year, 40
Contact David H. Kelley, President/CEO; 612-230-4100; Fax: 612-230-4200; E-mail: info@means.net

MEDTOX Laboratories, Inc.
402 West County Rd. D
Saint Paul, MN 55112
http://www.medtox.com
Founded: 1984
Total Employees: 300
Industries: Advanced Materials, Medical, Pharmaceuticals
Growth: Openings in past year, 25
Contact Ms. Jodi Spaulding, Human Resources Manager; 612-226-6311; Fax: 612-636-8284

Metaphase Technology, Inc.
4201 Lexington Ave. North
Arden Hills, MN 55126
http://www.sdrc.com/metaphase
Founded: 1992
Total Employees: 140
Annual Sales: $18 million

Industry: Computer Software
Growth: Openings in past year, 40
Contact Bob Nierman, President/CEO; 612-482-2171; Fax: 612-482-4348

MikroPrecision Instruments, Inc.
5480 Nathan Ln. North
Plymouth, MN 55442
http://www.mikroprecision. com
Founded: 1984
Total Employees: 80
Annual Sales: $12 million
Industries: Factory Automation, Photonics
Growth: Openings in past year, 30
Contact Ms. Lorie Anderson, Human Resources Representative; 612-593-0722; Fax: 612-593-0712; E-mail: info@mikroprecision.com

Milltronics Manufacturing Co.
1400 Mill Ln.
Waconia, MN 55387
Founded: 1973
Total Employees: 220
Annual Sales: $33 million
Industry: Factory Automation
Growth: Openings in past year, 60
Contact Timothy Rashleger, Operations Manager; 612-442-1410; Fax: 612-442-6457; E-mail: millitronic@aol. com

Minco Products, Inc.
7300 Commerce Ln.
Minneapolis, MN 55432
http://www.minco.com
Founded: 1956
Total Employees: 700
Annual Sales: $50 million
Industries: Energy, Subassemblies and Components, Test and Measurement

Growth: Openings in past year, 46
Contact Karl Schurr, President; 612-571-3121; Fax: 612-571-0927; E-mail: sales@minco. com

Miracle Ear, Inc.
4101 Dahlberg Dr.
Golden Valley, MN 55422
http://www.miracleear.com
Founded: 1948
Total Employees: 625
Annual Sales: $76 million
Industry: Medical
Growth: Openings in past year, 57
Contact Stuart Lyle, Director of Human Resources; 612-520-9500; Fax: 612-520-9522

Multi-Tech Systems, Inc.
2205 Woodale Dr.
Mounds View, MN 55112
http://www.multitech.com
Founded: 1970
Total Employees: 400
Industries: Computer Hardware, Telecommunications
Growth: Openings in past year, 30
Contact Dr. Raghu Sharma, President; 612-785-3500; Fax: 612-785-9874; E-mail: mtssales@ multitech.com

Multistream Systems, Inc.
6750 France Ave. South, Suite 360
Edina, MN 55435
http://www.multistream. com
Founded: 1987
Total Employees: 90
Industry: Computer Software
Growth: Openings in past year, 35
Contact Mario Griffith, President/CEO; 612-926-

3522; Fax: 612-926-3243; E-mail: mstream@ ens.net

Mycogen Seeds
1340 Corporate Center Curve
Saint Paul, MN 55121
http://www.mycogen.com
Founded: 1985
Total Employees: 650
Annual Sales: $70 million
Industry: Biotechnology
Growth: Openings in past year, 150
Contact Mike Muston, General Manager; 612-405-5800; Fax: 612-405-5815

NetCo Communications Corp.
333 North Washington Ave., Suite 102
Minneapolis, MN 55401
http://www.wamnet.com
Founded: 1994
Total Employees: 180
Industry: Telecommunications
Growth: Openings in past year, 140
Contact Ed Driscoll, President/CEO; 612-204-3100; Fax: 612-204-3257

Nonin Medical, Inc.
2605 Fernbrook Ln. North
Plymouth, MN 55447
http://www.nonin.com
Founded: 1985
Total Employees: 85
Annual Sales: $10 million
Industry: Medical
Growth: Openings in past year, 25
Contact Jerry Zweigbaum, Chief Executive Officer; 612-553-9968; Fax: 612-553-7807; E-mail: mail@ nonin.com

Nortech Systems, Inc.
4050 Norris Ct. Northwest
Bemidji, MN 56601
http://www.nortechsys.com
Founded: 1981
Total Employees: 503
Annual Sales: $26.182
million
Industries: Holding
Companies,
Subassemblies and
Components
Growth: Openings in past
year, 77
Contact Quent Finkelson,
President/CEO; 218-751-
0110; Fax: 218-759-0223;
E-mail: nortech@mail.
nortechsys.com

**Pace Analytical Services,
Inc.**
1700 Southeast Elm St.,
Suite 200
Minneapolis, MN 55414
Founded: 1978
Total Employees: 400
Annual Sales: $49 million
Industries: Biotechnology,
Environmental
Growth: Openings in past
year, 50
Contact Ms. LoAnn Grill,
Director of Human
Resources; 612-617-
6400; Fax: 612-617-
6444; E-mail: corpmktg@
pacelabs.com

Plastic Products Co., Inc.
30355 Akerson St.
Lindstrom, MN 55045
Founded: 1962
Total Employees: 700
Annual Sales: $92 million
Industry: Manufacturing
Equipment
Growth: Openings in past
year, 97
Contact Ms. Jacquie
Stendahl, Manager of
Human Resources; 612-
257-5980; Fax: 612-257-
9774

Quorum, Lanier, Inc.
3105 East 80th St., Suite
A2000
Bloomington, MN 55425
http://www.lanier.com
Founded: 1966
Total Employees: 150
Industry: Computer
Software
Growth: Openings in past
year, 50
Contact Ms. Lisa
Schwendinger, Human
Resources Director; 612-
858-6500; Fax: 612-858-
6566; E-mail: mgeorge@
qlanier.com

**Reuter Manufacturing,
Inc.**
410 11th Ave. South
Hopkins, MN 55343
http://www.reuterinc.com
Founded: 1949
Total Employees: 150
Annual Sales: $20 million
Industries: Manufacturing
Equipment, Medical
Growth: Openings in past
year, 35
Contact Ms. Anne
Johnson, Manager of
Human Resources; 612-
935-6921; Fax: 612-933-
5803

**Riverside Electronics,
Ltd.**
One Riverside Dr.
Lewiston, MN 55952
Founded: 1984
Total Employees: 375
Industries: Holding
Companies,
Subassemblies and
Components
Growth: Openings in past
year, 49
Contact Ms. Sandy
Creeley, Personnel
Manager; 507-523-3220;
Fax: 507-523-2831;
E-mail: jmcbride@rellw.
com

Schott Corp.
1000 Parkers Lake Rd.
Wayzata, MN 55391
http://www.schottcorp.com
Founded: 1951
Total Employees: 370
Annual Sales: $20 million
Industry: Subassemblies
and Components
Growth: Openings in past
year, 43
Contact O.W. Schott,
Chief Executive Officer;
612-475-1173; Fax: 612-
475-1786

Secure Computing Corp.
2675 Long Lake Rd.
Roseville, MN 55113
http://www.
securecomputing.com
Founded: 1989
Total Employees: 400
Annual Sales: $40.3
million
Industries: Computer
Software, Holding
Companies,
Telecommunications
Growth: Openings in past
year, 93
Contact Jeffrey H.
Waxman, COB/President/
CEO; 612-628-2700;
Fax: 612-628-2701;
E-mail: sales@
securecomputing.com

**Shared Resource
Management, Inc.**
3550 Lexington Ave.
North, Suite 300
Shoreview, MN 55126
http://www.srminc.com
Founded: 1988
Total Employees: 190
Annual Sales: $13 million
Industries: Computer
Hardware, Computer
Software
Growth: Openings in past
year, 40
Contact Leon E. Kline,
President; 612-486-0417;

Fax: 612-486-0418;
E-mail: visions@srminc.
com

ShowCase Corp.
4131 Hwy. 52 North, Suite
G-111
Rochester, MN 55901
http://www.showcasecorp.
com
Founded: 1989
Total Employees: 160
Annual Sales: $20 million
Industry: Computer
Software
Growth: Openings in past
year, 30
Contact Eric Schultz,
Human Resources
Manager; 507-288-5922;
Fax: 507-287-2803

**Spanlink
Communications, Inc.**
7125 Northland Terr.
Brooklyn Park, MN 55428
http://www.spanlink.com
Founded: 1988
Total Employees: 100
Annual Sales: $5.4 million
Industries: Computer
Software,
Telecommunications
Growth: Openings in past
year, 40
Contact Ms. Leah Stuart,
Human Resources
Manager; 612-971-2000;
Fax: 612-971-2300;
E-mail: mktg@spanlink.
com

**St. Jude Medical, Inc.,
Heart Valve Division**
One Lillehei Plaza
Saint Paul, MN 55117
http://www.sjm.com
Founded: 1988
Total Employees: 800
Annual Sales: $269 million
Industry: Medical
Growth: Openings in past
year, 99
Contact Ms. Jan Webster,
Director of Human
Resources; 612-483-

2000; Fax: 612-482-
8318; E-mail:
webmaster@sjm.com

St. Paul Software, Inc.
1450 Energy Park Dr.,
Suite 127
Saint Paul, MN 55108
http://www.stpaulsoftware.
com
Founded: 1981
Total Employees: 104
Annual Sales: $6.2 million
Industries: Computer
Software,
Telecommunications
Growth: Openings in past
year, 29
Contact Steve Waldron,
President/CEO; 612-603-
4400; Fax: 612-603-
4403; E-mail: info@
stpaulsoftware.com

**Summit Medical
Systems, Inc.**
10900 Red Circle Dr.
Minnetonka, MN 55343
http://www.summitmedical.
com
Founded: 1986
Total Employees: 215
Annual Sales: $20 million
Industries: Computer
Software, Holding
Companies
Growth: Openings in past
year, 39
Contact Dennis DeVal,
Director of Human
Resources; 612-939-
2200; Fax: 612-939-2799

SurVivaLink Corporation
5420 Feltl Rd.
Minneapolis, MN 55343
Founded: 1992
Total Employees: 90
Industry: Medical
Growth: Openings in past
year, 30
Contact R. Eric Bosler,
Chief Financial Officer;
612-939-4181; Fax: 612-
939-4191

Timesavers, Inc.
5270 Hanson Ct.
Minneapolis, MN 55429
Founded: 1946
Total Employees: 400
Industry: Factory
Automation
Growth: Openings in past
year, 34
Contact Raymond S. Vold,
President; 612-537-3611;
Fax: 612-537-9247

Tran Electronics Corp.
82 2nd Ave. Southeast
New Brighton, MN 55112
Founded: 1979
Total Employees: 70
Annual Sales: $5 million
Industry: Subassemblies
and Components
Growth: Openings in past
year, 30
Contact Hoa V. Tran,
President; 612-636-6286;
Fax: 612-631-2755

**Trane Company, Building
Automation Systems
Division**
4833 White Bear Pkwy.
Saint Paul, MN 55110
http://www.trane.com
Founded: 1977
Total Employees: 150
Annual Sales: $34 million
Industries: Computer
Software, Energy, Test
and Measurement
Growth: Openings in past
year, 29
Contact Ms. Sandy
Fellman, Human
Resources Supervisor;
612-407-4000; Fax: 612-
407-4192

**Twin City Fan
Companies, Ltd.**
5959 Trenton Ln.
Minneapolis, MN 55442
http://www.tcf.com
Founded: 1973

Total Employees: 800
Annual Sales: $100 million
Industries: Holding
Companies,
Subassemblies and
Components
Growth: Openings in past
year, 99
Contact Robert Bennett,
VP of Human Resources;
612-551-7600; Fax: 612-551-7501

Urologix, Inc.
14405 21st Ave. North
Minneapolis, MN 55447
http://www.urologix.com
Founded: 1991
Total Employees: 87
Annual Sales: $5.5 million
Industries: Medical,
Subassemblies and
Components
Growth: Openings in past
year, 37
Contact Jack E. Meyer,
President; 612-475-1400;
Fax: 612-475-1443;
E-mail: info@urologix.
com

USLink, Inc.
200 2nd St.
Pequot Lakes, MN 56472
http://www.uslink.net
Founded: 1986
Total Employees: 80
Annual Sales: $13 million
Industry:
Telecommunications
Growth: Openings in past
year, 30
Contact Jim Butman,
President; 218-568-4000;
Fax: 218-568-2225;
E-mail: info@uslink.net

Venturian Corp.
11111 Excelsior Blvd.
Hopkins, MN 55343
http://www.venturian.com
Founded: 1987
Total Employees: 140
Annual Sales: $28 million
Industry: Holding
Companies

Growth: Openings in past
year, 30
Contact Gary B.
Rappaport, COB/
President/CEO; 612-931-2500; Fax: 612-931-2402

Viratec Thin Films, Inc.
2150 Airport Dr,
Faribault, MN 55021
Founded: 1988
Total Employees: 300
Annual Sales: $39 million
Industries: Advanced
Materials, Photonics
Growth: Openings in past
year, 44
Contact Warren Planitzer,
Human Resources
Manager; 507-334-0051;
Fax: 507-334-0059;
E-mail: sales@viratec.
com

**ViroMed Laboratories,
Inc.**
6101 Blue Circle Dr.
Minneapolis, MN 55343
Founded: 1981
Total Employees: 210
Annual Sales: $22 million
Industries: Biotechnology,
Holding Companies,
Medical, Pharmaceuticals
Growth: Openings in past
year, 40
Contact Dr. Bonita L.
Baskin, Ph.D., President;
612-931-0077; Fax: 612-939-4215; E-mail: info@
viromedlabs.com

Wenger Corp.
555 Industrial Park Dr.
Owatonna, MN 55060
http://www.wengercorp.
com
Founded: 1946
Total Employees: 430
Industry:
Telecommunications
Growth: Openings in past
year, 100
Contact Bill Fierke, Direc-
tor of Human Resources;
507-455-4100; Fax: 507-455-4258

XATA Corp.
151 East Cliff Rd., Suite
10
Burnsville, MN 55337
http://www.xata.com
Founded: 1985
Total Employees: 96
Annual Sales: $10.3
million
Industries: Computer
Hardware, Computer
Software
Growth: Openings in past
year, 29
Contact Dennis R.
Johnson, Chief Executive
Officer; 612-894-3680;
Fax: 612-894-2463;
E-mail: info@xata.com

Mississippi

**Delta & Pine Land
Company**
PO Box 157
Scott, MS 38772
Founded: 1911
Total Employees: 800
Annual Sales: $153 million
Industry: Biotechnology
Growth: Openings in past
year, 99
Contact Roger D. Malkin,
COB/CEO; 601-742-4000; Fax: 601-742-3795

**Institute for Technology
Development, Inc.**
700 North State St., Suite
300
Jackson, MS 39202
Founded: 1988
Total Employees: 80
Annual Sales: $10 million
Industry: Holding
Companies
Growth: Openings in past
year, 25
Contact Len Vernamonti,
President; 601-960-3600;
Fax: 601-960-3605

Potter Production Corp.
3004 Hwy. 51 North
PO Box 337
Wesson, MS 39191

Founded: 1927
Total Employees: 160
Annual Sales: $21 million
Industry: Subassemblies and Components
Growth: Openings in past year, 40
Contact Clayton J. Hatzebuhler, Chief Financial Officer; 601-643-2215; Fax: 601-643-5126

Wireless One, Inc.
1080 River Oaks Dr., Suite A-150
Jackson, MS 39208
http://www.wireless-one.com
Founded: 1995
Total Employees: 850
Annual Sales: $11.4 million
Industry: Telecommunications
Growth: Openings in past year, 225
Contact Bill Hamblin, VP of Human Resources; 601-936-1515; Fax: 601-936-1517; E-mail: wireless@wireless-one.com

Missouri

Allied Healthcare Products, Inc.
1720 Sublette Ave.
Saint Louis, MO 63110
http://www.alliedhpi.com
Founded: 1947
Total Employees: 957
Annual Sales: $118.118 million
Industries: Holding Companies, Medical, Subassemblies and Components, Test and Measurement
Growth: Openings in past year, 125
Contact Uma Aggarwal, President/CEO; 314-771-2400; Fax: 314-771-0650

BHA Group, Inc.
8800 East 63rd St.
Kansas City, MO 64133
http://www.bhagroup.com
Founded: 1975
Total Employees: 800
Annual Sales: $121.308 million
Industries: Environmental, Test and Measurement
Growth: Openings in past year, 46
Contact James Lund, President/CEO; 816-356-8400; Fax: 816-353-1873

bioMerieux Vitek, Inc.
595 Anglum Dr.
Hazelwood, MO 63042
http://www.biomerieux-vitek.com
Founded: 1977
Total Employees: 750
Annual Sales: $91 million
Industry: Medical
Growth: Openings in past year, 29
Contact Philippe Archinard, President; 314-731-8500; Fax: 314-731-8700

Carboline Co.
350 Hanley Industrial Ct.
Saint Louis, MO 63144
Founded: 1947
Total Employees: 550
Annual Sales: $100 million
Industries: Advanced Materials, Test and Measurement
Growth: Openings in past year, 50
Contact Ms. Judith A. Hellman, VP of Corporate Services; 314-644-1000; Fax: 314-644-4617

Carmar Group, Inc.
PO Box 718
Carthage, MO 64836
Founded: 1987
Total Employees: 500

Annual Sales: $96 million
Industry: Holding Companies
Growth: Openings in past year, 73
Contact Ms. Suzanne Wolf, Director of Human Resources; 417-358-9027; Fax: 417-358-1274

Detroit Tool Metal Products
100 Carr Rd.
Lebanon, MO 65536
Founded: 1956
Total Employees: 265
Annual Sales: $33 million
Industry: Manufacturing Equipment
Growth: Openings in past year, 25
Contact Brad Morgan, President; 417-532-2142; Fax: 417-588-3405

Ecolab, Inc., Water Care Services Division
1345 Taney
North Kansas City, MO 64116
Founded: 1890
Total Employees: 120
Annual Sales: $31 million
Industry: Chemicals
Growth: Openings in past year, 30
Contact Ms. Diana Norris, Human Resources Manager; 816-842-0560; Fax: 816-842-6388

Electrovert USA Corp.
1O Box 709, Hwy. 5 South
Camdonton, MO 65020
http://www.electrovert.com
Founded: 1951
Total Employees: 650
Annual Sales: $81 million
Industries: Manufacturing Equipment, Test and Measurement
Growth: Openings in past year, 49
Contact David Campanini, Manager of Human Resources; 573-346-3341; Fax: 573-346-5554

Harvard Interiors Manufacturing Co., Electronic Products Facility
3000 Arnold Tenbrook Rd.
Arnold, MO 63010
Founded: 1970
Total Employees. 00
Annual Sales: $3.5 million
Industry: Subassemblies and Components
Growth: Openings in past year, 40
Contact Tony Stewart, President; 314-296-5417; Fax: 314-296-1967

Hitchiner Manufacturing Co., Inc., Nonferrous Division
600 Cannonball Ln.
O'Fallon, MO 63366
http://www.hitchiner.com
Founded: 1969
Total Employees: 155
Industry: Advanced Materials
Growth: Openings in past year, 30
Contact Allan Derhake, Controller; 314-272-6176; Fax: 314-272-6180

Jack Henry & Associates, Inc.
663 Hwy. 60
PO Box 807
Monett, MO 65708
http://www.jackhenry.com
Founded: 1976
Total Employees: 470
Annual Sales: $82.6 million
Industry: Computer Software
Growth: Openings in past year, 106
Contact Ms. Michelle Hunter, Benefits Administrator; 417-235-6652; Fax: 417-235-8406

Jones Medical Industries, Inc.
PO Box 46903
Saint Louis, MO 63146
Founded: 1981
Total Employees: 500
Annual Sales: $100 million
Industries: Holding Companies, Pharmaceuticals
Growth: Openings in past year, 148
Contact Dennis M. Jones, COB/CEO; 314-576-6100; Fax: 314-469-5749

Litton Industries, Inc., Inter-Pak Electronics Division
2500 Airport Commerce Dr.
Springfield, MO 65803
http://www.litton-aodipe.com
Founded: 1982
Total Employees: 196
Annual Sales: $51.7 million
Industries: Computer Hardware, Subassemblies and Components
Growth: Openings in past year, 72
Contact Ms. Sue Fuller, Director of Human Resources; 417-862-0751; Fax: 417-862-1528; E-mail: rschutz@acdipe.com

Litton Systems, Inc., Advanced Circuitry Division
4811 West Kearney St.
PO Box 2847CS
Springfield, MO 65803
http://www.littonocdips.com
Founded: 1963
Total Employees: 750
Annual Sales: $99 million
Industry: Subassemblies and Components
Growth: Openings in past year, 150

Contact Ms. Sue Fuller, Director of Human Resources; 417-862-0751; Fax: 417-862-0734

MAC Equipment, Inc.
10741 North West Ambassador Dr.
Kansas City, MO 64153
http://www.macequipment.com
Founded: 1969
Total Employees: 400
Annual Sales: $61 million
Industries: Environmental, Factory Automation
Growth: Openings in past year, 100
Contact Wes Kuhl, President; 816-891-9300; Fax: 816-891-8978; E-mail: www@macequipment.com

Precision Stainless, Inc.
3300 East Pythian St.
Springfield, MO 65802
Founded: 1984
Total Employees: 275
Industries: Factory Automation, Holding Companies, Manufacturing Equipment
Growth: Openings in past year, 25
Contact Tom Singleton, Chief Executive Officer; 417-865-2990; Fax: 417-865-0906

Sterling Direct, Document Division
1 American Eagle Plaza
Earth City, MO 63045
http://www.sterlingdirect.com
Founded: 1976
Total Employees: 140
Industries: Computer Hardware, Computer Software, Telecommunications
Growth: Openings in past year, 45
Contact Bill Ziercher, President; 314-344-3380; Fax: 314-344-9966

TranSystems Corp.
4600 Madison Ave., Suite
500
Kansas City, MO 64112
Founded: 1966
Total Employees: 380
Annual Sales: $40 million
Industry: Transportation
Growth: Openings in past
year, 160
Contact Dave Bertrand,
VP of Human Resources;
816-561-9800; Fax: 816-
561-5441; E-mail:
tsmail@transystems.com

Nebraska

Brumko Magnetics Corp.
150 Binfield St.
PO Box 673
Elkhorn, NE 68022
Founded: 1977
Total Employees: 170
Annual Sales: $35 million
Industry: Computer
Hardware
Growth: Openings in past
year, 70
Contact Ms. Vicki Hamke,
Personnel Coordinator;
402-289-2400; Fax: 402-
289-3676

CSG Systems, Inc.
2525 North 117 Ave.
PO Box 34965
Omaha, NE 68164
http://www.csgsys.com
Founded: 1985
Total Employees: 850
Industry: Computer
Software
Growth: Openings in past
year, 148
Contact Paul Shaddock,
VP of Human Resources;
402-431-7000; Fax: 402-
431-7254

Hastings Filter, Inc.
4400 East Hwy. 30
Kearney, NE 68848
http://www.hastingfilter.com
Founded: 1904
Total Employees: 200
Annual Sales: $40 million
Industry: Subassemblies
and Components
Growth: Openings in past
year, 50
Contact Richard Shrode,
President; 308-234-1951;
Fax: 800-828-4453

MDS Harris, Inc.
621 Rose St.
Lincoln, NE 68502
http://www.mdsharris.com
Founded: 1933
Total Employees: 525
Industries: Biotechnology,
Chemicals,
Environmental,
Pharmaceuticals
Growth: Openings in past
year, 25
Contact Sam Seever, VP
of Human Resources;
402-476-2811; Fax: 402-
476-7598

**PKS Information
Services, Inc.**
11707 Miracle Hills Rd.
Omaha, NE 68154
http://www.pksis.com
Founded: 1990
Total Employees: 500
Annual Sales: $100 million
Industries: Computer
Hardware,
Telecommunications
Growth: Openings in past
year, 100
Contact Raul Pupo,
President/CEO; 402-496-
8500; Fax: 402-496-8670

Snyder Industries, Inc.
PO Box 4583
Lincoln, NE 68504
http://www.snydernet.com

Founded: 1967
Total Employees: 300
Annual Sales: $45 million
Industries: Factory
Automation, Holding
Companies
Growth: Openings in past
year, 50
Contact Howard Gross,
COB/CEO; 402-467-
5221; Fax: 402-467-
6493; E-mail: siisales@
snydernet.com

Nevada

Casino Data Systems
3300 Birtcher Dr.
Las Vegas, NV 89118
Founded: 1991
Total Employees: 412
Annual Sales: $70.87
million
Industries: Computer
Hardware, Computer
Software, Holding
Companies, Photonics
Growth: Openings in past
year, 51
Contact Ms. Cathy
Dickerson, VP of Human
Resources; 702-269-
5000; Fax: 702-269-5165

Mikohn Gaming Corp.
PO Box 98686
Las Vegas, NV 89193
http://www.mikohn.com
Founded: 1976
Total Employees: 925
Annual Sales: $97 million
Industry: Holding
Companies
Growth: Openings in past
year, 100
Contact David J.
Thompson, COB/CEO/
President; 702-896-3890;
Fax: 702-263-1770

New Hampshire

Advanced Circuit Technology, Inc.
118 Northeastern Blvd.
PO Box 547X
Nashua, NH 03061
Founded: 1976
Total Employees: 200
Industry: Subassemblies and Components
Growth: Openings in past year, 25
Contact Ms. Betty Moody, Human Resources Manager; 603-880-6000; Fax: 603-880-1785

Affinity, Inc.
PO Box 1000
Ossipee, NH 03864
Founded: 1990
Total Employees: 70
Industry: Energy
Growth: Openings in past year, 40
Contact Fred Piehl, President; 603-539-3600; Fax: 603-539-8484; E-mail: rtozier@affii.com

Chemfab Corp.
701 Daniel Webster Hwy.
PO Box 1137
Merrimack, NH 03054
Founded: 1968
Total Employees: 550
Annual Sales: $83 million
Industries: Advanced Materials, Test and Measurement
Growth: Openings in past year, 46
Contact Duane C. Montopoli, President/CEO; 603-424-9000; Fax: 603-424-9028

Coda, Inc.
1155 Elm St.
Manchester, NH 03101
http://www.coda-financials.com

Founded: 1979
Total Employees: 450
Annual Sales: $52 million
Industry: Computer Software
Growth: Openings in past year, 75
Contact Robert Brown, Chief Executive Officer; 603-647-9600; Fax: 603-647-2634; E-mail: liberate@codainc.com

Dharma Systems, Inc.
436 Amherst St.
Nashua, NH 03063
http://www.dharma.com
Founded: 1987
Total Employees: 110
Industry: Computer Software
Growth: Openings in past year, 50
Contact J. Sasidhar, President; 603-886-1400; Fax: 603-883-6904; E-mail: info@@dharma.com

Diacom Corp.
5 Howe Dr.
Amherst, NH 03031
http://www.diacom.com
Founded: 1983
Total Employees: 100
Industry: Subassemblies and Components
Growth: Openings in past year, 35
Contact Don Comstock, President; 603-880-1900; Fax: 603-880-7616; E-mail: sales@diacom.com

Fibredyne, Inc.
47 Crosby Rd.
Dover, NH 03820
Founded: 1971
Total Employees: 95
Industries: Environmental, Manufacturing Equipment
Growth: Openings in past year, 35

Contact Robert W. Matchett, President; 603-749-1610; Fax: 603-749-2699

Hitchiner Manufacturing Co., Inc., Gas Turbine Division
PO Box 2001
Milford, NH 03055
http://www.hitchiner.com
Founded: 1985
Total Employees: 195
Industry: Advanced Materials
Growth: Openings in past year, 55
Contact William Brown, General Manager; 603-673-1100; Fax: 603-673-6928

Hubbard Farms, Inc.
Main St.
PO Box 415
Walpole, NH 03608
Founded: 1929
Total Employees: 275
Annual Sales: $29 million
Industry: Biotechnology
Growth: Openings in past year, 25
Contact John Gascoyne, President; 603-756-3311; Fax: 603-756-3184

Hypertherm, Inc.
PO Box 5010, Etna Rd.
Hanover, NH 03755
http://www.hypertherm.com
Founded: 1968
Total Employees: 425
Annual Sales: $65 million
Industry: Factory Automation
Growth: Openings in past year, 74
Contact Richard Couch, President; 603-643-3441; Fax: 603-643-5352; E-mail: info@hypertherm.com

Integrated Manufacturing by Design
540 North Commercial St.
Manchester, NH 03108
Founded: 1987
Total Employees: 80
Annual Sales: $10 million
Industry: Subassemblies and Components
Growth: Openings in past year, 30
Contact Jim Bell, Chief Executive Officer; 603-669-5224; Fax: 603-669-3826

KENDA Systems
1 Stiles Rd.
Salem, NH 03079
http://www.kenda.com/
Founded: 1984
Total Employees: 570
Annual Sales: $49.968 million
Industry: Computer Software
Growth: Openings in past year, 259
Contact Steve Kenda, President; 603-898-7884; Fax: 603-898-3016

Kingsbury Corp.
80 Laurel St.
PO Box 2020
Keene, NH 03431
Founded: 1916
Total Employees: 550
Annual Sales: $84 million
Industry: Holding Companies
Growth: Openings in past year, 50
Contact Jeff Toner, VP of Manufacturing; 603-352-5212; Fax: 603-352-8789

Kollsman, Inc.
220 Daniel Webster Hwy.
Merrimack, NH 03054
http://www.kollsman.com
Founded: 1995
Total Employees: 600

Annual Sales: $120 million
Industries: Computer Hardware, Defense, Factory Automation, Holding Companies, Medical, Test and Measurement, Telecommunications, Transportation
Growth: Openings in past year, 50
Contact Daniel Guerrette, Director of Human Resources; 603-889-2500; Fax: 603-889-7966

Lilly Software Associates, Inc.
500 Lafayette Rd.
Hampton, NH 03842
http://www.visualmfg.com
Founded: 1992
Total Employees: 225
Annual Sales: $18 million
Industry: Computer Software
Growth: Openings in past year, 95
Contact Richard T. Lilly, President/CEO; 603-926-9696; Fax: 603-926-9698; E-mail: info@visualmfg.com

Lonza Biologics, Inc.
101 International Dr.
Portsmouth, NH 03801
Founded: 1993
Total Employees: 95
Industry: Biotechnology
Growth: Openings in past year, 25
Contact David Gray, Human Resources Manager; 603-334-6100; Fax: 603-334-6262

M&I East Point Technology, Inc.
436 South River Rd.
Bedford, NH 03110
http://www.eastpoint.com
Founded: 1983
Total Employees: 80
Annual Sales: $10 million
Industry: Computer Software

Growth: Openings in past year, 35
Contact Dan Shannon, President; 603-647-2030; Fax: 603-669-8620; E-mail: info@eastpoint.com

MTL, Inc.
9 Merril Industrial Dr.
Hampton, NH 03842
Founded: 1987
Total Employees: 70
Industry: Factory Automation
Growth: Openings in past year, 30
Contact Ms. Michelle McCarthy, Accounting and Human Resources Mgr.; 603-926-0090; Fax: 603-926-1899

Newmarket Software Systems, Inc.
135 Commerce Way, Suite 300
Portsmouth, NH 03801
http://www.newsoft.com
Founded: 1985
Total Employees: 200
Industry: Computer Software
Growth: Openings in past year, 35
Contact Ms. Kate Lamphier, Director of Human Resources; 603-436-7500; Fax: 603-436-1826; E-mail: salesinfo@newsoft.com

Omtool, Ltd.
8 Industrial Way
Salem, NH 03079
http://www.omtool.com
Founded: 1991
Total Employees: 90
Annual Sales: $8.4 million
Industries: Computer Software, Telecommunications
Growth: Openings in past year, 40

Contact Bob Voelk, COB/
CEO; 603-898-8900;
Fax: 603-890-6756;
E-mail: info@omtool.com

P-Tech, Inc.
540 North Commercial St.
Manchester, NH 03101
Founded: 1987
Total Employees: 50
Annual Sales: $5 million
Industry:
Telecommunications
Growth: Openings in past
year, 29
Contact Michael Dobbins,
President; 603-645-1616;
Fax: 603-645-1424

Presstek, Inc.
8-9 Commercial St.
Hudson, NH 03051
Founded: 1987
Total Employees: 202
Annual Sales: $48.6
million
Industry: Photonics
Growth: Openings in past
year, 27
Contact Ms. Cathy
Cavanna, Human
Resources Manager;
603-595-7000; Fax: 603-
595-2602

Source Electronics Corp.
26 Clinton Dr.
Hollis, NH 03049
Founded: 1986
Total Employees: 125
Annual Sales: $28.3
million
Industries: Computer
Hardware, Manufacturing
Equipment,
Subassemblies and
Components
Growth: Openings in past
year, 45
Contact William
Wentworth, VP of Sales
and Marketing; 603-595-
2906; Fax: 603-595-
0068; E-mail: info@
sourcee.com

Spectra, Inc.
Etna Rd.
PO Box 68C
Hanover, NH 03755
Founded: 1985
Total Employees: 150
Annual Sales: $30 million
Industry: Computer
Hardware
Growth: Openings in past
year, 67
Contact Ms. Bonnie
Bauer, Human
Resources Manager;
603-643-4390; Fax: 603-
643-5430

WPI Group, Inc.
1155 Elm St.
Manchester, NH 03101
Founded: 1948
Total Employees: 410
Annual Sales: $47 million
Industries: Holding
Companies,
Subassemblies and
Components
Growth: Openings in past
year, 27
Contact Ms. Karen
Hebert, VP of Human
Resources; 603-627-
3500; Fax: 603-627-3150

New Jersey

**Advanced Digital Data,
Inc.**
6 Laurel Dr.
Flanders, NJ 07836
Founded: 1973
Total Employees: 85
Industries: Computer
Hardware, Computer
Software
Growth: Openings in past
year, 35
Contact Bruce Bott, Sr.,
President; 973-584-4026;
Fax: 973-584-3205

AIWA AMERICA, INC.
800 Corporate Dr.
Mahwah, NJ 07430
http://www.aiwa.com
Founded: 1978
Total Employees: 150
Annual Sales: $25 million
Industries: Computer
Hardware,
Telecommunications
Growth: Openings in past
year, 50
Contact Yukio Yamamoto,
President/CEO; 201-512-
3600; Fax: 201-512-3710

Alkon Corp.
45 U.S. Hwy. 46
PO Box 641
Pine Brook, NJ 07058
Founded: 1949
Total Employees: 100
Industries:
Subassemblies and
Components, Test and
Measurement
Growth: Openings in past
year, 65
Contact F.W. Winter,
COB/CEO; 973-808-
8686; Fax: 973-808-0444

AlphaNet Solutions, Inc.
7 Ridgedale Ave.
Cedar Knolls, NJ 07927
http://www.alphanetcorp.
com
Founded: 1984
Total Employees: 550
Annual Sales: $119.6
million
Industries: Computer
Hardware,
Telecommunications
Growth: Openings in past
year, 300
Contact Stan Gang, Chief
Executive Officer; 973-
267-0088; Fax: 973-267-
8675

Amano Cincinnati, Inc.
140 Harrison Ave.
Roseland, NJ 07068
http://www.amano.com
Founded: 1896
Total Employees: 225
Annual Sales: $46 million
Industries: Computer
  Hardware, Computer
  Software
Growth: Openings in past
  year, 25
Contact Junichi Minamoto,
  President; 973-403-1900;
  Fax: 973-364-1086

Anadigics, Inc.
35 Technology Dr.
Warren, NJ 07059
http://www.anadigics.com
Founded: 1985
Total Employees: 530
Annual Sales: $68.9
  million
Industry: Subassemblies
  and Components
Growth: Openings in past
  year, 231
Contact Ms. Andrea
  Foster, Director of
  Human Resources; 908-
  668-5000; Fax: 908-668-
  5132; E-mail: anadigics@
  attmail.com

Ariel Corp.
2540 Rte. 130
Cranbury, NJ 08512
http://www.ariel.com
Founded: 1982
Total Employees: 100
Annual Sales: $13 million
Industries: Computer
  Hardware,
  Telecommunications
Growth: Openings in past
  year, 25
Contact Anthony M.
  Agnello, Chief Executive
  Officer; 609-860-2900;
  Fax: 609-860-1155;
  E-mail: ariel@ariel.com

Audible, Inc.
65 Willow Brook Blvd.
Wayne, NJ 07470
http://www.audible.com
Founded: 1995
Total Employees: 40
Annual Sales: $6.8 million
Industry:
  Telecommunications
Growth: Openings in past
  year, 30
Contact Don Katz,
  President; 973-890-2442;
  Fax: 973-890-2442;
  E-mail: info@audible.com

Auric Corp.
470 Frelinghuysen Ave.
Newark, NJ 07114
Founded: 1941
Total Employees: 150
Annual Sales: $40 million
Industry: Holding
  Companies
Growth: Openings in past
  year, 50
Contact Maurice Bick,
  President/Director; 973-
  242-4110; Fax: 973-242-
  5796

Base Ten Systems, Inc.
1 Electronics Dr.
Trenton, NJ 08619
Founded: 1966
Total Employees: 213
Annual Sales: $14.8
  million
Industry: Holding
  Companies
Growth: Openings in past
  year, 43
Contact Myles M.
  Kranzler, COB/President;
  609-586-7010; Fax: 609-
  586-1593

**BEI Medical Systems
Co., Inc.**
83 Hobart St.
Hackensack, NJ 07601
http://www.beimedical.com
Founded: 1991

Total Employees: 90
Annual Sales: $10 million
Industry: Medical
Growth: Openings in past
  year, 30
Contact Richard W.
  Turner, President/CEO;
  201-489-4222; Fax: 201-
  488-5506; E-mail:
  service@beimedical.com

Bihler of America
55 Readington Rd.
North Branch, NJ 08876
Founded: 1974
Total Employees: 150
Annual Sales: $18 million
Industries: Factory
  Automation,
  Manufacturing
  Equipment,
  Subassemblies and
  Components
Growth: Openings in past
  year, 50
Contact Barry Littlewood,
  Vice President; 908-725-
  9000; Fax: 908-725-0457

Bluestone, Inc.
1000 Briggs Rd.
Mount Laurel, NJ 08054
http://www.bluestone.com
Founded: 1989
Total Employees: 270
Annual Sales: $34 million
Industries: Computer
  Hardware, Computer
  Software
Growth: Openings in past
  year, 100
Contact Ms. Amy Naples,
  Director of Human
  Resources; 609-727-
  4600; Fax: 609-725-
  5077; E-mail: info@
  bluestone.com

Certech, Inc.
1 Park Pl. West
Wood Ridge, NJ 07075
Founded: 1970
Total Employees: 350
Industry: Advanced
  Materials
Growth: Openings in past
  year, 23

Contact Edward J. Carchozza, CEO/ President; 201-939-7400; Fax: 201-939-1423

Commonwealth Long Distance
105 Carnegie Ctr.
Princeton, NJ 08540
Founded: 1897
Total Employees: 188
Annual Sales: $32 million
Industry:
Telecommunications
Growth: Openings in past year, 59
Contact Ken Knudsen, Senior Vice President; 609-734-3700; Fax: 609-734-3794

Commvault Systems
1 Industrial Way, Building D, Hov Park
Eatontown, NJ 07724
http://www.commvault.com
Founded: 1885
Total Employees: 200
Annual Sales: $36 million
Industry: Computer Hardware
Growth: Openings in past year, 100
Contact Scotty Neal, President; 732-935-8000; Fax: 732-935-8040

Computron Software, Inc.
301 Rte. 17 North
Rutherford, NJ 07070
http://www.ctronsoft.com
Founded: 1973
Total Employees: 450
Annual Sales: $54.3 million
Industry: Computer Software
Growth: Openings in past year, 49
Contact John A. Rade, President/CEO; 201-935-3400; Fax: 201-935-7678

Croda, Inc.
7 Century Dr.
Parsippany, NJ 07054
http://www.croda.com
Founded: 1961
Total Employees: 151
Annual Sales: $40 million
Industries: Advanced Materials, Biotechnology, Chemicals, Pharmaceuticals
Growth: Openings in past year, 31
Contact Ms. Marilyn C. Dunn, Personnel Manager; 973-644-4900; Fax: 973-644-9222; E-mail: marketing@crode.com

Desktop Engineering International, Inc.
1200 MacArthur Blvd.
Mahwah, NJ 07430
Founded: 1979
Total Employees: 40
Industry: Computer Software
Growth: Openings in past year, 30
Contact Daniel V. Schavello, President; 201-818-9700; Fax: 201-818-9707

Eclipse Internet Access
520 North Ave.
Plainfield, NJ 07061
http://www.eclipse.net
Founded: 1985
Total Employees: 30
Annual Sales: $5.1 million
Industry:
Telecommunications
Growth: Openings in past year, 27
Contact Erich Reinecker, President; 908-412-0700; Fax: 908-755-6379; E-mail: sales@eclipse.net

Edwards and Kelcey, Inc.
299 Madison Ave.
Morristown, NJ 07962
Founded: 1946
Total Employees: 547
Annual Sales: $68 million
Industries: Manufacturing Equipment, Telecommunications
Growth: Openings in past year, 80
Contact Ronald A. Wiss, COB/CEO; 973-267-0555; Fax: 973-267-3555; E-mail: edkel@ios.com

Emcore Corp.
394 Elizabeth Ave.
Somerset, NJ 08873
http://www.emcore.com
Founded: 1984
Total Employees: 210
Annual Sales: $27.8 million
Industries: Advanced Materials, Environmental, Manufacturing Equipment
Growth: Openings in past year, 70
Contact Reuben Richards, President/CEO; 732-271-9090; Fax: 732-271-9686

Epitaxx Optoelectronic Devices, Inc.
7 Graphics Dr.
West Trenton, NJ 08628
http://www.epitaxx.com
Founded: 1984
Total Employees: 200
Annual Sales: $25 million
Industry: Photonics
Growth: Openings in past year, 25
Contact N. Hiraguri, Chief Executive Officer; 609-538-1800; Fax: 609-538-1684; E-mail: jerry@epitaxx.com

Firmenich, Inc.
PO Box 5880
Princeton, NJ 08540
Founded: 1936
Total Employees: 750
Industry: Chemicals
Growth: Openings in past year, 50
Contact Alan D. Edenzon, Director of Human Resources; 609-452-1000; Fax: 609-452-0564

Heller Industries, Inc.
4 Vreeland Rd.
Florham Park, NJ 07932
http://www.hellerind.com
Founded: 1960
Total Employees: 150
Annual Sales: $18 million
Industry: Manufacturing Equipment
Growth: Openings in past year, 50
Contact David Heller, President; 973-377-6800; Fax: 973-377-3862; E-mail: hellerind@aol.com

Heyco Products, Inc.
1800 Industrial Way North
Toms River, NJ 08754
http://www.heyco.com
Founded: 1941
Total Employees: 160
Industries: Factory Automation, Subassemblies and Components
Growth: Openings in past year, 60
Contact Ed Cunningham, General Manager; 908-245-0033; Fax: 908-245-3238; E-mail: heyco@worldnet.com

Howmet Dover Casting
Roy St.
Dover, NJ 07801
Founded: 1948
Total Employees: 954

Annual Sales: $120 million
Industry: Transportation
Growth: Openings in past year, 203
Contact C.M. Prokto, Director of Human Resources; 973-361-0300; Fax: 973-328-2137

i-STAT Corp.
303 A College Rd. East
Princeton, NJ 08540
http://www.i-stat.com
Founded: 1983
Total Employees: 475
Annual Sales: $30 million
Industry: Medical
Growth: Openings in past year, 73
Contact William Beattie, Director of Human Resources; 609-243-9300; Fax: 609-243-0507; E-mail: marketing@i-stat.com

Icon CMT Corp.
1200 Harbor Blvd..
Weehawken, NJ 07083
http://www.icon.com
Founded: 1991
Total Employees: 220
Annual Sales: $38.1 million
Industry: Telecommunications
Growth: Openings in past year, 95
Contact Scott Baxter, President; 201-601-2000; Fax: 201-601-2018; E-mail: info@icon.com

Integratise, Inc.
100 Wood Ave. South, Suite 111
Iselin, NJ 08830
http://www.integratise.com
Founded: 1991
Total Employees: 176
Annual Sales: $22 million
Industries: Holding Companies, Telecommunications
Growth: Openings in past year, 36
Contact Fredrick Rozell, Manager of Personnel; 908-534-8929; Fax: 908-968-0067

Interferon Sciences, Inc.
783 Jersey Ave.
New Brunswick, NJ 08901
Founded: 1981
Total Employees: 135
Annual Sales: $2.092 million
Industry: Biotechnology
Growth: Openings in past year, 54
Contact Ms. Jeanne Howarth, Director of Human Resources; 732-249-3250; Fax: 732-249-6895

International Discount Telephone, Inc.
294 State St.
Hackensack, NJ 07601
http://www.idt.net
Founded: 1990
Total Employees: 360
Annual Sales: $135.187 million
Industries: Holding Companies, Telecommunications
Growth: Openings in past year, 33
Contact Jim Courter, President; 201-928-1000; Fax: 201-928-1057; E-mail: info@ids.net

Keptel, Inc.
56 Park Rd.
Tinton Falls, NJ 07724
Founded: 1983
Total Employees: 700
Annual Sales: $60 million
Industries: Factory Automation, Subassemblies and Components, Telecommunications
Growth: Openings in past year, 200
Contact David S. Stehlin, President; 732-389-8800; Fax: 732-460-5485

Killam Associates
27 Bleeker St.
PO Box 1008
Millburn, NJ 07041
http://www.killam.com
Founded: 1937
Total Employees: 400
Annual Sales: $70 million
Industry: Environmental
Growth: Openings in past year, 27
Contact Ms. Phyllis Carroll, Personnel Manager; 973-379-3400; Fax: 973-376-1072

Liposome Co., Inc.
One Research Way, Princeton Forrestal Ctr.
Princeton, NJ 08540
Founded: 1981
Total Employees: 400
Industry: Pharmaceuticals
Growth: Openings in past year, 50
Contact George Renton, VP of Human Resources; 609-452-7060; Fax: 609-452-1890

Logical Design Solutions, Inc.
465 South St., Suite 103
Morristown, NJ 07960
http://www.lds.com
Founded: 1990
Total Employees: 100
Annual Sales: $8 million
Industries: Computer Software, Holding Companies
Growth: Openings in past year, 60
Contact Ms. Mimi Brooks, President; 973-971-0100; Fax: 973-971-0103; E-mail: info@lds.com

Magic Solutions, Inc.
10 Forest Ave.
Paramus, NJ 07652
http://www.magicsolutions.com

Founded: 1988
Total Employees: 250
Annual Sales: $30 million
Industry: Computer Software
Growth: Openings in past year, 125
Contact Igal Lichtman, Chairman of the Board; 201-587-1515; Fax: 201-587-8005; E-mail: info@magicrx.com

Med-Link Technologies, Inc.
One Executive Dr.
Somerset, NJ 08873
Founded: 1991
Total Employees: 70
Industry: Telecommunications
Growth: Openings in past year, 30
Contact Jim Pickering, President; 732-560-1000; Fax: 732-560-0999; E-mail: info@medlink-linktech.com

MEGASOFT, Inc.
819 Hwy. 33 East
Freehold, NJ 07728
http://www.megasoft.com
Founded: 1983
Total Employees: 90
Industries: Computer Hardware, Computer Software
Growth: Openings in past year, 40
Contact Jon Sugarman, President; 732-431-5300; Fax: 732-845-0568; E-mail: details@megasoft.com

Metal Improvement Co., Inc.
10 Forest Ave.
Paramus, NJ 07652
http://www.metalimprovement.com
Founded: 1945
Total Employees: 950
Industries: Manufacturing Equipment,

Subassemblies and Components
Growth: Openings in past year, 46
Contact Gerald Nachman, President; 201-843-7800; Fax: 201-843-3460; E-mail: metalimp@ix.netcom.com

Metrologic Instruments, Inc.
PO Box 307
Bellmawr, NJ 08099
http://www.metrologic.com
Founded: 1968
Total Employees: 375
Annual Sales: $47 million
Industries: Computer Hardware, Holding Companies, Photonics
Growth: Openings in past year, 55
Contact John Patton, Director of Human Resources; 609-228-8100; Fax: 609-228-6673; E-mail: marketng@metrologic.com

Mettler-Toledo, Inc., Balances and Instruments Division
69 Princeton-Hightstown Rd.
PO Box 71
Hightstown, NJ 08520
http://www.mt.com
Founded: 1954
Total Employees: 200
Industries: Computer Software, Test and Measurement
Growth: Openings in past year, 25
Contact Ms. Patricia Houston, Manager of Employee Relations; 609-448-3000; Fax: 609-443-5972; E-mail: info@mico.mt.com

Music Semiconductors, Inc.
254B Mountain Ave.
Hackettstown, NJ 07840
http://www.music.com

Founded: 1986
Total Employees: 110
Annual Sales: $14 million
Industries: Holding
Companies,
Subassemblies and
Components
Growth: Openings in past
year, 45
Contact Stefan Stas,
President; 908-979-1010;
Fax: 908-979-1035;
E-mail: info@music.com

**Novo Nordisk
Pharmaceuticals, Inc.**
100 Overlook Ctr., Suite
200
Princeton, NJ 08540
http://www.novo.dk
Founded: 1982
Total Employees: 450
Industry: Biotechnology
Growth: Openings in past
year, 59
Contact Ms. Sarajane
Mackenzie, VP of Human
Resources; 609-987-
5800; Fax: 609-921-8082

**Paragon Computer
Professionals, Inc.**
20 Commerce Dr., Suite
226
Cranford, NJ 07016
http://www.paracomp.com
Founded: 1982
Total Employees: 815
Industry: Computer
Hardware
Growth: Openings in past
year, 189
Contact Dan O'Connor,
President/CEO; 908-709-
6767; Fax: 908-709-8071

Pharmacopeia, Inc.
101 College Rd. East
Princeton, NJ 08540
http://www.pcop.com
Founded: 1993
Total Employees: 200
Annual Sales: $14.7
million
Industries: Biotechnology,
Pharmaceuticals

Growth: Openings in past
year, 50
Contact Ken McCarthy,
VP of Human Resources;
609-452-3600; Fax: 609-
452-2434

**Positron Fiber Systems,
Inc.**
3000 Atrium Way, Suite
510 South
Mount Laurel, NJ 08054
http://www.positronfiber.
com
Founded: 1995
Total Employees: 120
Industry: Photonics
Growth: Openings in past
year, 55
Contact Don Gibbs,
President; 609-222-1288;
Fax: 609-222-1744;
E-mail: pfsales@positron.
com

**Princeton Financial
Systems, Inc.**
600 College Rd. East
Princeton, NJ 08540
http://www.psf.com
Founded: 1969
Total Employees: 210
Annual Sales: $27 million
Industry: Computer
Software
Growth: Openings in past
year, 35
Contact Will Mayhall,
President; 609-987-2400;
Fax: 609-987-9320;
E-mail: info@psf.com

**Princeton Instruments,
Inc.**
3660 Quaker Bridge Rd.
Trenton, NJ 08619
Founded: 1981
Total Employees: 125
Industries:
Subassemblies and
Components, Test and
Measurement
Growth: Openings in past
year, 25

Contact Ms. Sandy
Kapica, Office Manager;
609-587-9797; Fax: 609-
587-1970

PSM Fastener Corp.
7 Industrial Rd.
Fairfield, NJ 07004
Founded: 1958
Total Employees: 750
Industries: Factory
Automation,
Subassemblies and
Components
Growth: Openings in past
year, 98
Contact Joe Maziarski,
Vice President; 973-882-
7887; Fax: 973-227-7303

**Purepac Pharmaceutical
Co.**
200 Elmora Ave.
Elizabeth, NJ 07207
Founded: 1929
Total Employees: 350
Annual Sales: $53 million
Industry: Pharmaceuticals
Growth: Openings in past
year, 23
Contact Richard Moldin,
President/CEO; 908-527-
9100; Fax: 908-527-0649

RFE Industries, Inc.
19 Crows Mill Rd.
Keasbey, NJ 08832
Founded: 1967
Total Employees: 120
Annual Sales: $100 million
Industries: Chemicals,
Manufacturing
Equipment,
Subassemblies and
Components
Growth: Openings in past
year, 25
Contact Jack Leiner, Chief
Executive Officer; 732-
738-5200; Fax: 732-738-
5319

Sarnoff Corporation
CN5300
Princeton, NJ 08543
http://www.sarnoff.com
Founded: 1942
Total Employees: 835
Annual Sales: $140 million
Industries:
  Subassemblies and
  Components,
  Telecommunications
Growth: Openings in past
  year, 69
Contact Ms. Susan T.
  Gauff, VP of Human
  Resources & Com-
  munications; 609-734-
  2000; Fax: 609-734-2221

**Solkatronic Chemicals,
Inc.**
30 Two Bridges Rd.
Fairfield, NJ 07004
Founded: 1986
Total Employees: 100
Annual Sales: $20 million
Industry: Chemicals
Growth: Openings in past
  year, 33
Contact Jean Louis
  Aspach, President; 973-
  882-7900; Fax: 973-882-
  7967

Terumo Medical Corp.
2100 Cottontail Ln.
Somerset, NJ 08873
Founded: 1972
Total Employees: 591
Industry: Holding
  Companies
Growth: Openings in past
  year, 78
Contact Ms. Helene Katz,
  Manager of Corporate
  Human Resources; 732-
  302-4900; Fax: 732-302-
  3083

Transistor Devices, Inc.
85 Horsehill Rd.
Cedar Knolls, NJ 07927
http://www.transdev.com

Founded: 1960
Total Employees: 900
Annual Sales: $87 million
Industries: Factory
  Automation, Holding
  Companies,
  Subassemblies and
  Components
Growth: Openings in past
  year, 150
Contact Ms. Audrey
  Morse, Personnel
  Manager, 973-207 1000;
  Fax: 973-267-2047;
  E-mail: info@mailer.
  transdev.com

Virtual Reality, Inc.
333 Meadowlands Pkwy.
Secaucus, NJ 07094
Founded: 1988
Total Employees: 40
Industries: Computer
  Hardware, Computer
  Software, Photonics
Growth: Openings in past
  year, 33
Contact Martin Cardone,
  Chief Executive Officer;
  201-392-9800; Fax: 201-
  392-0156

Voxware, Inc.
305 College Rd. East
Princeton, NJ 08540
http://www.voxware.com
Founded: 1993
Total Employees: 100
Annual Sales: $7.8 million
Industry: Computer
  Software
Growth: Openings in past
  year, 85
Contact Dr. Bathsheba
  Malsheen, President/
  CEO; 609-514-4100;
  Fax: 609-514-4101;
  E-mail: vox@voxware.
  com

Wire Pro, Inc.
23 Front St.
Salem, NJ 08079
Founded: 1971
Total Employees: 615
Annual Sales: $44 million

Industry: Holding
  Companies
Growth: Openings in past
  year, 163
Contact Bob Barbera, Sr.,
  Chief Executive Officer;
  609-935-7560; Fax: 609-
  735-7555

**Wireless Telecom Group,
Inc.**
East Midland Ave.
Paramus, NJ 07652
Founded: 1985
Total Employees: 80
Annual Sales: $22.4
  million
Industries: Defense,
  Factory Automation, Test
  and Measurement,
  Telecommunications
Growth: Openings in past
  year, 31
Contact Dale Sydnor,
  COB/President/CEO;
  201-261-8797; Fax: 201-
  261-8339; E-mail:
  noisecom@haven.los.
  com

New Mexico

**Applied Research
Associates, Inc.**
4300 San Mateo
  Northeast, Suite A220
Albuquerque, NM 87110
http://www.ara.com
Founded: 1979
Total Employees: 385
Annual Sales: $34.8
  million
Industries: Computer
  Software, Defense,
  Environmental, Factory
  Automation,
  Manufacturing Equipment
Growth: Openings in past
  year, 65
Contact James A.
  Eddings, VP of Opera-
  tions; 505-881-8074; Fax:
  505-883-3673; E-mail:
  ara.com

New York

Bell Group, Inc.
7500 Bluewater Rd.
Northwest
Albuquerque, NM 87121
Founded: 1944
Total Employees: 300
Annual Sales: $45 million
Industry: Holding
Companies
Growth: Openings in past
year, 50
Contact Hugh Bell,
President; 505-839-3000;
Fax: 505-839-3001

**Los Alamos Technical
Associates, Inc.**
2400 Louisiana Dr., N.E.,
Bldg. 1, Suite 400
Albuquerque, NM 87110
http://www.lata.com
Founded: 1976
Total Employees: 450
Annual Sales: $50 million
Industries: Defense,
Environmental,
Manufacturing Equipment
Growth: Openings in past
year, 49
Contact D.B. Geran,
Assistant VP of
Administration; 505-884-
3800; Fax: 505-880-
3560; E-mail: ctdir@lata.
com

**Specialty
Teleconstructors, Inc.**
12001 State Hwy. 14 North
Cedar Crest, NM 87008
Founded: 1981
Total Employees: 500
Annual Sales: $65.627
million
Industries: Holding
Companies,
Telecommunications
Growth: Openings in past
year, 50
Contact Michael R.
Budagher, President;
505-281-2197; Fax: 505-
281-8652

A Consulting Team
200 Park Ave. South
New York, NY 10003
http://www.tact.com
Founded: 1983
Total Employees: 300
Annual Sales: $20.9
million
Industry: Computer
Software
Growth: Openings in past
year, 40
Contact Shmuel BenTov,
COB/CEO; 212-979-
8228; Fax: 212-979-8272

ABB Air Preheater, Inc.
Andover Rd.
PO Box 372
Wellsville, NY 14895
http://www.abb.com/
americas/usa
Founded: 1925
Total Employees: 625
Annual Sales: $140 million
Industries: Energy,
Environmental, Factory
Automation,
Manufacturing Equipment
Growth: Openings in past
year, 25
Contact Cory Guenter, VP
of Human Resources;
716-593-2700; Fax: 716-
593-2721

ABT Corp.
361 Broadway
New York, NY 10013
http://www.abtcorp.com
Founded: 1981
Total Employees: 325
Annual Sales: $42 million
Industry: Computer
Software
Growth: Openings in past
year, 25
Contact Ms. Daune
Drogin, Human
Resources Manager;
212-219-8945; Fax: 212-
219-3597

ACTS Testing Labs, Inc.
25 Anderson Rd.
Buffalo, NY 14225
http://www.acts-testing.
com
Founded: 1973
Total Employees: 550
Industries: Advanced
Materials, Biotechnology,
Manufacturing
Equipment, Test and
Measurement
Growth: Openings in past
year, 229
Contact Dr. Angelo M.
Fatta, Ph.D., President;
716-897-3300; Fax: 716-
897-0876

Aeroflex Incorporated
35 South Service Rd.
Plainview, NY 11803
http://www.aeroflex.com
Founded: 1961
Total Employees: 790
Annual Sales: $94.299
million
Industries: Defense,
Factory Automation,
Holding Companies,
Photonics,
Subassemblies and
Components
Growth: Openings in past
year, 85
Contact Harvey R. Blau,
COB/CEO; 516-694-
6700; Fax: 516-694-6771

AMTX, Inc.
5450 Campus Dr.
Canandaigua, NY 14425
http://www.amtx.com
Founded: 1989
Total Employees: 86
Annual Sales: $6.2 million
Industry: Manufacturing
Equipment
Growth: Openings in past
year, 41
Contact Ms. Grace Diaz-
Tubbs, CEO/President;
716-396-6974; Fax: 716-
396-6966; E-mail:
sales@mc.xerox.com

Anchor Computer, Inc.
1900 New Hwy.
Farmingdale, NY 11735
http://www.anchor-
computer.com
Founded: 1969
Total Employees: 155
Annual Sales: $20 million
Industry: Computer
Software
Growth: Openings in past
year, 48
Contact L. Schenker,
President; 516-293-6100;
Fax: 516-293-0891;
E-mail: info@anchor-
computer.com

Anorad Corp.
110 Oser Ave.
Hauppauge, NY 11788
Founded: 1972
Total Employees: 300
Annual Sales: $45 million
Industries: Factory
Automation,
Subassemblies and
Components, Test and
Measurement
Growth: Openings in past
year, 50
Contact Ms. Yolanda
Schweers, Personnel
Manager; 516-231-1990;
Fax: 516-435-1612

API AirTech, Inc.
91 North St.
PO Box 68
Arcade, NY 14006
Founded: 1985
Total Employees: 240
Industry: Energy
Growth: Openings in past
year, 80
Contact Jack Bellomo,
President/General
Manager; 716-496-5755;
Fax: 716-496-5776

**Applied Theory
Communications, Inc.**
40 Cuttermill Rd., Suite
405
Great Neck, NY 11021
http://www.appliedtheory.
com
Founded; 1996
Total Employees: 125
Annual Sales: $10 million
Industries: Computer
Hardware,
Telecommunications
Growth: Openings in past
year, 28
Contact Ms. Pat Foster,
Human Resources Direc-
tor; 516-466-8422; Fax:
516-466-8650; E-mail:
sales@appliedtheory.com

**APV Anhydro Separation
Technologies**
182 Wales Ave.
Tonawanda, NY 14150
Founded: 1972
Total Employees: 69
Industry: Test and
Measurement
Growth: Openings in past
year, 34
Contact Peter Worrall,
President; 716-692-3000;
Fax: 716-692-6416

**Astec America, Inc., ENI
Division**
100 Highpower Rd.
Rochester, NY 14623
http://www.enipower.com
Founded: 1969
Total Employees: 500
Annual Sales: $67 million
Industry: Subassemblies
and Components
Growth: Openings in past
year, 80
Contact John Stratakos,
President; 716-427-8300;
Fax: 716-427-7839

**Automatic Systems
Developers, Inc.**
1 Industry St.
Poughkeepsie, NY 12603
http://www.asdgroup.com
Founded: 1964
Total Employees: 225
Annual Sales: $25 million
Industries: Factory
Automation,
Manufacturing
Equipment,
Subassemblies and
Components
Growth: Openings in past
year, 52
Contact Bill Courchine,
Director of Personnel &
Human Resources; 914-
452-3000; Fax: 914-452-
5725; E-mail: sales@
asdgroup.com

Axiohm
950 Danby Rd.
Ithaca, NY 14850
http://www.axiohm.com
Founded: 1987
Total Employees: 490
Annual Sales: $97 million
Industry: Computer
Hardware
Growth: Openings in past
year, 53
Contact Paul Gardner,
Human Resources
Manager; 607-274-2500;
Fax: 607-274-2404;
E-mail: rosemary.
french@axiohm.com

**Balzers Tool Coating,
Inc.**
661 Erie Ave.
North Tonawanda, NY
14120
Founded: 1985
Total Employees: 300
Annual Sales: $37 million
Industry: Manufacturing
Equipment
Growth: Openings in past
year, 100
Contact Roger W. Bollier,
President/CEO; 716-693-
8557; Fax: 716-695-1995

BEC Group, Inc.
555 Theodore Fremd Ave.,
Suite B-302
Rye, NY 10580
http://www.becgroup.com
Founded: 1995
Total Employees: 380
Annual Sales: $66.996
million
Industry: Holding
Companies
Growth: Openings in past
year, 29
Contact Martin E. Frank-
lin, Chief Executive
Officer; 914-967-9400;
Fax: 914-967-9405;
E-mail: info@becgroup.
com

Belmay, Inc.
200 Corporate Blvd. South
Yonkers, NY 10701
Founded: 1932
Total Employees: 250
Industry: Chemicals
Growth: Openings in past
year, 55
Contact Theodore Kesten,
President; 914-376-1515;
Fax: 914-376-1784

CABLExpress Corp.
500 East Brighton Ave.
Syracuse, NY 13210
Founded: 1978
Total Employees: 195
Annual Sales: $33 million
Industries: Computer
Software, Factory
Automation,
Subassemblies and
Components,
Telecommunications
Growth: Openings in past
year, 50
Contact John M. Sabol,
Director of Human
Resources; 315-476-
3000; Fax: 315-476-
3034; E-mail: info@
cablexpress.com

**Cadus Pharmaceutical
Corp.**
777 Old Saw Mill River
Rd.
Tarrytown, NY 10591
http://www.cadus.com
Founded: 1992
Total Employees: 90
Annual Sales: $6.5 million
Industries: Biotechnology,
Pharmaceuticals
Growth: Openings in past
year, 28
Contact Jeremy Levin,
Ph.D., MD, COB/
President; 914-345-3344;
Fax: 914-345-3565

**Chromalloy Gas Turbine
Corp., Chromalloy New
York Division**
330 Blaisdell Rd.
Orangeburg, NY 10962
Founded: 1968
Total Employees: 600
Annual Sales: $75 million
Industries: Manufacturing
Equipment,
Subassemblies and
Components,
Transportation
Growth: Openings in past
year, 100
Contact Martin Feeney,
VP of Human Resources;
914-359-4700; Fax: 914-
359-4409

CIC International, Inc.
38-01 23rd Ave.
Astoria, NY 11105
Founded: 1930
Total Employees: 450
Annual Sales: $427 million
Industry: Holding
Companies
Growth: Openings in past
year, 196
Contact Michael Kane,
President; 718-204-0900;
Fax: 718-728-7663;
E-mail: 103227.250@
compuserve.com

**Columbia Technology
Corp.**
38-01 23rd Ave.
Astoria, NY 11105
Founded: 1995
Total Employees: 52
Annual Sales: $6.1 million
Industries: Defense,
Manufacturing Equipment
Growth: Openings in past
year, 48
Contact Joseph Ceva,
President; 718-204-0900;
Fax: 718-728-7663;
E-mail: 103227.250@
compuserve.com

**Components Specialties,
Inc.**
200 New Highway
Amityville, NY 11701
http://www.csi-speco.com/
csi
Founded: 1960
Total Employees: 55
Annual Sales: $15 million
Industries: Holding
Companies,
Subassemblies and
Components, Test and
Measurement
Growth: Openings in past
year, 25
Contact L.W. Keller,
President; 516-957-8700;
Fax: 516-957-9142

Compositech, Ltd.
120 Ricefield Ln.
Hauppauge, NY 11788
http://www.compositechltd.
com
Founded: 1984
Total Employees: 120
Annual Sales: $5.475
million
Industry: Advanced
Materials
Growth: Openings in past
year, 50
Contact Jonas Medney,
COB/CEO; 516-436-
5200; Fax: 516-436-
5203; E-mail: info@
compositechltd.com

CooperVision, Inc.
200 WillowBrook Office
Park
Fairport, NY 14450
http://www.coopervision.
com
Founded: 1980
Total Employees: 350
Annual Sales: $40 million
Industry: Medical
Growth: Openings in past
year, 100
Contact Tom Bender,
President/CEO; 716-385-
6810; Fax: 716-385-6145

**Creative Socio-Medics
Corp.**
146 Nassau Ave.
Islip, NY 11751
http://www.csmeoks.com
Founded: 1965
Total Employees: 105
Annual Sales: $8.4 million
Industry: Computer
Software
Growth: Openings in past
year, 30
Contact Jerry Koop, Chief
Executive Officer; 516-
968-2000; Fax: 516-968-
2123; E-mail:
apeldman@csmcorp.com

Curative Health Services
14 Research Way
PO Box 9052
East Setauket, NY 11733
Founded: 1987
Total Employees: 567
Annual Sales: $67.395
million
Industries: Biotechnology,
Medical, Pharmaceuticals
Growth: Openings in past
year, 117
Contact John Vakoutis,
President/CEO; 516-689-
7000; Fax: 516-689-7067

Curbell, Inc.
7 Cobham Dr.
Orchard Park, NY 14127

http://www.curbell.com
Founded: 1942
Total Employees: 300
Annual Sales: $22 million
Industry: Holding
Companies
Growth: Openings in past
year, 125
Contact Tom Leone,
President; 716-667-3377;
Fax: 716-667-7775

**Dayton T. Brown, Inc.,
Engineering and Test
Division**
555 Church St.
Bohemia, NY 11716
http://www.dtbrown.com
Founded: 1950
Total Employees: 250
Annual Sales: $33 million
Industries: Defense,
Factory Automation,
Manufacturing
Equipment, Test and
Measurement
Growth: Openings in past
year, 25
Contact Robert Single, VP
of Human Resources;
516-589-6300; Fax: 516-
589-3648; E-mail: test@
dtbrown.com

**Dielectric Laboratories,
Inc.**
2777 Rte. 20 East
Cazenovia, NY 13035
http://www.dilabs.com
Founded: 1977
Total Employees: 230
Industry: Subassemblies
and Components
Growth: Openings in past
year, 95
Contact Ms. Cheryl
Saunders, Personnel
Manager; 315-655-8710;
Fax: 315-655-8179;
E-mail: whautaniemi@
dilabs.com

**Dorling Kindersley
Publishing, Inc.**
95 Madison Ave.
New York, NY 10016
Founded: 1984
Total Employees: 103
Annual Sales: $15 million

Industries: Computer
Hardware, Computer
Software
Growth: Openings in past
year, 43
Contact Ms. Kristina
Peterson, Chief Execu-
tive Officer; 212-213-
4800; Fax: 212-213-5240

Dorne & Margolin, Inc.
2950 Veterans Memorial
Hwy.
Bohemia, NY 11716
http://www.dorne.com
Founded: 1947
Total Employees: 200
Annual Sales: $34 million
Industries: Test and
Measurement,
Telecommunications
Growth: Openings in past
year, 30
Contact Frank B. Russo,
President; 516-585-4000;
Fax: 516-585-4810

E-Z-EM, Inc.
717 Main St.
Westbury, NY 11590
http://www.ezem.com
Founded: 1961
Total Employees: 950
Annual Sales: $92 million
Industries: Chemicals,
Holding Companies,
Medical,
Pharmaceuticals, Test
and Measurement
Growth: Openings in past
year, 145
Contact Ms. Sandra
Baron, VP of Human
Resources; 516-333-
8230; Fax: 516-333-8278

EarthWeb, Inc.
3 Park Ave., 33rd Floor
New York, NY 10016
http://www.earthweb.com
Founded: 1994
Total Employees: 105
Annual Sales: $18 million
Industries: Computer
Software,
Telecommunications

Growth: Openings in past year, 65
Contact Jack D. Hidary, CEO/President/Co-Founder; 212-725-6550; Fax: 212-725-6559; E-mail: info@earthweb.com

Eastman Worldwide
779 Washington St.
Buffalo, NY 14203
http://www.eastmanww.com
Founded: 1893
Total Employees: 260
Annual Sales: $39 million
Industry: Factory Automation
Growth: Openings in past year, 30
Contact Robert Stevenson, President; 716-856-2200; Fax: 716-856-1140; E-mail: sales@eastmanww.com

Ellanef Manufacturing Corp.
97-11 50th Ave.
Corona, NY 11368
Founded: 1940
Total Employees: 600
Annual Sales: $75 million
Industries: Manufacturing Equipment, Transportation
Growth: Openings in past year, 60
Contact Ernest Constantine, Personnel Manager; 718-699-4000; Fax: 718-592-0722

Erdman, Anthony & Associates, Inc.
2165 Brighton Henrietta Town Line Rd.
Rochester, NY 14623
Founded: 1954
Total Employees: 235
Annual Sales: $18 million
Industries: Computer Hardware, Environmental, Manufacturing Equipment

Growth: Openings in past year, 35
Contact Ms. Helen A. MacLauchlan, Human Resources Administrator; 716-427-8888; Fax: 716-427-8914; E-mail: erdmana@eznet.net

Fiber Instrument Sales Inc.
161 Clear Rd.
Oriskany, NY 13424
http://www.fisfiber.com
Founded: 1985
Total Employees: 105
Annual Sales: $13 million
Industries: Factory Automation, Photonics, Subassemblies and Components
Growth: Openings in past year, 62
Contact Frank Giotto, President; 315-736-2206; Fax: 315-736-2285; E-mail: fisa@borg.com

Fiber Options, Inc.
80 Orville Dr., Suite 102
Bohemia, NY 11716
http://www.fiberoptions.com
Founded: 1987
Total Employees: 100
Annual Sales: $13 million
Industry: Photonics
Growth: Openings in past year, 35
Contact Ms. Karen Blankmeyer, Personnel Administrator; 516-567-8320; Fax: 516-567-8322; E-mail: info@fiberoptions.com

Fonar Corp.
110 Marcus Dr.
Melville, NY 11747
http://www.fonar.com
Founded: 1978
Total Employees: 400
Annual Sales: $17.633 million
Industry: Medical
Growth: Openings in past year, 75

Contact Raymond Damadian, MD, President/CEO/COB; 516-694-2929; Fax: 516-753-5150; E-mail: info@fonar.com

GEC Alsthom, Inc.
4 Skyline Dr.
Hawthorne, NY 10532
Founded: 1967
Total Employees: 589
Annual Sales: $77 million
Industries: Energy, Factory Automation, Subassemblies and Components, Transportation
Growth: Openings in past year, 39
Contact Paul J. Jancek, President; 914-347-5155; Fax: 914-347-5432

Gibraltar Steel Corp.
PO Box 2028
Buffalo, NY 14219
Founded: 1972
Total Employees: 911
Annual Sales: $342.974 million
Industry: Manufacturing Equipment
Growth: Openings in past year, 261
Contact Brian Lipke, COB/President; 716-826-6500; Fax: 716-826-1589

Globecomm Systems, Inc.
45 Oser Ave.
Hauppauge, NY 11788
http://www.worldcom.com
Founded: 1994
Total Employees: 88
Annual Sales: $36.2 million
Industries: Holding Companies, Telecommunications
Growth: Openings in past year, 28
Contact David E. Hershberg, COB/CEO; 516-231-9800; Fax: 516-231-1557

Hansford Manufacturing Corp.
3111 Winton Rd. South
Rochester, NY 14623
Founded: 1920
Total Employees: 260
Annual Sales: $39 million
Industry: Factory Automation
Growth: Openings in past year, 40
Contact Ms. Lisa Wiborg, Manager of Human Resources; 716-427-0660; Fax: 716-427-8610

Hasco Components International Corp.
24740 Jericho Tpke.
Bellerose Village, NY 11001
Founded: 1976
Total Employees: 400
Annual Sales: $12 million
Industry: Subassemblies and Components
Growth: Openings in past year, 175
Contact Tab Marcus, President; 516-328-4292; Fax: 516-326-9125

Hitachi America, Ltd., Power and Industrial Division
660 White Plains Rd.
Tarrytown, NY 10591
http://www.ha12.agency.com
Founded: 1975
Total Employees: 110
Industries: Factory Automation, Manufacturing Equipment, Subassemblies and Components
Growth: Openings in past year, 30
Contact Henry Takahashi, Vice President/General Manager; 914-631-0600; Fax: 914-631-3672

HSC Controls, Inc.
390 Youngs Rd.
Buffalo, NY 14221
Founded: 1974
Total Employees: 220
Annual Sales: $16 million
Industries:
Subassemblies and Components, Test and Measurement
Growth: Openings in past year, 29
Contact Mark Slimko, Accounting Manager; 716-631-9040; Fax: 716-631-8220

ICI/ADP / Fixed Income Division
420 Lexington Ave., Suite 1830
New York, NY 10163
Founded: 1977
Total Employees: 50
Industry: Computer Software
Growth: Openings in past year, 30
Contact William C. Bell, President; 212-973-6100; Fax: 212-983-5570

IFS International, Inc.
300 Jordan Rd.
Troy, NY 12180
http://www.ifsintl.com
Founded: 1981
Total Employees: 63
Annual Sales: $3.733 million
Industry: Computer Software
Growth: Openings in past year, 33
Contact Frank Pascuito, COB/CEO; 518-283-7900; Fax: 518-283-7336; E-mail: marketing@ifsintl.com

IKON Office Solutions, Inc., CTI Information Systems Division
90 West St., 14th Floor
New York, NY 10006
Founded: 1992
Total Employees: 150
Industries: Computer Hardware, Computer Software
Growth: Openings in past year, 50
Contact A. Broadus Anderson, III, President; 212-608-6200; Fax: 212-608-3200

Indotronix International Corp.
331 Main Mall
Poughkeepsie, NY 12601
http://www.iic.com
Founded: 1986
Total Employees: 350
Annual Sales: $45 million
Industry: Computer Software
Growth: Openings in past year, 175
Contact Babu R. Mandava, President; 914-473-1137; Fax: 914-473-1197

Innovir Laboratories, Inc.
510 East 73rd St.
New York, NY 10021
Founded: 1989
Total Employees: 54
Industry: Biotechnology
Growth: Openings in past year, 29
Contact Thomas Sharpe, President/CEO; 212-249-4703; Fax: 212-249-4513

Isogon Corp.
330 7th Ave.
New York, NY 10001
http://www.isogon.com
Founded: 1983
Total Employees: 65

Industry: Computer
Software
Growth: Openings in past
year, 30
Contact Robert Barritz,
President; 212-376-3200;
Fax: 212-376-3280;
E-mail: info@isogon.com

Jaco Electronics, Inc.
145 Oser Ave.
Hauppauge, NY 11788
http://www.jacoelectronics.
com
Founded: 1961
Total Employees: 438
Annual Sales: $155.098
million
Industries: Computer
Hardware, Holding
Companies
Growth: Openings in past
year, 25
Contact Ms. Diane
Eckhoff-Stickle, Human
Resources Manager;
516-273-5500; Fax: 516-
273-5506

K2 Design, Inc.
55 Broad St., 7th Floor
New York, NY 10004
http://www.k2design.com
Founded: 1993
Total Employees: 60
Annual Sales: $4 million
Industry:
Telecommunications
Growth: Openings in past
year, 35
Contact David J. Centner,
COB/CEO/Director; 212-
547-5234; Fax: 212-968-
0067; E-mail: info@
k2design.com

LeCroy Corp.
700 Chestnut Ridge Rd.
Chestnut Ridge, NY 10977
http://www.lecroy.com
Founded: 1964
Total Employees: 400
Annual Sales: $117.1
million
Industries: Computer
Hardware,
Subassemblies and

Components, Test and
Measurement
Growth: Openings in past
year, 50
Contact Warren Davis,
Director of Human
Resources; 914-578-
6020; Fax: 914-578-
5985; E-mail:
webmaster@lecroy.com

LPA Software, Inc.
290 Woodcliff Dr.
Fairport, NY 14450
http://www.lpa.com
Founded: 1972
Total Employees: 125
Annual Sales: $16 million
Industry: Computer
Software
Growth: Openings in past
year, 25
Contact Lawrence L.
Peckham, President;
716-248-9600; Fax: 716-
248-9199; E-mail:
kellym@lpa.com

MapInfo Corp.
1 Global View
Troy, NY 12180
http://www.mapinfo.com
Founded: 1986
Total Employees: 400
Annual Sales: $41.5
million
Industry: Computer
Software
Growth: Openings in past
year, 50
Contact John Cavalier,
President/CEO; 518-285-
6000; Fax: 518-285-
6060; E-mail: sales@
mapinfo.com

**Mediware Information
Systems, Inc.**
1121 Old Walt Whitman
Rd., Suite 305
Melville, NY 11747
http://www.mediware.com
Founded: 1981
Total Employees: 120
Annual Sales: $18.5
million

Industry: Holding
Companies
Growth: Openings in past
year, 30
Contact Les Dace,
President/CEO; 516-423-
7800; Fax: 516-423-
0161; E-mail: sales@
mediware.com

**Micro Modeling
Associates, Inc.**
115 Broadway, 14th Fl.
New York, NY 10006
http://www.micromodeling.
com
Founded: 1989
Total Employees: 160
Annual Sales: $20 million
Industries: Computer
Hardware, Computer
Software,
Telecommunications
Growth: Openings in past
year, 50
Contact Roy Wetterstrom,
President; 212-233-9890;
Fax: 212-233-9897;
E-mail: info@
micromodeling.com

**Micros-to-Mainframes,
Inc.**
614 Corporate Way
Valley Cottage, NY 10989
http://www.mtm.com
Founded: 1986
Total Employees: 120
Annual Sales: $58 million
Industries: Computer
Hardware, Computer
Software, Holding
Companies,
Telecommunications
Growth: Openings in past
year, 28
Contact Ms. Dorothy
Sloman, Personnel
Manager; 914-268-5000;
Fax: 914-268-9695;
E-mail: stever@mtm.com

**Mobius Management
Systems, Inc.**
One Ramada Plaza
New Rochelle, NY 10801
http://www.mobius-inc.com

Founded: 1981
Total Employees: 300
Annual Sales: $38 million
Industry: Computer Software
Growth: Openings in past year, 100
Contact Joseph Albracht, Executive Vice President; 914-637-7200; Fax: 914-632-1789

MovieFone, Inc.
335 Madison Ave., 27th Floor
New York, NY 10017
http://www.movielink.com
Founded: 1989
Total Employees: 100
Annual Sales: $16 million
Industries: Computer Hardware, Computer Software, Telecommunications
Growth: Openings in past year, 29
Contact Andrew Jarecki, Chief Executive Officer; 212-450-8000; Fax: 212-450-8001; E-mail: info@moviefone.com

MRC Bearings
PO Box 280
Jamestown, NY 14701
Founded: 1986
Total Employees: 930
Annual Sales: $120 million
Industry: Subassemblies and Components
Growth: Openings in past year, 28
Contact Michael Mistretta, Director of Human Resources; 716-661-2600; Fax: 716-661-2740

N2K Inc.
55 Broad St., 10th Fl.
New York, NY 10004
http://www.n2k.com
Founded: 1996
Total Employees: 208
Annual Sales: $1.7 million
Industries: Computer Hardware, Telecommunications

Growth: Openings in past year, 68
Contact Ms. Marian Quinn, VP of Human Resources; 212-378-5555; Fax: 212-742-1755; E-mail: pufo@n2k.com

Nalge Nunc International, Inc.
PO Box 20365
Rochester, NY 14602
Founded: 1949
Total Employees: 800
Annual Sales: $100 million
Industries: Biotechnology, Environmental, Pharmaceuticals, Subassemblies and Components, Test and Measurement
Growth: Openings in past year, 73
Contact Thomas Nientimp, VP of Personnel; 716-586-8800; Fax: 716-586-3294

Neuromedical Systems, Inc.
2 Executive Blvd., Suite 306
Suffern, NY 10901
Founded: 1988
Total Employees: 231
Annual Sales: $4.725 million
Industry: Medical
Growth: Openings in past year, 31
Contact Mark R. Rutenberg, COB/President/CEO; 914-368-3600

North Atlantic Instruments, Inc.
170 Wilbur Pl.
Bohemia, NY 11716
http://www.naii.com
Founded: 1992
Total Employees: 70
Annual Sales: $9.5 million
Industries: Subassemblies and

Components, Test and Measurement
Growth: Openings in past year, 25
Contact Bill Forman, Chief Executive Officer; 516-567-1100; Fax: 516-567-1823; E-mail: sales@naii.com

O'Brien & Gere Operations, Inc.
5000 Brittonfield Pkwy.
PO Box 4762
Syracuse, NY 13221
http://www.obg.com
Founded: 1984
Total Employees: 75
Annual Sales: $9.2 million
Industry: Environmental
Growth: Openings in past year, 40
Contact Peter W. McMaster, President; 315-437-8800; Fax: 315-463-7440

OK Industries, Inc.
4 Executive Plaza
Yonkers, NY 10701
http://www.okindustries.com
Founded: 1946
Total Employees: 400
Annual Sales: $50 million
Industries: Computer Hardware, Environmental, Factory Automation, Holding Companies, Manufacturing Equipment
Growth: Openings in past year, 100
Contact Ms. Barbara Albanese, Director of Administration; 914-969-6800; Fax: 914-969-6650; E-mail: info@okindustries.com

OnGard Systems, Inc.
40 Commerce Dr.
Hauppauge, NY 11788
Founded: 1989
Total Employees: 75
Annual Sales: $3.688 million

Industries: Holding
Companies, Medical
Growth: Openings in past
year, 32
Contact Ms. Priscilla
Perez, Administration
Manager; 516-231-8989;
Fax: 516-231-9124

Opkor, Inc.
740 Driving Park Ave.
Rochester, NY 14613
http://www.optics.org
Founded: 1989
Total Employees: 90
Annual Sales: $7.2 million
Industry: Photonics
Growth: Openings in past
year, 40
Contact Richard Mulcahy,
President/CEO; 716-458-
5390; Fax: 716-458-9282

Opus Core Corp.
141 Halstead Ave.
Mamaroneck, NY 10543
Founded: 1982
Total Employees: 50
Annual Sales: $5 million
Industries: Computer
Hardware, Computer
Software
Growth: Openings in past
year, 30
Contact Harvey Brofman,
President; 914-698-8444;
Fax: 914-698-8750

PAR Microsystems Corp.
8383 Seneca Tpke.
New Hartford, NY 13413
Founded: 1981
Total Employees: 600
Industry: Computer
Hardware
Growth: Openings in past
year, 83
Contact Kenneth Giffune,
VP of Human Resources;
315-738-0600; Fax: 315-
738-0562

PAR Technology Corp.
8383 Seneca Tpke.
New Hartford, NY 13413
http://www.partech.com
Founded: 1968
Total Employees: 924
Annual Sales: $118 million
Industry: Holding
Companies
Growth: Openings in past
year, 44
Contact Dr. Ken Giffune,
VP of Human Resources;
315-738-0600; Fax: 315-
738-0411; E-mail:
askpar@partech.com

PCB Piezotronics, Inc.
3425 Walden Ave.
Depew, NY 14043
http://www.pcb.com
Founded: 1967
Total Employees: 300
Annual Sales: $40 million
Industries: Holding
Companies,
Subassemblies and
Components, Test and
Measurement,
Transportation
Growth: Openings in past
year, 70
Contact Ms. Susan
Ruhland, Human
Resources Manager;
716-684-0001; Fax: 716-
684-0987

**Performance
Technologies, Inc.**
315 Science Pkwy.
Rochester, NY 14620
http://www.pt.com
Founded: 1981
Total Employees: 137
Annual Sales: $24.843
million
Industries: Computer
Hardware, Computer
Software, Holding
Companies,
Telecommunications
Growth: Openings in past
year, 37
Contact Donald Turrell,
President/CEO; 716-256-
0200; Fax: 716-256-
0791; E-mail: info@pt.
com

Periphonics Corp.
4000 Veterans Memorial
Hwy.
Bohemia, NY 11716
http://www.peri.com
Founded: 1970
Total Employees: 640
Annual Sales: $86.144
million
Industry:
Telecommunications
Growth: Openings in past
year, 98
Contact Ms. Janet
Anderson, Senior Direc-
tor of Human Resources;
516-468-9000; Fax: 516-
981-2689

**Philips Broadband
Networks, Inc.**
100 Fairgrounds Dr.
Manlius, NY 13104
Founded: 1988
Total Employees: 900
Annual Sales: $150 million
Industries: Manufacturing
Equipment, Photonics,
Telecommunications
Growth: Openings in past
year, 138
Contact Ms. Laurie
Palmiero, Manager of
Human Resources; 315-
682-9105; Fax: 315-682-
9006

Poppe Tyson, Inc.
40 West 23rd St.
New York, NY 10010
http://www.poppe.com
Founded: 1914
Total Employees: 300
Annual Sales: $41 million
Industry: Holding
Companies
Growth: Openings in past
year, 150
Contact Ms. Deborah
Shea, VP of Human
Resources; 212-367-
4000; Fax: 212-367-
4001; E-mail: cmarr@ny.
poppe.com

Porta Systems Corp.
575 Underhill Blvd.
Syosset, NY 11791
Founded: 1969
Total Employees: 416
Annual Sales: $57.987
million
Industries. Factory
Automation, Holding
Companies,
Subassemblies and
Components,
Telecommunications
Growth: Openings in past
year, 64
Contact William V.
Carney, COB/CEO; 516-
364-9300; Fax: 516-682-
4655

**Protective Closures Co.,
Inc., Caplug Division**
2150 Elmwood Ave.
Buffalo, NY 14207
http://www.caplugs.com
Founded: 1969
Total Employees: 250
Industries: Factory
Automation,
Subassemblies and
Components
Growth: Openings in past
year, 50
Contact Charlie Cole,
President; 716-876-9855;
Fax: 716-874-1680;
E-mail: sales@caplugs.
com

**Regeneron
Pharmaceuticals, Inc.**
777 Old Saw Mill River
Rd.
Tarrytown, NY 10591
Founded: 1988
Total Employees: 265
Annual Sales: $24.113
million
Industries: Biotechnology,
Pharmaceuticals
Growth: Openings in past
year, 39
Contact Dr. Leonard
Schleifer, MD, Ph.D.,
CEO/President; 914-347-
7000; Fax: 914-347-2113

Remee Products Corp.
PO Box 488
Florida, NY 10921
http://www.remee.com
Founded: 1972
Total Employees: 175
Annual Sales: $30 million
Industries: Holding
Companies,
Subassemblies and
Components
Growth: Openings in past
year, 40
Contact Al Muhlrad,
President; 914-651-4431;
Fax: 914-651-4160;
E-mail: rpcsale@aol.com

**Renaissance Software,
LLC**
1983 Marcus Ave., Suite
125
Lake Success, NY 11042
http://www.rensoftllc.com
Founded: 1979
Total Employees: 75
Industry: Computer
Software
Growth: Openings in past
year, 25
Contact Robert Schilt,
President; 516-466-5190;
Fax: 516-390-8888

Rome Cable Corp.
421 Ridge St.
Rome, NY 13440
http://www.romecable.com
Founded: 1936
Total Employees: 430
Annual Sales: $57 million
Industries: Manufacturing
Equipment,
Subassemblies and
Components
Growth: Openings in past
year, 40
Contact David Harvey,
COB/CEO; 315-337-
3000; Fax: 315-338-
6700; E-mail: dharvey@
romecable.com

Sandata, Inc.
26 Harbor Park Dr.
Port Washington, NY
11050
http://www.sandata.com
Founded: 1969
Total Employees: 150
Annual Sales: $11.881
million
Industry: Computer
Software
Growth: Openings in past
year, 50
Contact Richard Wilson,
Director of Human
Resources; 516-484-
0700; Fax: 516-484-
6084; E-mail: info@
sandata.com

**Schick Technologies,
Inc.**
31-00 47th Ave.
Long Island City, NY 11101
http://www.schicktech.com
Founded: 1992
Total Employees: 225
Annual Sales: $16 million
Industries: Computer
Software, Medical
Growth: Openings in past
year, 36
Contact Ms. Myra Fasner,
Human Resources Direc-
tor; 718-937-5765; Fax:
718-937-5962

Sear Brown Group, Inc.
85 Metro Park
Rochester, NY 14623
http://www.searbrown.com
Founded: 1929
Total Employees: 475
Industries: Environmental,
Manufacturing Equipment
Growth: Openings in past
year, 62
Contact Ms. Reva Riley,
Human Resources
Manager; 716-475-1440;
Fax: 716-272-1814;
E-mail: info@searbrown.
com

Sekisui America Corp.
666 Fifth Ave., 12th Floor
New York, NY 10103
Founded: 194/
Total Employees: 600
Annual Sales: $184 million
Industries: Advanced
Materials, Subassemblies
and Components
Growth: Openings in past
year, 50
Contact David G. Metro,
General Manager of
Human Resources; 212-
489-3500; Fax: 212-489-
5100

**Semiconductor Laser
International Corporation**
15 Link Dr.
Binghamton, NY 13904
http://www.slicorp.com
Founded: 1993
Total Employees: 45
Industries: Photonics,
Subassemblies and
Components
Growth: Openings in past
year, 35
Contact Geoffrey
Burnham, President/
CEO; 607-722-3800;
Fax: 607-722-3900;
E-mail: 76470.2336@
compuserve.com

**Semiconductor
Packaging Materials Co.,
Inc.**
1 Labriola Ct.
Armonk, NY 10504
Founded: 1966
Total Employees: 550
Annual Sales: $46 million
Industries: Holding
Companies,
Manufacturing
Equipment,
Subassemblies and
Components
Growth: Openings in past
year, 198
Contact Gilbert D. Raker,
COB/President/CEO;
914-273-5500; Fax: 914-
273-2065

**Sherwood, Taylor-
Wharton Gas Equipment
Division**
2111 Liberty Dr.
Niagara Falls, NY 14304
Founded: 1853
Total Employees: 500
Annual Sales: $67 million
Industries:
Subassemblies and
Components, Test and
Measurement
Growth: Openings in past
year, 50
Contact Kenneth Miller,
Vice President/General
Manager; 716-283-1010;
Fax: 716-283-5737

**Spellman High Voltage
Electronics Corp.**
475 Wireless Blvd.
Hauppauge, NY 11788
http://www.spellman.com
Founded: 1947
Total Employees: 350
Annual Sales: $47 million
Industries:
Subassemblies and
Components, Test and
Measurement
Growth: Openings in past
year, 29
Contact Ms. Carol
Stewart, Human
Resource Manager; 516-
630-3000; Fax: 516-435-
1620; E-mail: sales@
spellmanhv.com

STS Duotek, Inc.
336 Summit Point Dr.
Henrietta, NY 14467
Founded: 1978
Total Employees: 190
Annual Sales: $8.3 million
Industries: Biotechnology,
Chemicals, Holding
Companies,
Pharmaceuticals
Growth: Openings in past
year, 50
Contact Richard
Whitbourne, Chairman of
the Board; 716-321-1130;

Fax: 716-321-1575;
E-mail: sts@stsduotek.
com

**Syracuse Research
Corp.**
Merril Ln.
Syracuse, NY 13210
http://www.syrres.com
Founded: 1957
Total Employees: 251
Industries: Chemicals,
Computer Software,
Defense, Environmental,
Transportation
Growth: Openings in past
year, 51
Contact John Holland,
Manager of Human
Resources; 315-426-
3200; Fax: 315-426-
3352; E-mail: mailbox@
syrres.com

Systems Union, Inc.
10 Bank St.
White Plains, NY 10606
http://www.systemsunion.
com
Founded: 1981
Total Employees: 450
Annual Sales: $58 million
Industry: Computer
Software
Growth: Openings in past
year, 99
Contact Lawrence Helft,
Chief Executive Officer;
914-948-7770; Fax: 914-
948-7399

Taconic Farms, Inc.
273 Hover Ave.
Germantown, NY 12526
http://www.taconic.com
Founded: 1952
Total Employees: 260
Annual Sales: $19.5
million
Industry: Biotechnology
Growth: Openings in past
year, 30
Contact Ms. Patricia
Phelan, Personnel Direc-
tor; 518-537-6208; Fax:
518-537-7287; E-mail:
taconicser@aol.com

TelTech International Corp.
39 Broadway
New York, NY 10006
http://www.teletechinc.com
Founded: 1973
Total Employees: 475
Annual Sales: $57 million
Industries: Computer Hardware, Computer Software, Telecommunications
Growth: Openings in past year, 95
Contact Frank Tantillo, Vice President; 212-514-5600; Fax: 212-514-5504

TreaTek-CRA
2055 Niagara Falls Blvd., Suite 3
Niagara Falls, NY 14304
Founded: 1992
Total Employees: 215
Industries: Environmental, Manufacturing Equipment
Growth: Openings in past year, 115
Contact Anthony Ying, President; 716-297-2160; Fax: 716-297-2265; E-mail: jglazier@ttcra.com

Triple G Corporation
2 Rector St., 17th Floor
New York, NY 10008
http://www.tripleg.com
Founded: 1988
Total Employees: 80
Industry: Computer Software
Growth: Openings in past year, 50
Contact Lee Green, President; 888-874-7534; Fax: 888-778-3375; E-mail: info@tripleg.com

Ultrafem, Inc.
805 3rd Ave., 17th Fl.
New York, NY 10022
Founded: 1990

Total Employees: 103
Annual Sales: $3.534 million
Industry: Medical
Growth: Openings in past year, 61
Contact John W. Andersen, COB/President/CEO; 212-446-1400; Fax: 212-446-1401

US Computer Group, Inc.
4 Dubon Ct.
Farmingdale, NY 11735
Founded: 1987
Total Employees: 200
Annual Sales: $30 million
Industry: Computer Hardware
Growth: Openings in past year, 50
Contact Paul Eterno, Senior VP of Human Resources; 516-755-9400; Fax: 516-753-6105

Veeco Instruments, Inc.
Terminal Dr.
Plainview, NY 11803
http://www.veeco.com
Founded: 1946
Total Employees: 329
Annual Sales: $96.8 million
Industries: Factory Automation, Holding Companies, Photonics, Test and Measurement
Growth: Openings in past year, 58
Contact Edward Braun, President/CEO; 516-349-8300; Fax: 516-349-8321

Welch Allyn, Inc., Lighting Products Division
4619 Jordan Rd.
Skaneateles Falls, NY 13153
http://www.hi-lux.com
Founded: 1915
Total Employees: 150
Annual Sales: $19 million
Industries: Photonics, Subassemblies and Components

Growth: Openings in past year, 30
Contact Ms. Barb Emerson, Human Resources Manager; 315-685-4347; Fax: 315-685-2854; E-mail: babiarz@mail.welchallyn.com

Western New York Computing Systems, Inc.
1100 Pittsford-Victor Rd.
Pittsford, NY 14534
http://www.wnycs.com
Founded: 1971
Total Employees: 180
Industry: Computer Software
Growth: Openings in past year, 30
Contact Ray H. Hutch, President; 716-381-4120; Fax: 716-264-6041

WinStar Communications, Inc.
230 Park Ave.
New York, NY 10169
http://www.winstar.com
Founded: 1993
Total Employees: 873
Annual Sales: $68 million
Industries: Holding Companies, Telecommunications
Growth: Openings in past year, 621
Contact William Rouhana, COB/CEO; 212-687-7577; Fax: 212-867-1565

Zeitech, Inc.
500 5th Ave.
New York, NY 10110
http://www.zeitech.com
Founded: 1987
Total Employees: 550
Annual Sales: $50 million
Industries: Computer Hardware, Computer Software
Growth: Openings in past year, 200
Contact Michael Ornstein, President; 212-398-4100; Fax: 212-398-2075

North Carolina

Accipiter, Inc.
4000 Wake Forest Rd.,
Suite 200
Raleigh, NC 27609
http://www.accipiter.com
Founded: 1996
Total Employees: 35
Annual Sales: $4.5 million
Industry: Computer
Software
Growth: Openings in past
year, 30
Contact Chris Evans,
CEO/Founder; 919-872-
7755; Fax: 919-872-
5060; E-mail: info@
accipiter.com

Alliance of Professionals & Consultants, Inc.
8600 Caswell Ct.
Raleigh, NC 27613
http://www.apc-services.
com
Founded: 1993
Total Employees: 350
Industries: Computer
Hardware, Computer
Software,
Telecommunications
Growth: Openings in past
year, 49
Contact Roy L. Roberts,
COB/President/CEO;
919-847-6056; Fax: 919-
847-2705; E-mail: roy@
apc-services.com

Alphanumeric Systems, Inc.
3700 Barrett Dr.
Raleigh, NC 27609
http://www.alphanumeric.
com
Founded: 1979
Total Employees: 125
Annual Sales: $25 million
Industry: Computer
Hardware
Growth: Openings in past
year, 35
Contact Ms. Darleen M.
Johns, President; 919-
781-7575; Fax: 919-781-
7517

Alydaar Software Corp.
2101 West Rexford Rd.,
Suite 250
Charlotte, NC 28211
http://www.alydaar.com
Founded: 1982
Total Employees: 250
Industries: Computer
Hardware, Computer
Software
Growth: Openings in past
year, 239
Contact Ken Lanspery, VP
of Human Resources;
704-365-2324; E-mail:
info@alydaar.com

Angiosonics, Inc.
2200 Gateway Centre
Blvd., Suite 207
Morrisville, NC 27560
Founded: 1989
Total Employees: 50
Industry: Medical
Growth: Openings in past
year, 48
Contact Jonathan Ilany,
President/CEO; 919-468-
0049; Fax: 919-468-0216

Astor Corporation
8521 Six Forks Rd., Suite
105
Raleigh, NC 27615
Founded: 1948
Total Employees: 768
Annual Sales: $140 million
Industries: Advanced
Materials, Holding
Companies
Growth: Openings in past
year, 235
Contact Ms. Susan Bailey,
Director of Human
Resources; 919-846-
8011; Fax: 919-846-8283;
E-mail: astorcorp@
ntwrks.com

Basic Machinery Co., Inc.
1220 Harold Andrews Rd.
PO Box 688
Siler City, NC 27344
Founded: 1975
Total Employees: 125
Annual Sales: $15 million
Industries: Environmental,
Factory Automation,
Holding Companies,
Manufacturing Equipment
Growth: Openings in past
year, 25
Contact Harold Milholen,
President; 919-663-2244;
Fax: 919-663-2172

Cato Research Ltd.
200 Westpark Corporate
Ctr.
Durham, NC 27713
http://www.cato.com/cato
Founded: 1988
Total Employees: 160
Industries: Biotechnology,
Medical, Pharmaceuticals
Growth: Openings in past
year, 40
Contact Ms. Trisha
Whelan, Director of
Human Resources; 919-
361-2286; Fax: 919-361-
2290; E-mail: paha4@
mail.cato.com

Chloride Systems
126 Chloride Rd.
Burgaw, NC 28425
Founded: 1957
Total Employees: 175
Industries: Energy,
Subassemblies and
Components
Growth: Openings in past
year, 65
Contact Pat Hutchins,
General Manager; 910-
259-1000; Fax: 910-259-
1148

Cree Research, Inc.
2810 Meridian Pkwy.,
  Suite 176
Durham, NC 27713
http://www.cree.com
Founded: 1987
Total Employees: 210
Annual Sales: $28,973
  million
Industries: Holding
  Companies, Photonics,
  Subassemblies and
  Components
Growth: Openings in past
  year, 60
Contact Neal Hunter,
  COB/CEO/President;
  919-361-5709; Fax: 919-
  361-4630

**Engineered Sintered
Components, Inc.**
250 Old Murdock Rd.
Troutman, NC 28166
Founded: 1989
Total Employees: 300
Annual Sales: $40 million
Industry: Subassemblies
  and Components
Growth: Openings in past
  year, 50
Contact Dan Comer,
  Human Resources
  Manager; 704-528-7500;
  Fax: 704-528-7529

**Falk Integrated
Technologies, Inc.**
2275 Vanstory St., Suite
  306
Greensboro, NC 27403
Founded: 1986
Total Employees: 130
Annual Sales: $25 million
Industry: Computer
  Hardware
Growth: Openings in past
  year, 50
Contact Harry S. Falk,
  President; 910-852-0455;
  Fax: 910-852-0456

Interactive Magic, Inc.
PO Box 13491
Research Triangle Park,
  NC 27709
http://www.imagicgames.
  com
Founded: 1994
Total Employees: 90
Industries: Computer
  Software, Holding
  Companies
Growth: Openings in past
  year, 55
Contact Robert Pickens,
  President; 919-461-0722;
  Fax: 919-461-0723

LCI Corp.
PO Box 16348
Charlotte, NC 28297
Founded: 1961
Total Employees: 125
Industries: Biotechnology,
  Factory Automation,
  Manufacturing
  Equipment,
  Subassemblies and
  Components, Test and
  Measurement
Growth: Openings in past
  year, 25
Contact Ms. Pat Deering,
  VP of Human Resources;
  704-394-8341; Fax: 704-
  393-8590; E-mail: info@
  lcicorp.com

**Lydall, Inc., Westex
Division**
Brooks Crossroads
Hamptonville, NC 27020
http://www.lydall.com
Founded: 1879
Total Employees: 180
Annual Sales: $22 million
Industries: Advanced
  Materials, Medical,
  Subassemblies and
  Components
Growth: Openings in past
  year, 30
Contact Ms. Maria
  Morrison, Personnel
  Manager; 910-468-8522;
  Fax: 910-468-8555

**Magellan Laboratories,
Inc.**
PO Box 13341
Research Triangle Park,
  NC 27709
Founded: 1992
Total Employees: 140
Annual Sales: $21 million
Industries: Biotechnology,
  Chemicals,
  Pharmaceuticals
Growth: Openings in past
  year, 40
Contact W. Lowry Caudill,
  Ph.D., Co-President;
  919-481-4855; Fax: 919-
  481-4908

Metasys Inc.
2550 West Tyvola Rd.,
  Suite 500
Charlotte, NC 28217
http://www.metasys.com
Founded: 1991
Total Employees: 170
Annual Sales: $22 million
Industry: Computer
  Software
Growth: Openings in past
  year, 60
Contact Patrick Thean,
  President/CEO; 704-423-
  7200; Fax: 704-423-
  7176; E-mail: info@
  metasys.com

**Novo Nordisk BioChem
North America, Inc.**
77 Perry Chapel Rd.
Franklinton, NC 27525
http://www.novo.dk
Founded: 1978
Total Employees: 325
Industries: Biotechnology,
  Chemicals
Growth: Openings in past
  year, 90
Contact Ms. Joanne
  Steiner, Director of
  Human Resources; 919-
  494-3000; Fax: 919-494-
  3450

Rexam Custom
PO Box 368
Matthews, NC 28106
http://www.rexamcustom.
com
Founded: 1959
Total Employees: 600
Industry: Manufacturing
Equipment
Growth: Openings in past
year, 178
Contact Mitch Weiss,
Director of Human
Resources; 704-847-
9171; Fax: 704-845-
4333; E-mail: rexinfo@
custom.rexam.com

**SunGard Trust Systems,
Inc.**
PO Box 240882
Charlotte, NC 28224
http://www.sungard.com/
trust
Founded: 1975
Total Employees: 200
Annual Sales: $25 million
Industries: Computer
Hardware, Computer
Software
Growth: Openings in past
year, 72
Contact Robert F. Clark,
President; 704-527-6300;
Fax: 704-527-9741

**Great Plains Software,
Inc.**
1701 Southwest 38th St.
Fargo, ND 58103
http://www.gps.com
Founded: 1980
Total Employees: 550
Annual Sales: $57.12
million
Industry: Computer
Software
Growth: Openings in past
year, 50
Contact Ms. Jodie
Uecker-Rust, VP of
Employee Services; 701-
281-0550; Fax: 701-281-
3700; E-mail: info@gps.
com

RF Micro Devices, Inc.
7625 Thorndike Rd.
Greensboro, NC 27409
http://www.rfmd.com
Founded: 1991
Total Employees: 125
Annual Sales: $9.5 million
Industry: Subassemblies
and Components
Growth: Openings in past
year, 45
Contact Ms. Liz Moore,
Human Resources
Manager; 910-664-1233;
Fax: 910-664-0839;
E-mail: info@rfmd.com

**Zurn Industries, Inc.,
Flush Valve Operations
Division**
5900 Elwien Buchanan Dr.
Sanford, NC 27330
Founded: 1900
Total Employees: 100
Annual Sales: $13 million
Industry: Subassemblies
and Components
Growth: Openings in past
year, 40
Contact Jerry Markijohn,
Plant Manager; 919-775-
2255; Fax: 919-775-3541

**Phoenix International
Corporation**
1441 44th St. Northwest
Fargo, ND 58102
http://www.phoeintl.com
Founded: 1987
Total Employees: 300
Annual Sales: $39 million
Industries: Computer
Software, Environmental,
Manufacturing
Equipment,
Transportation
Growth: Openings in past
year, 70
Contact Barry Batcheller,
President/CEO; 701-282-
9364; Fax: 701-282-9365

**Strategic Technologies,
Inc.**
301 Gregson Dr.
Cary, NC 27511
http://www.stratech.com
Founded: 1988
Total Employees: 110
Industry: Computer
Hardware
Growth: Openings in past
year, 25
Contact Mike Shook,
President/CEO; 919-481-
9797; Fax: 919-481-
2203; E-mail: info@
stratech.com

North Dakota

Fargo Assembly Co., Inc.
1402 43rd St. Northwest
Fargo, ND 58102
Founded: 1975
Total Employees: 500
Industry: Subassemblies
and Components
Growth: Openings in past
year, 199
Contact Ron Bergan,
Chief Executive Officer;
701-298-3803; Fax: 701-
298-3806

Ohio

3X Corporation
760 Lakeview Plaza Blvd.
Worthington, OH 43085
Founded: 1970
Total Employees: 160
Annual Sales: $10 million
Industries: Computer
Hardware, Computer
Software
Growth: Openings in past
year, 68
Contact Ms. Polly
Hartsough, Director of

Human Resources; 614-433-9406; Fax: 614-433-9430

Accu-Med Services, Inc.
300 Techne Center Dr., Suite A
Milford, OH 45150
Founded: 1994
Total Employees: 60
Annual Sales: $7.7 million
Industry: Computer Software
Growth: Openings in past year, 30
Contact Gerald A. McKenzie, President/CEO; 513-831-1207; Fax: 513-831-1370

Advanced Assembly Automation, Inc.
313 Mound St.
Dayton, OH 45407
Founded: 1978
Total Employees: 240
Annual Sales: $48 million
Industries: Factory Automation, Test and Measurement
Growth: Openings in past year, 40
Contact Robert Douglas, President; 937-222-3030; Fax: 937-222-2931

Aeronca, Inc.
1712 Germantown Rd.
Middletown, OH 45042
Founded: 1928
Total Employees: 267
Annual Sales: $15 million
Industry: Transportation
Growth: Openings in past year, 67
Contact David Caudill, Director of Human Resources; 513-422-2751; Fax: 513-422-0812

Aircraft Braking Systems Corp.
1204 Massillon Rd.
Akron, OH 44306

Founded: 1923
Total Employees: 890
Industries: Test and Measurement, Transportation
Growth: Openings in past year, 26
Contact Ed Searle, Director of Human Resources; 330-796-4400; Fax: 330-796-9805

Allen Telecom, Inc., Antenna Specialists Division
30500 Bruce Industrial Pkwy.
Solon, OH 44139
http://www.allentele.com
Founded: 1953
Total Employees: 600
Annual Sales: $120 million
Industries:
Subassemblies and Components, Telecommunications
Growth: Openings in past year, 198
Contact Ms. Susan Van Dale, Director of Personnel; 440-349-8400; Fax: 440-349-8407

Allied Mineral Products, Inc.
2700 Scioto Pkwy.
Columbus, OH 43221
Founded: 1960
Total Employees: 210
Industry: Advanced Materials
Growth: Openings in past year, 25
Contact Jon K. Tabor, COB/President; 614-876-0244; Fax: 614-876-0981

Argo-Tech Corp.
23555 Euclid Ave.
Cleveland, OH 44117
Founded: 1987
Total Employees: 618
Annual Sales: $69 million
Industry: Transportation
Growth: Openings in past year, 99

Contact Michael Lipscomb, President/CEO; 216-692-6000; Fax: 216-692-5293

Associated Enterprises
1382 West Jackson St.
Painesville, OH 44077
Founded: 1968
Total Employees: 225
Industry: Holding Companies
Growth: Openings in past year, 25
Contact T. Martz, Personnel Manager; 440-354-2106; Fax: 440-354-0687; E-mail: 76311.2313@compuserve.com

Automated Packaging Systems, Inc.
10175 Philipp Pkwy.
Streetsboro, OH 44241
http://www.autopro.com
Founded: 1963
Total Employees: 700
Industries: Manufacturing Equipment, Medical, Pharmaceuticals, Subassemblies and Components
Growth: Openings in past year, 200
Contact Bernie Lerner, President/CEO; 330-342-2000; Fax: 330-342-2400

Automatic Feed Co.
476 East Riverview Ave.
Napoleon, OH 43545
http://www.automaticfeed.com
Founded: 1948
Total Employees: 175
Annual Sales: $15 million
Industry: Factory Automation
Growth: Openings in past year, 45
Contact Kim Beck, President/CEO; 419-592-0050; Fax: 419-592-8590; E-mail: sales@automaticfeed.com

**Bailey Transportation
Products, Inc.**
333 Gore Rd.
Conneaut, OH 44030
Founded: 1969
Total Employees: 400
Industry: Manufacturing
Equipment
Growth: Openings in past
year, 50
Contact Jack Young,
Personnel Director; 440-
599-8131; Fax: 440-599-
7870

CCPI, Inc.
838 Cherry St.
Blanchester, OH 45107
http://www.ceramics.com/
ccpi
Founded: 1957
Total Employees: 160
Annual Sales: $21 million
Industries: Holding
Companies, Test and
Measurement
Growth: Openings in past
year, 40
Contact Robert Sollars,
Vice President; 937-783-
2476; Fax: 937-783-
2539; E-mail: ccpi@
ceramics.com

Colormatrix Corp.
3005 Chester Ave.
Cleveland, OH 44114
Founded: 1979
Total Employees: 120
Annual Sales: $31 million
Industries: Advanced
Materials, Chemicals
Growth: Openings in past
year, 45
Contact John Haugh,
Chief Executive Officer;
216-622-0100; Fax: 216-
622-0502

Com Net, Inc.
522 Clinton St.
Defiance, OH 43512
http://www.bright.net

Founded: 1993
Total Employees: 34
Industry:
Telecommunications
Growth: Openings in past
year, 28
Contact Mark Rekers,
Chief Executive Officer;
419-784-9422; Fax: 419-
784-9452

**Computer Output
Microfilm Corp.**
6802 West Snowville Rd.
Cleveland, OH 44141
Founded: 1969
Total Employees: 85
Industry: Computer
Hardware
Growth: Openings in past
year, 25
Contact William F.
Zimmerman, President/
CEO; 440-546-4266;
Fax: 440-546-4282

**Computer Systems Co.,
Inc.**
6802 West Snowville Rd.
Cleveland, OH 44141
http://www.csc-papars.com
Founded: 1964
Total Employees: 135
Annual Sales: $17 million
Industries: Computer
Software, Holding
Companies,
Telecommunications
Growth: Openings in past
year, 35
Contact William F.
Zimmerman, President/
CEO; 440-546-4272;
Fax: 440-546-4282

CTL-Aerospace, Inc.
5616 Spellmire Dr.
Cincinnati, OH 45246
Founded: 1946
Total Employees: 280
Industry: Advanced
Materials
Growth: Openings in past
year, 105

Contact James C. Irwin,
COB/CEO/President;
513-874-7900; Fax: 513-
874-2499

Cyberex, Inc.
7171 Industrial Park Blvd.
Mentor, OH 44060
http://www.cyberex.com
Founded: 1968
Total Employees: 150
Industries: Energy,
Subassemblies and
Components
Growth: Openings in past
year, 40
Contact Gus Stevens,
President/COO; 440-946-
1783; Fax: 440-946-
5963; E-mail: sales@
cyberex.com

Danieli Wean
3805 Henricks Rd.
PO Box 180
Youngstown, OH 44501
Founded: 1914
Total Employees: 225
Industries: Factory
Automation,
Manufacturing Equipment
Growth: Openings in past
year, 75
Contact W.W. Stasik,
President/CEO; 330-797-
2000; Fax: 330-797-2068

**Entek IRD International
Corporation**
1700 Edison Dr.
Milford, OH 45150
http://www.entekird.com
Founded: 1981
Total Employees: 400
Industries: Computer
Software, Factory
Automation
Growth: Openings in past
year, 50
Contact Scott Bowers,
Manager of Human
Resources & Admin.;
513-576-6151; Fax: 513-
576-6104

Eurand America, Inc.
845 Center Dr.
Vandalia, OH 45377
http://www.eurand.com
Founded: 1979
Total Employees: 311
Industry: Pharmaceuticals
Growth: Openings in past year, 29
Contact Ms. Dorothy Homan, Manager of Personnel Services; 937-898-9669; Fax: 937-898-9529

Imperial Adhesives, Inc.
6315 Wiehe Rd.
Cincinnati, OH 45237
http://www.
  imperialadhesives.com
Founded: 1960
Total Employees: 220
Annual Sales: $43 million
Industry: Advanced Materials
Growth: Openings in past year, 24
Contact Robert D. Johnson, President; 513-351-1300; Fax: 513-351-1994

Kendle International, Inc.
700 Carew Tower, 441 Vine St.
Cincinnati, OH 45202
http://www.kendle.com
Founded: 1981
Total Employees: 450
Annual Sales: $12.959 million
Industries: Biotechnology, Computer Software, Pharmaceuticals
Growth: Openings in past year, 350
Contact Stephen Scheurer, Director of Human Resources; 513-381-5550; Fax: 513-381-5870; E-mail: info@kendle.com

Gorman-Rupp Co.
305 Bowman St.
PO Box 1217
Mansfield, OH 44901
http://www.gormanrupp.com
Founded: 1933
Total Employees: 994
Annual Sales: $155.187 million
Industry: Holding Companies
Growth: Openings in past year, 29
Contact Lee A. Wilkins, Personnel Director; 419-755-1011; Fax: 419-755-1233; E-mail: grsales@gormanrupp.com

ITW Ransburg Electrostatic Systems
PO Box 913
Toledo, OH 43697
http://www.itwransburg.com
Founded: 1888
Total Employees: 200
Annual Sales: $30 million
Industry: Factory Automation
Growth: Openings in past year, 50
Contact Ms. Lois Christopher, Director of Human Resources; 419-470-2000; Fax: 800-949-6886; E-mail: marketing@itwransburg.com

Kindt-Collins Co.
12651 Elmwood Ave.
Cleveland, OH 44111
Founded: 1914
Total Employees: 90
Annual Sales: $13 million
Industries: Advanced Materials, Factory Automation, Subassemblies and Components
Growth: Openings in past year, 25
Contact John Lindseth, COB/CEO; 216-252-4122; Fax: 216-252-5639

Honda Engineering North America, Inc.
24000 Honda Pkwy.
Marysville, OH 43040
Founded: 1987
Total Employees: 250
Annual Sales: $32 million
Industries: Manufacturing Equipment, Transportation
Growth: Openings in past year, 50
Contact T. Imura, President; 937-642-5000; Fax: 937-644-6608

KDI Precision Products, Inc.
3975 McMann Rd.
Cincinnati, OH 45245
Founded: 1946
Total Employees: 356
Annual Sales: $48 million
Industry: Subassemblies and Components
Growth: Openings in past year, 30
Contact Sal Mira, President; 513-943-2000; Fax: 513-943-2317

Kinetico Incorporated
10845 Kinsman Rd.
Newbury, OH 44065
http://www.kinetico.com
Founded: 1970
Total Employees: 330
Industries: Environmental, Holding Companies
Growth: Openings in past year, 69
Contact Ms. Judy Sedivy, VP of Human Resources; 440-564-9111; Fax: 440-564-9541; E-mail: custserv@kinetico.com

LanVision Systems, Inc.
One Financial Way, Suite
400
Cincinnati, OH 45242
http://www.lanvision.com
Founded: 1989
Total Employees: 111
Annual Sales: $10 million
Industry: Computer
Software
Growth: Openings in past
year, 29
Contact Alan J. Hartman,
General Counsel; 513-
794-7100; Fax: 513-794-
7272

LDA Systems, Inc.
6650 West Snowville Rd.
Brecksville, OH 44141
Founded: 1979
Total Employees: 200
Industry: Computer
Software
Growth: Openings in past
year, 70
Contact Steve Sweetnich,
President; 440-838-8200;
Fax: 440-838-4144

Lehr Precision, Inc.
11230 Deerfield Rd.
Cincinnati, OH 45242
Founded: 1956
Total Employees: 285
Industry: Transportation
Growth: Openings in past
year, 85
Contact Don Wright,
Sales Manager; 513-489-
9800; Fax: 513-489-2409

Liquid Control Corp.
7576 Freedom Ave.
Northwest
PO Box 2747
North Canton, OH 44720
http://www.liquidcontrol.
com
Founded: 1975
Total Employees: 130
Annual Sales: $19 million

Industries: Factory
Automation, Holding
Companies
Growth: Openings in past
year, 27
Contact William Schiltz,
President; 330-494-1313;
Fax: 330-494-5383

M.K. Morse Co.
PO Box 8677
Canton, OH 44711
Founded: 1964
Total Employees: 285
Annual Sales: $43 million
Industries: Advanced
Materials, Factory
Automation
Growth: Openings in past
year, 35
Contact James T.
Batchelder, President;
330-453-8187; Fax: 330-
453-1111

MedPlus, Inc.
8805 Governor's Hill Dr.
Cincinnati, OH 45299
http://www.medplus.com
Founded: 1991
Total Employees: 120
Annual Sales: $10.9
million
Industry: Computer
Software
Growth: Openings in past
year, 50
Contact Ms. Amy Seltz,
Director of Personnel;
513-583-0500; Fax: 513-
583-8885; E-mail: info@
medplus.com

Minster Machine Co.
240 West Fifth St.
PO Box 120
Minster, OH 45865
Founded: 1896
Total Employees: 950
Annual Sales: $140 million
Industries: Factory
Automation,
Subassemblies and
Components
Growth: Openings in past
year, 46

Contact Stephen C. Kill,
VP of Human Resources;
419-628-2331; Fax: 419-
628-3517

Motoman, Inc.
805 Liberty Ln.
West Carrollton, OH 45449
http://www.motoman.com
Founded: 1989
Total Employees: 400
Industry: Factory
Automation
Growth: Openings in past
year, 100
Contact Ms. D. Myers,
Senior Director of
Personnel; 937-847-
3300; Fax: 937-847-3288

Ohio Semitronics, Inc.
4242 Reynolds Dr.
Hilliard, OH 43026
Founded: 1964
Total Employees: 112
Annual Sales: $8 million
Industries:
Subassemblies and
Components, Test and
Measurement
Growth: Openings in past
year, 32
Contact Dr. W.E. Bulman,
President/CEO; 614-777-
1005; Fax: 614-777-4511

OnRamp Group
One Internet Way
Girard, OH 44420
http://www.theonramp.net
Founded: 1995
Total Employees: 70
Annual Sales: $12 million
Industry:
Telecommunications
Growth: Openings in past
year, 30
Contact Ms. Pam
Chambers, Director of
Finance; 330-539-7800;
Fax: 330-539-2122;
E-mail: sales@
theonramp.net

Process Technology, Inc.
7010 Lindsay Dr.
Mentor, OH 44060
http://www.process-
 technology.com
Founded: 1978
Total Employees: 140
Annual Sales: $17 million
Industries: Energy,
 Manufacturing
 Equipment, Test and
 Measurement
Growth: Openings in past
 year, 25
Contact Ms. Barbara
 Henderson, Personnel
 Director; 440-946-9500;
 Fax: 440-974-9561

**RELTEC Corp., RELTEC
Services Division**
38683 Taylor Woods
 Industrial Pkwy.
North Ridgeville, OH
 44039
Founded: 1983
Total Employees: 450
Annual Sales: $74 million
Industry:
 Telecommunications
Growth: Openings in past
 year, 79
Contact Nicholas Camino,
 Vice President/General
 Manager; 440-353-2000;
 Fax: 440-353-2188

**Rexroth Corp., Mobile
Hydraulics Division**
1700 Old Mansfield Rd.
PO Box 394
Wooster, OH 44691
Founded: 1955
Total Employees: 550
Annual Sales: $130 million
Industries: Computer
 Hardware,
 Subassemblies and
 Components, Test and
 Measurement
Growth: Openings in past
 year, 50
Contact Dave Deremer,
 Personnel Manager; 330-
 263-3300; Fax: 330-263-
 3333

**Reynolds and Reynolds
Company, Healthcare
Systems Division**
PO Box 1537
Dayton, OH 45401
http://www.reyrey.com/
 healthcare
Founded: 1974
Total Employees: 454
Annual Sales: $58 million
Industry: Computer
 Software
Growth: Openings in past
 year, 53
Contact Tim Bailey, VP of
 Human Resources; 937-
 485-4600; Fax: 937-485-
 4862; E-mail: healthcare-
 info@reyrey.com

**Sawyer Research
Products, Inc.**
35400 Lakeland Blvd.
Eastlake, OH 44095
Founded: 1956
Total Employees: 175
Industries: Advanced
 Materials, Holding
 Companies
Growth: Openings in past
 year, 25
Contact Ms. Viann Hite,
 Human Resources
 Manager; 440-951-8770;
 Fax: 440-951-1480

Sealtron, Inc.
9705 Reading Rd.
Cincinnati, OH 45215
Founded: 1953
Total Employees: 175
Annual Sales: $23 million
Industry: Subassemblies
 and Components
Growth: Openings in past
 year, 40
Contact Norm Allard,
 President/General
 Manager; 513-733-8400;
 Fax: 513-733-0131

Solomon Software
200 East Hardin St.
Findlay, OH 45840
http://www.solomon.com
Founded: 1980
Total Employees: 220
Annual Sales: $28 million
Industry: Computer
 Software
Growth: Openings in past
 year, 40
Contact Gary Harpst,
 COB/President; 419-424-
 0422; Fax: 419-424-
 3400; E-mail: sales@
 solomon.com

Sygnet Wireless, Inc.
6550 Seville Dr.
Canfield, OH 44406
Founded: 1991
Total Employees: 403
Annual Sales: $44.758
 million
Industry: Holding
 Companies
Growth: Openings in past
 year, 44
Contact Albert H. Pharis,
 President/CEO; 330-565-
 5000

**Symix Computer
Systems Inc.**
2800 Corporate Exchange
 Dr.
Columbus, OH 43231
Founded: 1979
Total Employees: 488
Annual Sales: $65.7
 million
Industry: Computer
 Software
Growth: Openings in past
 year, 137
Contact Robert Williams,
 VP of Human Resources;
 614-523-7000; Fax: 614-
 895-2504

Unibus, Inc.
145 Keep Ct.
Elyria, OH 44035

Founded: 1987
Total Employees: 125
Industry: Subassemblies and Components
Growth: Openings in past year, 50
Contact T.C. Burtnett, President; 440-324-9452; Fax: 440-324-9458

Vickers Electronic Systems
1151 West Mason-Morrow Rd.
Lebanon, OH 45036
Founded: 1955
Total Employees: 550
Annual Sales: $69 million
Industries: Factory Automation, Subassemblies and Components, Test and Measurement
Growth: Openings in past year, 50
Contact Ken Schuebeler, Division Manager; 513-494-1200; Fax: 513-494-5400

Waterlink, Inc.
4100 Holiday St. Northwest, Suite 201
Canton, OH 44718
http://www.waterlink.com
Founded: 1994
Total Employees: 310
Annual Sales: $19.8 million
Industry: Holding Companies
Growth: Openings in past year, 150
Contact Chet S. Ross, President; 330-649-4000; Fax: 330-649-4008; E-mail: waterlink@waterlink.com

Will-Burt Co.
169 South Main St.
Orrville, OH 44667
http://www.willburt.com
Founded: 1918
Total Employees: 400
Annual Sales: $31.6 million

Industries: Holding Companies, Manufacturing Equipment
Growth: Openings in past year, 100
Contact Karl Lewis, Director of Human Resources; 330-682-7015; Fax: 330-684-1190

Zehrco Plastics, Inc.
5500 Washington Ave.
Ashtabula, OH 44004
Founded: 1950
Total Employees: 175
Annual Sales: $21 million
Industry: Manufacturing Equipment
Growth: Openings in past year, 25
Contact Barry Royko, Director of Human Resources; 440-998-5774; Fax: 440-992-2430; E-mail: zpi@interlaced.net

Oklahoma

AAON, Inc.
2425 South Yukon Ave.
Tulsa, OK 74107
http://www.aaon.com
Founded: 1988
Total Employees: 800
Annual Sales: $62.845 million
Industries: Energy, Holding Companies
Growth: Openings in past year, 199
Contact Ms. Martha Lenard, Personnel Manager; 918-583-2266; Fax: 918-583-6094; E-mail: aaon@aaon.com

Callidus Technologies Inc.
7130 South Lewis, Suite 635
Tulsa, OK 74136
Founded: 1957
Total Employees: 286

Industries: Environmental, Factory Automation
Growth: Openings in past year, 46
Contact William P. Bartlett, President; 918-496-7599; Fax: 918-496-7587

Central Plastics Co., Inc.
PO Box 3129
Shawnee, OK 74801
Founded: 1955
Total Employees: 550
Annual Sales: $74 million
Industries: Environmental, Factory Automation, Holding Companies, Subassemblies and Components
Growth: Openings in past year, 76
Contact Ms. Melani Clifton, Human Resources Manager; 405-273-6302; Fax: 800-733-5993; E-mail: tjones@centralplastics.com

GEA Rainey Corp.
5202 West Channel Rd.
Catoosa, OK 74015
Founded: 1965
Total Employees: 300
Industries: Energy, Holding Companies
Growth: Openings in past year, 40
Contact Charles E. Curtis, President/CEO; 918-266-3060; Fax: 918-266-2464

GEA Rainey Corp., Package Cooler Division
5320 North Cimarron Rd.
Catoosa, OK 74015
Founded: 1988
Total Employees: 84
Annual Sales: $19 million
Industry: Energy
Growth: Openings in past year, 33
Contact Phil Snodgrass, Vice President/General

Manager; 918-266-0266;
Fax: 918-266-0275;
E-mail: dls@webzone.net

KF Industries, Inc.
1500 Southeast 89th St.
PO Box 95249
Oklahoma City, OK 73143
Founded: 1874
Total Employees: 343
Annual Sales: $78 million
Industries: Energy,
Subassemblies and
Components
Growth: Openings in past
year, 32
Contact Bob Paulkner,
Human Resources
Manager; 405-631-1533;
Fax: 405-631-5034

LB&M Associates, Inc.
211 Southwest A Ave.
Lawton, OK 73501
http://www.lbm.com
Founded: 1982
Total Employees: 280
Annual Sales: $13 million
Industries: Computer
Hardware, Computer
Software, Defense,
Telecommunications,
Transportation
Growth: Openings in past
year, 30
Contact Ms. Dena Riede,
Director of HR &
Administrative Services;
405-355-1471; Fax: 405-
357-9360; E-mail:
lawton@lbm.com

Mertz, Inc.
PO Box 150
Ponca City, OK 74602
Founded: 1948
Total Employees: 225
Annual Sales: $18 million
Industries: Energy,
Manufacturing Equipment
Growth: Openings in past
year, 75
Contact Forrest Mertz,
President; 405-762-5646;
Fax: 405-767-8411;
E-mail: ljones@mertzok.
com

Norris Sucker Rods
4801 West 49th St.
PO Box 1496
Tulsa, OK 74101
Founded: 1909
Total Employees: 250
Industry: Energy
Growth: Openings in past
year, 60
Contact Dan Bisett,
Personnel Manager; 918-
445-7600; Fax: 918-445-
7692

Temtrol, Inc.
15 East Oklahoma Ave.
Okarche, OK 73762
Founded: 1955
Total Employees: 275
Industry: Energy
Growth: Openings in past
year, 40
Contact Ms. Vicki
Hoebing, Personnel
Manager; 405-263-7286;
Fax: 405-263-4924

TMS, Inc.
206 West 6th Ave.
PO Box 1358
Stillwater, OK 74076
http://www.tmsinc.com
Founded: 1981
Total Employees: 111
Annual Sales: $5.6 million
Industries: Computer
Hardware, Computer
Software
Growth: Openings in past
year, 35
Contact Maxwell
Steinhardt, COB/
President/CEO; 405-377-
0880; Fax: 405-377-
0452; E-mail:
contact_us@tmsinc.com

Vyvx, Inc.
111 East First St., Suite
200
Tulsa, OK 74103
http://www.vyvx.com
Founded: 1990

Total Employees: 175
Annual Sales: $32 million
Industry:
Telecommunications
Growth: Openings in past
year, 75
Contact Dell Bothof,
President; 918-588-5760;
Fax: 918-588-5761

Westwood Corp.
12437 East 60th St.
PO Box 35493
Tulsa, OK 74153
Founded: 1986
Total Employees: 375
Annual Sales: $31 million
Industry: Holding
Companies
Growth: Openings in past
year, 25
Contact Ernest McKee,
Chief Executive Officer;
918-524-0002; Fax: 918-
524-0006

Oregon

ABC Technologies, Inc.
16100 Northwest Cornell
Rd., Suite 200
Beaverton, OR 97006
http://www.abctech.com
Founded: 1989
Total Employees: 110
Annual Sales: $14 million
Industry: Computer
Software
Growth: Openings in past
year, 45
Contact Chris M. Pieper,
Chief Executive Officer;
503-617-7100; Fax: 503-
617-7200; E-mail: ernie@
abctech.com

ADC Kentrox
14375 Northwest Science
Park Dr.
Portland, OR 97229
http://www.kentrox.com
Founded: 1967
Total Employees: 530
Industries: Photonics,
Telecommunications

Growth: Openings in past year, 35
Contact Ms. Karen Callin, Director of Human Resources; 503-643-1681; Fax: 503-641-3341; E-mail: info@kentrox.com

Advanced Machine Vision Corp.
PO Box 1666
Medford, OR 97501
Founded: 1987
Total Employees: 190
Annual Sales: $30 million
Industry: Holding Companies
Growth: Openings in past year, 29
Contact William J. Young, COB/President/CEO; 541-776-7700; Fax: 541-779-6838; E-mail: arccap@cdsnet.net

Analogy, Inc.
9205 Southwest Gemini Dr.
Beaverton, OR 97008
http://www.analogy.com
Founded: 1985
Total Employees: 200
Annual Sales: $23 million
Industry: Computer Software
Growth: Openings in past year, 35
Contact Terrence Rixford, VP of Finance and Administration; 503-626-9700; Fax: 503-643-3361

Cascade Microtech, Inc.
14255 Southwest Brigadoon Ct.
Beaverton, OR 97005
http://www.cmicro.com
Founded: 1984
Total Employees: 200
Annual Sales: $30 million
Industries: Factory Automation, Photonics, Test and Measurement
Growth: Openings in past year, 50

Contact Eric W. Strid, President; 503-626-8245; Fax: 503-626-6023; E-mail: sales@cmicro.com

CFI ProServices, Inc.
400 Southwest Sixth Ave.
Portland, OR 97204
http://www.cfipro.com
Founded: 1978
Total Employees: 540
Annual Sales: $59.949 million
Industries: Computer Software, Holding Companies
Growth: Openings in past year, 63
Contact Ms. Shannon Lynch, Human Resources Manager; 503-274-7280; Fax: 503-790-9293

Claremont Technology Group, Inc.
1600 Northwest Compton Dr., Suite 210
Beaverton, OR 97006
http://www.clrmnt.com
Founded: 1989
Total Employees: 749
Annual Sales: $48.091 million
Industries: Computer Hardware, Computer Software
Growth: Openings in past year, 195
Contact Paul Cosgrave, COB/President/CEO; 503-690-4000; Fax: 503-690-4004

Columbia Gorge Center
2940 Thomsen Rd.
Hood River, OR 97031
Founded: 1967
Total Employees: 90
Industry: Subassemblies and Components
Growth: Openings in past year, 30

Contact William F. Uhlman, Executive Director; 541-386-3520; Fax: 541-386-7788

FaxBack, Inc.
1100 Northwest Compton Dr., Suite 200
Beaverton, OR 97006
http://www.faxback.com
Founded: 1990
Total Employees: 50
Annual Sales: $4 million
Industry: Computer Software
Growth: Openings in past year, 27
Contact Art King, President; 503-645-1114; Fax: 503-614-5399; E-mail: info@faxback.com

Fiber Optic Technologies of the Northwest
14976 Northwest Greenbrier Pkwy.
Beaverton, OR 97006
Founded: 1985
Total Employees: 125
Annual Sales: $17 million
Industry: Telecommunications
Growth: Openings in past year, 25
Contact Thomas E. Ardell, General Manager; 503-690-6500; Fax: 503-645-3800; E-mail: first_last@foti.com

Flight Dynamics
16600 Southwest 72nd St.
Portland, OR 97224
Founded: 1979
Total Employees: 198
Industries: Defense, Test and Measurement, Transportation
Growth: Openings in past year, 48
Contact John P. Desmond, President/CEO; 503-684-5384; Fax: 503-684-0169

FLIR Systems, Inc.
16505 Southwest 72nd Ave.
Portland, OR 97224
http://www.flir.com
Founded: 1978
Total Employees: 450
Annual Sales: $66.017 million
Industries: Defense, Factory Automation, Holding Companies, Photonics, Test and Measurement, Telecommunications, Transportation
Growth: Openings in past year, 85
Contact Robert Daltry, COB/CEO; 503-684-3731; Fax: 503-684-3207

GemStone Systems, Inc.
20575 Northwest Von Neuman Dr.
Beaverton, OR 97006
http://www.gemstone.com
Founded: 1982
Total Employees: 160
Industry: Computer Software
Growth: Openings in past year, 40
Contact Rick Baird, Director of Human Resources; 503-533-3000; Fax: 503-690-7205; E-mail: info@gemstone.com

Hanard Machine, Inc.
8597 9th Northwest St.
Salem, OR 97304
Founded: 1968
Total Employees: 100
Industry: Factory Automation
Growth: Openings in past year, 30
Contact Frank Kirsch, President; 503-364-3952; Fax: 503-371-8238

In Focus Systems, Inc.
27700B Southwest Parkway Ave.
Wilsonville, OR 97070
http://www.infocus.com
Founded: 1986
Total Employees: 450
Annual Sales: $258.5 million
Industry: Telecommunications
Growth: Openings in past year, 49
Contact Ms. Susan L. Thompson, VP of Human Resources; 503-685-8888; Fax: 503-685-8887

La Cie, Ltd.
22985 Northwest Evergreen Pkwy.
Hillsboro, OR 97124
http://www.lacie.com
Founded: 1986
Total Employees: 110
Industry: Computer Hardware
Growth: Openings in past year, 50
Contact Philippe Spruch, President/General Manager; 503-844-4500; Fax: 503-844-4501; E-mail: sales@lacie.com

Lattice Semiconductor Corp.
5555 Northeast Moore Ct.
Hillsboro, OR 97124
Founded: 1983
Total Employees: 531
Annual Sales: $204 million
Industry: Subassemblies and Components
Growth: Openings in past year, 31
Contact Cyrus Tsui, COB/CEO/President; 503-681-0118; Fax: 503-681-0347

Laughlin-Wilt Group, Inc.
9825 Southwest Sunshine Ct.
Beaverton, OR 97005
Founded: 1988
Total Employees: 280
Annual Sales: $30 million
Industry: Subassemblies and Components
Growth: Openings in past year, 30
Contact Joe Laughlin, President/CEO; 503-644-4808; Fax: 503-641-9145

Phoenix Gold International, Inc.
1 Phoenix Gold Way, 9300 North Decatur St.
Portland, OR 97203
http://www.phoenixgoldcorp.com
Founded: 1991
Total Employees: 290
Annual Sales: $26.5 million
Industries: Subassemblies and Components, Telecommunications
Growth: Openings in past year, 60
Contact Daniel A. Anderson, Manager of Human Resources; 503-288-2008; Fax: 503-978-3381

Planar Systems, Inc.
1400 Northwest Compton Dr.
Beaverton, OR 97006
http://www.planar.com
Founded: 1983
Total Employees: 800
Annual Sales: $120.37 million
Industries: Computer Hardware, Holding Companies, Photonics
Growth: Openings in past year, 46
Contact Ms, Iris Newman, Personnel Manager; 503-

690-1100; Fax: 503-690-1244; E-mail: sales@planar.com

Precision Interconnect
16640 Southwest 72nd Ave.
Portland, OR 97224
http://www.precision.com
Founded: 1972
Total Employees: 950
Annual Sales: $120 million
Industry: Subassemblies and Components
Growth: Openings in past year, 95
Contact Ms. Holly Borden, Personnel Manager; 503-620-9400; Fax: 503-620-7131

Protocol Systems, Inc.
8500 Southwest Creekside Pl.
Beaverton, OR 97008
http://www.protocol.com
Founded: 1985
Total Employees: 405
Annual Sales: $66.89 million
Industry: Medical
Growth: Openings in past year, 155
Contact Allen L. Oyler, VP of Human Resources & Administration; 503-526-8500; Fax: 503-526-4200

RadiSys Corp.
5445 North East Dawson Creek Dr.
Hillsboro, OR 97124
http://www.radisys.com
Founded: 1987
Total Employees: 400
Annual Sales: $81 million
Industries: Computer Hardware, Holding Companies
Growth: Openings in past year, 216
Contact Dr. Glen Myers, Ph.D., President; 503-615-1100; Fax: 503-615-1150; E-mail: info@radisys.com

Scientific Imaging Technology, Inc.
PO Box 569
Beaverton, OR 97075
http://www.site-inc.com
Founded: 1993
Total Employees: 85
Annual Sales: $11 million
Industry: Photonics
Growth: Openings in past year, 33
Contact Ms. Beth Gudeman, Chief Executive Officer; 503-644-0688; Fax: 503-649-0798

Tactica Corp.
10450 Southwest Nimbus Ave.
Portland, OR 97223
http://www.tactica.com
Founded: 1990
Total Employees: 100
Annual Sales: $12 million
Industry: Computer Software
Growth: Openings in past year, 75
Contact Ms. Linn-Dee Bricker, Manager of Human Resources; 503-620-7800; Fax: 503-603-6801; E-mail: info@tactica.com

Toshiba Ceramics America, Inc.
6701 Northeast Campus St.
Hillsboro, OR 97124
Founded: 1982
Total Employees: 81
Annual Sales: $10 million
Industry: Manufacturing Equipment
Growth: Openings in past year, 30
Contact Nishi Mura, President; 503-640-0806; Fax: 503-681-0929

TriQuint Semiconductor, Inc.
2300 Northeast Brookwood Pkwy.
Hillsboro, OR 97124
http://www.tqs.com
Founded: 1985
Total Employees: 345
Annual Sales: $60 million
Industries: Holding Companies, Manufacturing Equipment, Subassemblies and Components
Growth: Openings in past year, 69
Contact Dick Zeller, Personnel Director; 503-615-9000; Fax: 503-615-8900; E-mail: sales@tqs.com

Valmont Microflect
3575 25th St. Southeast
PO Box 12985
Salem, OR 97309
http://www.microflect.com
Founded: 1956
Total Employees: 250
Annual Sales: $42 million
Industry: Telecommunications
Growth: Openings in past year, 74
Contact Ms. Terrie Bigness, Personnel Coordinator; 503-363-9267; Fax: 503-363-4613; E-mail: custinfo@microflect.com

WARN Industries, Inc.
12900 South Capps Rd.
Clackamas, OR 97015
http://www.warn.com
Founded: 1948
Total Employees: 675
Industries: Subassemblies and Components, Transportation
Growth: Openings in past year, 148
Contact Ms. Kim King, Human Resources Team

Leader; 503-722-1200;
Fax: 800-638-8126;
E-mail: warn@teleport.
com

Pennsylvania

ACCU WEATHER, Inc.
619 West College Ave.
State College, PA 16801
http://www.accuweather.
com
Founded: 1962
Total Employees: 320
Annual Sales: $39 million
Industries: Computer
Hardware, Computer
Software, Environmental,
Telecommunications
Growth: Openings in past
year, 30
Contact Ms. Bev Grothy,
Assistant Vice President;
814-237-0309; Fax: 814-
231-0621; E-mail:
intemail@accuwx.com

Accu-Sort Systems, Inc.
511 School House Rd.
Telford, PA 18969
Founded: 1971
Total Employees: 407
Annual Sales: $62 million
Industries: Computer
Hardware, Factory
Automation
Growth: Openings in past
year, 27
Contact Albert Wurz,
Chief Executive Officer;
215-723-0981; Fax: 215-
723-1515

Adhesives Research, Inc.
Rte. 216, West of I-83
PO Box 100
Glen Rock, PA 17327
http://www.
adhesivesresearch.com
Founded: 1960
Total Employees: 251
Annual Sales: $48 million
Industry: Holding
Companies

Growth: Openings in past
year, 35
Contact Edward L.
Daisey, President; 717-
235-7979; Fax: 717-235-
8320

AGR International, Inc.
PO Box 149
Butler, PA 16003
Founded: 1936
Total Employees: 250
Industry: Factory
Automation
Growth: Openings in past
year, 25
Contact Dwight Byers,
Personnel Director; 412-
482-2163; Fax: 412-482-
2767

Allegheny Plastics, Inc.
17 Ave. A
Leetsdale, PA 15056
Founded: 1962
Total Employees: 220
Industries: Environmental,
Holding Companies
Growth: Openings in past
year, 70
Contact Dennis Hoffman,
Human Resources
Manager; 412-749-0700;
Fax: 412-749-9530

**Allegheny Powder
Metallurgy, Inc.**
Rte. 950 South
PO Box 376
Falls Creek, PA 15840
Founded: 1982
Total Employees: 100
Industries: Factory
Automation,
Subassemblies and
Components
Growth: Openings in past
year, 40
Contact Francis
Grieneisen, President;
814-371-0184; Fax: 814-
371-4640

Alphametrics Corp.
PO Box 2566
Bala Cynwyd, PA 19004
Founded: 1978
Total Employees: 110
Annual Sales: $14 million
Industry: Computer
Software
Growth: Openings in past
year, 35
Contact Dr. Charles G.
Renfro, President/
Director of Marketing;
610-664-0386; Fax: 610-
667-8390; E-mail: 74242.
2260@compuserve.com

Analytical Graphics, Inc.
660 American Ave.
King of Prussia, PA 19406
http://www.stk.com
Founded: 1989
Total Employees: 100
Industry: Computer
Software
Growth: Openings in past
year, 30
Contact Ms. Lisa Velte,
Director of Human
Resources; 610-337-
3055; Fax: 610-337-
3058; E-mail: paul@stk.
com

Ansoft Corporation
Four Station Sq., Suite
660
Pittsburgh, PA 15219
http://www.ansoft.com
Founded: 1984
Total Employees: 150
Annual Sales: $15 million
Industries: Computer
Software, Holding
Companies
Growth: Openings in past
year, 50
Contact Nick Csendes,
President/CEO; 412-261-
3200; Fax: 412-471-
9427; E-mail: info@
ansoft.com

ANSYS, Inc.
275 Technology Dr.
Canonsburg, PA 15317
http://www.ansys.com
Founded: 1970
Total Employees: 250
Annual Sales: $47 million
Industry: Computer
Software
Growth: Openings in past
year, 80
Contact Ms. Karen
Harker, Director of
Human Resources; 412-
746-3304; Fax: 412-514-
9494; E-mail: ansysinfo@
ansys.com

Astea International Inc.
455 Business Center Dr.
Horsham, PA 19044
http://www.astea.com
Founded: 1979
Total Employees: 594
Annual Sales: $62 million
Industry: Computer
Software
Growth: Openings in past
year, 91
Contact Ms. Eileen
Pierson, Human
Resources Director; 215-
682-2500; Fax: 215-682-
2515; E-mail: info@
astea.com

Aydin Telemetry
47 Friends Ln.
PO Box 328
Newtown, PA 18940
http://www.aydinvector.com
Founded: 1969
Total Employees: 435
Annual Sales: $74 million
Industries:
Subassemblies and
Components, Test and
Measurement,
Telecommunications,
Transportation
Growth: Openings in past
year, 60
Contact Ms. Joan
Wenyon, Manager of
Administration; 215-497-
8000; Fax: 215-968-
3214; E-mail: aydin@
aydinvector.com

Bentley Systems, Inc.
690 Pennsylvania Dr.
Exton, PA 19341
http://www.bentley.com
Founded: 1984
Total Employees: 650
Annual Sales: $114 million
Industries: Computer
Software, Holding
Companies
Growth: Openings in past
year, 49
Contact Scott Bentley, VP
of Operations and
Services; 610-458-5000;
Fax: 610-458-1060;
E-mail: family@bentley.
com

Berk-Tek
132 White Oak Rd.
New Holland, PA 17557
Founded: 1961
Total Employees: 674
Annual Sales: $200 million
Industries: Photonics,
Subassemblies and
Components
Growth: Openings in past
year, 103
Contact Warren Moore,
VP of Human Resources;
717-354-6200; Fax: 717-
354-7944

**Biocontrol Technology,
Inc.**
2275 Swallow Hill Rd.
Pittsburgh, PA 15220
http://www.bico.com
Founded: 1972
Total Employees: 165
Industries: Holding
Companies, Medical
Growth: Openings in past
year, 24
Contact Ms. Adele
Bobbish, Manager of
Administration; 412-429-
0673; Fax: 412-279-9690

Black Box Corporation
PO Box 12800.
Pittsburgh, PA 15241
http://www.blackbox.com
Founded: 1976
Total Employees: 650
Annual Sales: $232.2
million
Industries: Computer
Hardware, Photonics,
Subassemblies and
Components,
Telecommunications
Growth: Openings in past
year, 49
Contact Jeffrey Boetticher,
CEO/President; 412-746-
5500; Fax: 800-321-0746

**Cagelec AEG Automation
Systems Corp.**
701 Technology Dr.
Canonsburg, PA 15317
http://www.cegelec-asc.
com
Founded: 1989
Total Employees: 300
Industry: Factory
Automation
Growth: Openings in past
year, 25
Contact Bob Percival, VP
of Personnel; 412-873-
9300; Fax: 412-873-
9416; E-mail: asco@
nauticonn.net

Carnegie Group, Inc.
5 PPG Pl.
Pittsburgh, PA 15222
http://www.cgi.com
Founded: 1984
Total Employees: 300
Annual Sales: $28.4
million
Industries: Computer
Hardware, Computer
Software
Growth: Openings in past
year, 80
Contact Dennis
Yablonsky, President/
CEO; 412-642-6900;
Fax: 412-642-6906;
E-mail: info@cgi.com

CCX, Inc., Hanover Wire Cloth Division
500 East Middle St.
Hanover, PA 17331
Founded: 1903
Total Employees: 280
Annual Sales: $45 million
Industries: Advanced Materials, Factory Automation
Growth: Openings in past year, 30
Contact Richard Rinaldi, President/CEO; 717-637-3795; Fax: 717-637-4766

Centocor, Inc.
200 Great Valley Pkwy.
Malvern, PA 19355
http://www.centocor.com
Founded: 1979
Total Employees: 650
Annual Sales: $135.5 million
Industry: Holding Companies
Growth: Openings in past year, 150
Contact Michael Melore, Director of Human Resources; 610-651-6000; Fax: 610-651-6100

CFM Technologies, Inc.
1336 Enterprise Dr.
West Chester, PA 19380
http://www.cfmtech.com
Founded: 1984
Total Employees: 359
Annual Sales: $44 million
Industry: Manufacturing Equipment
Growth: Openings in past year, 108
Contact Ms. Kim Egdin, Director of Human Resources; 610-696-8300; Fax: 610-696-8309; E-mail: info@cfmtech.com

Chromalloy T.A.D.
1400 North Cameron St.
Harrisburg, PA 17103
Founded: 1951
Total Employees: 500
Annual Sales: $65 million
Industry: Transportation
Growth: Openings in past year, 50
Contact Bradlee McClimanus, Vice President; 717-255-3400; Fax: 717-255-3448

Computer Resource Associates, Inc.
650 Wilson Ln., Suite 200
Mechanicsburg, PA 17055
http://www.cra-online.com
Founded: 1983
Total Employees: 150
Annual Sales: $10.25 million
Industries: Computer Software, Holding Companies
Growth: Openings in past year, 50
Contact Kenneth Podd, President; 717-691-5500; Fax: 717-691-7102; E-mail: crainc@cra-online.com

CorNet International, Ltd.
701 Main St.
Stroudsburg, PA 18360
http://www.cornetltd.com
Founded: 1986
Total Employees: 210
Annual Sales: $11 million
Industries: Computer Hardware, Computer Software
Growth: Openings in past year, 75
Contact Ms. Patricia H. Kennedy, VP of Human Resources; 717-420-0800; Fax: 717-420-0818; E-mail: info@cornetltd.com

Corporate Word, Inc.
7 Parkway Ctr., Suite 125
Pittsburgh, PA 15220
http://www.corpword.com
Founded: 1979
Total Employees: 50
Annual Sales: $15 million
Industries: Computer Hardware, Computer Software
Growth: Openings in past year, 29
Contact Thomas Blondi, President; 412-922-9151; Fax: 412-922-9155

D.H. Marketing and Consulting, Inc.
H677 Box 394B, Rtes. 6 & 209
Milford, PA 18337
Founded: 1993
Total Employees: 50
Annual Sales: $2.1 million
Industry: Holding Companies
Growth: Openings in past year, 30
Contact David D. Hagen, President/CEO; 717-786-9613; Fax: 610-366-8589

Delta Health Systems
PO Box 1824
Altoona, PA 16603
http://www.deltahealth.com
Founded: 1968
Total Employees: 275
Annual Sales: $26 million
Industry: Computer Software
Growth: Openings in past year, 44
Contact Deane Mann, Human Resource Manager; 814-944-1651; Fax: 814-942-0125

Dentsply International, Inc., Preventive Care Division
1301 Smile Way
York, PA 17404
Founded: 1899
Total Employees: 225
Annual Sales: $27 million
Industry: Medical

Growth: Openings in past year, 35
Contact James G. Mosch, Vice President/General Manager; 717-767-8500; Fax: 717-767-8250

Diamond Management Systems, Inc.
101 Greenwood Ave., Suite 600
Jenkintown, PA 19046
Founded: 1967
Total Employees: 125
Industry: Computer Software
Growth: Openings in past year, 50
Contact Tom Altman, Chief Executive Officer; 215-887-2515; Fax: 215-572-9908

DRS Laurel Technologies
423 Walters Ave.
Johnstown, PA 15904
http://www.rltech.com
Founded: 1993
Total Employees: 280
Annual Sales: $37 million
Industry: Subassemblies and Components
Growth: Openings in past year, 115
Contact John J. Donnelly, President; 814-269-4141; Fax: 814-269-4661; E-mail: rclark@lrltech.com

Dynamics Corporation of America, Reeves-Hoffman Division
400 West North St.
Carlisle, PA 17013
Founded: 1941
Total Employees: 220
Industries: Subassemblies and Components, Test and Measurement
Growth: Openings in past year, 24
Contact Ms. Mary Gettle, Personnel Manager; 717-

243-5929; Fax: 717-243-0079; E-mail: kbstone@pipeline.com

Electro-Science Laboratories, Inc.
416 East Church Rd.
King of Prussia, PA 19406
http://www.electroscience.com
Founded: 1962
Total Employees: 130
Annual Sales: $24 million
Industries: Advanced Materials, Photonics, Test and Measurement
Growth: Openings in past year, 30
Contact Franklin Golberg, Director of Human Resources; 610-272-8000; Fax: 610-272-6759; E-mail: sales@electroscience.com

Equimed, Inc.
2171 Sandy Dr.
State College, PA 16803
Founded: 1991
Total Employees: 235
Annual Sales: $99.115 million
Industry: Holding Companies
Growth: Openings in past year, 35
Contact Douglas R. Colkitt, MD, COB/CEO/President; 814-238-0375; Fax: 814-238-4632

Ever-Tite Coupling Co., Inc.
2240 West 15th St.
Erie, PA 16505
Founded: 1937
Total Employees: 75
Annual Sales: $10 million
Industry: Subassemblies and Components
Growth: Openings in past year, 25
Contact Jon Whiteman, President/COO; 814-459-1741; Fax: 814-453-5155

Extrude Hone Corp.
8075 Pennsylvania Ave.
PO Box 527
Irwin, PA 15642
http://www.extrudehone.com
Founded: 1966
Total Employees: 280
Annual Sales: $42 million
Industries: Factory Automation, Holding Companies, Manufacturing Equipment
Growth: Openings in past year, 30
Contact C. Gary Dinsel, VP of Operations; 412-863-5900; Fax: 412-863-8759; E-mail: exhone@extrudehone.com

Flinchbaugh Engineering, Inc.
4387 Run Way
York, PA 17406
Founded: 1978
Total Employees: 180
Annual Sales: $20 million
Industry: Manufacturing Equipment
Growth: Openings in past year, 30
Contact Todd Marsteller, Controller; 717-755-1900; Fax: 717-757-9437; E-mail: fei@fei-york.com

FMC Corp., Pharmaceutical Division
1735 Market St.
Philadelphia, PA 19103
http://www.avicel.com
Founded: 1961
Total Employees: 325
Industries: Advanced Materials, Biotechnology, Chemicals
Growth: Openings in past year, 25
Contact Ms. Josephine Fala, Human Resources Director; 215-299-6000; Fax: 215-299-6821

**Fogel/Jordan
Refrigerator Co.**
2200 Kennedy St.
Philadelphia, PA 19137
Founded: 1899
Total Employees: 450
Industries: Energy,
Holding Companies
Growth: Openings in past
year, 49
Contact George Dresch,
Chief Executive Officer;
215-535-8300; Fax: 215-
289-1597

**Greene, Tweed & Co.,
Inc.**
2570 Detwiler Rd.
Kulpsville, PA 19443
http://www.gtweed.com
Founded: 1863
Total Employees: 850
Industries: Holding
Companies,
Subassemblies and
Components
Growth: Openings in past
year, 49
Contact Phil Paino,
President; 215-256-9521;
Fax: 215-256-0189

Herley Industries, Inc.
10 Industry Dr.
Lancaster, PA 17603
http://www.herley.com
Founded: 1965
Total Employees: 250
Annual Sales: $29 million
Industries: Defense,
Holding Companies,
Telecommunications
Growth: Openings in past
year, 35
Contact Lee N. Blatt,
COB/CEO; 717-397-
2777; Fax: 717-397-4475

Herley Vega Systems
10 Industry Dr.
Lancaster, PA 17603
http://www.herley.com
Founded: 1963

Total Employees: 180
Annual Sales: $21 million
Industries: Defense,
Telecommunications
Growth: Openings in past
year, 30
Contact Myron Levy,
President; 717-397-2777;
Fax: 717-397-4475

Hussey Copper, Ltd.
100 Washington St.
Leetsdale, PA 15056
Founded: 1984
Total Employees: 500
Industries: Advanced
Materials, Holding
Companies
Growth: Openings in past
year, 50
Contact Robert Peterson,
VP of Human Resources;
412-251-4200; Fax: 412-
251-4243

Hycon Corp.
2280 City Line Rd.
Bethlehem, PA 18017
http://www.hydac.com
Founded: 1976
Total Employees: 100
Industries:
Subassemblies and
Components, Test and
Measurement
Growth: Openings in past
year, 35
Contact Matthias Mueller,
Executive VP/General
Manager; 610-266-0100;
Fax: 610-264-3540;
E-mail: hydac@freedom.
net

**IBAH Bio-Pharm
Pharmaceutics Services,
Inc.**
425 Delaware Dr.
Fort Washington, PA
19034
Founded: 1993
Total Employees: 60
Annual Sales: $9.2 million
Industry: Pharmaceuticals
Growth: Openings in past
year, 25

Contact John L. Santoro,
President; 215-646-1226;
Fax: 215-646-6509

IBAH, Inc.
4 Valley Square, 512
Township Line Rd.
Blue Bell, PA 19422
http://www.ibah.oom
Founded: 1985
Total Employees: 755
Annual Sales: $35.260
million
Industry: Holding
Companies
Growth: Openings in past
year, 50
Contact Dr. Geraldine A.
Henwood, Chief Execu-
tive Officer; 215-283-
0770; Fax: 215-283-0733

Infonautics, Inc.
900 West Valley Rd., Suite
1000
Wayne, PA 19087
http://www.infonautics.com
Founded: 1992
Total Employees: 150
Annual Sales: $1.4 million
Industry:
Telecommunications
Growth: Openings in past
year, 100
Contact Marvin
Weinberger, COB/CEO;
610-971-8840; Fax: 610-
971-8859; E-mail: info@
infonautics.com

**Innovative Tech
Systems, Inc.**
444 Jacksonville Rd., Suite
200
Warminster, PA 18974
http://www.spanfm.com
Founded: 1986
Total Employees: 120
Annual Sales: $8.903
million
Industry: Computer
Software
Growth: Openings in past
year, 26
Contact William
Thompson, COB/CEO;

215-441-5600; Fax: 215-441-5989; E-mail: sales@spanfm.com

Instrument Specialties Co., Inc.
Shielding Way
PO Box 650
Delaware Water Gap, PA 18327
http://www.instrumentspecialties.com
Founded: 1938
Total Employees: 560
Annual Sales: $75 million
Industries: Manufacturing Equipment, Subassemblies and Components
Growth: Openings in past year, 42
Contact Frank Rushen, President; 717-424-8510; Fax: 717-424-6213; E-mail: info@instrumentspecialties.com

InterDigital Communications Corp.
781 Third Ave.
King of Prussia, PA 19406
http://www.interdigital.com
Founded: 1972
Total Employees: 250
Annual Sales: $53.693 million
Industries: Manufacturing Equipment, Telecommunications
Growth: Openings in past year, 50
Contact Ms. Deborah Hayes, Director of Human Resources; 610-878-7800; Fax: 610-992-9432

Interlectric Corporation
1401 Lexington Ave.
Warren, PA 16365
http://www.interlectric.com
Founded: 1940
Total Employees: 160
Annual Sales: $21 million
Industry: Photonics
Growth: Openings in past year, 40

Contact Steven Rothenberg, CEO/President; 814-723-6061; Fax: 814-723-6069; E-mail: ic@interlectric.com

Kensey Nash Corporation
55 East Uwchlan Ave., Suite 204
Exton, PA 19341
Founded: 1984
Total Employees: 88
Annual Sales: $3 million
Industries: Biotechnology, Medical
Growth: Openings in past year, 31
Contact Joe Kaufmann, President; 610-524-0188; Fax: 610-524-0265

Koppel Steel Corp.
Sixth & Mount Sts.
PO Box 750
Beaver Falls, PA 15010
http://www.koppelsteel.com
Founded: 1988
Total Employees: 800
Annual Sales: $150 million
Industries: Advanced Materials, Subassemblies and Components
Growth: Openings in past year, 46
Contact James Barger, Manager of Human Resources; 412-843-7100; Fax: 412-847-4071; E-mail: sales@koppelsteel.com

Kras Corp.
88 Canal Rd.
Fairless Hills, PA 19030
Founded: 1960
Total Employees: 410
Annual Sales: $49 million
Industries: Factory Automation, Manufacturing Equipment
Growth: Openings in past year, 90
Contact Lonny Plummer, Chief Executive Officer;

215-736-0981; Fax: 215-736-8953; E-mail: info@kras.sprint.com

Krautkramer Branson
50 Industrial Park Rd.
Lewistown, PA 17044
http://www.krautkramer.com
Founded: 1946
Total Employees: 260
Annual Sales: $35 million
Industries: Factory Automation, Medical, Subassemblies and Components, Test and Measurement
Growth: Openings in past year, 30
Contact Darrin Woodruff, Human Resources Administrator; 717-242-0327; Fax: 717-242-2606; E-mail: kb-ltn.mhs.compuserve.com

Kurt J. Lesker Co.
1515 Worthington Ave.
Clairton, PA 15025
http://www.lesker.com
Founded: 1954
Total Employees: 175
Annual Sales: $30 million
Industry: Holding Companies
Growth: Openings in past year, 25
Contact Kurt J. Lesker, III, President; 412-233-4200; Fax: 412-233-4275; E-mail: sales@lesker.com

L&N Metallurgical Products
6th St. and Jamison Ave.
Ellport, PA 16117
Founded: 1980
Total Employees: 200
Annual Sales: $27 million
Industry: Test and Measurement
Growth: Openings in past year, 50

Contact Dave S. Araneicka, President; 412-758-4541; Fax: 412-758-1423

Lancaster Laboratories
2425 New Holland Pike
PO Box 12425
Lancaster, PA 17605
http://www.lancasterlabs. com
Founded: 1961
Total Employees: 580
Annual Sales: $38 million
Industries: Biotechnology, Chemicals, Environmental, Pharmaceuticals
Growth: Openings in past year, 48
Contact J. Wilson Hershey, Ph.D., President; 717-656-2300; Fax: 717-656-2681

Longview Solutions, Inc.
301 Lindenwood Dr., Suite 300
Malvern, PA 19355
http://www.longview.com
Founded: 1986
Total Employees: 80
Annual Sales: $10 million
Industries: Computer Hardware, Computer Software
Growth: Openings in past year, 50
Contact Matthew Townley, President; 610-889-9380; Fax: 610-889-2422; E-mail: david_weiss@ markham.longview.ca

Loranger International Corp.
817 Fourth Ave.
Warren, PA 16365
Founded: 1968
Total Employees: 125
Annual Sales: $19 million
Industry: Factory Automation
Growth: Openings in past year, 25
Contact Ms. Joanne Firestone, VP of

Administration; 814-723-2250; Fax: 814-723-5391; E-mail: licsales@ loranger.com

Management Science Associates, Inc.
6565 Penn Ave. at 5th
Pittsburgh, PA 15206
http://www.msa.com
Founded: 1963
Total Employees: 550
Industries: Computer Hardware, Computer Software
Growth: Openings in past year, 100
Contact Viv Penninti, President/CEO; 412-362-2000; Fax: 412-363-5598; E-mail: info@msa. com

Medrad, Inc.
One Medrad Dr.
Indianola, PA 15051
http://www.medrad.com
Founded: 1964
Total Employees: 770
Annual Sales: $111 million
Industry: Medical
Growth: Openings in past year, 70
Contact Gary W. Bucciarelli, VP of Human Resources/Treasurer; 412-767-2400; Fax: 412-767-4128

Met-Pro Corp.
160 Cassell Rd.
Harleysville, PA 19438
http://www.met-pro.com
Founded: 1966
Total Employees: 407
Annual Sales: $60.853 million
Industries: Environmental, Holding Companies
Growth: Openings in past year, 27
Contact William L. Kacin, President/CEO; 215-723-6751; Fax: 215-723-6758

Neutronics, Inc.
456 Creamery Way
Exton, PA 19341
Founded: 1976
Total Employees: 159
Annual Sales: $16 million
Industry: Holding Companies
Growth: Openings in past year, 49
Contact Ms. Carol Nye, Personnel Director; 610-524-8800; Fax: 610-524-8807; E-mail: ntron@ erols.com

Oberg Manufacturing, Inc.
PO Box 368
Freeport, PA 16229
http://www.oberg.com
Founded: 1948
Total Employees: 600
Annual Sales: $91 million
Industries: Factory Automation, Holding Companies, Manufacturing Equipment
Growth: Openings in past year, 100
Contact Ms. Melissa Croll, Director of Human Resources; 412-295-2121; Fax: 412-295-2588

OmniComp, Inc.
220 Regent Ct.
State College, PA 16801
http://www.omni-comp.com
Founded: 1981
Total Employees: 70
Annual Sales: $3 million
Industry: Computer Software
Growth: Openings in past year, 30
Contact Steven D. Heinz, President; 814-238-4181; Fax: 814-238-4673; E-mail: omnicomp.@ vicon.net

Oppenheimer Precision Products
173 Centennial Plaza
Horsham, PA 19044
http://www.voicenet.com/
~oppi
Founded: 1971
Total Employees: 125
Annual Sales: $15 million
Industry: Transportation
Growth: Openings in past year, 25
Contact Ms. Linda Urban, Personnel Manager; 215-674-9100; Fax: 215-674-0423; E-mail: oppi@ voicenet.com

Pentamation Enterprises, Inc.
One Bethlehem Plaza
Bethlehem, PA 18018
Founded: 1970
Total Employees: 260
Industries: Computer Hardware, Holding Companies
Growth: Openings in past year, 40
Contact Ms. Mary Boyle, Personnel Manager; 610-691-3616; Fax: 610-691-1031

PHB, Inc., Molding Division
8152 West Ridge Rd.
Fairview, PA 16415
Founded: 1984
Total Employees: 100
Annual Sales: $12 million
Industry: Manufacturing Equipment
Growth: Openings in past year, 35
Contact William Hilbert, Sr., President/CEO; 814-474-2683; Fax: 814-474-5868

Phoenix Contact Inc.
PO Box 4100
Harrisburg, PA 17111

http://www.phoenix.
contact.com
Founded: 1981
Total Employees: 300
Industries: Factory Automation, Subassemblies and Components
Growth: Openings in past year, 100
Contact Ms. Melissa Tsenoff, Human Resources Manager; 717-944-1300; Fax: 717-944-1625; E-mail: info@ phoenixcon.com

Pilling Weck
420 Delaware Dr.
Fort Washington, PA 19034
Founded: 1814
Total Employees: 240
Annual Sales: $29 million
Industry: Medical
Growth: Openings in past year, 40
Contact John Murdock, President; 215-643-2600; Fax: 215-646-0340

Polycom Huntsman, Inc.
90 West Chestnut St.
Washington, PA 15301
Founded: 1977
Total Employees: 325
Annual Sales: $62 million
Industries: Advanced Materials, Chemicals
Growth: Openings in past year, 25
Contact Ms. Barbara Hooten, Controller; 412-225-2220; Fax: 412-225-7170

Prophet 21, Inc.
19 West College Ave.
Yardley, PA 19067
http://www.p21.com
Founded: 1967
Total Employees: 278
Annual Sales: $36.4 million
Industries: Computer Hardware, Computer Software

Growth: Openings in past year, 28
Contact Charles L. Boyle, III, CEO/President; 215-493-8900; Fax: 215-321-8008

Quadritek Systems, Inc.
10 Valley Stream Pkwy., Suite 300
Malvern, PA 19355
http://www.quadritek.com
Founded: 1993
Total Employees: 70
Annual Sales: $9.1 million
Industry: Computer Software
Growth: Openings in past year, 45
Contact Joe D'Andrea, President/Co-Founder; 610-725-8535; Fax: 610-725-8559; E-mail: info@ quadritek.com

Quality Chemicals, Inc.
PO Box 216
Tyrone, PA 16686
Founded: 1957
Total Employees: 162
Annual Sales: $43 million
Industry: Chemicals
Growth: Openings in past year, 38
Contact Scott Martin, President; 814-684-4310; Fax: 814-684-2532

RAM Industries, Inc.
PO Box 629
Leesport, PA 19533
http://www.1usa.com/ram1/
Founded: 1971
Total Employees: 275
Annual Sales: $55 million
Industries:
Subassemblies and Components, Test and Measurement
Growth: Openings in past year, 44
Contact David Walton, President; 610-916-3939; Fax: 610-916-0156; E-mail: ram1@1usa.com

Reality Online, Inc.
1000 Madison Ave.
Norristown, PA 19403
http://www.moneynet.com
Founded: 1987
Total Employees: 250
Annual Sales: $49 million
Industry: Computer
   Hardware
Growth: Openings in past
   year, 40
Contact Chad Weimer,
   Director of Human
   Resources; 610-650-
   8600; Fax: 610-650-
   8170; E-mail: info@
   moneynet.com

Red Lion Controls, Inc.
20 Willow Springs Cir.
York, PA 17402
http://www.redlion-controls.
   com
Founded: 1975
Total Employees: 250
Annual Sales: $35 million
Industries: Photonics,
   Subassemblies and
   Components, Test and
   Measurement
Growth: Openings in past
   year, 60
Contact Lester Goodman,
   President; 717-767-6961;
   Fax: 717-764-0839

Resolite Polyglas
1575 Lebanon School Rd.
West Mifflin, PA 15122
Founded: 1987
Total Employees: 100
Annual Sales: $15 million
Industries: Manufacturing
   Equipment,
   Subassemblies and
   Components
Growth: Openings in past
   year, 52
Contact C.H. Norris, Jr.,
   President; 412-466-8611;
   Fax: 412-466-8640

Robicon
500 Hunt Valley Dr.
New Kensington, PA
   15068
http://www.robicon.com
Founded: 1964
Total Employees: 446
Annual Sales: $60 million
Industries: Energy,
   Subassemblies and
   Components, Test and
   Measurement
Growth: Openings in past
   year, 81
Contact Bob Bell, VP of
   Human Resources; 412-
   339-9500; Fax: 412-339-
   8100

**Sandvik Steel Co.,
Welding and Wire
Division**
PO Box 1220
Scranton, PA 18501
Founded: 1919
Total Employees: 350
Annual Sales: $47 million
Industries: Factory
   Automation,
   Subassemblies and
   Components
Growth: Openings in past
   year, 23
Contact Ms. Rosemary
   Chromey, Director of
   Human Resources; 717-
   587-5191; Fax: 717-586-
   8183

**Schott Glass
Technologies, Inc.**
400 York Ave.
Duryea, PA 18642
http://www.schottglasstech.
   com
Founded: 1969
Total Employees: 450
Industries: Advanced
   Materials, Photonics
Growth: Openings in past
   year, 22
Contact Joseph Frankel,
   Director of Personnel;
   717-457-7485; Fax: 717-
   457-6960; E-mail: sgt@
   sg230ll.attmail.com

SCIREX Corp.
587 Skippack Pike
Blue Bell, PA 19422
Founded: 1983
Total Employees: 250
Annual Sales: $38 million
Industries: Biotechnology,
   Medical, Pharmaceuticals
Growth: Openings in past
   year, 50
Contact Michael Choukas,
   President/CEO; 215-646-
   4117; Fax: 215-646-4673;
   E-mail: levyb@nmrc.mhs.
   compuserve.com

SCT Education Systems
4 Country View Rd.
Malvern, PA 19355
Founded: 1968
Total Employees: 500
Annual Sales: $64 million
Industries: Computer
   Software,
   Telecommunications
Growth: Openings in past
   year, 38
Contact Roy Zatcoff,
   President; 610-647-5930;
   Fax: 610-640-5102

**Sentient Systems
Technology, Inc.**
2100 Wharton St., Suite
   630
Pittsburgh, PA 15203
http://www.sentient-sys.
   com
Founded: 1983
Total Employees: 66
Industry: Computer
   Hardware
Growth: Openings in past
   year, 26
Contact Tilden Bennett,
   President; 412-381-4883;
   Fax: 412-381-5121;
   E-mail: sstsales@
   sentient-sys.com

Sermatech International, Inc.
155 South Limerick Rd.
Limerick, PA 19468
http://www.sermatech.com
Founded: 1944
Total Employees: 525
Annual Sales: $99 million
Industries: Advanced Materials, Manufacturing Equipment
Growth: Openings in past year, 25
Contact Stephen Holland, VP of Human Resources; 610-948-5100; Fax: 610-948-0811; E-mail: 102214@2247@compuserve.com

ServiceWare Inc.
333 Allegheny St.
Oakmont, PA 15139
http://www.serviceware.com
Founded: 1991
Total Employees: 120
Annual Sales: $15 million
Industry: Computer Software
Growth: Openings in past year, 50
Contact Jeff Pepper, Chief Executive Officer; 412-826-1158; Fax: 412-826-0577; E-mail: info@serviceware.com

Solid State Measurements, Inc.
110 Technology Dr.
Pittsburgh, PA 15275
Founded: 1970
Total Employees: 70
Annual Sales: $14 million
Industries: Factory Automation, Manufacturing Equipment
Growth: Openings in past year, 38
Contact Charles A. Thomas, President; 412-787-0620; Fax: 412-787-0630

Spirax Sarco Engineered Systems, Inc.
1951 Glenwood St. Southwest
PO Box 119
Allentown, PA 18105
http://www.spirax-sarco.com
Founded: 1913
Total Employees: 385
Annual Sales: $52 million
Industries: Subassemblies and Components, Test and Measurement
Growth: Openings in past year, 85
Contact Ms. Jennifer Davis, Human Resources Manager; 610-797-5830; Fax: 610-433-1346

Spree.com Corp.
381 Brinton Lake Rd.
Pharton, PA 19373
http://www.spree.com
Founded: 1996
Total Employees: 50
Annual Sales: $8.5 million
Industry: Telecommunications
Growth: Openings in past year, 45
Contact Mike Dever, Founder/President; 610-361-3000; Fax: 610-361-3001

STC Technologies, Inc.
1745 Eaton Ave.
Bethlehem, PA 18018
Founded: 1987
Total Employees: 75
Annual Sales: $9.1 million
Industry: Medical
Growth: Openings in past year, 25
Contact Michael J. Gausling, President; 610-882-1820; Fax: 610-882-1830

Strategic Management Group, Inc.
3624 Market St., University City Science Ctr.
Philadelphia, PA 19104

http://www.smginc.com
Founded: 1981
Total Employees: 162
Annual Sales: $20 million
Industry: Computer Software
Growth: Openings in past year, 47
Contact Dr. Leslie L. Spero, COB/CEO; 215-387-4000; Fax: 215-387-3653; E-mail: christG@smginc.com

SunGard Recovery Services, Inc.
1285 Drummers Ln.
Wayne, PA 19087
http://www.recovery.sungard.com
Founded: 1978
Total Employees: 600
Annual Sales: $120 million
Industry: Computer Hardware
Growth: Openings in past year, 100
Contact Ms. Karen Bilinski, VP of Human Resources; 610-341-8700; Fax: 610-341-8739

Systems & Computer Technology Corp., Technology Management Division
4 Country View Rd.
Malvern, PA 19355
Founded: 1968
Total Employees: 974
Annual Sales: $200 million
Industry: Computer Hardware
Growth: Openings in past year, 120
Contact Ms. Cathy Welsh, President; 610-647-5930; Fax: 610-648-7491

Teva Pharmaceuticals USA, Inc.
650 Cathill Rd.
Sellersville, PA 18960
Founded: 1945
Total Employees: 700
Annual Sales: $100 million
Industry: Pharmaceuticals

Growth: Openings in past year, 122
Contact William Fletcher, President/CEO; 215-256-8400; Fax: 215-256-7855

Thermal Transfer Corp
1100 Rico Rd.
Monroeville, PA 15146
Founded: 1952
Total Employees: 80
Industry: Energy
Growth: Openings in past year, 35
Contact Tim Ottie, VP of Sales; 412-351-3013; Fax: 412-856-0256

Titanium Hearth Technologies, Inc.
Hemlock Rd., Morgantown Business Park
Morgantown, PA 19543
Founded: 1984
Total Employees: 312
Annual Sales: $59 million
Industries: Advanced Materials, Manufacturing Equipment
Growth: Openings in past year, 112
Contact Ms. Betty J. Dare, Director of Human Resources; 610-286-6100

Tollgrade Communications, Inc.
493 Nixon Rd.
Cheswick, PA 15024
Founded: 1986
Total Employees: 185
Annual Sales: $37.5 million
Industry: Computer Hardware
Growth: Openings in past year, 50
Contact Chris Allison, Chief Executive Officer; 412-274-2156; Fax: 412-274-8014

Transarc Corporation
Gulf Tower, 707 Grant St.
Pittsburgh, PA 15219
http://www.transarc.com
Founded: 1989
Total Employees: 330
Industry: Computer Software
Growth: Openings in past year, 80
Contact Dione Kennedy, VP of Operations; 412-338-4400; Fax: 412-338-4404; E-mail: sales@transarc.com

Triumph Controls, Inc.
205 Church Rd.
PO Box 2100
North Wales, PA 19454
Founded: 1943
Total Employees: 288
Annual Sales: $37 million
Industries: Energy, Subassemblies and Components, Test and Measurement, Transportation
Growth: Openings in past year, 38
Contact Lee Baggett, Director of Human Resources; 215-699-4861; Fax: 215-699-2595

Vertex Inc.
1041 Old Cassatt Rd.
Berwyn, PA 19312
http://www.vertexinc.com
Founded: 1976
Total Employees: 300
Annual Sales: $30 million
Industry: Computer Software
Growth: Openings in past year, 75
Contact Bill Boyer, Executive Director of Admin. & Finance; 610-640-4200; Fax: 610-640-2761; E-mail: info@vertexinc.com

W.B. Saunders Co.
The Curtis Ctr.,
Independence Sq. West
Philadelphia, PA 19106

http://www.wbsaunders.com
Founded: 1888
Total Employees: 590
Industry: Computer Software
Growth: Openings in past year, 77
Contact Lewis Reines, President; 215-238-7800; Fax: 215-238-7883; E-mail: wbsinfo@wbsaunders.com

Western Atlas Inc., Landis/Gardner/CITCO Division
20 East 6th St.
Waynesboro, PA 17268
http://www.westatlas.com
Founded: 1996
Total Employees: 650
Annual Sales: $120 million
Industries: Advanced Materials, Factory Automation, Subassemblies and Components
Growth: Openings in past year, 49
Contact Jim Herrman, President; 717-762-2161; Fax: 717-765-5143

Rhode Island

Atlantic Cellular Management Co.
15 Westminster St., Suite 830
Providence, RI 02903
Founded: 1989
Total Employees: 211
Industry: Telecommunications
Growth: Openings in past year, 81
Contact Ms. Pamela Morais, VP of Human Resources; 401-458-1900; Fax: 401-421-9260

Comtec Information Systems, Inc.
30 Plan Way
Warwick, RI 02886

http://www.comtecinfosys.
com
Founded: 1959
Total Employees: 230
Annual Sales: $47 million
Industry: Computer
Hardware
Growth: Openings in past
year, 30
Contact Alfred J. Petteruti,
President; 401-739-5800;
Fax: 401-732-2586;
E-mail: sales@comtecis.
com

Daly & Wolcott, Inc.
1 Hospital Trust Plaza,
21st Floor
Providence, RI 02903
http://www.dalywolcott.com
Founded: 1977
Total Employees: 225
Annual Sales: $29 million
Industry: Computer
Software
Growth: Openings in past
year, 25
Contact Steve Loffredo,
VP of Human Resources;
401-351-8400; Fax: 401-
351-8484; E-mail:
webmaster@dalywolcott.
com

**Dome Publishing Co.,
Inc.**
10 New England Way
PO Box 1220
Warwick, RI 02887
Founded: 1940
Total Employees: 100
Industry: Computer
Software
Growth: Openings in past
year, 30
Contact Nicholas
Picchione, II, President;
401-738-7900; Fax: 401-
732-5377

Early Cloud and Co.
Aquidneck Corporate Park
Middletown, RI 02842
http://www.earlycloud.com
Founded: 1981
Total Employees: 280
Annual Sales: $50 million

Industries: Computer
Hardware, Computer
Software
Growth: Openings in past
year, 80
Contact Bob Pardini,
Director of Business
Operations; 401-849-
0500; Fax: 401-849-1190

EFD, Inc.
977 Waterman Ave.
East Providence, RI 02914
Founded: 1963
Total Employees: 210
Industries: Factory
Automation,
Manufacturing Equipment
Growth: Openings in past
year, 29
Contact Thomas
O'Connell, VP of
Finance; 401-434-1680;
Fax: 401-431-0237

**Everett Charles
Technologies, Ostby-
Barton Pylon Division**
487 Jefferson Blvd.
Warwick, RI 02886
http://www.ectinfo.com
Founded: 1986
Total Employees: 70
Annual Sales: $10 million
Industries: Factory
Automation,
Transportation
Growth: Openings in past
year, 30
Contact David Van Loan,
CEO/President; 401-739-
7310; Fax: 401-732-4937

Lance Industries, Inc.
20 Moshassock Rd.
Lincoln, RI 02865
http://www.foamtech.com
Founded: 1982
Total Employees: 90
Annual Sales: $17 million
Industry: Holding
Companies
Growth: Openings in past
year, 25
Contact Ms. Eileen
Lancia, Comptroller/
Bookkeeper; 401-723-
3626; Fax: 401-726-
3490; E-mail: foamtech@
ids.net

Schroff, Inc.
170 Commerce Dr.
Warwick, RI 02886
http://www.schroffus.com
Founded: 1982
Total Employees: 250
Annual Sales: $33 million
Industries: Manufacturing
Equipment,
Subassemblies and
Components
Growth: Openings in past
year, 50
Contact John Abbott,
President; 401-732-3770;
Fax: 401-738-7988

Tanury Industries
6 New England Way
Lincoln, RI 02865
Founded: 1946
Total Employees: 200
Industry: Manufacturing
Equipment
Growth: Openings in past
year, 40
Contact Michael Akkaoui,
President/CEO; 401-333-
9400; Fax: 401-333-3042

Technical Materials, Inc.
5 Wellington Rd.
Lincoln, RI 02865
Founded: 1968
Total Employees: 200
Annual Sales: $38 million
Industry: Advanced
Materials
Growth: Openings in past
year, 50
Contact Al Lubrano,
President; 401-333-1700;
Fax: 401-333-2848

South Carolina

**Advanced Automation,
Inc.**
600 Airport Rd.
Greenville, SC 29607

http://www.aautomation.
com
Founded: 1976
Total Employees: 240
Annual Sales: $31 million
Industry: Factory
Automation
Growth: Openings in past
year, 90
Contact Bill Schulze,
Human Resources
Manager; 864-627-0900;
Fax: 864-297-3734;
E-mail: info@
aautomation.com

Ambac International, Inc.
PO Box 85
Columbia, SC 29202
Founded: 1986
Total Employees: 435
Annual Sales: $50 million
Industry: Subassemblies
and Components
Growth: Openings in past
year, 29
Contact Nick Drayer,
Human Resources
Manager; 803-735-1400;
Fax: 803-735-2163;
E-mail: ambac@aol.com

Blackbaud, Inc.
4401 Belle Oaks Dr.
Charleston, SC 29405
http://www.blackbaud.com
Founded: 1981
Total Employees: 400
Annual Sales: $26.0
million
Industry: Computer
Software
Growth: Openings in past
year, 80
Contact Anthony E.
Bakker, President; 803-
740-5400; Fax: 803-740-
5410; E-mail: sales@
blackbaud.com

**Datastream Systems,
Inc.**
50 Datastream Plaza
Greenville, SC 29605
http://www.dstm.com
Founded: 1982
Total Employees: 400

Annual Sales: $32 million
Industry: Computer
Software
Growth: Openings in past
year, 100
Contact Larry Blackwell,
COB/CEO/President;
864-422-5001; Fax: 864-
422-5000

**Enterprise Computer
Systems, Inc.**
One Independence Pointe
PO Box 2383
Greenville, SC 29602
http://www.ecs-inc.com
Founded: 1978
Total Employees: 162
Annual Sales: $20 million
Industry: Computer
Software
Growth: Openings in past
year, 37
Contact Jim Sobeck,
President; 864-234-7676;
Fax: 864-987-6400

**Fuentez Systems
Concepts, Inc.**
2460 Remount Rd., Suite
102
North Charleston, SC
29406
http://www.fuentez.com
Founded: 1983
Total Employees: 120
Annual Sales: $15 million
Industries: Computer
Hardware, Computer
Software, Defense,
Manufacturing Equipment
Growth: Openings in past
year, 40
Contact Raymond M.
Fuentez, President; 803-
745-9496; Fax: 803-566-
9372; E-mail: quality@
fuentez.com

Huffman Corp.
1050 Huffman Way
Clover, SC 29710
http://www.huffman.com
Founded: 1980
Total Employees: 120
Annual Sales: $18 million

Industries: Factory
Automation, Photonics
Growth: Openings in past
year, 25
Contact Roger H. Hayes,
President; 803-222-4561;
Fax: 803-222-7599

**Jacobs Chuck
Manufacturing Co.**
One Jacobs Rd.
Clemson, SC 29633
Founded: 1902
Total Employees: 500
Annual Sales: $76 million
Industry: Factory
Automation
Growth: Openings in past
year, 50
Contact John Townsley,
Director of Human
Resources; 864-654-
5926; Fax: 864-654-7568

Marley Electric Heating
470 Beauty Spot Rd. E
Bennettsville, SC 29512
Founded: 1882
Total Employees: 400
Annual Sales: $92 million
Industry: Energy
Growth: Openings in past
year, 75
Contact Dennis Porzio,
President; 803-479-4006;
Fax: 803-479-8912

SCT Utility Systems
9 Science Ct.
Columbia, SC 29203
http://www.sctcorp.com
Founded: 1980
Total Employees: 290
Industries: Computer
Hardware, Computer
Software
Growth: Openings in past
year, 80
Contact Bill Mahoney,
President; 803-935-8000;
Fax: 803-935-8033

Sequa Chemicals, Inc.
1 Sequa Dr.
Chester, SC 29706
Founded: 1928
Total Employees: 303
Annual Sales: $80 million
Industries: Advanced
Materials, Chemicals
Growth: Openings in past
year, 57
Contact Ray Smith,
Human Resources
Manager; 803-385-5181;
Fax: 803-377-3542

U.S. Engine Valve Co.
7039 South Hwy. 11
Westminster, SC 29693
Founded: 1988
Total Employees: 250
Annual Sales: $33 million
Industry: Subassemblies
and Components
Growth: Openings in past
year, 50
Contact Ms. Mary Ann
Craft, Human Resources
Manager; 864-647-2061;
Fax: 864-647-2649

South Dakota

EROS Data Center
Mundt Federal Building
Sioux Falls, SD 57198
http://www.edc.cr.usgs.gov/
eros-home.html
Founded: 1972
Total Employees: 450
Industries: Environmental,
Photonics
Growth: Openings in past
year, 99
Contact Ms. Gail Hanson,
Personnel Specialist;
605-594-6511; Fax: 605-
594-6589; E-mail: eros@
edcserve.cr.usgs.gov

**Midco Communications,
Inc.**
410 South Phillips Ave.
Sioux Falls, SD 57104
http://comm.midco.net
Founded: 1982
Total Employees: 150
Annual Sales: $28 million
Industry:
Telecommunications
Growth: Openings in past
year, 50
Contact W. Tom
Simmons, Vice President/
General Manager; 605-
334-1200; Fax: 605-339-
4919

OEM Worldwide
400 Cessna St.
PO Box 430
Watertown, SD 57201
Founded: 1989
Total Employees: 150
Industry: Subassemblies
and Components
Growth: Openings in past
year, 80
Contact Ms. Lisa Turbak,
Human Resources
Manager; 605-886-2519;
Fax: 605-886-5123

**Portec, Inc.,
Construction Equipment
Division**
700 West 21st St.
Yankton, SD 57078
http://www.portec-ced.com
Founded: 1965
Total Employees: 345
Industry: Factory
Automation
Growth: Openings in past
year, 35
Contact Jerry Deel,
President/General
Manager; 605-665-9311;
Fax: 605-665-2623;
E-mail: mail@portec-ced.
com

Tennessee

**Buckman Laboratories
International, Inc.**
1256 North McLean Blvd.
Memphis, TN 38108
http://www.buckman.com
Founded: 1987
Total Employees: 187
Industry: Chemicals
Growth: Openings in past
year, 29
Contact Edson Peredo,
President; 901-278-0330;
Fax: 901-276-5343;
E-mail: knetix@buckman.
com

Celcore, Inc.
8001 Centerview Pkwy.,
Suite 201
Memphis, TN 38118
http://www.celcore.com
Founded: 1992
Total Employees: 200
Annual Sales: $34 million
Industry:
Telecommunications
Growth: Openings in past
year, 70
Contact Tom Berger,
President; 901-759-5155;
Fax: 901-759-5177;
E-mail: marketing@
celcore.com

Ceramspeed, Inc.
1227 McArthur Rd.
Maryville, TN 37804
Founded: 1991
Total Employees: 100
Annual Sales: $45 million
Industry: Energy
Growth: Openings in past
year, 92
Contact J.R. McWilliams,
Chairman/Managing
Director; 423-681-7070;
Fax: 423-681-0102

**Commercial Data
Corporation**
3600 Regal Blvd.
Memphis, TN 38118

Founded: 1967
Total Employees: 50
Industries: Computer Hardware, Computer Software
Growth: Openings in past year, 25
Contact Carroll L. Lewis, President; 901-375-1000; Fax: 901-375-9197

Computational Systems, Inc.
835 Innovation Dr.
Knoxville, TN 37932
http://www.compsys.com
Founded: 1984
Total Employees: 430
Annual Sales: $50 million
Industries: Computer Hardware, Computer Software, Factory Automation, Holding Companies, Photonics, Test and Measurement
Growth: Openings in past year, 60
Contact Ronald Canada, COB/CEO; 423-675-2110; Fax: 423-675-3100

CTI, Inc.
810 Innovation Dr.
Knoxville, TN 37932
http://www.cti-pet.com
Founded: 1984
Total Employees: 200
Annual Sales: $50 million
Industries: Holding Companies, Medical
Growth: Openings in past year, 64
Contact Terry Douglass, Ph.D., President; 423-966-7539; Fax: 423-966-8955

Cullom Machine Tool & Die, Inc.
1701 Hardeman Ln.
Cleveland, TN 37311
Founded: 1984
Total Employees: 80
Industries: Factory Automation, Manufacturing Equipment

Growth: Openings in past year, 30
Contact Heinrich Dichet, President; 423-476-2982; Fax: 423-479-6368

ENVOY Corporation
15 Century Blvd., Suite 600
Nashville, TN 37214
http://www.envoy-neic.com
Founded: 1981
Total Employees: 460
Annual Sales: $76.6 million
Industries: Computer Software, Telecommunications
Growth: Openings in past year, 60
Contact Fred C. Goad, Jr., COB/Co-CEO; 615-885-3700; Fax: 615-889-9955

Learning Co., Foreign Language Software Division
314 Erin Dr.
Knoxville, TN 37919
Founded: 1988
Total Employees: 200
Annual Sales: $25 million
Industry: Computer Software
Growth: Openings in past year, 50
Contact William Mackenzie, Director of Human Resources; 423-558-8270; Fax: 423-450-2105

Manufacturing Sciences Corp.
804 Kerr Hollow Rd.
Oak Ridge, TN 37830
http://www.mnsci.com
Founded: 1982
Total Employees: 200
Annual Sales: $20. million
Industries: Advanced Materials, Environmental
Growth: Openings in past year, 60
Contact Allen Liby, President; 423-481-0455;

Fax: 423-481-3142;
E-mail: mlundberg@mnsci.com

Micro Craft, Inc.
PO Box 370
Tullahoma, TN 37388
http://www.microcraft.com
Founded. 1950
Total Employees: 650
Annual Sales: $52 million
Industries: Holding Companies, Manufacturing Equipment, Subassemblies and Components, Transportation
Growth: Openings in past year, 100
Contact Ms. Brenda Craig, Director of Human Resources; 931-455-2664; Fax: 931-455-7060; E-mail: webmaster@microcraft.com

PAI Corp.
116 Milan Way
Oak Ridge, TN 37830
Founded: 1983
Total Employees: 340
Annual Sales: $16 million
Industry: Environmental
Growth: Openings in past year, 29
Contact Doan L. Phung, Chief Executive Officer; 423-483-0666; Fax: 423-481-0003; E-mail: paicorphq@aol.com

TennMark Telecommunications, Inc.
903 Industrial Dr.
Murfreesboro, TN 37129
Founded: 1983
Total Employees: 140
Annual Sales: $24 million
Industry: Telecommunications
Growth: Openings in past year, 40

Contact Terry Blakemore, President; 615-890-3505; Fax: 615-890-3575

Texas

ACS Dataline
1287 North Post Oak Rd., Suite 160
Houston, TX 77055
Founded: 1985
Total Employees: 450
Industry:
Telecommunications
Growth: Openings in past year, 150
Contact Robby Sawyer, Chief Executive Officer; 713-956-4894; Fax: 713-956-8425

Airborn, Inc.
4321 Airborn Dr.
PO Box 519
Addison, TX 75001
http://www.airborn.com
Founded: 1958
Total Employees: 450
Industry: Subassemblies and Components
Growth: Openings in past year, 150
Contact Ms. Dee Goleman, Human Resources Manager; 972-931-3200; Fax: 972-931-9305; E-mail: airborn@airborn.com

Allen Telecom, Inc., Decibel Products Division
8635 North Stemmons Frwy.
Dallas, TX 75247
http://www. decibelproducts.com
Founded: 1947
Total Employees: 700
Industries:
Subassemblies and Components, Telecommunications
Growth: Openings in past year, 46

Contact Dr. Peter Mailandt, President; 214-631-0310; Fax: 214-631-4706; E-mail: dbsales@ flash.net

Alpha Technologies Group, Inc.
330 Barker Cypress Rd., Suite 270
Houston, TX 77094
Founded: 1969
Total Employees: 816
Annual Sales: $70.237 million
Industry: Holding Companies
Growth: Openings in past year, 119
Contact Ms. Tricia Teed, Manager of Human Resources; 281-647-9941; Fax: 281-647-0587

AMBAC Connect, Inc.
9130 Jollyville Rd., Suite 355
Austin, TX 78759
http://www.ambac-connect. com
Founded: 1985
Total Employees: 40
Annual Sales: $3.0 million
Industry: Computer Software
Growth: Openings in past year, 26
Contact David Tucker, Comptroller; 512-338-0091; Fax: 512-343-0131

American Eurocopter Corp.
2701 Forum Dr.
Grand Prairie, TX 75052
http://www.eurocopterusa. com
Founded: 1973
Total Employees: 300
Annual Sales: $39 million
Industry: Transportation
Growth: Openings in past year, 40
Contact Christian Gras, President; 972-641-0000;

Fax: 972-641-3761; E-mail: breuland@ eurocopterusa.com

American Telco, Inc.
100 Waugh Dr., Suite 200
Houston, TX 77007
http://www.amtelco.com
Founded: 1983
Total Employees: 280
Annual Sales: $51 million
Industry:
Telecommunications
Growth: Openings in past year, 80
Contact Ron Henriksen, Chief Executive Officer; 713-862-2000; Fax: 713-868-4906

AMX Corporation
11995 Forestgate Dr.
Dallas, TX 75243
http://www.amx.com
Founded: 1982
Total Employees: 240
Annual Sales: $30.274 million
Industries: Holding Companies, Telecommunications
Growth: Openings in past year, 70
Contact Ms. Karen Thomas, Director of Human Resources; 972-644-3048; Fax: 972-907-2053; E-mail: info@amx. com

ANATEC, Inc.
10777 Westheimer Rd., Suite 810
Houston, TX 77042
Founded: 1982
Total Employees: 325
Annual Sales: $67 million
Industries: Computer Hardware, Computer Software
Growth: Openings in past year, 75
Contact Joe Springer, VP of Human Resources; 713-978-6848; Fax: 713-978-6408

ATX Technologies, Inc.
10010 San Pedro, Suite 200
San Antonio, TX 78216
http://www.track.com
Founded: 1994
Total Employees: 80
Industries: Computer Hardware, Test and Measurement
Growth: Openings in past year, 40
Contact Steven W. Riebel, President/CEO; 210-979-4999; Fax: 210-979-4979; E-mail: corpcom@track.com

Benchmarq Microelectronics, Inc.
17919 Waterview Pkwy.
Dallas, TX 75252
http://www.benchmarq.com
Founded: 1989
Total Employees: 240
Annual Sales: $40 million
Industry: Subassemblies and Components
Growth: Openings in past year, 42
Contact Al Schuele, President; 972-437-9195; Fax: 972-437-9198; E-mail: benchmarq@benchmarq.com

CANTEX, Inc.
PO Box 340
Mineral Wells, TX 76068
http://www.cantexinc.com
Founded: 1853
Total Employees: 550
Annual Sales: $74 million
Industry: Subassemblies and Components
Growth: Openings in past year, 149
Contact Don Wirtanen, President/CEO; 940-325-3344; Fax: 940-325-4644

Carreker-Antinori
14001 North Dallas Pkwy., Suite 1100
Dallas, TX 75240
http://www.carreker.com
Founded: 1978
Total Employees: 150
Annual Sales: $19 million
Industry: Computer Software
Growth: Openings in past year, 70
Contact Ms. Shirley Avina, Human Resources Manager; 972-458-1981; Fax: 972-701-0758

B.R. Blackmarr & Associates, Inc.
2515 McKinney Ave., LB17
Dallas, TX 75201
http://www.brba.com
Founded: 1954
Total Employees: 150
Industry: Computer Software
Growth: Openings in past year, 50
Contact Brian R. Blackmarr, President; 214-922-9030; Fax: 214-922-8118

Bindview Development Corp.
3355 West Alabama, 12th Floor
Houston, TX 77098
http://www.bindview.com
Founded: 1990
Total Employees: 120
Industry: Computer Software
Growth: Openings in past year, 35
Contact Eric Pulaski, President; 713-789-0882; Fax: 713-977-9111; E-mail: info@bindview.com

Carrington Laboratories, Inc.
2001 Walnut Hill Ln.
Irving, TX 75038
Founded: 1974
Total Employees: 250
Annual Sales: $24 million
Industries: Biotechnology, Medical, Pharmaceuticals
Growth: Openings in past year, 50
Contact Ms. Carol Kitchell, Personnel Manager; 972-518-1300; Fax: 972-518-1020

Barrios Technology, Inc.
1331 Gemini Ave., Suite 300
Houston, TX 77058
http://www.barrios.com
Founded: 1980
Total Employees: 250
Annual Sales: $11 million
Industries: Computer Software, Telecommunications, Transportation
Growth: Openings in past year, 50
Contact Ms. Sandra Plash, Director of Human Resources; 281-480-1889; Fax: 281-280-1901

Cal Dive International, Inc.
400 North Sam Houston Pkwy., East, Suite 400
Houston, TX 77060
Founded: 1984
Total Employees: 385
Annual Sales: $76.1 million
Industries: Energy, Environmental
Growth: Openings in past year, 35
Contact Owen Kratz, President/CEO; 281-618-0400; Fax: 281-618-0500

CFAN Co.
1000 Technology Way
San Marcos, TX 78666
Founded: 1993
Total Employees: 218

Industry: Transportation
Growth: Openings in past year, 58
Contact Ms. Linda Porter, Manager of Human Resources; 512-353-2832; Fax: 512-353-2838

Cimarron Software Services, Inc.
1830 NASA Rd. 1
Houston, TX 77058
http://www.phoenix.net/ ~cimarron
Founded: 1981
Total Employees: 210
Industries: Computer Hardware, Computer Software, Telecommunications
Growth: Openings in past year, 35
Contact Ms. Alene Albright, Human Resources Manager; 281-335-5800; Fax: 281-335-5890; E-mail: cimarron@phoenix.net

Clinicor, Inc.
1717 West Sixth St., Suite 400
Austin, TX 78703
http://www.clinicor.com
Founded: 1992
Total Employees: 200
Annual Sales: $15 million
Industries: Biotechnology, Medical, Pharmaceuticals
Growth: Openings in past year, 150
Contact Thomas P. O'Donnell, COB/CEO; 512-344-3300; Fax: 512-477-9449; E-mail: info@ clinicor.com

Consulting Partners, Inc.
6750 Hillcrest Plaza Dr., Suite 315
Dallas, TX 75230
http://www. consultingpartners.com
Founded: 1990
Total Employees: 125
Annual Sales: $10.6 million

Industry: Computer Software
Growth: Openings in past year, 25
Contact Ms. Chris Drake, Director of Professional Staffing; 972-386-7858; Fax: 972-386-8667; E-mail: partners@dallas. net

Control Specialties, Inc.
5939 Nunn St.
Houston, TX 77087
Founded: 1966
Total Employees: 100
Industry: Test and Measurement
Growth: Openings in past year, 35
Contact Randy Pennington, Jr., President; 713-644-5353; Fax: 713-845-1515

Control Systems International, Inc.
1625 West Crosby Rd.
Carrollton, TX 75006
http://www.control-systems.com
Founded: 1965
Total Employees: 500
Annual Sales: $99 million
Industries: Computer Hardware, Energy
Growth: Openings in past year, 153
Contact Ms. Jennifer Olivier, Human Resources Manager; 972-323-1111; Fax: 972-242-0026

Cybertek, Inc.
7800 North Stemmons Frwy., Suite 800
Dallas, TX 75247
http://www.cybertek.com
Founded: 1969
Total Employees: 600
Annual Sales: $77 million
Industry: Computer Software
Growth: Openings in past year, 100

Contact Hugh Browning, Chief Executive Officer; 214-637-1540; Fax: 214-638-4407

Cynara Co.
2925 Briarpark, Suite 1200
Houston, TX 77042
Founded: 1981
Total Employees: 60
Industry: Energy
Growth: Openings in past year, 30
Contact Ralph M. Kelly, Chief Executive Officer; 713-975-8881; Fax: 713-975-9611

Dan-Lock Industrial, Inc.
725 North Drennan Rd.
PO Box 292
Houston, TX 77001
Founded: 1961
Total Employees: 235
Annual Sales: $31 million
Industry: Subassemblies and Components
Growth: Openings in past year, 53
Contact Wayne Curington, President; 713-224-5811; Fax: 713-224-1833

Deja News, Inc.
9430 Research Blvd., Echelon II, Suite 350
Austin, TX 78759
http://www.dejanews.com
Founded: 1995
Total Employees: 65
Annual Sales: $11 million
Industry: Telecommunications
Growth: Openings in past year, 50
Contact Steve Madere, President/Founder; 512-343-6397; Fax: 512-502-8889; E-mail: sales@ dejanews.com

Denali, Inc.
1360 Post Oak Blvd.,
  Suite 2470
Houston, TX 77056
http://www.denaliholdings.
  com
Founded: 1994
Total Employees: 750
Annual Sales. $104.9
  million
Industry: Environmental
Growth: Openings in past
  year, 136
Contact Stephen T.
  Harcrow, COB/CEO; 713-
  627-0933; Fax: 713-627-
  0937

Denison Industries, Inc.
5511 Fielder St.
Denison, TX 75020
Founded: 1972
Total Employees: 130
Annual Sales: $16 million
Industries: Advanced
  Materials, Manufacturing
  Equipment,
  Subassemblies and
  Components
Growth: Openings in past
  year, 30
Contact Kurt Friedmann,
  President; 903-786-4444;
  Fax: 903-786-6646

**Diagnostic Systems
Laboratories, Inc.**
445 Medical Center Blvd.
Webster, TX 77598
http://www.dslabs.com
Founded: 1981
Total Employees: 92
Annual Sales: $15 million
Industries: Chemicals,
  Medical
Growth: Openings in past
  year, 27
Contact Gopal Savjani,
  President; 281-332-9678;
  Fax: 281-338-1895;
  E-mail: mktg@dslabs.
  com

Dril-Quip, Inc.
13550 Hempstead Hwy.
Houston, TX 77040
Founded: 1981
Total Employees: 926
Annual Sales: $115.9
  million
Industry: Energy
Growth: Openings in past
  year, 19
Contact Larry E. Reimert,
  President; 713-939-7711;
  Fax: 713-939-8063

Eagle Geophysical, Inc.
50 Briar Hollow Ln., 6th
  Floor West
Houston, TX 77027
Founded: 1992
Total Employees: 330
Annual Sales: $90.9
  million
Industry: Energy
Growth: Openings in past
  year, 30
Contact Jay N. Silverman,
  Chief Executive Officer;
  713-627-1990; Fax: 713-
  627-1020

**Eagle Traffic Control
Systems**
8004 Cameron Rd.
Austin, TX 78754
http://www.eagletes.com
Founded: 1958
Total Employees: 200
Annual Sales: $30 million
Industry: Transportation
Growth: Openings in past
  year, 50
Contact R. Gregg Evans,
  Director of Human
  Resources; 512-837-
  8310; Fax: 512-837-
  0196; E-mail: info@
  eagletes.com

**EG&G Automotive
Research, Inc.**
5404 Bandera Rd.
San Antonio, TX 78238
http://www.egginc.com

Founded: 1953
Total Employees: 450
Annual Sales: $61 million
Industries: Advanced
  Materials, Test and
  Measurement
Growth: Openings in past
  year, 99
Contact Alexander L.
  Rice, Director of Human
  Resources; 210-684-
  2310; Fax: 210-684-6074

**Electric & Gas
Technology, Inc.**
13636 Neutron Rd.
Dallas, TX 75244
Founded: 1985
Total Employees: 460
Annual Sales: $34 million
Industry: Holding
  Companies
Growth: Openings in past
  year, 60
Contact S. Mort
  Zimmerman, COB/
  President; 972-934-8797;
  Fax: 972-991-3265

Ensemble Corp.
12655 North Central
  Expwy., Suite 700
Dallas, TX 75243
http://www.ensemble.net
Founded: 1991
Total Employees: 60
Annual Sales: $7.7 million
Industries: Computer
  Hardware, Computer
  Software
Growth: Openings in past
  year, 30
Contact Tony Goodman,
  President; 972-960-2700;
  Fax: 972-960-2704;
  E-mail: tchapman@
  ensemble.net

EPI Technologies, Inc.
2901 Summit Ave.
Plano, TX 75074
Founded: 1980
Total Employees: 125
Annual Sales: $6.3 million
Industries: Manufacturing
  Equipment,

Subassemblies and Components

Growth: Openings in past year, 40

Contact Larry Kern, Executive VP of Finance/CFO; 972-398-5500; Fax: 972-398-5501; E-mail: lkern@cyberramp.net

ErgoBilt, Inc.
9244 Markville Dr.
Dallas, TX 75243
http://www.ergobilt.com
Founded: 1995
Total Employees: 175
Annual Sales: $17.5 million
Industry: Holding Companies
Growth: Openings in past year, 39
Contact Gerard Smith, CEO/President; 972-889-3742; Fax: 972-671-3742

Eurosoft, Inc.
1705 South Capital of Texas Hwy., Suite 202
Austin, TX 78746
http://www.euro-soft.com
Founded: 1991
Total Employees: 50
Annual Sales: $1.7 million
Industry: Computer Software
Growth: Openings in past year, 43
Contact Mrs. Marianne Metzner, President; 512-329-8100; Fax: 512-329-6776; E-mail: staffing@eurosoft-inc.com

Evolutionary Technologies International
4301 West Bank Dr., Bldg. B
Austin, TX 78746
http://www.eti.com
Founded: 1991
Total Employees: 180
Annual Sales: $25.5 million
Industry: Computer Software
Growth: Openings in past year, 45
Contact Ric Collins, Human Resources Direc-

tor; 512-327-6994; Fax: 512-327-6117; E-mail: information@eti.com

EXE Technologies, Inc.
12740 Hillcrest Rd.
Dallas, TX 75230
http://www.exe.com
Founded: 1980
Total Employees: 360
Annual Sales: $46 million
Industries: Computer Hardware, Computer Software
Growth: Openings in past year, 60
Contact Ms. Dorothy Jones, VP of Human Resources; 972-233-3761; Fax: 972-788-4208

Flagship Systems, Inc.
14315 Inwood Rd., Suite 101
Dallas, TX 75244
http://www.flagsys.com
Founded: 1994
Total Employees: 200
Industry: Computer Software
Growth: Openings in past year, 50
Contact Peter Bell, VP of Sales; 972-458-8828; Fax: 972-458-8728; E-mail: sales@flagsys.com

ForeFront Group, Inc.
1330 Post Oak Blvd., Suite 1300
Houston, TX 77056
http://www.ffg.com
Founded: 1992
Total Employees: 190
Annual Sales: $13.7 million
Industries: Computer Software, Holding Companies
Growth: Openings in past year, 50
Contact David Sikora, CEO/President; 713-961-1101; Fax: 713-961-1149; E-mail: asirlin@ffg.com

Fugro-McClelland Marine Geosciences, Inc.
PO Box 740010
Houston, TX 77274
Founded: 1955
Total Employees: 120
Annual Sales: $14 million
Industries: Energy, Environmental, Transportation
Growth: Openings in past year, 35
Contact W. Scott Rainey, President; 713-778-5500; Fax: 713-778-5573

Gagemaker, Inc.
712 East Southmore
Pasadena, TX 77502
Founded: 1980
Total Employees: 58
Industries: Factory Automation, Test and Measurement
Growth: Openings in past year, 28
Contact Jeff Wright, General Manager; 713-472-7360; Fax: 713-472-7241

GHG Corporation
1100 Hercules Ave., Suite 290
Houston, TX 77058
http://www.ghgcorp.com
Founded: 1979
Total Employees: 265
Annual Sales: $12 million
Industries: Computer Software, Telecommunications
Growth: Openings in past year, 45
Contact Ms. Suzanne Daly, Director of Operations; 281-488-8806; Fax: 281-488-1838

GlobeSet, Inc.
1250 Capital of Texas Hwy. South, Bldg. 1, Ste. 300
Austin, TX 78746
http://www.globeset.com
Founded: 1994
Total Employees: 60
Annual Sales: $7.7 million
Industry: Computer Software
Growth: Openings in past year, 48
Contact Michael Cation, COB/CEO; 512-427-5100; Fax: 512-427-5101; E-mail: info@globeset.com

HAC Corp.
537 Camden Dr.
Grand Prairie, TX 75051
Founded: 1970
Total Employees: 186
Annual Sales: $24 million
Industry: Transportation
Growth: Openings in past year, 56
Contact John Haran, President; 972-263-4387; Fax: 972-642-9772

Healthpoint, Ltd.
2400 Handley Ederville Rd.
Fort Worth, TX 76118
Founded: 1938
Total Employees: 100
Industries: Medical, Pharmaceuticals
Growth: Openings in past year, 60
Contact Paul Dorman, COB/CEO; 817-595-0394; Fax: 817-595-0921

HR Industries, Inc.
1302 East Collins Blvd.
Richardson, TX 75081
Founded: 1976
Total Employees: 300
Annual Sales: $29 million

Industries: Computer Hardware, Subassemblies and Components
Growth: Openings in past year, 70
Contact Ms. Kathleen Kolb, Secretary/Treasurer; 972-301-6620; Fax: 972-699-3704

Hudson Products Corporation
PO Box 36100
Houston, TX 77236
http://www.mcdermott.com/sig/hudson/
Founded: 1946
Total Employees: 375
Annual Sales: $73 million
Industries: Energy, Subassemblies and Components
Growth: Openings in past year, 25
Contact Bob Niles, Manager of Personnel; 713-914-5700; Fax: 713-914-5991; E-mail: hudson.products@mcdermott.com

IEX Corporation
2425 North Central Expwy.
Richardson, TX 75080
http://www.iex.com
Founded: 1988
Total Employees: 200
Annual Sales: $34 million
Industries: Computer Hardware, Computer Software, Telecommunications
Growth: Openings in past year, 75
Contact Ms. Carolyn Holmberg, Director of Human Resources; 972-301-1300; Fax: 972-301-1200; E-mail: info@iex.com

InfoEdge Technology, Inc.
9101 Burnet Rd., Suite 202
Austin, TX 78758

Founded: 1990
Total Employees: 75
Industries: Computer Hardware, Computer Software
Growth: Openings in past year, 50
Contact Paul Cliff, President; 512-833-5588; Fax: 512-832-0302; E-mail: infoedge@nfo.com

Intactix International, Inc.
3021 Gateway Dr., Suite 200
Irving, TX 75063
http://www.intactix.com
Founded: 1988
Total Employees: 170
Annual Sales: $22 million
Industry: Computer Software
Growth: Openings in past year, 90
Contact Dale Byrne, Chief Executive Officer; 972-580-1733; Fax: 972-580-0709

Intelect Network Technologies
1100 Executive Dr.
Richardson, TX 75081
http://www.intelectinc.com
Founded: 1964
Total Employees: 200
Industries: Photonics, Subassemblies and Components, Telecommunications
Growth: Openings in past year, 82
Contact Ms. Shirley Hudnal, Human Resources; 972-367-2100; Fax: 972-367-2200; E-mail: infocenter@intelectinc.com

Interliant, Inc.
1301 Frannin, Suite 700
Houston, TX 77002
http://www.interliant.com
Founded: 1992
Total Employees: 100

Industry:
Telecommunications
Growth: Openings in past
year, 70
Contact James M.
Lidestri, President/CEO;
713-650-6522; E-mail:
info@interllant.com

Interphase Corporation
13800 Senlac Dr.
Dallas, TX 75234
http://www.iphase.com/
Founded: 1974
Total Employees: 275
Annual Sales: $56.7
million
Industries:
Subassemblies and
Components,
Telecommunications
Growth: Openings in past
year, 50
Contact Stephen Polley,
COB/CEO/President;
214-654-5000; Fax: 214-
654-5500; E-mail:
fastnet@iphase.com

InterVoice, Inc.
17811 Waterview Pkwy.
Dallas, TX 75252
http://www.intervoice.com
Founded: 1983
Total Employees: 600
Annual Sales: $104.8
million
Industries: Computer
Hardware,
Telecommunications
Growth: Openings in past
year, 74
Contact Harold D. Brown,
VP of Human Resources;
972-454-8000; Fax: 972-
454-8905; E-mail: mktg@
intervoice.com

IRI International Corp.
PO Box 1101
Pampa, TX 79065
Founded: 1985
Total Employees: 575
Industries: Advanced
Materials, Energy,
Manufacturing Equipment

Growth: Openings in past
year, 123
Contact L.I. Howard, VP
of Human Resources;
806-665-3701; Fax: 806-
665-3216

**IXC Communications,
Inc.**
5000 Plaza on the Lake,
Suite 200
Austin, TX 78746
http://www.ixc-comm.net
Founded: 1986
Total Employees: 507
Annual Sales: $203 million
Industry:
Telecommunications
Growth: Openings in past
year, 200
Contact Benjamin Scott,
President/CEO; 512-328-
1112; Fax: 512-328-4717;
E-mail: info@ixc-comm.
net

Kobelco America, Inc.
12755 S Kirkwood Rd.
Stafford, TX 77477
Founded: 1984
Total Employees: 400
Industry: Factory
Automation
Growth: Openings in past
year, 40
Contact S. Yoshida,
President; 281-240-4800;
Fax: 281-240-4906

Laboratory Tops, Inc.
3206 North Main St
PO Box 232
Taylor, TX 76574
http://www.labtops.com
Founded: 1970
Total Employees: 164
Annual Sales: $16 million
Industry: Test and
Measurement
Growth: Openings in past
year, 28
Contact Ms. Kelli
Strickland, Vice
President; 512-352-5591;
Fax: 512-352-9523;
E-mail: info@labtops.com

Lepco, Inc.
1750 Stebbins Dr.
Houston, TX 77043
http://www.lapcoinc.com
Founded: 1968
Total Employees: 145
Industries: Environmental,
Manufacturing
Equipment, Test and
Measurement
Growth: Openings in past
year, 45
Contact Charles W. Soltis,
Chief Executive Officer;
713-461-1131; Fax: 713-
464-1148; E-mail:
rearlos@lepcoinc.com

LTI Technologies, Inc.
Armour Dr.
Houston, TX 77020
http://www.ltitech.com
Founded: 1976
Total Employees: 99
Annual Sales: $4.3 million
Industry: Holding
Companies
Growth: Openings in past
year, 39
Contact Ms. Jan S.
Gardner, Vice President;
713-671-3549; Fax: 713-
675-4771; E-mail: info@
litech.com

**Ludlum Measurements,
Inc.**
501 Oak St.
Sweetwater, TX 79556
Founded: 1962
Total Employees: 150
Annual Sales: $20 million
Industries: Holding
Companies, Test and
Measurement
Growth: Openings in past
year, 25
Contact Don Ludlum,
President; 915-235-5494;
Fax: 915-235-4672;
E-mail: ludlum@camalott.
com

MagRabbit, Inc.
3815 Jarrett Way, Bldg.
 B220
Austin, TX 78728
http://www.magrabbit.com
Founded: 1985
Total Employees: 110
Industries: Computer
 Hardware, Computer
 Software, Holding
 Companies,
 Telecommunications
Growth: Openings in past
 year, 25
Contact William Witt,
 President; 512-310-9903;
 Fax: 512-310-8497;
 E-mail: mail@magrabbit.
 com

Marlow Industries, Inc.
10451 Vista Park Rd.
Dallas, TX 75238
http://www.marlow.com
Founded: 1973
Total Employees: 270
Industries: Energy,
 Subassemblies and
 Components, Test and
 Measurement
Growth: Openings in past
 year, 45
Contact Ms. Pamela J.
 Jennett, Assistant Vice
 President; 214-340-4900;
 Fax: 214-341-5212

**McDonald Technologies
International, Inc.**
2434 McIver Ln.
Carrollton, TX 75006
Founded: 1986
Total Employees: 800
Industries: Computer
 Hardware, Holding
 Companies,
 Subassemblies and
 Components
Growth: Openings in past
 year, 150
Contact Pip Sivakumar,
 President; 972-243-6767;
 Fax: 972-241-2643

MetaSolv Software, Inc.
14900 Landmark, Suite
 530
Dallas, TX 75240
http://www.metasolv.com
Founded: 1992
Total Employees: 75
Annual Sales: $9.7 million
Industry: Computer
 Software
Growth: Openings in past
 year, 45
Contact Ms. Julie Black,
 Human Resources
 Manager; 972-239-0623;
 Fax: 972-239-0653;
 E-mail: sales@metasolv.
 com

Metrowerks, Inc.
2201 Donley Dr., Suite 310
Austin, TX 78758
http://www.metrowerks.
 com
Founded: 1985
Total Employees: 150
Annual Sales: $18.3
 million
Industry: Computer
 Software
Growth: Openings in past
 year, 60
Contact Jim Welch, VP of
 Finance/CFO; 512-873-
 4700; Fax: 512-873-
 4900; E-mail: sales@
 metrowerks.com

ObjectSpace, Inc.
1488 Quorum Dr., Suite
 400
Dallas, TX 75240
http://www.objectspace.
 com
Founded: 1992
Total Employees: 180
Annual Sales: $23 million
Industry: Computer
 Software
Growth: Openings in past
 year, 100
Contact David Norris,
 President; 972-934-2496;
 Fax: 972-663-9099

**Oceaneering
International, Inc.,
Multiflex Division**
11911 Farmed Market 529
Houston, TX 77041
Founded: 1977
Total Employees: 350
Industry: Subassemblies
 and Components
Growth: Openings in past
 year, 49
Contact Jeff White, VP of
 Sales and Marketing;
 713-329-4500; Fax: 713-
 329-4951

**Oceaneering
International, Inc.,
Production Systems
Division**
11911 Farmed Market 529
Houston, TX 77041
http://www.oceaneering.
 com
Founded: 1988
Total Employees: 350
Annual Sales: $80 million
Industries: Energy,
 Subassemblies and
 Components, Test and
 Measurement,
 Transportation
Growth: Openings in past
 year, 49
Contact Bruce Crager,
 Senior Vice President;
 713-329-4500; Fax: 713-
 329-4951; E-mail:
 userid@ops.oceaneering.
 com

**Oceaneering Space
Systems**
16665 Space Center Blvd.
Houston, TX 77058
Founded: 1988
Total Employees: 230
Annual Sales: $30 million
Industries: Advanced
 Materials, Factory
 Automation,
 Telecommunications,
 Transportation
Growth: Openings in past
 year, 45

Contact Ms. Jane Robertson, Manager of Contracts and Administration; 281-488-9080; Fax: 281-488-6485

Optical Data Systems, Inc.
1101 East Arapaho Rd.
Richardson, TX 75081
http://www.ods.com
Founded: 1983
Total Employees: 387
Annual Sales: $117.9 million
Industry: Telecommunications
Growth: Openings in past year, 36
Contact Ms. Donna Combs, Director of Administration; 972-234-6400; Fax: 972-234-1467; E-mail: sales@ods. com

Perry Equipment Corp., Flow Measurement Division
1 Peco Pl., Wolters Industrial Park
Mineral Wells, TX 76068
Founded: 1936
Total Employees: 350
Annual Sales: $47 million
Industry: Test and Measurement
Growth: Openings in past year, 23
Contact Ms. Laine Perry, President; 940-325-2575; Fax: 940-325-4622; E-mail: fm@pecousa.com

Pervasive Software, Inc.
8834 Capital of Texas Hwy. North, Suite 300
Austin, TX 78759
http://www.btrieve.com
Founded: 1994
Total Employees: 180
Annual Sales: $24.5 million
Industry: Computer Software
Growth: Openings in past year, 59

Contact Ms. Meiling Newman, Director of Human Resources; 512-794-1719; Fax: 512-794-1778; E-mail: info@ pervasive-sw.com

Pioneer Companies, Inc.
700 Louisiana St., Suite 4200
Houston, TX 77002
Founded: 1988
Total Employees: 900
Annual Sales: $209 million
Industry: Holding Companies
Growth: Openings in past year, 208
Contact Jerry B. Bradley, VP of Human Resources; 713-225-3831; Fax: 713-225-4426

Poco Graphite, Inc.
1601 South State St.
Decatur, TX 76234
Founded: 1964
Total Employees: 330
Annual Sales: $63 million
Industry: Advanced Materials
Growth: Openings in past year, 48
Contact Michael Collar, Human Resources Manager; 940-627-2121; Fax: 940-393-8337

Pollak Engineered Products Group, Transportation Electronics Division
11801 Miriam Dr., Suite B1
El Paso, TX 79936
Founded: 1925
Total Employees: 720
Annual Sales: $94 million
Industries: Subassemblies and Components, Telecommunications, Transportation
Growth: Openings in past year, 130
Contact Judson Caruthers, Director of HR

and Organization; 915-592-5700; Fax: 915-593-7379

Powell Electrical Manufacturing Company
PO Box 12818
Houston, TX 77217
http://www.powl.com
Founded: 1947
Total Employees: 900
Annual Sales: $170 million
Industries: Energy, Holding Companies, Subassemblies and Components
Growth: Openings in past year, 150
Contact Robert Murphy, Director of Human Resources; 713-944-6900; Fax: 713-944-4453; E-mail: info@powl. com

Power Computing Corp.
2400 South Interstate 35
Round Rock, TX 78681
http://www.powercc.com
Founded: 1993
Total Employees: 690
Annual Sales: $140 million
Industry: Computer Hardware
Growth: Openings in past year, 40
Contact Savino Ferrales, VP of Human Resources; 512-388-6868; Fax: 512-388-6798; E-mail: info@ powercc.com

Precision Tube Technology, Inc.
PO Box 24746
Houston, TX 77229
Founded: 1990
Total Employees: 100
Annual Sales: $13 million
Industry: Subassemblies and Components
Growth: Openings in past year, 30
Contact Lawrence W. Smith, President; 281-

458-2883; Fax: 281-458-2886; E-mail: precision@precision.com

Progressive System Technologies, Inc.
11000 North Mopac
Expwy., Suite 100
Austin, TX 78759
Founded: 1990
Total Employees: 130
Annual Sales: $18 million
Industries: Computer Software, Factory Automation, Manufacturing Equipment
Growth: Openings in past year, 70
Contact Tony DiNapoli, President; 512-342-2000; Fax: 512-342-2010; E-mail: sales@pst-inc.com

RELTEC Corp., RELTEC Transmission Products
2100 Reliance Pkwy.
PO Box 919
Bedford, TX 76021
Founded: 1988
Total Employees: 775
Annual Sales: $130 million
Industries: Computer Software, Factory Automation, Telecommunications
Growth: Openings in past year, 124
Contact Patrick Welker, Vice President/General Manager; 817-267-3141; Fax: 817-540-9766

RF Monolithics, Inc.
4441 Sigma Rd.
Dallas, TX 75244
http://www.rfm.com
Founded: 1979
Total Employees: 556
Annual Sales: $47.6 million
Industries:
Subassemblies and Components, Test and Measurement, Telecommunications

Growth: Openings in past year, 56
Contact Ms. Diana Handler, Director of Human Resources; 972-233-2903; Fax: 972-404-9476

Rothe Development, Inc.
4614 Sinclair Rd.
San Antonio, TX 78222
Founded: 1968
Total Employees: 200
Annual Sales: $23 million
Industries: Computer Software, Manufacturing Equipment
Growth: Openings in past year, 40
Contact Ms. Suzanne Phtenaude, President; 210-648-1817; Fax: 210-648-4091

Sai Software Consultants, Inc.
2313 Timber Shadows, Suite 200
Kingwood, TX 77339
http://www.saisoft.com
Founded: 1984
Total Employees: 375
Annual Sales: $30 million
Industries: Computer Hardware, Computer Software
Growth: Openings in past year, 75
Contact Siva P. Tayi, President; 281-358-1858; Fax: 281-358-8952

Sawyer Research Products, Inc., Sawyer Crystal Systems Division
1601 Airport Rd.
Conroe, TX 77301
Founded: 1979
Total Employees: 110
Annual Sales: $21 million
Industry: Advanced Materials
Growth: Openings in past year, 50

Contact Kelley Scott, General Manager; 409-756-8886; Fax: 409-756-4914

SH Leggitt, Inc.
1000 Civic Center Dr.
San Marcos, TX 78666
Founded: 1945
Total Employees: 425
Annual Sales: $53 million
Industries: Holding Companies, Subassemblies and Components
Growth: Openings in past year, 25
Contact Tim Nicholson, VP of Operations; 512-396-0707; Fax: 512-396-3064

Shaffer, Inc.
12950 West Little York St.
Houston, TX 77041
Founded: 1891
Total Employees: 450
Annual Sales: $100 million
Industries: Energy, Test and Measurement
Growth: Openings in past year, 142
Contact Ms. Lonna Moore, Director of Human Resources; 713-937-5000; Fax: 713-937-5779

SMART Technologies, Inc.
11701 Stonehollow Dr.
Austin, TX 78758
http://www.smartdna.com
Founded: 1995
Total Employees: 140
Annual Sales: $18 million
Industry: Computer Software
Growth: Openings in past year, 110
Contact Jeffrey Decoux, President/CEO; 512-719-9100; Fax: 512-719-9167; E-mail: info@smartdna.com

Source Media, Inc.
8140 Walnut Hill Ln., Suite 1000
Dallas, TX 75231
Founded: 1987
Total Employees: 153
Annual Sales: $18.5 million
Industry: Telecommunications
Growth: Openings in past year, 31
Contact Timothy Peters, Chief Executive Officer; 214-890-9050; Fax: 214-890-9014

Stelax Industries, Ltd.
4004 Beltline Rd., Suite 107
Dallas, TX 75244
http://www.stelax.co.uk
Founded: 1987
Total Employees: 32
Industry: Advanced Materials
Growth: Openings in past year, 27
Contact Harmon S. Hardy, COB/President/CEO/COO; 972-233-6041; Fax: 972-991-8483

Technical Directions, Inc.
3030 L.B.J. Frwy.
Dallas, TX 75234
http://www.td-inc.com
Founded: 1985
Total Employees: 655
Industries: Computer Hardware, Computer Software, Telecommunications
Growth: Openings in past year, 105
Contact John Hammerbeck, President; 972-243-1020; Fax: 972-243-3660; E-mail: dallas@td-inc.com

Standard Manufacturing Co., Inc.
4012 West Illinois Ave.
PO Box 210300
Dallas, TX 75211
Founded: 1938
Total Employees: 160
Annual Sales: $14 million
Industry: Manufacturing Equipment
Growth: Openings in past year, 40
Contact N.D. Oswald, President; 214-337-8911; Fax: 214-330-5932

Symtx, Inc.
1301 Capitol of Texas Hwy. South, Suite B224
Austin, TX 78746
http://www.symtx.com
Founded: 1981
Total Employees: 90
Annual Sales: $11 million
Industries: Computer Software, Factory Automation, Manufacturing Equipment
Growth: Openings in past year, 40
Contact Paul Hiller, President; 512-328-7799; Fax: 512-328-7778; E-mail: salest@symtx.com

Tekram Technology Corp.
11500 Metric Blvd., Suite 190
Austin, TX 78758
Founded: 1991
Total Employees: 100
Annual Sales: $20 million
Industry: Computer Hardware
Growth: Openings in past year, 30
Contact Ms. Betty Noell, Office Manager; 512-833-6550; Fax: 512-833-7276

Tex-Tube Co.
1503 North Post Oak Rd.
Houston, TX 77270
Founded: 1951
Total Employees: 160
Annual Sales: $21 million
Industry: Subassemblies and Components
Growth: Openings in past year, 60
Contact Gerald Merfish, President; 713-686-4351; Fax: 713-681-5256

STEAG MicroTech, Inc.
8305 Cross Park Dr.
Austin, TX 78754
http://www.steag.com
Founded: 1990
Total Employees: 120
Annual Sales: $15 million
Industries: Factory Automation, Manufacturing Equipment, Test and Measurement
Growth: Openings in past year, 25
Contact Ms. Elfi Mavronicles, Human Resources Manager; 512-438-1300; Fax: 512-438-1399

Tanknology-NDE Corp.
8900 Shoal Creek Blvd., Bldg. 200
Austin, TX 78757
http://www.tanknde.com
Founded: 1981
Total Employees: 320
Annual Sales: $16 million
Industries: Environmental, Holding Companies
Growth: Openings in past year, 70
Contact Daniel Sharplin, President; 512-451-6334; Fax: 512-459-1459

Texas Hydraulics
PO Box 1067
Temple, TX 76503
Founded: 1968
Total Employees: 388

Industry: Subassemblies and Components
Growth: Openings in past year, 68
Contact Ms. Lanelle Mersiozski, Personnel Director; 254-778-4701; Fax: 254-774-9940

Texstar, Inc.
802 Ave. J East
PO Box 534036
Grand Prairie, TX 75053
http://www.texstar.com
Founded: 1945
Total Employees: 300
Industries: Manufacturing Equipment, Transportation
Growth: Openings in past year, 40
Contact David Rollings, President; 972-647-1366; Fax: 972-641-2800; E-mail: texstar@texstar. com

TexTek Plastics
9800 West Commerce
San Antonio, TX 78227
Founded: 1971
Total Employees: 350
Annual Sales: $43 million
Industry: Manufacturing Equipment
Growth: Openings in past year, 49
Contact Jim Heyde, Vice President; 210-675-4950; Fax: 210-675-4650

Thermalloy, Inc.
PO Box 810839
Dallas, TX 75381
http://www.thermalloy.com
Founded: 1958
Total Employees: 382
Industry: Subassemblies and Components
Growth: Openings in past year, 25
Contact Chris Hallmark, Personnel Manager; 972-243-4321; Fax: 972-241-4656

Travel Technologies Group, L.P.
5550 LBJ Frwy., Suite 950
Dallas, TX 75240
http://www.ttgwest.com
Founded: 1988
Total Employees: 50
Annual Sales: $6.4 million
Industry. Computer Software
Growth: Openings in past year, 25
Contact John Farrier, President; 972-702-1015; Fax: 972-702-1023

Tyrex Manufacturing Group LLP
2433 Rutland Dr., Suite 150
Austin, TX 78758
http://www.tyrexmfg.com
Founded: 1994
Total Employees: 100
Industries: Holding Companies, Subassemblies and Components
Growth: Openings in past year, 75
Contact Andrew Cooper, President; 512-835-1200; Fax: 512-835-1344

Vesuvius Lava Co.
1812 East Duncan St.
Tyler, TX 75702
Founded: 1986
Total Employees: 120
Annual Sales: $23 million
Industry: Advanced Materials
Growth: Openings in past year, 42
Contact Jim Hoppe, Regional Manager; 903-597-7237; Fax: 903-597-3531

Vignette Corp.
3410 Far West Blvd., Suite 300
Austin, TX 78731

http://www.vignette.com
Founded: 1995
Total Employees: 53
Annual Sales: $6.8 million
Industry: Computer Software
Growth: Openings in past year, 49
Contact Ross Garber, Chief Executive Officer; 512-502-0223; Fax: 512-502-0280; E-mail: info@ vignette.com

Voice Control Systems, Inc.
14140 Midway Rd., Suite 100
Dallas, TX 75244
http://www.voicecontrol. com
Founded: 1978
Total Employees: 120
Annual Sales: $13.6 million
Industries: Computer Hardware, Computer Software
Growth: Openings in past year, 60
Contact Peter J. Foster, CEO/President; 972-726-1200; Fax: 972-726-1267; E-mail: sales@ vcsi.com

VTEL Corp.
108 Wild Basin Rd. South
Austin, TX 78746
http://www.vtel.com
Founded: 1984
Total Employees: 500
Annual Sales: $90.8 million
Industry: Telecommunications
Growth: Openings in past year, 50
Contact Ms. Judy A. Wallace, VP of Human Resources; 512-314-2700; Fax: 512-314-2792

Web America Networks, Inc.
17250 Dallas Pkwy.
Dallas, TX 75248

http://www.wans.net
Founded: 1996
Total Employees: 30
Annual Sales: $5.1 million
Industry:
Telecommunications
Growth: Openings in past
year, 28
Contact Philip Midkiff,
President; 972-738-6000;
Fax: 972-733-0756;
E-mail: sales@wans.net

**Weston Brothers
Software, Inc.**
12300 Ford Rd., Suite 410
Dallas, TX 75234
Founded: 1986
Total Employees: 75
Annual Sales: $9.7 million
Industries: Computer
Hardware, Computer
Software
Growth: Openings in past
year, 25
Contact Jim Alkire,
General Manager; 972-
241-3307; Fax: 972-241-
2053

Utah

Access Software, Inc.
4750 Wiley Post Way,
Bldg. 1, Suite 200
Salt Lake City, UT 84116
http://www.accesssoftware.
com
Founded: 1982
Total Employees: 150
Annual Sales: $19 million
Industry: Computer
Software
Growth: Openings in past
year, 50
Contact Dave Curtain,
Personnel Director; 801-
359-2900; Fax: 801-359-
2968

Auto-Soft Corp.
International Ctr., 5245
Yeager Rd.
Salt Lake City, UT 84116
http://www.autosoft.com

Founded: 1985
Total Employees: 233
Annual Sales: $30 million
Industry: Computer
Software
Growth: Openings in past
year, 83
Contact Greg Schaack,
Director of Human
Resources; 801-322-
2069; Fax: 801-322-1846

Caldera(R), Inc.
633 South 550 East
Provo, UT 84606
http://www.caldera.com
Founded: 1994
Total Employees: 60
Annual Sales: $7.7 million
Industry: Computer
Software
Growth: Openings in past
year, 40
Contact Bryan Sparks,
President/CEO; 801-377-
7687; Fax: 801-377-
8752; E-mail: info@
caldera.com

**CallWare Technologies,
Inc.**
8911 South Sandy Pkwy.
Sandy, UT 84070
http://www.callware.com
Founded: 1994
Total Employees: 125
Annual Sales: $16 million
Industry: Computer
Software
Growth: Openings in past
year, 35
Contact Reino Kerttula,
President/CEO; 801-984-
1100; Fax: 801-984-1120;
E-mail: info@callware.
com

**Capsoft Development
Corp.**
732 East Utah Valley Dr.,
Suite 400
American Fork, UT 84003
http://www.capsoft.com
Founded: 1987
Total Employees: 90
Industry: Computer
Software

Growth: Openings in past
year, 30
Contact Ms. Cherie St.
John, Personnel
Manager; 801-763-3900;
Fax: 801-763-3999;
E-mail: reps@capsoft.
com

Ceramatec, Inc.
2425 South 900 West
Salt Lake City, UT 84119
Founded: 1976
Total Employees: 125
Annual Sales: $16 million
Industries: Medical,
Subassemblies and
Components, Test and
Measurement
Growth: Openings in past
year, 25
Contact Jim Davis, Chief
Executive Officer; 801-
972-2455; Fax: 801-972-
1925

**Computer Marketing
Corp.**
2450 East Fort Union Blvd.
Salt Lake City, UT 84121
http://www.cmcflex.com
Founded: 1978
Total Employees: 65
Annual Sales: $8.4 million
Industry: Computer
Software
Growth: Openings in past
year, 25
Contact Fred Holcomb,
President/Marketing
Director; 801-365-5000;
Fax: 801-365-5100;
E-mail: cmcmail@
cmcflex.com

**Dentrix Dental Systems,
Inc.**
732 East Utah Valley Dr.,
Suite 500
American Fork, UT 84003
http://www.dentrix.com
Founded: 1985
Total Employees: 104
Annual Sales: $10.3
million
Industry: Computer
Software

Growth: Openings in past year, 30
Contact Ms. Pat Reece, Human Resources Manager; 801-763-9300; Fax: 801-763-9336; E-mail: info@dentrix.com

EMC Corp., Jetway Systems Division
PO Box 9368
Ogden, UT 84409
Founded: 1928
Total Employees: 600
Annual Sales: $78 million
Industry: Transportation
Growth: Openings in past year, 178
Contact Art Belinger, Director of Human Resources; 801-627-6600; Fax: 801-629-3474

fonix(tm) corporation
1225 Eagle Gate Towers, 60 East South Temple
Salt Lake City, UT 84111
http://www.fonix.com
Founded: 1993
Total Employees: 80
Industries: Computer Hardware, Computer Software
Growth: Openings in past year, 35
Contact Thomas A. Murdock, President/CEO; 801-328-0161; Fax: 801-328-8778

GSE Erudite Software, Inc.
406 West & 10600 South, Suite 460
South Jordan, UT 84095
http://www.erudite.com
Founded: 1989
Total Employees: 157
Annual Sales: $28 million
Industries: Computer Hardware, Computer Software
Growth: Openings in past year, 82
Contact Gene Loveridge, President/CEO; 801-576-8800; Fax: 801-576-8815

KeyLabs, Inc.
633 South 550 East
Provo, UT 84606
http://www.keylabs.com
Founded: 1996
Total Employees: 40
Industries: Computer Hardware, Computer Software, Telecommunications
Growth: Openings in past year, 35
Contact Jan Newman, President/CEO; 801-377-5484; Fax: 801-377-5439; E-mail: info@keylabs.com

Myriad Genetic Laboratories, Inc.
390 Wakara Way
Salt Lake City, UT 84108
http://www.myriad.com
Founded: 1991
Total Employees: 205
Annual Sales: $15.236 million
Industry: Biotechnology
Growth: Openings in past year, 80
Contact Ms. Barbara Perry, Director of Personnel; 801-582-3400; Fax: 801-584-3640

NACT Telecommunications, Inc.
191 West 5200 North
Provo, UT 84604
http://www.nact.com
Founded: 1982
Total Employees: 95
Annual Sales: $16.3 million
Industries: Computer Hardware, Computer Software
Growth: Openings in past year, 38
Contact Ms. Suzette Lundgren, Director of Human Resources; 801-802-3000; Fax: 801-802-2000

OEC Medical Systems, Inc.
384 Wright Brothers Dr.
Salt Lake City, UT 84116
http://www.oecmed.com
Founded: 1983
Total Employees: 580
Annual Sales: $128 million
Industry. Medical
Growth: Openings in past year, 58
Contact Ms. Susan Transtrum, Senior Manager of Human Resources; 801-328-9300; Fax: 801-328-4300; E-mail: webmaster@oecmed.com

Oldham Associates, Inc.
500 West 1200 South
Orem, UT 84058
Founded: 1960
Total Employees: 250
Annual Sales: $32 million
Industry: Holding Companies
Growth: Openings in past year, 25
Contact Ms. Joanne Froelich, President; 801-226-2984; Fax: 801-226-8438

Open Market, Inc., Folio Division
5072 North 300 West
Provo, UT 84604
http://www.folio.com
Founded: 1986
Total Employees: 180
Annual Sales: $23 million
Industry: Computer Software
Growth: Openings in past year, 30
Contact Bill Bennett, President/CEO; 801-229-6700; Fax: 801-229-6787; E-mail: sales@folio.com

Raytheon Aircraft Montek Company
2268 South 3270 West
Salt Lake City, UT 84119

Founded: 1955
Total Employees: 570
Annual Sales: $58.660 million
Industries: Defense, Subassemblies and Components, Transportation
Growth: Openings in past year, 43
Contact A.B. Buchanan, Director of Human Resources; 801-973-4300; Fax: 801-974-7581

Smith Megadiamond Co.
275 West 2230 North
Provo, UT 84604
Founded: 1966
Total Employees: 180
Annual Sales: $29 million
Industry: Manufacturing Equipment
Growth: Openings in past year, 30
Contact Kesh Keshavan, General Manager; 801-377-3474; Fax: 801-377-2071

Vermont

Carris Financial Corp.
PO Box 696
Rutland, VT 05702
http://www.carris.com
Founded: 1956
Total Employees: 800
Industry: Holding Companies
Growth: Openings in past year, 73
Contact Ms. Karin McGrath, Personnel Manager; 802-773-9111; Fax: 802-770-3581

Casella Waste Systems, Inc.
25 Greens Hill Ln.
Rutland, VT 05701
http://www.casella.com
Founded: 1976
Total Employees: 891
Annual Sales: $73.2 million
Industry: Environmental
Growth: Openings in past year, 190

Contact John W. Casella, COB/President/CEO; 802-775-0325; Fax: 802-775-3290; E-mail: feedback@casella.com

Clifford of Vermont, Inc.
PO Box 51
Bethel, VT 05032
Founded: 1946
Total Employees: 100
Annual Sales: $40 million
Industry: Holding Companies
Growth: Openings in past year, 57
Contact Maynard Nelson, President; 802-234-9921; Fax: 802-234-5006; E-mail: cablesales@clifcom.com

Virginia

AC&E Ltd.
14101 Sullyfield Cir.
Chantilly, VA 20151
http://www.aceltd.com
Founded: 1985
Total Employees: 80
Annual Sales: $5 million
Industries: Computer Hardware, Computer Software
Growth: Openings in past year, 25
Contact Ms. Terri Lynn Murphy, Director of Human Resources; 703-968-5700; Fax: 703-968-4331

Access Teleconferencing International, Inc.
1861 Wiehle Ave.
Reston, VA 20190
Founded: 1987
Total Employees: 120
Annual Sales: $20 million
Industry: Telecommunications
Growth: Openings in past year, 30
Contact C. Raymond Marvin, President/CEO; 703-736-7100; Fax: 703-736-7150

Advanced Engineering & Management Associates, Inc., Aerospace Engineering Division
1919 South Eads St., Suite 400
Arlington, VA 22202
Founded: 1993
Total Employees: 90
Industry: Computer Software
Growth: Openings in past year, 43
Contact Bernie Doyle, Director of Information Technology; 703-486-1993; Fax: 703-486-0793

Advanced Marine Enterprises, Inc.
1725 Jefferson Davis Hwy., Suite 1300
Arlington, VA 22202
http://www.advmar.com
Founded: 1976
Total Employees: 350
Annual Sales: $46 million
Industries: Defense, Manufacturing Equipment, Transportation
Growth: Openings in past year, 49
Contact Ms. Patti Schaeffer, Manager of Human Resources; 703-413-9200; Fax: 703-413-9221; E-mail: info@advmar.com

Advanced Technology Systems, Inc.
7915 Jones Branch Dr.
Mc Lean, VA 22102
http://www.atsva.com
Founded: 1978
Total Employees: 660
Annual Sales: $85 million
Industries: Computer Hardware, Computer Software
Growth: Openings in past year, 208

Contact Ms. Elsie M. Love, Personnel Manager; 703-506-0088; Fax: 703-903-0415

Analytical & Research Technology, Inc.
8110 Gatehouse Rd., Suite 100E
Falls Church, VA 22042
Founded: 1988
Total Employees: 50
Annual Sales: $9.9 million
Industry: Computer Hardware
Growth: Openings in past year, 25
Contact Kevin T. Keyes, President; 703-573-5001; Fax: 703-260-2466; E-mail: artinc@erols.com

ANS Communications, Inc.
1875 Campus Commons Dr., Suite 220
Reston, VA 22091
http://www.ans.net
Founded: 1991
Total Employees: 200
Annual Sales: $34 million
Industry: Telecommunications
Growth: Openings in past year, 50
Contact Bruce Bond, President/CEO; 703-758-7724; Fax: 703-758-7717; E-mail: info@ans.net

Automata, Inc.
1200 Severn Way
Sterling, VA 20166
http://www.automata.com
Founded: 1975
Total Employees: 450
Annual Sales: $60 million
Industry: Subassemblies and Components
Growth: Openings in past year, 99
Contact John Milks, President/CEO; 703-450-2600; Fax: 703-450-5871; E-mail: info@automata.com

Best Software, Inc.
1413 Isaac Newton Sq. Southwest
Reston, VA 22090
http://www.bestsoftware.com
Founded: 1982
Total Employees: 350
Annual Sales: $39.4 million
Industry: Holding Companies
Growth: Openings in past year, 66
Contact Tim Davenport, President/CEO; 703-709-5200; Fax: 703-709-9359

Betac International Corp.
2001 North Beauregard St.
Alexandria, VA 22311
http://www.betac.com
Founded: 1977
Total Employees: 470
Annual Sales: $36 million
Industries: Defense, Holding Companies, Manufacturing Equipment
Growth: Openings in past year, 69
Contact Earl F. Lockwood, President/CEO; 703-824-3100; Fax: 703-824-0333; E-mail: bahnsen@betac.com

Blessings Corp.
200 Enterprise Dr.
Newport News, VA 23603
Founded: 1944
Total Employees: 495
Annual Sales: $158.135 million
Industry: Holding Companies
Growth: Openings in past year, 33
Contact Ken Hudson, VP of Human Resources; 757-887-2100; Fax: 757-887-3787

CENCOR
5252 Cherokee Ave., Suite 300
Alexandria, VA 22312
http://www.cencoriss.com
Founded: 1987
Total Employees: 110
Annual Sales: $4.5 million
Industry: Computer Software
Growth: Openings in past year, 35
Contact Ms. Carolyn Wall, Administration Manager; 703-941-5916; Fax: 703-941-4309

Claritas Inc.
1525 Wilson Blvd., Suite 1000
Arlington, VA 22209
http://www.claritas.com
Founded: 1970
Total Employees: 375
Industries: Computer Hardware, Computer Software
Growth: Openings in past year, 150
Contact Tom Dailey, President/CEO; 703-812-2700; Fax: 703-812-2701; E-mail: info@claritas.com

CMDS
1661 Virginia Ave.
Harrisonburg, VA 22801
http://www.cmds.com
Founded: 1980
Total Employees: 130
Industry: Computer Software
Growth: Openings in past year, 30
Contact Dwight Wyse, President; 540-432-5200; Fax: 540-432-5275; E-mail: sales@cmds.com

Comdial Corp.
1180 Seminole Trail
PO Box 7266
Charlottesville, VA 22906
http://www.comdial.com
Founded: 1977
Total Employees: 830
Annual Sales: $102 million
Industries: Energy,
Holding Companies,
Telecommunications
Growth: Openings in past
year, 32
Contact Joe D. Ford,
Director of Human
Resources; 804-978-
2200; Fax: 804-978-2512

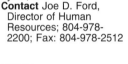

**Communication Systems
Technology, Inc.,
Manufacturing Services
& Integration Division**
8500 Phoenix Dr.
Manassas, VA 20110
Founded: 1986
Total Employees: 90
Annual Sales: $9.1 million
Industry: Subassemblies
and Components
Growth: Openings in past
year, 40
Contact Michael Kennett,
President; 703-369-6167;
Fax: 703-369-5124

**Comprehensive
Technologies
International, Inc.**
3951 Pender Dr., Suite
120
Fairfax, VA 22030
http://www.cti.com
Founded: 1980
Total Employees: 230
Industries: Computer
Hardware, Manufacturing
Equipment
Growth: Openings in past
year, 30
Contact Ms. Suzanne
Berthay, Director of
Human Resources; 703-
383-7200; Fax: 703-352-
6765; E-mail:
celbeltran@cti.com

**COMSAT RSI, Inc.,
Plexsys Wireless
Systems**
607 Herndon Pkwy., Suite
201
Herndon, VA 20170
Founded: 1991
Total Employees: 96
Annual Sales: $16 million
Industry:
Telecommunications
Growth: Openings in past
year, 41
Contact Ms. Karen
DeLeo, Director of
Human Resources; 703-
904-4000; Fax: 703-904-
0980; E-mail: csrcare@
plexsys-wireless.com

Cornet, Inc.
6800 Versar Ctr., Suite
216
Springfield, VA 22151
Founded: 1989
Total Employees: 60
Industries: Factory
Automation,
Telecommunications
Growth: Openings in past
year, 30
Contact Nat Kumar,
President; 703-658-3400;
Fax: 703-658-3440

CyberCash, Inc.
2100 Reston Pkwy., Third
Floor
Reston, VA 22091
http://www.cybercash.com
Founded: 1994
Total Employees: 200
Annual Sales: $127.439
million
Industry: Computer
Software
Growth: Openings in past
year, 130
Contact William Melton,
President/CEO; 703-620-
4200; Fax: 703-620-
4215; E-mail: info@
cybercash.com

DCS Corp.
1330 Braddock Pl.
Alexandria, VA 22314
http://www.dcscorp.com
Founded: 1977
Total Employees: 365
Annual Sales: $29.4
million
Industries: Computer
Hardware, Defense,
Factory Automation,
Manufacturing
Equipment, Photonics,
Subassemblies and
Components,
Transportation
Growth: Openings in past
year, 42
Contact James T. Wood,
President; 703-683-8430;
Fax: 703-684-7229

Deltek Systems, Inc.
8280 Greensboro Dr., 3rd
Floor
Mc Lean, VA 22102
http://www.deltek.com
Founded: 1983
Total Employees: 268
Annual Sales: $34.8
million
Industry: Computer
Software
Growth: Openings in past
year, 43
Contact Ken de Laski,
President/CEO; 703-734-
8606; Fax: 703-734-1146;
E-mail: mktgues@deltek.
com

**Dimensions
International, Inc.**
4501 Ford Ave., Suite
1200
Alexandria, VA 22302
http://www.dimen-intl.com
Founded: 1985
Total Employees: 300
Annual Sales: $37 million
Industries: Computer
Hardware, Computer
Software, Defense,
Manufacturing
Equipment,
Subassemblies and

Components,
Telecommunications
Growth: Openings in past
year, 30
Contact Dr. Robert L.
Wright, President/CEO;
703-998-0098; Fax: 703-
379-1695; E-mail:
rlwright@dimen-intl.com

**Electronic Warfare
Associates, Inc.**
13873 Park Center Rd.
Herndon, VA 22071
http://www.ewa.com
Founded: 1977
Total Employees: 400
Annual Sales: $62 million
Industries: Defense,
Subassemblies and
Components
Growth: Openings in past
year, 50
Contact Carl N. Guerreri,
President; 703-904-5700;
Fax: 703-904-5779

ENSCO, Inc.
5400 Port Royal Rd.
Springfield, VA 22151
http://www.ensco.com
Founded: 1969
Total Employees: 520
Industry: Holding
Companies
Growth: Openings in past
year, 98
Contact Ms. Joanne
McDonald, VP of Human
Resources and
Administration; 703-321-
9000; Fax: 703-321-
4529; E-mail: info@
ensco.com

ENVIRON Corp.
4350 North Fairfax Dr.
Arlington, VA 22203
Founded: 1982
Total Employees: 350
Industry: Environmental
Growth: Openings in past
year, 23
Contact Ms. Penny Wil-
liams, Human Resources
Administrator; 703-516-
2300; Fax: 703-516-2345

**Erol's Internet &
Computer**
7921 Woodruff Ct.
Springfield, VA 22151
http://www.erols.com
Founded: 1963
Total Employees: 500
Industry:
Telecommunications
Growth: Openings in past
year, 375
Contact Dennis Spina,
Chief Executive Officer;
703-321-8000; Fax: 703-
321-8316; E-mail:
sales@erols.com

**Excalibur Technologies
Corp.**
1921 Gallows Rd., Suite
200
Vienna, VA 22182
http://www.excalib.com
Founded: 1980
Total Employees: 173
Annual Sales: $20.2
million
Industry: Computer
Software
Growth: Openings in past
year, 43
Contact Pat Condo,
President; 703-761-3700;
Fax: 703-761-1990;
E-mail: info@excalib.com

**Export Software
International**
PO Box 10836
Chantilly, VA 20153
http://www.esi2000.com
Founded: 1992
Total Employees: 78
Industry: Computer
Software
Growth: Openings in past
year, 43
Contact Ms. Kimberly
Walsh, Human
Resources Manager;
703-661-9006; Fax: 703-
742-4580; E-mail:
sales@esi2000.com

Fuisz Technologies Ltd.
3810 Concorde Pkwy.,
Suite 100
Chantilly, VA 20151
http://www.fuisz.com
Founded: 1988
Total Employees: 116
Annual Sales: $8.526
million
Industries: Chemicals,
Pharmaceuticals
Growth: Openings in past
year, 56
Contact Kenneth W.
McVey, President/CEO;
703-803-3260; Fax: 703-
803-6460; E-mail: info@
fuisz.com

GTSI
4100 Lafayette Center Dr.
Chantilly, VA 20151
http://www.gtsi.com
Founded: 1983
Total Employees: 400
Annual Sales: $492 million
Industry: Computer
Hardware
Growth: Openings in past
year, 50
Contact H. Robert Boehm,
VP of Human Resources;
703-502-2000; Fax: 703-
222-5210

Halifax Corporation
5250 Cherokee Ave.
PO Box 11904
Alexandria, VA 22312
http://www.hxcorp.com
Founded: 1967
Total Employees: 660
Annual Sales: $76.278
million
Industries: Computer
Hardware, Holding
Companies,
Telecommunications
Growth: Openings in past
year, 208
Contact Howard Mills,
President; 703-750-2202;
Fax: 703-658-2411;
E-mail: halifax@hxcorp.
com

Hayes, Seay, Mattern & Mattern, Inc.
PO Box 13446
Roanoke, VA 24034
Founded: 1947
Total Employees: 450
Industries: Environmental, Manufacturing Equipment
Growth: Openings in past year, 30
Contact T. Howard Noel, President/CEO; 540-857-3100; Fax: 540-857-3180; E-mail: hsmm@roanoke.infi.net

Information Analysis, Inc.
11240 Waples Mill Rd., Suite 400
Fairfax, VA 22030
http://www.infoa.com
Founded: 1979
Total Employees: 110
Annual Sales: $11.2 million
Industry: Computer Software
Growth: Openings in past year, 30
Contact Sandor Rosenberg, President; 703-383-3000; Fax: 703-293-7979

IPC Technologies, Inc.
7200 Glen Forest Dr.
Richmond, VA 23226
http://www.ipctech.com
Founded: 1981
Total Employees: 235
Annual Sales: $20 million
Industries: Computer Hardware, Computer Software, Holding Companies
Growth: Openings in past year, 40
Contact Stormy Hamlin, Director of Strategic Services; 804-285-9300; Fax: 804-285-4492

HSI GeoTrans, Inc.
46050 Manekin Plaza., Suite 100
Sterling, VA 20166
http://www.hsigeotrans.com
Founded: 1979
Total Employees: 210
Annual Sales: $25 million
Industries: Computer Software, Energy, Environmental
Growth: Openings in past year, 35
Contact Charles Faust, President; 703-444-7000; Fax: 703-444-1685

INTECS International, Inc.
440 Viking Dr., Suite 250
Virginia Beach, VA 23452
http://www.intecs.com
Founded: 1988
Total Employees: 98
Annual Sales: $12 million
Industries: Computer Hardware, Computer Software, Manufacturing Equipment
Growth: Openings in past year, 53
Contact Ms. Pat Tsao, President/CEO; 757-486-5889; Fax: 757-486-7313; E-mail: intecs@infi.net

ITT Industries, Inc., ITT Night Vision Division
7635 Plantation Rd.
Roanoke, VA 24019
Founded: 1959
Total Employees: 800
Annual Sales: $130 million
Industries: Defense, Subassemblies and Components, Telecommunications
Growth: Openings in past year, 160
Contact Donald Hershey, Vice President/Dir. of Human Resources; 540-563-0371; Fax: 540-366-9015

InfiNet Co.
740 Duke St.
Norfolk, VA 23510
http://www.infi.net
Founded: 1994
Total Employees: 225
Annual Sales: $38 million
Industry:
Telecommunications
Growth: Openings in past year, 45
Contact David Richards, President; 757-664-2239; Fax: 757-628-1050

InteliData Technologies Corp.
13100 Worldgate Dr.
Herndon, VA 20170
http://www.intelidata.com
Founded: 1996
Total Employees: 370
Annual Sales: $70 million
Industry: Computer Software
Growth: Openings in past year, 60
Contact Ms. Cathy Carney Peters, Director of Human Resources; 703-834-8500; Fax: 703-834-8510; E-mail: info@intellidata.com

JIL Information Systems, Inc.
1608 Spring Hill Rd., Suite 300
Vienna, VA 22182
Founded: 1985
Total Employees: 188
Industries: Computer Hardware, Computer Software, Defense, Manufacturing Equipment
Growth: Openings in past year, 26
Contact Ms. Doria Ridick, Human Resources Manager; 703-749-1260; Fax: 703-749-1270; E-mail: jilsyst@databank.com

Jouan, Inc.
170 Marcel Dr.
Winchester, VA 22602
Founded: 1984
Total Employees: 80
Annual Sales: $8.1 million
Industries:
Subassemblies and
Components, Test and
Measurement
Growth: Openings in past
year, 30
Contact Charles Vestal,
Human Resources Direc-
tor; 540-869-8623; Fax:
540-869-8626

**Kasten Chase Applied
Research, Inc.**
12110 Sunset Hills Rd.,
Suite 450
Reston, VA 22090
http://www.kastenchase.
com
Founded: 1987
Total Employees: 175
Annual Sales: $30 million
Industry:
Telecommunications
Growth: Openings in past
year, 55
Contact Paul Hyde,
President/CEO; 703-715-
3197; Fax: 703-471-0760

**Kollmorgen Motion
Technologies Group**
501 First St.
Radford, VA 24141
http://www.kollmorgen.com
Founded: 1948
Total Employees: 750
Annual Sales: $110 million
Industries: Factory
Automation,
Subassemblies and
Components, Test and
Measurement
Growth: Openings in past
year, 50
Contact Dennis Mabes,
VP of Human Resources;
800-777-3788; Fax: 540-
731-0847; E-mail: kmtg@
kollmorgen.com

LCC International, Inc.
2300 Clarendon Blvd.,
Suite 800
Arlington, VA 22201
http://www.lccinc.com
Founded: 1983
Total Employees: 850
Annual Sales: $141.6
million
Industries: Computer
Software, Factory
Automation,
Manufacturing
Equipment,
Telecommunications
Growth: Openings in past
year, 148
Contact Riyush Sodha,
President/CEO; 703-351-
6666; Fax: 703-516-4950

**Logicon Ultrasystems,
Inc.**
14175 Sully Field Cir.,
Suite 700
Chantilly, VA 20151
http://www.logicon.com
Founded: 1969
Total Employees: 250
Annual Sales: $32 million
Industries: Computer
Software, Defense,
Manufacturing
Equipment,
Transportation
Growth: Openings in past
year, 65
Contact Donald Hard,
President/CEO; 703-222-
3225; Fax: 703-968-5549

Microdyne Corp.
3601 Eisenhower Ave.
Alexandria, VA 22304
http://www.mcdy.com
Founded: 1968
Total Employees: 742
Annual Sales: $99.2
million
Industries: Computer
Hardware, Holding
Companies,
Telecommunications
Growth: Openings in past
year, 68

Contact Ms. Heide
Steiner, Director of
Human Resources; 703-
329-3700; Fax: 703-329-
3722; E-mail:
webmaster@mcdy.com

MicroStrategy, Inc.
8000 Towers Crescent Dr.
Vienna, VA 22182
http://www.strategy.com
Founded: 1989
Total Employees: 547
Annual Sales: $25 million
Industry: Computer
Software
Growth: Openings in past
year, 366
Contact Michael J. Saylor,
President/CEO; 703-848-
8600; Fax: 703-848-
8610; E-mail: info@
strategy.com

Mystech Associates, Inc.
5205 Leesburg Pike, Suite
1200
Falls Church, VA 22041
http://www.mystech.com
Founded: 1971
Total Employees: 320
Annual Sales: $27.1
million
Industries: Computer
Software, Defense,
Environmental, Factory
Automation,
Manufacturing Equipment
Growth: Openings in past
year, 35
Contact Ms. Sandra
Danis, Personnel
Manager; 703-671-8680;
Fax: 703-671-8932

**Nautilus International,
Inc.**
709 Powerhouse Rd.
Independence, VA 24348
Founded: 1971
Total Employees: 300
Annual Sales: $36 million
Industry: Medical
Growth: Openings in past
year, 50
Contact Ms. Tammy
Webb, Director of Human
Resources; 540-773-
2881; Fax: 540-773-3306

NCI Information Systems, Inc.
8260 Greensboro Dr., Suite 400
Mc Lean, VA 22102
http://www.nciinc.com
Founded: 1986
Total Employees: 933
Annual Sales: $52 million
Industries: Computer Hardware, Computer Software, Manufacturing Equipment, Photonics, Telecommunications
Growth: Openings in past year, 136
Contact Ms. Maureen Fitgerald, VP of Human Resources; 703-903-0325; Fax: 703-903-9750; E-mail: busdev@nciinc.com

NetStart, Inc.
11495 Sunset Hills Rd.
Reston, VA 20190
http://www.netstartinc.com
Founded: 1995
Total Employees: 55
Annual Sales: $7.1 million
Industries: Computer Software, Telecommunications
Growth: Openings in past year, 35
Contact Robert McGovern, President/CEO; 703-709-1001; Fax: 703-709-1004; E-mail: kate@netstartinc.com

Orbital Communications Corp.
21700 Atlantic Blvd.
Dulles, VA 20166
http://www.orbcomm.net
Founded: 1990
Total Employees: 118
Annual Sales: $20 million
Industry: Telecommunications
Growth: Openings in past year, 50

Contact Alan Parker, President; 703-406-6000; Fax: 703-406-3504

Prosoft, Inc.
200 Golden Oak Ct., Reflections II, Suite 100
Virginia Beach, VA 23452
http://www.prosoft-eng.com
Founded: 1984
Total Employees: 260
Industries: Computer Hardware, Computer Software, Manufacturing Equipment, Telecommunications
Growth: Openings in past year, 89
Contact Paul K. Wong, President; 757-431-2400; Fax: 757-463-1071; E-mail: rhou@prosoft-eng.com

PSINet, Inc.
510 Huntmar Park Dr.
Herndon, VA 20170
http://www.psi.net
Founded: 1989
Total Employees: 550
Annual Sales: $89.6 million
Industry: Telecommunications
Growth: Openings in past year, 41
Contact William L. Schrader, COB/President/CEO; 703-904-4100; Fax: 703-904-4200; E-mail: info@psi.com

Quality Specialties, Inc.
PO Box 46
Hopewell, VA 23860
Founded: 1986
Total Employees: 125
Industry: Environmental
Growth: Openings in past year, 50
Contact D. Bowen Hyatt, President; 804-458-2733; Fax: 804-458-8521

Quality Systems, Inc.
8201 Greensboro Dr., Suite 1200
Mc Lean, VA 22102
http://www.qsi.com
Founded: 1981
Total Employees: 650
Annual Sales: $62 million
Industries: Computer Hardware, Computer Software
Growth: Openings in past year, 150
Contact William Shernit, Chief Executive Officer; 703-847-5820; Fax: 703-847-5887

Questech, Inc.
7600-W Leesburg Pike
Falls Church, VA 22043
Founded: 1968
Total Employees: 600
Annual Sales: $72.4 million
Industries: Computer Hardware, Computer Software, Defense
Growth: Openings in past year, 163
Contact Vincent L. Salvatori, COB/CEO; 703-760-1000; Fax: 703-760-1062

S.T. Research Corp.
8419 Terminal Rd.
Newington, VA 22122
http://www.stresearch.com
Founded: 1971
Total Employees: 150
Industries: Computer Hardware, Subassemblies and Components, Telecommunications
Growth: Openings in past year, 30
Contact S.R. Perrino, President; 703-550-7000; Fax: 703-550-0883

SETA Corp.
6862 Elm St., Suite 600
Mc Lean, VA 22101
http://www.seta.com
Founded: 1987
Total Employees: 450
Annual Sales: $33 million
Industries: Computer
Hardware, Computer
Software, Manufacturing
Equipment,
Telecommunications
Growth: Openings in past
year, 99
Contact Ranvir K. Trehan,
President; 703-821-8178;
Fax: 703-821-8274

SPOT Image Corp.
1897 Preston White Dr.
Reston, VA 20191
http://www.spot.com
Founded: 1982
Total Employees: 200
Annual Sales: $41 million
Industry:
Telecommunications
Growth: Openings in past
year, 150
Contact Neal Carney, VP
of Finance and
Administration; 703-715-
3100; Fax: 703-648-1813

**TMA Corporation,
Resources Division**
8201 Greensboro Dr.,
Suite 900
Mc Lean, VA 22102
http://www.tmaresources.
com
Founded: 1973
Total Employees: 80
Industry: Computer
Software
Growth: Openings in past
year, 40
Contact Thomas
Brantigan, Senior Vice
President; 703-847-2800;
Fax: 703-847-2899

**SMS Data Products
Group, Inc.**
1501 Farm Credit Dr.
Mc Lean, VA 22102
Founded: 1976
Total Employees: 135
Industries: Computer
Hardware, Defense
Growth: Openings in past
year, 65
Contact Albert Rosecan,
President; 703-709-9898;
Fax: 703-356-4831

**Stanford
Telecommunications,
Inc., Reston Division**
1761 Business Center Dr.
Reston, VA 22090
http://www.stel.com
Founded: 1973
Total Employees: 400
Industries: Computer
Hardware,
Telecommunications
Growth: Openings in past
year, 50
Contact Leonard
Schuchman, General
Manager; 703-438-8000;
Fax: 703-438-7900

**Universal Systems &
Technology, Inc.**
12450 Fair Lakes Cir.,
Suite 625
Fairfax, VA 22033
http://www.unitech1.com
Founded: 1988
Total Employees: 194
Annual Sales: $21.6
million
Industries: Computer
Hardware,
Telecommunications
Growth: Openings in past
year, 39
Contact Earl W. Stafford,
President; 703-502-9600;
Fax: 703-502-9300

Solutions By Design, Inc.
8603 Westwood Center
Dr., Suite 300
Vienna, VA 22182
http://www.sbd.com
Founded: 1987
Total Employees: 53
Annual Sales: $3.6 million
Industries: Computer
Hardware, Computer
Software,
Telecommunications
Growth: Openings in past
year, 33
Contact Ms. Kathy Sayer,
Director of Human
Resources; 703-827-
0300; Fax: 703-734-
8704; E-mail: asaeedi@
sbd.com

Template Software, Inc.
45365 Vintage Park Plaza,
Suite 100
Dulles, VA 20166
http://www.template.com
Founded: 1978
Total Employees: 130
Annual Sales: $14 million
Industry: Computer
Software
Growth: Openings in past
year, 50
Contact Linwood Pearce,
Chief Executive Officer;
703-318-1000; Fax: 703-
318-7378; E-mail: info@
template.com

University Online, Inc.
105 West Broad St., Suite
301, George Mason Sq.
Falls Church, VA 22046
http://www.uol.com
Founded: 1984
Total Employees: 150
Annual Sales: $19 million
Industry: Computer
Software
Growth: Openings in past
year, 110
Contact Nat P. Kannan,
COB/CEO; 703-893-
7800; Fax: 703-893-
1905; E-mail: info@uol.
com

User Technology Associates, Inc.
4301 North Fairfax Dr., Suite 400
Arlington, VA 22203
http://www.utanet.com
Founded: 1985
Total Employees: 750
Annual Sales: $97 million
Industries: Computer Hardware, Computer Software, Telecommunications
Growth: Openings in past year, 150
Contact Paul Bonolis, Director of Human Resources; 703-522-5132; Fax: 703-522-6457; E-mail: utahq@utanet.com

Vanguard Research, Inc.
10400 Eaton Pl., Suite 450
Fairfax, VA 22030
Founded: 1984
Total Employees: 160
Annual Sales: $19 million
Industries: Computer Software, Environmental, Holding Companies, Test and Measurement, Telecommunications
Growth: Openings in past year, 25
Contact Mel Chaskin, President; 703-934-6300; Fax: 703-273-9398; E-mail: vri@vriffx.com

Versatility, Inc.
11781 Lee Jackson Memorial Hwy., Suite 600
Fairfax, VA 22033
http://www.versatility.com
Founded: 1981
Total Employees: 230
Annual Sales: $27.4 million
Industry: Computer Software
Growth: Openings in past year, 80
Contact Ron Charnock, President; 703-591-2900; Fax: 703-591-2992

VIDAR Systems Corp.
460 Spring Park Pl.
Herndon, VA 20170
http://www.vidar.com
Founded: 1984
Total Employees: 130
Annual Sales: $26 million
Industry: Computer Hardware
Growth: Openings in past year, 30
Contact Ms. Sherry Cowart, Personnel Manager; 703-471-7070; Fax: 703-471-1165; E-mail: info@vidar.com

Virginia Transformer Corp.
220 Glade View Dr.
Roanoke, VA 24012
Founded: 1971
Total Employees: 240
Industries: Energy, Subassemblies and Components
Growth: Openings in past year, 65
Contact Larry Rush, Manager of Human Resources; 540-345-9892; Fax: 540-342-7694; E-mail: vtc@roanoke.infi.net

Walter Grinders, Inc.
5160 Ladland Dr.
Fredericksburg, VA 22407
Founded: 1981
Total Employees: 97
Annual Sales: $14 million
Industry: Factory Automation
Growth: Openings in past year, 27
Contact Dietmar Weselin, President; 540-898-3700; Fax: 540-898-2811

WIN Laboratories, Ltd.
11090 Industrial Rd.
Manassas, VA 22110
http://www.win-labs.com

Founded: 1980
Total Employees: 180
Industries: Computer Hardware, Telecommunications
Growth: Openings in past year, 55
Contact Ms. Christianne Tan, Vice President; 703-330-1426; Fax: 703-330-9967; E-mail: ha@win-labs.com

Xybernaut Corporation
12701 Fair Lakes Cir., Suite 550
Fairfax, VA 22033
http://www.xybernaut.com
Founded: 1990
Total Employees: 50
Annual Sales: $1.093 million
Industry: Computer Hardware
Growth: Openings in past year, 25
Contact Ms. Cheryl Nierregger, Director of Human Resources; 703-631-6925; Fax: 703-631-6734; E-mail: sales@xybernaut.com

Zimmerman Associates, Inc.
8229 Boone Blvd., Suite 200
Vienna, VA 22182
Founded: 1977
Total Employees: 300
Industry: Holding Companies
Growth: Openings in past year, 80
Contact Ms. Mary Blevins, Chief Executive Officer; 703-883-0506; Fax: 703-883-0526; E-mail: zaiamelex@aol.com

Washington

Active Voice Corp.
2901 3rd Ave., Suite 500
Seattle, WA 98121

Founded: 1983
Total Employees: 221
Annual Sales: $49.5 million
Industry: Computer Software
Growth: Openings in past year, 46
Contact Ms. Debra Faulkner, Director of Administration; 206-441-4700; Fax: 206-441-4784

Alpha Technologies, Inc.
3767 Alpha Way
Bellingham, WA 98226
http://www.alpha.com
Founded: 1977
Total Employees: 900
Industry: Energy
Growth: Openings in past year, 400
Contact Ms. Kim Harle, Human Resources Coordinator; 360-647-2360; Fax: 360-671-4936

Applied Voice Technology, Inc.
PO Box 97025
Kirkland, WA 98083
http://www.appliedvoice.com
Founded: 1982
Total Employees: 225
Annual Sales: $44 million
Industries: Computer Hardware, Holding Companies, Telecommunications
Growth: Openings in past year, 75
Contact Ms. Shannon Koenig, Human Resources Manager; 425-820-6000; Fax: 425-820-4040

Asymetrix Learning Systems, Inc.
110-110th Ave. Northeast, Suite 700
Bellevue, WA 98004
http://www.asymetrix.com
Founded: 1985
Total Employees: 300
Annual Sales: $38 million

Industry: Computer Software
Growth: Openings in past year, 25
Contact Jim Billmaier, President/CEO; 425-462-0501; Fax: 425-455-3071

Cascade Design Automation Corp.
3650 131st Ave. Southeast, Suite 650
Bellevue, WA 98006
http://www.cdac.com
Founded: 1991
Total Employees: 170
Annual Sales: $22 million
Industry: Computer Software
Growth: Openings in past year, 60
Contact Ms. Carri Virek, Director of Personnel; 425-643-0200; Fax: 425-649-7600; E-mail: info@cdac.com

Cell Therapeutics, Inc.
201 Elliott Ave., Suite 400
Seattle, WA 98119
http://www.cticseattle.com
Founded: 1992
Total Employees: 134
Industry: Biotechnology
Growth: Openings in past year, 37
Contact Ms. Susan Moore, Executive Vice President/Director of HR; 206-282-7100; Fax: 206-282-6206; E-mail: invest@cticseattle.com

Cellular Technical Services Co., Inc.
2401 Fourth Ave., Suite 808
Seattle, WA 98121
Founded: 1993
Total Employees: 177
Annual Sales: $12.5 million
Industry: Computer Software
Growth: Openings in past year, 77

Contact Ms. Lynne Sederholm, Human Resources Manager; 206-443-6400; Fax: 206-443-1550; E-mail: info@celtech.com

Clean-Pak International
4170 Lind Ave. Southwest
Renton, WA 98058
Founded: 1950
Total Employees: 450
Annual Sales: $75 million
Industries: Energy, Environmental, Manufacturing Equipment, Subassemblies and Components
Growth: Openings in past year, 49
Contact Ko Izumi, Chief Executive Officer; 206-251-8483; Fax: 206-251-9781

Columbia Analytical Services, Inc.
1317 South 13th Ave.
Kelso, WA 98626
http://www.caslab.com
Founded: 1986
Total Employees: 250
Annual Sales: $22 million
Industries: Chemicals, Environmental
Growth: Openings in past year, 40
Contact Ms. Alicia Pulaski, Human Resources Manager; 360-577-7222; Fax: 360-636-1068; E-mail: cas@caslab.com

CompuServe, Inc., Internet Division
3535 128th Ave. Southeast
Bellevue, WA 98006
http://www.sprynet.com
Founded: 1987
Total Employees: 200
Annual Sales: $34 million
Industry: Telecommunications
Growth: Openings in past year, 35

Contact Ms. Rita Moore, Human Resources Generalist; 425-957-8000; Fax: 425-957-6000; E-mail: feedback@sprynet.com

Corixa Corporation
1124 Columbia St., Suite 200
Seattle, WA 98104
Founded: 1994
Total Employees: 82
Annual Sales: $5.8 million
Industry: Pharmaceuticals
Growth: Openings in past year, 32
Contact Steven Gillis, Ph.D., President/CEO; 206-667-5711; Fax: 206-667-5715

Cymbolic Sciences International, Inc.
147 C St.
PO Box 4147
Blaine, WA 98231
Founded: 1986
Total Employees: 215
Annual Sales: $44 million
Industries: Computer Hardware, Factory Automation
Growth: Openings in past year, 65
Contact Rob Tarnowski, Director of Human Resources; 360-332-4054; Fax: 360-332-8032; E-mail: info@cymbolic.com

Dealer Information Systems Corp.
114 West Magnolia, Suite 500
Bellingham, WA 98225
http://www.dis-corp.com/~dis
Founded: 1980
Total Employees: 150
Annual Sales: $15 million
Industry: Computer Software
Growth: Openings in past year, 30

Contact Robert H. Brim, President/COB; 360-733-7610; Fax: 360-647-6921; E-mail: dis@dis-corp.com

Hytek Finishes Co.
8127 South 216th St.
Kent, WA 98032
http://www.hytekfinishes.com
Founded: 1928
Total Employees: 205
Industry: Manufacturing Equipment
Growth: Openings in past year, 65
Contact Clif Johnson, President; 253-872-7160; Fax: 253-872-7214

iCat Corp.
1420 5th Ave., Suite 1800
Seattle, WA 98101
http://www.icat.com
Founded: 1993
Total Employees: 120
Annual Sales: $15 million
Industry: Computer Software
Growth: Openings in past year, 40
Contact Craig Danuloff, President/CEO; 206-505-8800; Fax: 206-505-8810; E-mail: info@icat.com

IDD Aerospace Corp.
18225 Northeast 76th St.
PO Box 97056
Redmond, WA 98073
Founded: 1965
Total Employees: 165
Annual Sales: $21 million
Industries: Energy, Photonics, Subassemblies and Components, Transportation
Growth: Openings in past year, 65
Contact James Van Osdol, COB/CEO/President; 425-885-4353;

Fax: 425-883-0387; E-mail: mktg@iddmail.attmail.com

Immunex Corp.
51 University St.
Seattle, WA 98101
http://www.immunex.com
Founded: 1981
Total Employees: 834
Annual Sales: $151.198 million
Industry: Biotechnology
Growth: Openings in past year, 33
Contact Ms. Kathy Spencer, VP of Human Resources; 206-587-0430; Fax: 206-587-0606

Irwin Research & Development, Inc.
PO Box 10668
Yakima, WA 98909
Founded: 1975
Total Employees: 420
Industry: Factory Automation
Growth: Openings in past year, 28
Contact Jere Irwin, President; 509-248-0194; Fax: 509-248-3503

Itronix Corp.
801 South Stevens St.
Spokane, WA 99204
http://www.itronix.com
Founded: 1992
Total Employees: 300
Annual Sales: $61 million
Industry: Computer Hardware
Growth: Openings in past year, 100
Contact Steven L. Gevurtz, President/CEO; 509-624-6600; Fax: 509-626-4203

Key Technology, Inc.
150 Avery St.
Walla Walla, WA 99362
Founded: 1947

Total Employees: 490
Annual Sales: $54.341 million
Industry: Factory Automation
Growth: Openings in past year, 68
Contact Ms. Sherri Masen, Human Resources Manager; 509-529-2161; Fax: 509-522-3378

Korry Electronics Co.
901 Dexter Ave. North
Seattle, WA 98109
http://www.korry.com
Founded: 1937
Total Employees: 500
Industries: Computer Hardware, Photonics, Subassemblies and Components, Test and Measurement, Transportation
Growth: Openings in past year, 100
Contact Ms. Marlene Winter, Personnel Director; 206-281-1300; Fax: 206-281-1365; E-mail: info@korry.com

Luxar Corp.
11911 Northcreek Pkwy., Suite 200
Bothell, WA 98011
http://www.escmed.com
Founded: 1987
Total Employees: 170
Annual Sales: $20 million
Industries: Medical, Photonics
Growth: Openings in past year, 70
Contact Ms. Janet Mills, Director of Human Resources; 425-483-4142; Fax: 425-483-6844

MDS Panlabs
11804 North Creek Pkwy. South
Bothell, WA 98011
http://www.panlabs.com
Founded: 1970
Total Employees: 300

Annual Sales: $46 million
Industry: Holding Companies
Growth: Openings in past year, 50
Contact Nicholas Dykstra, Executive VP of Finance & Administration; 425-487-8200; Fax: 425-487-3787; E-mail: panlabs@panlabs.com

Metawave Communications Corporation
8700 148th Ave. Northeast
Redmond, WA 98052
http://www.metawave.com
Founded: 1995
Total Employees: 140
Industries: Computer Software, Telecommunications
Growth: Openings in past year, 100
Contact Dr. Douglas O. Reudink, President/CTO; 425-702-5600; Fax: 425-702-5970; E-mail: info@metawave.com

Mosaix, Inc.
6464 185th Ave. Northeast
Redmond, WA 98052
http://www.mosaix.com
Founded: 1978
Total Employees: 600
Annual Sales: $120 million
Industries: Computer Hardware, Computer Software, Telecommunications
Growth: Openings in past year, 100
Contact Nicholas Tiliacos, President/CEO; 425-881-7544; Fax: 206-558-6000

NeoPath, Inc.
8271 154th Ave. Northeast
Redmond, WA 98052
Founded: 1989
Total Employees: 190
Annual Sales: $2 million
Industries: Medical, Pharmaceuticals

Growth: Openings in past year, 35
Contact Rick Karnofski, Director of Human Resources; 425-869-7284; Fax: 425-869-5325

NEXTLINK Communications, Inc.
155 108th Ave., 8th Floor
Bellevue, WA 98004
http://www.nextlink.net
Founded: 1994
Total Employees: 845
Annual Sales: $25.7 million
Industry: Telecommunications
Growth: Openings in past year, 41
Contact Wayne M. Perry, Chief Executive Officer; 425-519-8900; Fax: 425-519-8910

Pathogenesis Corporation
201 Elliott Ave. West
Seattle, WA 98119
Founded: 1991
Total Employees: 110
Industry: Pharmaceuticals
Growth: Openings in past year, 40
Contact Ms. Joan Duggan, Director of Human Resources; 206-467-8100; Fax: 206-282-5065

Primex Technologies, Inc., Aerospace & Electronics Division
PO Box 97009
Redmond, WA 98073
http://www.rocket.com
Founded: 1959
Total Employees: 750
Annual Sales: $96 million
Industries: Defense, Subassemblies and Components, Test and Measurement, Transportation
Growth: Openings in past year, 50

Contact C.D. Walker, VP of Human Resources; 425-885-5000; Fax: 425-882-5804; E-mail: yan@vocher.com

Pyrotek, Inc.
9503 East Montgomery Ave.
Spokane, WA 99206
http://www.pyrotek-inc.com
Founded: 1956
Total Employees: 575
Industry: Advanced Materials
Growth: Openings in past year, 75
Contact Allan Roy, President; 509-926-6212; Fax: 509-927-2408; E-mail: jctinfo@pyrotek-inc.com

Quinton Instrument Co.
3303 Monte Villa Pkwy.
Bothell, WA 98021
Founded: 1961
Total Employees: 700
Industry: Medical
Growth: Openings in past year, 40
Contact Ed Schnebele, Director of Personnel; 425-402-2000; Fax: 425-402-2001

RealNetworks, Inc.
1111 Third Ave., Suite 2900
Seattle, WA 98101
http://www.real.com
Founded: 1994
Total Employees: 200
Industry: Computer Software
Growth: Openings in past year, 115
Contact Rob Glaser, Chief Executive Officer; 206-674-2700; Fax: 206-674-2699; E-mail: info@prognet.com

Sarif, Inc.
501 Southeast Columbia Shores Blvd.
Vancouver, WA 98661
http://www.sarif.com
Founded: 1994
Total Employees: 102
Annual Sales: $17 million
Industries: Photonics, Telecommunications
Growth: Openings in past year, 72
Contact Steve Hix, President; 360-750-0242; Fax: 360-750-0244

SeaMED Corp.
14500 Northeast 87th St.
Redmond, WA 98052
http://www.seamed.com
Founded: 1976
Total Employees: 325
Annual Sales: $32.9 million
Industry: Medical
Growth: Openings in past year, 175
Contact W. Robert Berg, President/CEO; 425-867-1818; Fax: 425-867-0622

SECOR International, Incorporated
11061 Noetheast 2nd St., Suite 102
Bellevue, WA 98004
http://www.secor.com
Founded: 1989
Total Employees: 690
Annual Sales: $84 million
Industries: Environmental, Factory Automation
Growth: Openings in past year, 40
Contact Ms. Marguerite Shuffelton, VP of Human Resources; 425-646-0231; Fax: 425-462-7592; E-mail: webmaster@secor.com

SelfServe USA
3605 132nd Ave. Southeast, Suite 150
Bellevue, WA 98006
http://www.cdi.net
Founded: 1995
Total Employees: 50
Industry: Computer Software
Growth: Openings in past year, 40
Contact Toby Tobaccowala, Chief Executive Officer; 425-313-3143; Fax: 425-649-1709; E-mail: njclark@cdi.net

Siemens Medical Systems, Inc., Ultrasound Group
22010 Southeast 51st St.
PO Box 7002
Issaquah, WA 98027
Founded: 1982
Total Employees: 490
Industry: Medical
Growth: Openings in past year, 82
Contact Lothar Koob, Group Vice President; 425-392-9180; Fax: 425-391-8362

SolutionsIQ
1260 116th Ave. Northeast
Bellevue, WA 98004
http://www.solutionsiq.com
Founded: 1979
Total Employees: 235
Annual Sales: $20 million
Industry: Holding Companies
Growth: Openings in past year, 35
Contact Douglas Wright, President/CEO; 425-451-2727; Fax: 425-451-2728; E-mail: connxfiles@solutionsiq.com

Sonus Pharmaceuticals, Inc.
22026 20th Ave.
  Southeast, Suite 102
Bothell, WA 98021
http://www.sonuspharma.
  com
Founded: 1991
Total Employees: 58
Industry: Chemicals
Growth: Openings in past
  year, 29
Contact Steven C. Quay,
  MD, Ph.D., President/
  CEO; 425-487-9500;
  Fax: 425-489-0626

Spectra Lux Corp.
11825 120th Ave.
  Northeast
Kirkland, WA 98034
Founded: 1976
Total Employees: 200
Industry: Transportation
Growth: Openings in past
  year, 75
Contact Brian Abell, VP of
  Finance/Treasurer; 425-
  823-6857; Fax: 425-821-
  3193

ST Labs, Inc.
3535 128th Ave. SE,
  Sterling Plaza, 3rd Fl.
Bellevue, WA 98006
http://www.stlabs.com
Founded: 1993
Total Employees: 200
Annual Sales: $6.9 million
Industries: Computer
  Hardware, Computer
  Software
Growth: Openings in past
  year, 140
Contact Phil Herres,
  President; 425-974-0174;
  Fax: 425-974-0150;
  E-mail: info@stlabs.com

Starwave Corp.
13810 Southeast Eastgate
  Way, Suite 400
Bellevue, WA 98005

http://www.starwave.com
Founded: 1992
Total Employees: 300
Annual Sales: $61 million
Industries: Computer
  Hardware, Computer
  Software,
  Telecommunications
Growth: Openings in past
  year, 75
Contact Mike Slade,
  President/CEO; 425-957-
  2000; Fax: 425-957-2009

Sygenex, Inc.
15446 Bel-red Rd., Suite
  450
Redmond, WA 98052
Founded: 1984
Total Employees: 65
Industries: Computer
  Hardware, Computer
  Software, Defense,
  Manufacturing
  Equipment,
  Transportation
Growth: Openings in past
  year, 25
Contact Ms. Donna L.
  Roberts, President/CEO;
  425-881-5500; Fax: 425-
  869-2837; E-mail:
  sygenex@ix.netcom.com

Telect, Inc.
2111 North Molter Rd.
PO Box 665
Liberty Lake, WA 99019
http://www.telect.com
Founded: 1982
Total Employees: 747
Annual Sales: $75 million
Industries: Factory
  Automation,
  Subassemblies and
  Components, Test and
  Measurement,
  Telecommunications
Growth: Openings in past
  year, 135
Contact Ms. Colleen
  Connors, Director of
  Human Resources; 509-
  926-6000; Fax: 509-926-
  8915; E-mail: getinfo@
  telect.com

UniTrek Corp.
3000 Lewis & Clark Hwy.,
  Suite 2
Vancouver, WA 98661
Founded: 1990
Total Employees: 125
Industry: Subassemblies
  and Components
Growth: Openings in past
  year, 25
Contact Juan Sifontes,
  Finance and Accounting
  Manager; 360-699-7277;
  Fax: 360-694-9230

Virtual Spin, LLC.
1307 120th Ave. Northeast
Bellevue, WA 98004
http://www.virtualspin.com
Founded: 1995
Total Employees: 45
Industries: Computer
  Software,
  Telecommunications
Growth: Openings in past
  year, 30
Contact Ms. Vicki Foster,
  Director of Technology
  Support; 206-974-1100;
  Fax: 206-974-1200;
  E-mail: info@virtualspin.
  com

Visio Corp.
520 Pike St., Suite 1800
Seattle, WA 98101
http://www.visio.com
Founded: 1990
Total Employees: 235
Annual Sales: $59.7
  million
Industry: Computer
  Software
Growth: Openings in past
  year, 60
Contact Jeremy A. Jaech,
  COB/CEO/President;
  206-521-4500; Fax: 206-
  521-4501

WRQ, Inc.
1500 Dexter Ave. North
Seattle, WA 98109

http://www.wrq.com
Founded: 1981
Total Employees: 675
Annual Sales: $130 million
Industry: Computer
Software
Growth: Openings in past
year, 73
Contact Ms. Char
Harrington, Director of
Project & Property
Mgmt.; 206-217-7500;
Fax: 206-217-0293;
E-mail: info@wrq.com

Zetron, Inc.
PO Box 97004
Redmond, WA 98073
http://www.zetron.com
Founded: 1981
Total Employees: 350
Annual Sales: $40 million
Industries: Computer
Software,
Telecommunications
Growth: Openings in past
year, 70
Contact John Reece,
President; 425-820-6363;
Fax: 425-820-7031;
E-mail: zetron@zetron.
com

West Virginia

**Pierce Companies, Inc.,
Micross Division**
3 Bryan Dr.
Wheeling, WV 26003
http://www.microsswv.com
Founded: 1962
Total Employees: 85
Annual Sales: $13.5
million
Industry: Computer
Hardware
Growth: Openings in past
year, 25
Contact Ken Jordan, Vice
President/General
Manager; 304-232-0899;
Fax: 304-232-0996;
E-mail: micross@ovnet.
com

Wisconsin

**ABB Flexible
Automation, Inc.**
2487 South Commerce Dr.
New Berlin, WI 53151
http://www.abb.se/flexible/
welcome.htm
Founded: 1984
Total Employees: 450
Industries: Factory
Automation, Holding
Companies
Growth: Openings in past
year, 49
Contact Silas Nichols,
President; 414-785-3400;
Fax: 414-785-0342

**Automating Peripherals,
Inc.**
310 North Wilson Ave.
Hartford, WI 53027
http://www.api-wi.com
Founded: 1981
Total Employees: 88
Industry: Computer
Software
Growth: Openings in past
year, 27
Contact Luis Garcia,
President; 414-673-6815;
Fax: 414-673-2650

CMD Corp.
2901 East Pershing St.
PO Box 1279
Appleton, WI 54912
Founded: 1980
Total Employees: 120
Industries: Factory
Automation,
Manufacturing Equipment
Growth: Openings in past
year, 25
Contact Ms. Julaine
Kluever, Human
Resources Administrator;
920-730-6888; Fax: 920-
730-6880

Converter Concepts, Inc.
100 Industrial Pkwy.
Pardeeville, WI 53954

Founded: 1976
Total Employees: 190
Annual Sales: $23 million
Industries: Energy,
Subassemblies and
Components
Growth: Openings in past
year, 35
Contact Joe Felder,
Human Resources
Manager; 608-429-3000;
Fax: 608-429-9241

Eder Industries, Inc.
2250 West Southbranch
Blvd.
Oak Creek, WI 53154
http://www.execpc.com/
~eder
Founded: 1953
Total Employees: 220
Industry: Subassemblies
and Components
Growth: Openings in past
year, 29
Contact Ron Rutowski,
Human Resources
Manager; 414-761-0400;
Fax: 414-761-0582;
E-mail: eder@execpc.
com

**Electronic Theatre
Controls, Inc.**
3030 Laura Ln.
Middleton, WI 53562
http://www.etcconnect.com
Founded: 1975
Total Employees: 470
Annual Sales: $98 million
Industry: Energy
Growth: Openings in past
year, 250
Contact Fred Foster,
President; 608-831-4116;
Fax: 608-836-1736;
E-mail: mail@etcconnect.
com

**Enterprise
Communications, Inc.**
21045 Enterprise Ave.
Brookfield, WI 53045
http://www.e-c.net
Founded: 1994
Total Employees: 195

Industry:
Telecommunications
Growth: Openings in past year, 34
Contact J.J. Blonien, President; 414-860-6300; Fax: 414-860-6305; E-mail: info@e-c.net

Findley Adhesives, Inc.
11326 Watertown Plank Rd.
Wauwatosa, WI 53226
http://www.atofindley.com
Founded: 1912
Total Employees: 490
Industry: Advanced Materials
Growth: Openings in past year, 37
Contact Michael Klonne, President/CEO; 414-774-2250; Fax: 414-774-8075; E-mail: info@atofindley.com

Flodar Fluid Power Fittings, Inc.
1864 Nagle Ave.
PO Box 1810
Manitowoc, WI 54221
Founded: 1960
Total Employees: 150
Industry: Subassemblies and Components
Growth: Openings in past year, 50
Contact Mark Lukas, President; 920-684-0011; Fax: 920-684-7210

Great Lakes Instruments, Inc.
9020 West Dean Rd.
Milwaukee, WI 53224
Founded: 1970
Total Employees: 230
Annual Sales: $31 million
Industries: Environmental, Test and Measurement
Growth: Openings in past year, 30
Contact Chris Dreher, President; 414-355-3601; Fax: 414-355-8346

J.J. Keller & Associates, Inc.
3003 West Breezewood Ln.
PO Box 368
Neenah, WI 54957
http://www.jjkeller.com
Founded: 1953
Total Employees. 800
Annual Sales: $110 million
Industry: Computer Software
Growth: Openings in past year, 31
Contact Tony La Malfa, Corporate Personnel Manager; 920-722-2848; Fax: 920-727-7526; E-mail: sales@jjkeller.com

Koss Corp.
4129 North Port Washington Ave.
Milwaukee, WI 53212
http://www.koss.com
Founded: 1958
Total Employees: 260
Annual Sales: $39.554 million
Industry:
Telecommunications
Growth: Openings in past year, 28
Contact Ms. Cheryl Mike, Director of Human Resources; 414-964-5000; Fax: 414-964-8615

Lunar Corp.
313 West Beltline Hwy.
Madison, WI 53713
http://www.lunarcorp.com
Founded: 1978
Total Employees: 270
Annual Sales: $81.4 million
Industry: Medical
Growth: Openings in past year, 40
Contact Ms. Ann Trainor, Human Resources Manager; 608-274-2663; Fax: 608-274-5374; E-mail: us.sales@lunarcorp.com

MagneTek Drives & Systems
16555 West Ryerson Rd.
New Berlin, WI 53151
Founded: 1901
Total Employees: 450
Annual Sales: $61 million
Industries:
Subassemblies and Components, Test and Measurement
Growth: Openings in past year, 99
Contact Ms. Beth Johnson, Director of Human Resources; 414-782-0200; Fax: 414-782-1283

Milsco Manufacturing Co., Inc.
9009 North 51st St.
Milwaukee, WI 53223
Founded: 1925
Total Employees: 428
Annual Sales: $52 million
Industry: Manufacturing Equipment
Growth: Openings in past year, 53
Contact Dave Anderson, President; 414-354-0500; Fax: 414-354-0508

MTI Electronics, Inc.
W133 N5139 Campbell Dr.
Menomonee Falls, WI 53051
http://www.mti-intl.com
Founded: 1978
Total Employees: 500
Industry: Subassemblies and Components
Growth: Openings in past year, 100
Contact Gregory S. Martinek, President/CEO; 414-783-6080; Fax: 414-783-4959

Nicolet Instrument Corp.
5225 Verona Rd.
Madison, WI 53711
http://www.nicolet.com
Founded: 1967
Total Employees: 570
Annual Sales: $77 million

Industries: Photonics, Test and Measurement
Growth: Openings in past year, 118
Contact Fred Walder, General Manager; 608-276-6100; Fax: 608-273-5046; E-mail: nicinfo@nicolet.com

Osmonics, Autotrol Corp.
5730 North Glenn Park Rd.
Milwaukee, WI 53209
Founded: 1967
Total Employees: 250
Annual Sales: $30 million
Industry: Environmental
Growth: Openings in past year, 40
Contact Ms. Laura Rasmussen, Human Resources Supervisor; 414-238-4400; Fax: 414-238-4402

Persoft, Inc.
465 Science Dr.
Madison, WI 53711
http://www.persoft.com
Founded: 1982
Total Employees: 150
Annual Sales: $19 million
Industry: Computer Software
Growth: Openings in past year, 50
Contact Ms. Bonnie McMullen-Lawton, Personnel Director; 608-273-6000; Fax: 608-273-8227; E-mail: sales@persoft.com

Rockwell Automation, Rockwell Software, Inc.
2424 South 102nd St.
West Allis, WI 53227

http://www.software.rockwell.com
Founded: 1985
Total Employees: 350
Industry: Computer Software
Growth: Openings in past year, 75
Contact Scott Zifferer, President/CEO; 414-321-8000; Fax: 414-321-2211

Waukesha Cherry-Burrell
611 Sugar Creek Rd.
Delavan, WI 53115
http://www.waukesha-cb.com
Founded: 1995
Total Employees: 840
Annual Sales: $143 million
Industries: Energy, Subassemblies and Components
Growth: Openings in past year, 227
Contact Bob Summers, VP of Human Resources; 414-728-1900; Fax: 800-252-5012; E-mail: custserv@waukesha-cb.com

Wisconsin Machine Tool Corp.
445 South Curtis Rd.
West Allis, WI 53214
http://www.machine-tool.com
Founded: 1945

Total Employees: 225
Annual Sales: $23 million
Industry: Factory Automation
Growth: Openings in past year, 25
Contact Ms. Tiffany Dietz, Human Resources Manager; 414-302-3200; Fax: 414-302-3210

Wollard Airport Equipment Co., Inc.
PO Box 265
Eau Claire, WI 54702
Founded: 1917
Total Employees: 150
Industries: Factory Automation, Transportation
Growth: Openings in past year, 50
Contact Kevin Steingart, President; 715-835-3151; Fax: 715-835-6625

Wyoming

Data Broadcasting Corp.
3490 Clubhouse Dr., Box I-2
Jackson, WY 83001
http://www.dbc.com
Founded: 1982
Total Employees: 805
Annual Sales: $92.480 million
Industries: Holding Companies, Telecommunications
Growth: Openings in past year, 146
Contact Alan J. Hirschfield, Co-COB/Co-CEO; 307-733-9742; Fax: 307-733-4935

HIDDEN JOB MARKET 1999

Indexes

In the preceding part of *Peterson's Hidden Job Market 1999,* company profiles appear alphabetically within each state, providing a geographic directory of the fastest-growing technology companies in the United States. To make your search for the right job opportunity even easier, this section features three indexes.

The first, the **Industry Index,** lists all companies in this book according to the industry or industries in which they are active, along with the page number of their detailed description. Because of the diversity of opportunities offered by high-tech companies, you might find the kind of position you are looking for in more than one area. Don't limit your possibilities!

The second index, the **Company Index,** lists all companies in *Peterson's Hidden Job Market 1999* alphabetically, giving their state abbreviation and the page number on which their detailed description appears.

The third index, the **Metropolitan Area Index,** lists the country's major metropolitan areas and the companies located within these areas. Areas usually span several cities and/or states and are defined by the dominant metropolitan area. For instance, Florence, Kentucky would be found under "Cincinnati" because Cincinnati dominates this particular metropolitan area.

INDUSTRY INDEX

Advanced Materials

ACMI Michigan Casting Center, 142
ACTS Testing Labs, Inc., 166
Advanced Packaging Technology of America, 30
Alliance Pharmaceutical Corp., 31
Allied Mineral Products, Inc., 181
AlliedSignal Inc., AlliedSignal Advanced Microelectronic Materials, 31
American Synthetic Rubber Corp., 118
Amoco Polymer, Inc., 99
Astor Corporation, 178
Atlas Electric Devices Co., 105
Auto-Air Composites, Inc., 143
BYK-Chemie, USA, 85
Cabaco, Inc., 26
Carboline Co., 154
Casting Technology Co., 112
CCX, Inc., Hanover Wire Cloth Division, 193
Ceradyne, Inc., 38
Certech, Inc., 160
Cesar Color, Inc., 38
Chemfab Corp., 157
Coherent, Inc., Auburn Group, 39
Colormatrix Corp., 182
Compositech, Ltd., 168
CONAM Inspection, Inc., 40
Counter Point Furniture Products, Inc., 143
Croda, Inc., 161
CTL-Aerospace, Inc., 182
Cuming Corp., 129
Denison Industries, Inc., 209
DSM Desotech Inc., 106
EG&G Automotive Research, Inc., 209
Electronic Designs, Inc., 130

Electro-Science Laboratories, Inc., 194
Ellison Surface Technologies, 118
Emcore Corp., 161
Emerson and Cuming Composite Materials, Inc., 131
Fansteel, Inc., Wellman Dynamics Division, 114
Findley Adhesives, Inc., 235
FMC Corp., Pharmaceutical Division, 194
Geltech, Inc., 95
Gold Shield, Inc., 49
Hanson Engineers, Inc., 107
Hemlock Semiconductor Corp., 144
Heraeus Amersil, Inc., 100
Hitchiner Manufacturing Co., Inc., Gas Turbine Division, 157
Hitchiner Manufacturing Co., Inc., Nonferrous Division, 155
Howmet Corp., Ti-Cast Division, 144
Hughes Manufacturing, Inc., 95
Hussey Copper, Ltd., 195
Imperial Adhesives, Inc., 183
Industrial Dielectrics, Inc., 113
IRI International Corp., 212
Kindt-Collins Co., 183
Kleinfelder, Inc., 54
Koppel Steel Corp., 196
Lifecore Biomedical, Inc., Oral Restorative Division, 149
Lydall, Inc., Westex Division, 179
Manufacturing Sciences Corp., 205
M.C. Gill Corp., 56
MEDTOX Laboratories, Inc., 149
M.K. Morse Co., 184
Nanophase Technologies Corporation, 109
Nuclear Metals, Inc., 136

Oceaneering Space Systems, 213
Pilkington Aerospace, Inc., 64
Plastic Fabricating Co., Inc., 117
Poco Graphite, Inc., 214
Polycom Huntsman, Inc., 198
Pyrotek, Inc., 232
Quality Assurance Engineering, Inc., 66
Quest International Flavors & Food Ingredients, 109
Reinhold Industries, Inc., 68
Remel, Inc., 117
Rodel, Inc., 91
Sawyer Research Products, Inc., 185
Sawyer Research Products, Inc., Sawyer Crystal Systems Division, 215
Schott Glass Technologies, Inc., 199
Seal Products, Inc., 89
Sekisui America Corp., 176
Sequa Chemicals, Inc., 204
Sermatech International, Inc., 200
SGL Technic, Inc., 71
SPARTA, Inc., 73
Spiveco, Inc., 73
Springborn Testing and Research, Inc., 89
Stelax Industries, Ltd., 216
Technical Materials, Inc., 202
Titanium Hearth Technologies, Inc., 201
Velsicol Chemical Corp., 111
Vesuvius Lava Co., 217
Viratec Thin Films, Inc., 153
Western Atlas Inc., Landis/Gardner/CITCO Division, 201

Biotechnology

ACTS Testing Labs, Inc., 166

Chemicals

Computer Hardware

Computer Software

Defense

Factory Automation

Allied Products Corp.,
Verson Division, 104
Alloyd Co., Inc., 104
Amada Engineering
Services, Inc., 32
American Science and
Engineering, Inc., 127
American Technical
Molding Corp., 92
Ameritec Corp., 32
AMETEK, Inc., Dixson
Division, 82
Anorad Corp., 167
Applied Research
Associates, Inc., 165
Asymtek, 33
Atlas Electric Devices Co.,
105
Automatic Feed Co., 181
Automatic Systems
Developers, Inc., 167
Autosplice, Inc., 34
Barnstead, Thermolyne
Corp., 114
Basic Machinery Co., Inc.,
178
Baystate/Sterling, Inc., 128
Bell Technologies, Inc., 92
Berg Chilling Systems,
Inc., 105
Berghof/America, 35
B.F. Goodrich Aerospace
Test Systems, JCAir, 116
Bihler of America, 160
Blue Grass Manufacturing
Co. of Lexington, Inc.,
118
Burnham Products, Inc.,
116
Cabaco, Inc., 26
CABLExpress Corp., 168
Cagelec AEG Automation
Systems Corp., 192
Callidus Technologies Inc.,
186
Carl Zeiss IMT Corp., 147
Cascade Microtech, Inc.,
188
CCX, Inc., Hanover Wire
Cloth Division, 193
CD Associates, Inc., 37
Central Plastics Co., Inc.,
186
Ceradyne, Inc., 38
Channel Commercial
Corp., 38
Chantland Co., 114
CMD Corp., 234
Cognex Corp., 129

Coherent, Inc., Auburn
Group, 39
Computational Systems,
Inc., 205
Consolidated Devices,
Inc., 40
Cornet, Inc., 222
Credence Systems Corp.,
41
Cullom Machine Tool &
Die, Inc., 205
Cymbolic Sciences
International, Inc., 230
Danieli Wean, 182
Daniel Woodhead Co., 106
Dayton T. Brown, Inc.,
Engineering and Test
Division, 169
DCS Corp., 222
Detroit Tool and
Engineering, Peer
Division, 143
Deublin Co., 106
DICKEY-john Corp., 106
Durr Automation, Inc., 144
Dynetics, Inc., 24
Eastman Worldwide, 170
EDAC Technologies Corp.,
86
EFD, Inc., 202
Electroglas, Inc., 45
Electronic Designs, Inc.,
130
Electronic Retailing
Systems International,
Inc., 86
Energy Sciences, Inc., 131
Entek IRD International
Corporation, 182
Equipe Technologies, Inc.,
46
E-TEK Dynamics, Inc., 45
Everett Charles
Technologies, Ostby-
Barton Pylon Division,
202
Exclusive Design Co., Inc.,
47
Extrude Hone Corp., 194
Fiber Instrument Sales
Inc., 170
FLIR Systems, Inc., 189
Fusion Semiconductor
Systems, 122
Gagemaker, Inc., 210
GEC Alsthom, Inc., 170
Genesis Systems Group,
115
Gerber Optical, Inc., 87

GMT Corp., 115
GSE Systems, Inc., 122
Hanard Machine, Inc., 189
Hansford Manufacturing
Corp., 171
Heyco Products, Inc., 162
Hitachi America, Ltd.,
Power and Industrial
Division, 171
Huffman Corp., 203
Hypertherm, Inc., 157
Ingersoll Cutting Tool Co.,
107
Inspex, Inc., 133
Interactive Video Systems,
Inc., 133
International Business
Machines Corp.,
Manufacturing
Technology Center, 96
Irwin Research &
Development, Inc., 230
ITW Ransburg
Electrostatic Systems,
183
Jacobs Chuck
Manufacturing Co., 203
Keptel, Inc., 162
Key Technology, Inc., 230
Kindt-Collins Co., 183
Kobelco America, Inc., 212
Kollmorgen Motion
Technologies Group, 225
Kollsman, Inc., 158
Kras Corp., 196
Krautkramer Branson, 196
LCC International, Inc.,
225
LCI Corp., 179
LESCO, 55
Lindgren RF Enclosures,
Inc., 108
Liquid Control Corp., 184
Loranger International
Corp., 197
MAC Equipment, Inc., 155
Mag-Tek, Inc., 56
Mansur Industries Inc., 96
Manufacturing Technology,
Inc., 56
Marsh Co., 108
Mazak Corp., 118
McClain Industries, Inc.,
145
Medar, Inc., 145
Mestek, Inc., Cooper-
Weymouth, Peterson
Division, 119

Holding Companies

Terracon Companies, Inc., 117
Terumo Medical Corp., 165
Thermedics Detection, Inc., 140
Transact Technologies, Inc., 90
Transistor Devices, Inc., 165
Trans-Lux Corp., 90
Trek Industries, Inc., 77
Tricon Industries, Inc., 111
Trio-Tech International, 77
TriQuint Semiconductor, Inc., 190
Twin City Fan Companies, Ltd., 152
Tyrex Manufacturing Group LLP, 217
UltraViolet Devices, Inc., 78
Unicomp, Inc., 103
United Oil Recovery, Inc., 90
USWeb Corp., 79
U.S. Wireless Corp., 78
Vanguard Research, Inc., 228
Veeco Instruments, Inc., 177
Venturian Corp., 153
Viktron West Chicago, 111
ViroMed Laboratories, Inc., 153
Visigenic Software, Inc., 80
Vulcan Engineering Co., 25
Waterlink, Inc., 186
Watson Pharmaceuticals, Inc., 81
WavePhore, Inc., 29
Westwood Corp., 187
Will-Burt Co., 186
Wilton Corp., 111
WinStar Communications, Inc., 177
Wire Pro, Inc., 165
World Access, Inc., 104
Worldtalk Corp., 81
WPI Group, Inc., 159
Zimmerman Associates, Inc., 228
Zygo Corp., 91

Manufacturing Equipment

ABB Air Preheater, Inc., 166

AB Plastics, 29
Ace Metal Fabricators, Inc., 126
Acme Laundry Products, Inc., 29
ACMI Michigan Casting Center, 142
ACTS Testing Labs, Inc., 166
Advanced Manufacturing Technologies, Inc., 91
Advanced Marine Enterprises, Inc., 220
Ahntech, Inc., 31
Airtronics Metal Products, Inc., 31
Allied Products Corp., Verson Division, 104
AlliedSignal Inc.,
AlliedSignal Advanced Microelectronic Materials, 31
Alloyd Co., Inc., 104
Alphatech, Inc., 127
A&M Engineering Plastics, Inc., 91
American Technical Molding Corp., 92
AMETEK, Inc., Dixson Division, 82
AMTX, Inc., 166
Annapolis Micro Systems, Inc., 120
Applied Films Corporation, 82
Applied Research Associates, Inc., 165
Applied Science and Technology, Inc., 127
Asyst Technologies, Inc., 33
Atcor Corporation, 34
Automated Packaging Systems, Inc., 181
Automatic Systems Developers, Inc., 167
Avedon Engineering, Inc., 82
Bailey Transportation Products, Inc., 182
Balzers Tool Coating, Inc., 167
Basic Machinery Co., Inc., 178
bd Systems, Inc., 35
Betac International Corp., 221
Bihler of America, 160

Blue Grass Manufacturing Co. of Lexington, Inc., 118
Blue Star Plastics, Inc., 118
Boeing Cummings Research Park, 24
Brooks Automation, Inc., 128
BTD Manufacturing, Inc., 147
Cabaco, Inc., 26
Casting Technology Co., 112
CFM Technologies, Inc., 193
Chip Express Corp., 38
Chromalloy Gas Turbine Corp., Caval Tool Division, 85
Chromalloy Gas Turbine Corp., Chromalloy New York Division, 168
Clean-Pak International, 229
CMD Corp., 234
Coherent, Inc., Auburn Group, 39
Columbia Technology Corp., 168
Comprehensive Technologies International, Inc., 222
CONAM Inspection, Inc., 40
Contract Machining & Manufacturing Co., Inc., 118
Counter Point Furniture Products, Inc., 143
Credence Systems Corp., 41
Cullom Machine Tool & Die, Inc., 205
Danieli Wean, 182
Dayton T. Brown, Inc., Engineering and Test Division, 169
DCS Corp., 222
Denison Industries, Inc., 209
Detroit Tool Metal Products, 154
Dimensions International, Inc., 222
Discas, Inc., 86
D-Velco Manufacturing of Arizona, Inc., 26

Medical

Pharmaceuticals

Photonics

Total Control Products, Inc., 111
Trans-Lux Corp., 90
TRUMPF Inc., 90
TRW Inc., Automotive Electronics Group, 146
UDT Sensors, Inc., 78
UNC Johnson Technology, 146
Veeco Instruments, Inc., 177
Veeco Process Meterology, 28
Viratec Thin Films, Inc., 153
Virtual Reality, Inc., 165
Welch Allyn, Inc., Lighting Products Division, 177
Whelen Engineering Co., 91
Zygo Corp., 91

Subassemblies and Components

ABB CEAG Power Supplies, 91
Accu-Tech Corporation, 99
ACT Networks, Inc., 30
Advanced Circuit Technology, Inc., 157
Advanced Energy Industries, Inc., 82
Advanced Filtration Concepts, Inc., 117
Advanced Packaging Technology of America, 30
Aeroflex Incorporated, 166
Airborn, Inc., 206
Airtronics Metal Products, Inc., 31
Alflex Corp., 31
Alkon Corp., 159
Allegheny Powder Metallurgy, Inc., 191
Allen Telecom, Inc., Antenna Specialists Division, 181
Allen Telecom, Inc., Decibel Products Division, 206
Allied Healthcare Products, Inc., 154
Allomatic Products Co., Inc., 112
Alpha Industries, Inc., 126
Alteon Networks, Inc., 31
Ambac International, Inc., 203

Anadigics, Inc., 160
Annapolis Micro Systems, Inc., 120
Anorad Corp., 167
Applied Science and Technology, Inc., 127
Astec America, Inc., ENI Division, 167
Automata, Inc., 221
Automated Packaging Systems, Inc., 181
Automatic Systems Developers, Inc., 167
Autosplice, Inc., 34
Avibank Mfg., Inc., 34
Aydin Telemetry, 192
Bal Seal Engineering Co., Inc., 34
Barnstead, Thermolyne Corp., 114
BEI Sensors & Systems Co., Systron Donner Inertial Division, 35
Belkin Components, 35
Bell Technologies, Inc., 92
Benchmarq Microelectronics, Inc., 207
Berg Chilling Systems, Inc., 105
Berg Electronics Corp., Cable Assembly Division, 85
Berghof/America, 35
Berk-Tek, 192
Bihler of America, 160
Bimba Manufacturing Co., 105
Black Box Corporation, 192
Bowmar Instrument Corp., White Microelectronics Division, 25
Burge Electronics, Inc., RF Coaxial Division, 112
Burnham Products, Inc., 116
Cabaco, Inc., 26
CABLExpress Corp., 168
Calex Manufacturing Co., Inc., 36
Cal Quality Electronics, Inc., 36
CANTEX, Inc., 207
Carley Lamps, Inc., 37
Celeritek, Inc., 37
Central Plastics Co., Inc., 186
Ceradyne, Inc., 38

Ceramatec, Inc., 218
Chantland Co., 114
Chip Express Corp., 38
Chips and Technologies, Inc., 38
Chloride Systems, 178
Chromalloy Gas Turbine Corp., Chromalloy New York Division, 168
Circle Seal Controls, Inc., 39
Clairson Industries Corp., 93
Clean-Pak International, 229
Climco Coils Co., 105
Columbia Gorge Center, 188
Columbia Technical Services, 129
Communication Systems Technology, Inc., Manufacturing Services & Integration Division, 222
Components Specialties, Inc., 168
Compressor Controls Corp., 114
Computer Products Power Conversion America, 129
Conax Florida Corp., 93
Condor Reliability Services, Inc., 40
Continental Circuits, Inc., 94
Continuum Electro Optics, Inc., Scientific Division, 41
Converter Concepts, Inc., 234
Corcom, Inc., 106
Crane Co., Hydro-Aire Division, 41
Cree Research, Inc., 179
Cristek Interconnects, Inc., 41
CSD Industries, 42
CTS Corp., Microelectronics, 112
Cyberex, Inc., 182
Daniel Woodhead Co., 106
Dan-Lock Industrial, Inc., 208
DCS Corp., 222
Denison Industries, Inc., 209
Denro, Inc., 121
Details, Inc., 43

Semiconductor Laser International Corporation, 176

Semiconductor Packaging Materials Co., Inc., 176

Semiconductor Packaging Materials Corp., Retconn Division, 89

Senior Flexonics, Katema Division, 70

Senior Systems Technology, Inc., 70

Sherwood, Taylor-Wharton Gas Equipment Division, 176

SH Leggitt, Inc., 215

Sigma Circuits, Inc., 71

Silicon Power Corp., 72

Silicon Storage Technology, Inc., 72

SMC Pneumatics, Inc., 113

Solitron, Vector Microwave Products, Inc., 98

Somnus Medical Technologies, Inc., 73

Source Electronics Corp., 159

Specialty Plastics, Inc., 119

SpecTran Corp., 139

Spectrian Corp., 73

Spectrum Astro, Inc., 28

Spellman High Voltage Electronics Corp., 176

Spirax Sarco Engineered Systems, Inc., 200

Springborn Testing and Research, Inc., 89

Stanford Telecommunications, Inc., 73

Steel Parts Corp., 113

S.T. Research Corp., 226

Structural North America, Codeline Division, 74

Sturman Industries, 84

Sun Hydraulics Corp., 98

SUPERMICRO Computer, Inc., 75

Supertex, Inc., 75

TA Manufacturing Co., 75

Tech Etch, Inc., 140

TelCom Semiconductor, Inc., 75

Telect, Inc., 233

Teleflex Fluid Systems, Inc., 89

Tessera, Inc., 76

Texas Hydraulics, 216

Tex-Tube Co., 216

Thermalloy, Inc., 217

T.M. Morris Manufacturing Co., Inc., 113

Total Control Products, Inc., 111

Tran Electronics Corp., 152

Transcon Technologies, Inc., 140

Transistor Devices, Inc., 165

Trek Industries, Inc., 77

Trident Microsystems, Inc., 77

TriQuint Semiconductor, Inc., 190

Triumph Controls, Inc., 201

Trompeter Electronics, Inc., 77

Tru-Turn Corp., 146

TRW Inc., Automotive Electronics Group, 146

TUV Product Service, Inc., 141

Twin City Fan Companies, Ltd., 152

Tyrex Manufacturing Group LLP, 217

UDT Sensors, Inc., 78

UIP Engineered Products, 111

Unibus, Inc., 185

UniTrek Corp., 233

Universal Security Instruments, Inc., 125

Urologix, Inc., 153

U.S. Assemblies New England, 141

U.S. Engine Valve Co., 204

Vadem, Inc., 79

Valley-Todeco, 79

Varian Tempe Electronics Center, 28

Vernitron Corp., Motion Controls Group, 79

Vertek International, Inc., 80

VertiCom, Inc., 80

Vickers Electronic Systems, 186

Viktron West Chicago, 111

Virginia Transformer Corp., 228

Vitesse Semiconductor Corporation, 80

V-Tron Electronics Corp., 141

Warner Electric, Superior Electric Divsion, 90

WARN Industries, Inc., 190

Waukesha Cherry-Burrell, 236

Welch Allyn, Inc., Lighting Products Division, 177

Wells Electronics, Inc., 114

Western Atlas Inc., Landis/Gardner/CITCO Division, 201

World Access, Inc., 104

WPI Group, Inc., 159

Zoran Corp., 82

Zurn Industries, Inc., Flush Valve Operations Division, 180

Telecommunications

AAC Corp., 29

Access Teleconferencing International, Inc., 220

ACCU WEATHER, Inc., 191

ACE*COMM Corp., 119

ACS Dataline, 206

ACT Networks, Inc., 30

Adaptive Optics Associates, Inc., 126

ADC Kentrox, 187

AdiCom Wireless, Inc., 30

Advanced Computer Communications, 30

Advanced Modular Solutions, Inc., 126

AIWA AMERICA, INC., 159

Allen Telecom, Inc., Antenna Specialists Division, 181

Allen Telecom, Inc., Decibel Products Division, 206

Alliance of Professionals & Consultants, Inc., 178

Allied Group, Inc., 85

Alpha Industries, Inc., 126

AlphaNet Solutions, Inc., 159

Alpine Computer Systems, Inc., 127

Alteon Networks, Inc., 31

American Information Systems, Inc., 105

American Megatrends, Inc., 99

Test and Measurement

Schlumberger Industries, Meter Communications Systems Division, 103

Schumacher, 70

Science Applications International Corp., Radeco Division, 70

Sensitech, Inc., 139

Shaffer, Inc., 215

Sherwood, Taylor-Wharton Gas Equipment Division, 176

Shomiti Systems, Inc., 71

Silicon Power Corp., 72

Somanetics Corp., 146

Spellman High Voltage Electronics Corp., 176

Spirax Sarco Engineered Systems, Inc., 200

Springborn Testing and Research, Inc., 89

STEAG MicroTech, Inc., 216

Sun Hydraulics Corp., 98

Techsonic Industries, Inc., 25

TelCom Semiconductor, Inc., 75

Telect, Inc., 233

Thermedics Detection, Inc., 140

Total Control Products, Inc., 111

Trane Company, Building Automation Systems Division, 152

Trek Industries, Inc., 77

Triumph Controls, Inc., 201

TRW Inc., Automotive Electronics Group, 146

TUV Product Service, Inc., 141

UDT Sensors, Inc., 78

Unisyn Technologies, Inc., 141

Universal Security Instruments, Inc., 125

Vanguard Research, Inc., 228

Vasco Corp., 111

VEDA Systems, Inc., 125

Veeco Instruments, Inc., 177

Veeco Process Meterology, 28

Vernitron Corp., Motion Controls Group, 79

Vickers Electronic Systems, 186

Warner Electric, Superior Electric Divsion, 90

Whelen Engineering Co., 91

Wireless Telccom Group, Inc., 165

Zygo Corp., 91

Transportation

Accessory Controls and Equipment Corp., 84

Advanced Aerodynamics & Structures, Inc., 30

Advanced Marine Enterprises, Inc., 220

Aeronautical Systems, Inc., 30

Aeronca, Inc., 181

Aircraft Braking Systems Corp., 181

Airport Systems International, Inc., 115

American Eurocopter Corp., 206

American Science and Engineering, Inc., 127

Argo-Tech Corp., 181

ASD-Simula, 25

Ashtech, Inc., 33

Auto-Air Composites, Inc., 143

Avibank Mfg., Inc., 34

Aydin Telemetry, 192

Ayres Corp., 99

Barrios Technology, Inc., 207

bd Systems, Inc., 35

BEI Sensors & Systems Co., Systron Donner Inertial Division, 35

Boeing Cummings Research Park, 24

Buderus Sell Aviation, Inc., 116

Burnham Products, Inc., 116

Ceradyne, Inc., 38

CFAN Co., 207

Chromalloy Gas Turbine Corp., Caval Tool Division, 85

Chromalloy Gas Turbine Corp., Chromalloy New York Division, 168

Chromalloy T.A.D., 193

Circle Seal Controls, Inc., 39

Communication Systems Technology, Inc., 121

Condor Systems, Inc., 40

Crane Co., Hydro-Aire Division, 41

Crestview Aerospace Corp., 91

DCS Corp., 222

Denro, Inc., 121

DICKEY-john Corp., 106

Display Solutions, Inc., 100

D-Velco Manufacturing of Arizona, Inc., 26

Dynacs Engineering Co., Inc., 94

Eagle Traffic Control Systems, 209

Econolite Control Products, Inc., 45

EDAC Technologies Corp., 86

EG&G Astrophysics Research Corp., 45

Electrodynamics, Inc., 106

Ellanef Manufacturing Corp., 170

Etak, Inc., 46

Everett Charles Technologies, Ostby-Barton Pylon Division, 202

Federal APD, Inc., 144

Flight Dynamics, 188

FLIR Systems, Inc., 189

FMC Corp., Jetway Systems Division, 219

Fugro-McClelland Marine Geosciences, Inc., 210

GEC Alsthom, Inc., 170

GHSP, 144

Global Engineering & Technology, Inc., 116

HAC Corp., 211

Honda Engineering North America, Inc., 183

Howmet Corp., Ti-Cast Division, 144

Howmet Dover Casting, 162

IDD Aerospace Corp., 230

Kaiser Electroprecision, 54

Kollsman, Inc., 158

Korry Electronics Co., 231

LB&M Associates, Inc., 187

Lehr Precision, Inc., 184

Litton Industries, Inc., Life Support Division, 115

COMPANY INDEX

A

AAC Corp. (CA), 29
AAON, Inc. (OK), 186
ABB Air Preheater, Inc. (NY), 166
ABB CEAG Power Supplies (FL), 91
ABB Flexible Automation, Inc. (WI), 234
ABC Technologies, Inc. (OR), 187
AB Plastics (CA), 29
ABT Corp. (NY), 166
Access Graphics, Inc. (CO), 82
Accessory Controls and Equipment Corp. (CT), 84
Access Software, Inc. (UT), 218
Access Teleconferencing International, Inc. (VA), 220
Accipiter, Inc. (NC), 178
ACCRAM, Inc. (AZ), 25
Accu-Fab California Systems, Inc. (CA), 29
AccuMed International, Inc. (IL), 104
Accu-Med Services, Inc. (OH), 181
Accu-Sort Systems, Inc. (PA), 191
Accu-Tech Corporation (GA), 99
ACCU WEATHER, Inc. (PA), 191
ACE*COMM Corp. (MD), 119
AC&E Ltd. (VA), 220
Ace Metal Fabricators, Inc. (MA), 126
Acme Laundry Products, Inc. (CA), 29
ACMI Michigan Casting Center (MI), 142
ACS Dataline (TX), 206
Active Voice Corp. (WA), 228
ACT Networks, Inc. (CA), 30
ACTS Testing Labs, Inc. (NY), 166
ADAC Laboratories (CA), 30

Adaptive Optics Associates, Inc. (MA), 126
ADC Kentrox (OR), 187
Adhesives Research, Inc. (PA), 191
AdiCom Wireless, Inc. (CA), 30
AdminStar, Inc. (KY), 117
ADP-Integrated Medical Solutions, Inc. (MD), 120
ADS Environmental Services, Inc. (AL), 24
Advanced Aerodynamics & Structures, Inc. (CA), 30
Advanced Assembly Automation, Inc. (OH), 181
Advanced Automation, Inc. (SC), 202
Advanced Bioresearch Associates (CA), 30
Advanced Circuit Technology, Inc. (NH), 157
Advanced Computer Communications (CA), 30
Advanced Digital Data, Inc. (NJ), 159
Advanced Energy Industries, Inc. (CO), 82
Advanced Engineering & Management Associates, Inc., Aerospace Engineering Division (VA), 220
Advanced Filtration Concepts, Inc. (KY), 117
Advanced Machine Vision Corp. (OR), 188
Advanced Manufacturing Technologies, Inc. (FL), 91
Advanced Marine Enterprises, Inc. (VA), 220
Advanced Modular Solutions, Inc. (MA), 126
Advanced Packaging Technology of America (CA), 30
Advanced Technology Systems, Inc. (VA), 220

Advanced Visual Systems, Inc. (MA), 126
Advent Software, Inc. (CA), 30
Aeroflex Incorporated (NY), 166
Aeronautical Systems, Inc. (CA), 30
Aeronca, Inc. (OH), 181
AETRIUM, Incorporated (MN), 147
Affinity, Inc. (NH), 157
Affymetrix, Inc. (CA), 30
Agile Software Corp. (CA), 31
AGR International, Inc. (PA), 191
Ahntech, Inc. (CA), 31
Airborn, Inc. (TX), 206
Aircraft Braking Systems Corp. (OH), 181
Airport Systems International, Inc. (KS), 115
Airtronics Metal Products, Inc. (CA), 31
AIWA AMERICA, INC. (NJ), 159
Alflex Corp. (CA), 31
Alias, Wavefront (CA), 31
Alkon Corp. (NJ), 159
Allaire Corp. (MA), 126
ALLDATA Corp. (CA), 31
Allegheny Plastics, Inc. (PA), 191
Allegheny Powder Metallurgy, Inc. (PA), 191
Allen Telecom, Inc., Antenna Specialists Division (OH), 181
Allen Telecom, Inc., Decibel Products Division (TX), 206
Alliance of Professionals & Consultants, Inc. (NC), 178
Alliance Pharmaceutical Corp. (CA), 31
Allied Group, Inc. (CT), 85
Allied Healthcare Products, Inc. (MO), 154
Allied Mineral Products, Inc. (OH), 181
Allied Products Corp., Verson Division (IL), 104

Clayton Industries, Inc. (CA), 39

Clean-Pak International (WA), 229

Clear Communications Corp. (IL), 105

Clifford of Vermont, Inc. (VT), 220

Climco Coils Co. (IL), 105

CliniComp International (CA), 39

Clinicor, Inc. (TX), 208

CLONTECH Laboratories, Inc. (CA), 39

Clover Communications (MI), 143

CMD Corp. (WI), 234

CMDS (VA), 221

CMI-Competitive Solutions, Inc. (MI), 143

CMS, Inc. (FL), 93

CNET: The Computer Network (CA), 39

Coda, Inc. (NH), 157

Cognex Corp. (MA), 129

Coherent, Inc., Auburn Group (CA), 39

Collagen Corp. (CA), 39

Collagenesis, Inc. (MA), 129

COLLEGIS (FL), 93

Colorado Memory Systems, Inc. (CO), 83

Colormatrix Corp. (OH), 182

Columbia Analytical Services, Inc. (WA), 229

Columbia Gorge Center (OR), 188

Columbia Technical Services (MA), 129

Columbia Technology Corp. (NY), 168

Comdial Corp. (VA), 222

Command Data, Incorporated (AL), 24

Command Software Systems, Inc. (FL), 93

Command Systems, Inc. (CT), 85

Commercial Data Corporation (TN), 204

CommNet Cellular, Inc. (CO), 83

Commonwealth Long Distance (NJ), 161

Commonwealth Technology, Inc. (KY), 118

Communication Intelligence Corp. (CA), 39

Communication Systems Technology, Inc., Manufacturing Services & Integration Division (VA), 222

Communication Systems Technology, Inc. (MD), 121

Commvault Systems (NJ), 161

COMNET Corporation (MD), 121

Com Net, Inc. (OH), 182

Compaction America, Inc. (IL), 105

Compass Plastics & Technologies, Inc. (CA), 39

Components Specialties, Inc. (NY), 168

Compositech, Ltd. (NY), 168

Comprehensive Technologies International, Inc. (VA), 222

Compressor Controls Corp. (IA), 114

Compris Technologies, Inc. (GA), 100

CompuServe, Inc., Internet Division (WA), 229

Computational Systems, Inc. (TN), 205

Computech, Inc. (MD), 121

Computech, Inc. (MI), 143

Computer Information Technology Corp. (AZ), 26

Computer Intelligence (CA), 40

Computerized Structural Analysis & Research Corp. (CA), 40

Computer Marketing Corp. (UT), 218

Computer Merchant Ltd. (MA), 129

Computer Network Technology Corp. (MN), 147

Computer Output Microfilm Corp. (OH), 182

COMPUTERPEOPLE, Inc., RPM Systems Division (CA), 40

Computer Products Power Conversion America (MA), 129

Computer Resource Associates, Inc. (PA), 193

Computer Systems Co., Inc. (OH), 182

Computhink, Inc. (IL), 105

Computone Corp. (GA), 100

Computron Software, Inc. (NJ), 161

COMSAT RSI, Inc., Plexsys Wireless Systems (VA), 222

Comtec Information Systems, Inc. (RI), 201

CONAM Inspection, Inc. (CA), 40

Conax Florida Corp. (FL), 93

Concord Communications, Inc. (MA), 129

Condor Reliability Services, Inc. (CA), 40

Condor Systems, Inc. (CA), 40

Connect Computer Co. (MN), 147

ConsenSys Software Corporation (CA), 40

Consolidated Devices, Inc. (CA), 40

Constellar Corp. (CA), 40

Consulting Partners, Inc. (TX), 208

A Consulting Team (NY), 166

Continental Circuits, Inc. (FL), 94

Continental Resources, Inc. (MA), 129

Continuum Electro Optics, Inc., Scientific Division (CA), 41

Contract Machining & Manufacturing Co., Inc. (KY), 118

Control Specialties, Inc. (TX), 208

Control Systems International, Inc. (TX), 208

Converter Concepts, Inc. (WI), 234

Coopers & Lybrand, LLP, SysteCon Division (GA), 100

CooperVision, Inc. (NY),
169
Copper Mountain
Networks, Inc. (CA), 41
Corcom, Inc. (IL), 106
Corixa Corporation (WA),
230
Cornet, Inc. (VA), 222
CorNet International, Ltd.
(PA), 193
Corporate Word, Inc. (PA),
193
Corsair Communications,
Inc. (CA), 41
CoSystems Inc. (CA), 41
Counter Point Furniture
Products, Inc. (MI), 143
CPSI (AL), 24
Crane Co., Hydro-Aire
Division (CA), 41
Creative Computer
Solutions, Inc. (CA), 41
Creative Labs, Inc. (CA),
41
Creative Socio-Medics
Corp. (NY), 169
Credence Systems Corp.
(CA), 41
Credit Management
Solutions, Inc. (MD), 121
Cree Research, Inc. (NC),
179
Crestview Aerospace
Corp. (FL), 94
Cristek Interconnects, Inc.
(CA), 41
Croda, Inc. (NJ), 161
CSD Industries (CA), 42
CSG Systems, Inc. (NE),
156
CSG Systems
International, Inc. (CO),
83
CSS Laboratories, Inc.
(CA), 42
CTI, Inc. (TN), 205
CTL-Aerospace, Inc. (OH),
182
CTS Corp.,
Microelectronics (IN),
112
Cullom Machine Tool &
Die, Inc. (TN), 205
Cuming Corp. (MA), 129
CuraGen Corp. (CT), 86
Curative Health Services
(NY), 169
Curbell, Inc. (NY), 169

C.W. Costello &
Associates, Inc. (MA),
128
Cyanotech Corporation
(HI), 104
CyberCash, Inc. (VA), 222
Cyberex, Inc. (OH), 182
CyberGate, Inc. (FL), 94
CyberMedia Inc. (CA), 42
Cybertek, Inc. (TX), 208
Cyborg Systems, Inc. (IL),
106
Cyclades Corp. (CA), 42
Cygnus Solutions, Inc.
(CA), 42
Cylink Corp. (CA), 42
Cymbolic Sciences
International, Inc. (WA),
230
Cymer, Inc. (CA), 42
Cynara Co. (TX), 208
Cynosure, Inc. (MA), 130
Cytyc Corp. (MA), 130

D

Dako Corp. (CA), 42
Dalloz Safety (FL), 94
Daly & Wolcott, Inc. (RI),
202
Danieli Wean (OH), 182
Daniel Woodhead Co. (IL),
106
Dan-Lock Industrial, Inc.
(TX), 208
DASCOM, Inc. (CA), 42
Database Technologies,
Inc. (MA), 130
Data Broadcasting Corp.
(WY), 236
Datamax International
Corp. (FL), 94
Datastream Systems, Inc.
(SC), 203
Data Systems Marketing
Corp. (MD), 121
Data Systems Network
Corp. (MI), 143
DataTools, Inc. (CA), 43
Data Tree Corp. (CA), 43
DataWorks Corporation
(CA), 43
Datum, Inc. (CA), 43
Davidson & Associates,
Inc. (CA), 43
Dayton T. Brown, Inc.,
Engineering and Test
Division (NY), 169
DCS Corp. (VA), 222

DDL Electronics, Inc. (CA),
43
Dealer Information
Systems Corp. (WA),
230
Decision Research Corp.
(HI), 104
Decision Systems, Inc.
(MN), 147
Deja News, Inc. (TX), 208
Delta & Pine Land
Company (MS), 153
Delta Health Systems
(PA), 193
Deltek Systems, Inc. (VA),
222
Denali, Inc. (TX), 209
Denison Industries, Inc.
(TX), 209
Denro, Inc. (MD), 121
Dentrix Dental Systems,
Inc. (UT), 218
Dentsply International,
Inc., Preventive Care
Division (PA), 193
DePuy Orthopedic
Technology, Inc. (CA), 43
Desktop Engineering
International, Inc. (NJ),
161
Details, Inc. (CA), 43
Detroit Tool and
Engineering, Peer
Division (MI), 143
Detroit Tool Metal Products
(MO), 154
Deublin Co. (IL), 106
Devtec Corp. (CT), 86
Dharma Systems, Inc.
(NH), 157
D.H. Marketing and
Consulting, Inc. (PA),
193
Diacom Corp. (NH), 157
Diagnostic Chemicals
Limited (USA) (CT), 86
Diagnostic Systems
Laboratories, Inc. (TX),
209
Diamond Lane
Communications Corp.
(CA), 43
Diamond Management
Systems, Inc. (PA), 194
Diamond Multimedia
Systems, Inc. (CA), 44
Diamond Products, Inc.
(FL), 94
Diba, Inc. (CA), 44

T

Taconic Farms, Inc. (NY), 176

Tactica Corp. (OR), 190

TA Manufacturing Co. (CA), 75

Tangent Computer, Inc. (CA), 75

Tanknology-NDE Corp. (TX), 216

Tanury Industries (RI), 202

Tatung Co. of America (CA), 75

TAXWARE International, Inc. (MA), 140

Team Personnel, Inc. (FL), 98

Tech Etch, Inc. (MA), 140

Technical Directions, Inc. (TX), 216

Technical Materials, Inc. (RI), 202

Techsonic Industries, Inc. (AL), 25

Tecom Industries, Inc. (CA), 75

Teklogix, Inc. (KY), 119

Tekno, Inc. (KY), 119

Teknowledge Corp. (CA), 75

Tekram Technology Corp. (TX), 216

TelCom Semiconductor, Inc. (CA), 75

Telco Systems, Inc. (MA), 140

Telect, Inc. (WA), 233

Teleflex Fluid Systems, Inc. (CT), 89

Telegen Corp. (CA), 76

Telegra Corp. (CA), 76

Telegroup, Inc. (IA), 115

Telepartner International North America, Inc. (CT), 90

TelTech International Corp. (NY), 177

Teltronics, Inc. (FL), 99

Template Software, Inc. (VA), 227

Temtrol, Inc. (OK), 187

Tenax Corporation (MD), 125

TennMark Telecommunications, Inc. (TN), 205

Teradyne, Inc., Assembly Test/Walnut Creek Division (CA), 76

Terasys, Inc. (IL), 110

Terex Handlers (MI), 146

Terracon Companies, Inc. (KS), 117

Terumo Medical Corp. (NJ), 165

Tessera, Inc. (CA), 76

Teva Pharmaceuticals USA, Inc. (PA), 200

Texas Hydraulics (TX), 216

Texstar, Inc. (TX), 217

TexTek Plastics (TX), 217

Tex-Tube Co. (TX), 216

3Com Corp., Palm Computing, Inc. (CA), 29

3D Systems, Inc. (CA), 29

Thermalloy, Inc. (TX), 217

Thermal Transfer Corp. (PA), 201

Therma-Wave, Inc. (CA), 76

Thermedics Detection, Inc. (MA), 140

Thermogenesis Corp. (CA), 76

Thermwood Corp. (IN), 114

Thoratec Laboratories Corp. (CA), 76

3X Corporation (OH), 180

Timesavers, Inc. (MN), 152

Titanium Hearth Technologies, Inc. (PA), 201

TLF Associates, Inc. (CT), 90

TMA Corporation, Resources Division (VA), 227

TMCI Electronics, Inc. (CA), 76

T.M. Morris Manufacturing Co., Inc. (IN), 113

TMS, Inc. (OK), 187

T-NETIX Inc. (CO), 84

Tollgrade Communications, Inc. (PA), 201

TomaHawk II, Inc. (CA), 76

Tom Snyder Productions (MA), 140

Topeka Metal Specialties, Inc. (KS), 117

Toshiba Ceramics America, Inc. (OR), 190

Total Control Products, Inc. (IL), 111

Trane Company, Building Automation Systems Division (MN), 152

Tran Electronics Corp. (MN), 152

Transact Technologies, Inc. (CT), 90

Trans-Ameritech (CA), 77

Transarc Corporation (PA), 201

Transcon Technologies, Inc. (MA), 140

Transistor Devices, Inc. (NJ), 165

Trans-Lux Corp. (CT), 90

TranSystems Corp. (MO), 156

Travel Technologies Group, L.P. (TX), 217

TreaTek-CRA (NY), 177

Trek Industries, Inc. (CA), 77

Tricon Industries, Inc. (IL), 111

Trident Microsystems, Inc. (CA), 77

Trigem America Corp. (CA), 77

Tri-Industries, Inc. (IN), 114

Trillium Digital Systems, Inc. (CA), 77

Trio-Tech International (CA), 77

Triple G Corporation (NY), 177

Triple-I, Inc. (KS), 117

TriQuint Semiconductor, Inc. (OR), 190

Triumph Controls, Inc. (PA), 201

Trompeter Electronics, Inc. (CA), 77

True Software, Inc. (MA), 140

TRUMPF Inc. (CT), 90

Trusted Information Systems, Inc. (MD), 125

Tru-Turn Corp. (MI), 146

TRW Inc., Automotive Electronics Group (MI), 146

TSI International Software, Ltd. (CT), 90

TSW International, Inc. (GA), 103

Tumbleweed Software Corporation (CA), 77

Tut Systems, Inc. (CA), 77

TUV Product Service, Inc. (MA), 141
TV/COM International, Inc. (CA), 78
Twin City Fan Companies, Ltd. (MN), 152
TYAN Computer Corp. (CA), 78
Tyrex Manufacturing Group LLP (TX), 217

U

UCS, Inc. (FL), 99
UDT Sensors, Inc. (CA), 78
UIP Engineered Products (IL), 111
Ulead Systems, Inc. (CA), 78
Ultra Clean Technology (CA), 78
Ultradata Corporation (CA), 78
Ultrafem, Inc. (NY), 177
Ultranet Communications, Inc. (MA), 141
Ultratech Stepper, Inc. (CA), 78
UltraViolet Devices, Inc. (CA), 78
UMAX Technologies, Inc. (CA), 78
UNC Johnson Technology (MI), 146
Unibus, Inc. (OH), 185
Unicomp, Inc. (GA), 103
UNIFAB International, Inc. (LA), 119
UNIFI Communications, Inc. (MA), 141
Unison Software, Inc. (CA), 79
Unisyn Technologies, Inc. (MA), 141
Unitech Systems, Inc. (IL), 111
United Oil Recovery, Inc. (CT), 90
United States Diamond Wheel Co. (IL), 111
United States Filter Corp., Davis Fabrication Division (GA), 104
Unitrac Software Corporation (MI), 146
UniTrek Corp. (WA), 233
Universal Security Instruments, Inc. (MD), 125

Universal Systems & Technology, Inc. (VA), 227
Universal Tax Systems, Inc. (GA), 104
University Online, Inc. (VA), 227
Urologix, Inc. (MN), 153
UroMed Corporation (MA), 141
U.S. Assemblies New England (MA), 141
US Computer Group, Inc. (NY), 177
U.S. Engine Valve Co. (SC), 204
User Technology Associates, Inc. (VA), 228
USLink, Inc. (MN), 153
USWeb Corp. (CA), 79
U S WEST Interactive (CO), 84
U.S. Wireless Corp. (CA), 78
Utimaco Mergent (CT), 90
Utopia Technology Partners, Inc. (CA), 79

V

Vadem, Inc. (CA), 79
Vality(R) Technology, Inc. (MA), 141
Valley-Todeco (CA), 79
Valmont Microflect (OR), 190
Vanguard Research, Inc. (VA), 228
Varian Tempe Electronics Center (AZ), 28
Vasco Corp. (IL), 111
VEDA Systems, Inc. (MD), 125
Veeco Instruments, Inc. (NY), 177
Veeco Process Meterology (AZ), 28
Vela Research, Inc. (FL), 99
Velsicol Chemical Corp. (IL), 111
Venturian Corp. (MN), 153
Verilink Corp. (CA), 79
VeriSign, Inc. (CA), 79
VERITAS Software Corp. (CA), 79
Vernitron Corp., Motion Controls Group (CA), 79

Versant Object Technology (CA), 80
Versatility, Inc. (VA), 228
Vertek International, Inc. (CA), 80
Vertex Inc. (PA), 201
VertiCom, Inc. (CA), 80
Vesuvius Lava Co. (TX), 217
ViaSat, Inc. (CA), 80
Vickers Electronic Systems (OH), 186
VIDAR Systems Corp. (VA), 228
VideoServer, Inc. (MA), 141
Viewlogic Systems, Inc. (MA), 141
Vignette Corp. (TX), 217
Viisage Technology, Inc. (MA), 142
Viking Components, Inc. (CA), 80
Viktron West Chicago (IL), 111
Viratec Thin Films, Inc. (MN), 153
Virginia Transformer Corp. (VA), 228
ViroMed Laboratories, Inc. (MN), 153
Virtual Reality, Inc. (NJ), 165
Virtual Spin, LLC. (WA), 233
Visibility Inc. (MA), 142
Visigenic Software, Inc. (CA), 80
Visio Corp. (WA), 233
Visual Networks, Inc. (MD), 125
VITCO, Inc. (IN), 114
Vitech America, Inc. (FL), 99
Vitesse Semiconductor Corporation (CA), 80
VIVUS, Inc. (CA), 80
Voice Control Systems, Inc. (TX), 217
Voicetek Corporation (MA), 142
Voxware, Inc. (NJ), 165
VPNet Technologies, Inc. (CA), 80
VTEL Corp. (TX), 217
V-Tron Electronics Corp. (MA), 141
Vulcan Engineering Co. (AL), 25

METROPOLITAN INDEX

Laboratory Tops, Inc. (TX), 212

MagRabbit, Inc. (TX), 213

Metrowerks, Inc. (TX), 213

Pervasive Software, Inc. (TX), 214

Power Computing Corp. (TX), 214

Progressive System Technologies, Inc. (TX), 215

SH Leggitt, Inc. (TX), 215

SMART Technologies, Inc. (TX), 215

STEAG MicroTech, Inc. (TX), 216

Symtx, Inc. (TX), 216

Tanknology-NDE Corp. (TX), 216

Tekram Technology Corp. (TX), 216

Tyrex Manufacturing Group LLP (TX), 217

Vignette Corp. (TX), 217

VTEL Corp. (TX), 217

BAKERSFIELD, CA

Scaled Composites, Inc. (CA), 70

BALTIMORE, MD

American Environmental Network, Inc. (MD), 120

Annapolis Micro Systems, Inc. (MD), 120

California Microwave, Inc., Airborne Systems Integration (MD), 120

Communication Systems Technology, Inc. (MD), 121

Credit Management Solutions, Inc. (MD), 121

EOG, Inc. (MD), 122

Estimation, Inc. (MD), 122

FiberTech Medical, Inc. (MD), 122

Forensic Technologies International Corp. (MD), 122

GSE Systems, Inc. (MD), 122

Guilford Pharmaceuticals Inc. (MD), 122

Hittman Materials & Medical Components, Inc. (MD), 122

Hunter Group (MD), 123

LB & B Associates (MD), 123

MCI Systemhouse Lerning Technology (MD), 123

Meridian Medical Technologies, Inc. (MD), 123

Nichols Research, CSSI (MD), 124

Osiris Therapeutics, Inc. (MD), 124

PATS, Inc. (MD), 124

Peri Formwork Systems, Inc. (MD), 124

RDA Consultants, Ltd. (MD), 124

RPM Consulting, Inc. (MD), 124

RWD Technologies, Inc. (MD), 124

Sherwin-Williams Co., Cleaning Solutions Group (MD), 125

Tenax Corporation (MD), 125

Trusted Information Systems, Inc. (MD), 125

Universal Security Instruments, Inc. (MD), 125

Ward Machinery Co. (MD), 126

XDB Systems, Inc. (MD), 126

BARNSTABLE-YARMOUTH, MA

Infinium Software, Inc. (MA), 133

SENCORP SYSTEMS, Inc. (MA), 139

BATON ROUGE, LA

Specialty Plastics, Inc. (LA), 119

BELLINGHAM, WA

Alpha Technologies, Inc. (WA), 229

Cymbolic Sciences International, Inc. (WA), 230

Dealer Information Systems Corp. (WA), 230

BENTON HARBOR, MI

Detroit Tool and Engineering, Peer Division (MI), 143

BERGEN-PASSAIC COUNTIES, NJ

AIWA AMERICA, INC. (NJ), 159

Audible, Inc. (NJ), 160

BEI Medical Systems Co., Inc. (NJ), 160

Certech, Inc. (NJ), 160

Computron Software, Inc. (NJ), 161

Desktop Engineering International, Inc. (NJ), 161

International Discount Telephone, Inc. (NJ), 162

Magic Solutions, Inc. (NJ), 163

Metal Improvement Co., Inc. (NJ), 163

Wireless Telecom Group, Inc. (NJ), 165

BINGHAMTON, NY

Semiconductor Laser International Corporation (NY), 176

BIRMINGHAM, AL

Command Data, Incorporated (AL), 24

Revere, Inc. (AL), 25

Vulcan Engineering Co. (AL), 25

BOSTON, MA-NH

Adaptive Optics Associates, Inc. (MA), 126

Advanced Modular Solutions, Inc. (MA), 126

Advanced Visual Systems, Inc. (MA), 126

Allaire Corp. (MA), 126

Alpha Industries, Inc. (MA), 126

Alphatech, Inc. (MA), 127

Alpine Computer Systems, Inc. (MA), 127

CINCINNATI, OH-KY-IN

CLEVELAND-LORAIN-ELYRIA, OH

COLUMBIA, SC

COLUMBUS, OH

DALLAS, TX

Star Cutter Co. (MI), 146
TRW Inc., Automotive
  Electronics Group (MI),
  146

DUBUQUE, IA

Barnstead, Thermolyne
  Corp. (IA), 114

DUTCHESS COUNTY, NY

Automatic Systems
  Developers, Inc. (NY),
  167
Indotronix International
  Corp. (NY), 171

EAU CLAIRE, WI

Wollard Airport Equipment
  Co., Inc. (WI), 236

ELKHART-GOSHEN, IN

VITCO, Inc. (IN), 114

EL PASO, TX

Pollak Engineered
  Products Group,
  Transportation
  Electronics Division (TX),
  214

ERIE, PA

Ever-Tite Coupling Co.,
  Inc. (PA), 194
PHB, Inc., Molding
  Division (PA), 198

FARGO-MOORHEAD, ND-MN

Fargo Assembly Co., Inc.
  (ND), 180
Great Plains Software, Inc.
  (ND), 180
Phoenix International
  Corporation (ND), 180

FAYETTEVILLE-SPRINGDALE-ROGERS, AR

INDUTEC Corp. (AR), 29
Pel-Freez, Inc. (AR), 29

FORT COLLINS-LOVELAND, CO

Advanced Energy
  Industries, Inc. (CO), 82
Atrix Laboratories, Inc.
  (CO), 82
Colorado Memory
  Systems, Inc. (CO), 83

FORT LAUDERDALE, FL

Andrx Corp. (FL), 92
Andrx Pharmaceuticals,
  Inc. (FL), 92
AquaCare Systems, Inc.
  (FL), 92
Aquagenix Land-Water
  Technology, Inc. (FL), 92
Citrix Systems, Inc. (FL),
  93
CyberGate, Inc. (FL), 94
Guardian International,
  Inc. (FL), 95
ProxyMed, Inc. (FL), 97
UCS, Inc. (FL), 99

FORT WALTON BEACH, FL

Crestview Aerospace
  Corp. (FL), 94

FORT WAYNE, IN

Steel Parts Corp. (IN), 113

FORT WORTH-ARLINGTON, TX

Healthpoint, Ltd. (TX), 211
RELTEC Corp., RELTEC
  Transmission Products
  (TX), 215

GARY, IN

Point Medical Corp. (IN),
  113

GRAND JUNCTION, CO

AMETEK, Inc., Dixson
  Division (CO), 82

GRAND RAPIDS-MUSKEGON-HOLLAND, MI

ACMI Michigan Casting
  Center (MI), 142
CMI-Competitive Solutions,
  Inc. (MI), 143
Counter Point Furniture
  Products, Inc. (MI), 143
GHSP (MI), 144
Howmet Corp., Ti-Cast
  Division (MI), 144
Prein & Newhof, Inc. (MI),
  146
UNC Johnson Technology
  (MI), 146

GREENSBORO—WINSTON-SALEM—HIGH POINT, NC

Falk Integrated
  Technologies, Inc. (NC),
  179
Lydall, Inc., Westex
  Division (NC), 179
RF Micro Devices, Inc.
  (NC), 180

GREENVILLE-SPARTANBURG-ANDERSON, SC

Advanced Automation, Inc.
  (SC), 202
Datastream Systems, Inc.
  (SC), 203
Enterprise Computer
  Systems, Inc. (SC), 203
Jacobs Chuck
  Manufacturing Co. (SC),
  203

HAMILTON-MIDDLETOWN, OH

Aeronca, Inc. (OH), 181

HARRISBURG-LEBANON-CARLISLE, PA

Chromalloy T.A.D. (PA),
  193

MEDFORD-ASHLAND, OR

Advanced Machine Vision
Corp. (OR), 188

MELBOURNE-TITUSVILLE-PALM BAY, FL

Advanced Manufacturing
Technologies, Inc. (FL),
91
AmPro Corp. (FL), 92
Johnson Matthey
Electronic Assembly
Services, Inc. (FL), 96
Q-bit Corp. (FL), 97
Software Technology, Inc.
(FL), 98

MEMPHIS, TN-AR-MS

Buckman Laboratories
International, Inc. (TN),
204
Celcore, Inc. (TN), 204
Commercial Data
Corporation (TN), 204

MIAMI, FL

Arnet Pharmaceutical
Corp. (FL), 92
Equitrac Corp. (FL), 94
FDP Corp. (FL), 95
Hi-Rise Recycling
Systems, Inc. (FL), 95
Holographic Dimensions,
Inc. (FL), 95
Internet Communications
of America, Inc. (FL), 96
Mansur Industries Inc.
(FL), 96
Omega Research, Inc.
(FL), 97
Raltron Electronics Corp.
(FL), 98
Renex Corp. (FL), 98
Vitech America, Inc. (FL),
99

MIDDLESEX-SOMERSET-HUNTERDON COUNTIES, NJ

Anadigics, Inc. (NJ), 160
Ariel Corp. (NJ), 160

Bihler of America (NJ), 160
Emcore Corp. (NJ), 161
Integratise, Inc. (NJ), 162
Interferon Sciences, Inc.
(NJ), 162
Med-Link Technologies,
Inc. (NJ), 163
RFE Industries, Inc. (NJ),
164
Terumo Medical Corp.
(NJ), 165

MILWAUKEE-WAUKESHA, WI

ABB Flexible Automation,
Inc. (WI), 234
Automating Peripherals,
Inc. (WI), 234
Eder Industries, Inc. (WI),
234
Enterprise
Communications, Inc.
(WI), 234
Findley Adhesives, Inc.
(WI), 235
Great Lakes Instruments,
Inc. (WI), 235
Koss Corp. (WI), 235
MagneTek Drives &
Systems (WI), 235
Milsco Manufacturing Co.,
Inc. (WI), 235
MTI Electronics, Inc. (WI),
235
Osmonics, Autotrol Corp.
(WI), 236
Rockwell Automation,
Rockwell Software, Inc.
(WI), 236
Wisconsin Machine Tool
Corp. (WI), 236

MINNEAPOLIS-SAINT PAUL, MN-WI

AETRIUM, Incorporated
(MN), 147
Angeion Corp. (MN), 147
Caire, Inc. (MN), 147
Carl Zeiss IMT Corp.
(MN), 147
Computer Network
Technology Corp. (MN),
147
Connect Computer Co.
(MN), 147

Decision Systems, Inc.
(MN), 147
Digital River, Inc. (MN),
147
DISC Acquisition Corp.
(MN), 147
DRS Ahead Technology,
Inc. (MN), 147
EMA Services, Inc. (MN),
148
ENStar Inc. (MN), 148
Fourth Shift Corp. (MN),
148
Honeywell Inc., Solid State
Electronic Center (MN),
148
Hypro Corporation (MN),
148
Innovex, Inc., Precision
Products Division (MN),
148
Integ Incorporated (MN),
148
INTERCIM Corp. (MN),
148
IntraNet Solutions, Inc.
(MN), 149
ITI Technologies, Inc.
(MN), 149
Lifecore Biomedical, Inc.,
Oral Restorative Division
(MN), 149
Lucht, Inc. (MN), 149
Manufacturers' Services
Ltd., Central US
Operations (MN), 149
McKechnie Plastic
Components (MN), 149
MEANS Telcom (MN), 149
MEDTOX Laboratories,
Inc. (MN), 149
Metaphase Technology,
Inc. (MN), 149
MikroPrecision
Instruments, Inc. (MN),
150
Milltronics Manufacturing
Co. (MN), 150
Minco Products, Inc. (MN),
150
Miracle Ear, Inc. (MN), 150
Multistream Systems, Inc.
(MN), 150
Multi-Tech Systems, Inc.
(MN), 150
Mycogen Seeds (MN), 150
NetCo Communications
Corp. (MN), 150

Kobe Precision, Inc. (CA), 54

Manufacturers' Services Ltd., Fremont Division (CA), 56

Matrix Pharmaceutical, Inc. (CA), 57

Maxis, Inc. (CA), 57

MDL Information Systems, Inc. (CA), 57

Metabyte, Inc. (CA), 57

MicroProse, Inc. (CA), 58

Netwave Technologies, Inc. (CA), 60

Pangea Systems, Inc. (CA), 63

PEDCOM, Inc. (CA), 63

PREMENOS (CA), 65

Premisys Communications, Inc. (CA), 65

ProBusiness Services, Inc. (CA), 66

Quality Assurance Engineering, Inc. (CA), 66

Quester Technology, Inc. (CA), 67

RedCreek Communications, Inc. (CA), 68

RSP Manufacturing Corp. (CA), 69

Scopus Technology, Inc. (CA), 70

SIIG, Inc. (CA), 71

SMART Modular Technologies, Inc. (CA), 72

SSD, Inc. (CA), 73

SteriGenics International (CA), 74

Teradyne, Inc., Assembly Test/Walnut Creek Division (CA), 76

Therma-Wave, Inc. (CA), 76

Thoratec Laboratories Corp. (CA), 76

Trigem America Corp. (CA), 77

Tut Systems, Inc. (CA), 77

Ultradata Corporation (CA), 78

UMAX Technologies, Inc. (CA), 78

U.S. Wireless Corp. (CA), 78

Versant Object Technology (CA), 80

Wind River Systems, Inc. (CA), 81

Wintec Industries, Inc. (CA), 81

OCALA, FL

Clairson Industries Corp. (FL), 93

OKLAHOMA CITY, OK

Central Plastics Co., Inc. (OK), 186

KF Industries, Inc. (OK), 187

OMAHA, NE-IA

Brumko Magnetics Corp. (NE), 156

CSG Systems, Inc. (NE), 156

PKS Information Services, Inc. (NE), 156

ORANGE COUNTY, CA

AAC Corp. (CA), 29

Anabolic, Inc. (CA), 32

Bal Seal Engineering Co., Inc. (CA), 34

Cal Quality Electronics, Inc. (CA), 36

CD Associates, Inc. (CA), 37

Ceradyne, Inc. (CA), 38

Cristek Interconnects, Inc. (CA), 41

CSS Laboratories, Inc. (CA), 42

Datum, Inc. (CA), 43

Details, Inc. (CA), 43

D-Link Systems, Inc. (CA), 42

Econolite Control Products, Inc. (CA), 45

Epoch Internet, Inc. (CA), 46

HC Power, Inc. (CA), 49

HID Corp. (CA), 50

I-Flow Corp. (CA), 50

International Circuits and Components, Inc. (CA), 53

Kaiser Electroprecision (CA), 54

KDS USA (CA), 54

Kingston Technology Co. (CA), 54

Linfinity Microelectronics Inc. (CA), 55

Litronic, Inc. (CA), 55

MAG InnoVision Co., Inc. (CA), 56

Micro Motors, Inc., Industrial Motors Division (CA), 58

Mustek, Inc. (CA), 59

National Telephone & Communications, Inc. (CA), 59

NetSoft (CA), 60

Nichols Institute Diagnostics (CA), 61

PairGain Technologies, Inc. (CA), 63

Plastic Engineered Components, Inc., PEC Los Angeles Division (CA), 65

Powerwave Technologies, Inc. (CA), 65

Printrak International Inc. (CA), 65

Quality Systems, Inc. (CA), 67

Quest International, Inc. (CA), 67

Racal Instruments, Inc. (CA), 67

Rainbow Technologies, Inc. (CA), 67

Safety Components International, Inc., Automotive Division (CA), 69

Scantron Corp. (CA), 70

SELECT Software Tools, Inc. (CA), 70

Simple Technology, Inc. (CA), 72

SPARTA, Inc. (CA), 73

Spiveco, Inc. (CA), 73

Steri-Oss, Inc. (CA), 74

Subscriber Computing, Inc. (CA), 74

Viking Components, Inc. (CA), 80

ORLANDO, FL

Bell Technologies, Inc. (FL), 92

COLLEGIS (FL), 93

Continental Circuits, Inc. (FL), 94

SAN FRANCISCO, CA

Teknowledge Corp. (CA), 75
Telegen Corp. (CA), 76
Tumbleweed Software Corporation (CA), 77
Ultra Clean Technology (CA), 78
Utopia Technology Partners, Inc. (CA), 79
Visigenic Software, Inc. (CA), 80
VIVUS, Inc. (CA), 80

SAN JOSE, CA

ADAC Laboratories (CA), 30
Affymetrix, Inc. (CA), 30
Agile Software Corp. (CA), 31
Airtronics Metal Products, Inc. (CA), 31
AlliedSignal Inc., AlliedSignal Advanced Microelectronic Materials (CA), 31
Alteon Networks, Inc. (CA), 31
Arbor Software Corp. (CA), 32
ArrayComm, Inc. (CA), 33
ArthroCare Corp. (CA), 33
Asante Technologies, Inc. (CA), 33
Ashtech, Inc. (CA), 33
Aspect Development, Inc. (CA), 33
Asyst Software, Inc. (CA), 33
Atcor Corporation (CA), 34
Aurum Software, Inc. (CA), 34
BEA Systems, Inc. (CA), 35
Bizcon Electronics, Inc. (CA), 35
BroadVision, Inc. (CA), 36
Business Objects, Inc. (CA), 36
Cadence Design Systems, Inc., Alta Division (CA), 36
Caere Corp. (CA), 36
Cardiac Pathways Corp. (CA), 37
CardioThoracic Systems, Inc. (CA), 37
CeLAN Technology, Inc. (CA), 37
Celeritek, Inc. (CA), 37

Centigram Communications Corp. (CA), 38
Chip Express Corp. (CA), 38
Chips and Technologies, Inc. (CA), 38
CIDCO Incorporated (CA), 38
Condor Reliability Services, Inc. (CA), 40
Condor Systems, Inc. (CA), 40
ConsenSys Software Corporation (CA), 40
Continuum Electro Optics, Inc., Scientific Division (CA), 41
Corsair Communications, Inc. (CA), 41
CoSystems Inc. (CA), 41
Creative Labs, Inc. (CA), 41
Cygnus Solutions, Inc. (CA), 42
Cylink Corp. (CA), 42
DataTools, Inc. (CA), 43
Diamond Multimedia Systems, Inc. (CA), 44
Digital Link Corp. (CA), 44
DiviCom, Inc. (CA), 44
Duet Technologies, Inc. (CA), 45
Electroglas, Inc. (CA), 45
Equipe Technologies, Inc. (CA), 46
E-TEK Dynamics, Inc. (CA), 45
Exclusive Design Co., Inc. (CA), 47
Finjan, Inc. (CA), 47
FORCE COMPUTERS, Inc. (CA), 48
Gadzoox Networks, Inc. (CA), 48
Gigalabs, Inc. (CA), 48
Harmonic Lightwaves, Inc. (CA), 49
Hewlett-Packard Company, Santa Clara Division (CA), 50
Hotmail (CA), 50
Identix, Inc. (CA), 51
IKOS Systems, Inc. (CA), 51
ILOG, Inc. (CA), 51
Incyte Pharmaceuticals, Inc. (CA), 51

Indigo Technologies, Inc. (CA), 51
Infinity Financial Technology, Inc. (CA), 51
Infoseek Corporation (CA), 52
InnoMedia, Inc. (CA), 52
InnovaCom, Inc. (CA), 52
Integrated Silicon Solution, Inc. (CA), 52
Integrated Systems, Inc. (CA), 52
i-Planet, Inc. (CA), 50
Ipsilon Networks (CA), 53
KIVA Software Corp. (CA), 54
Lambda Advanced Analog, Inc. (CA), 54
Larscom Incorporated (CA), 55
Lightwave Electronics Corp. (CA), 55
Lightwave Microsystems Corp. (CA), 55
Logos Corp. (CA), 55
Lumisys, Inc. (CA), 56
Marimba, Inc. (CA), 56
Matheson-Semi-Gas Systems (CA), 56
MatriDigm Corp. (CA), 57
Mercury Interactive Corp. (CA), 57
Metricom, Inc. (CA), 57
Microcide Pharmaceuticals, Inc. (CA), 58
Micro Lithography, Inc. (CA), 58
MicroTel International, Inc. (CA), 58
Mitsubishi Electronics America, Inc., Electronic Device Group (CA), 58
Molecular Dynamics, Inc. (CA), 59
Motorola Indala Corp. (CA), 59
NETCOM On-Line Communication Services, Inc. (CA), 59
Netro Corp. (CA), 60
Objectivity, Inc. (CA), 61
OnTrak Systems, Inc. (CA), 62
Optivision, Inc. (CA), 62
Orbit Semiconductor, Inc. (CA), 62
Pacific Monolithics, Inc. (CA), 63

WATERBURY, CT

WATERLOO-CEDAR FALLS, IA

WEST PALM BEACH-BOCA RATON, FL

WHEELING, WV-OH

WICHITA, KS

All items are due on latest date stamped. A charge is
made for each day, including Sundays and holidays,
that this item is overdue.

420-1-8/91